SFAKIA

A history of the region in its Cretan context

2015 © Mystis Editions, A. Tsintaris & Co.
Industrial Area, Heraklion
Crete, Greece, 71601

Tel. +30 2810 346451
Email: info@mystis.gr

Website : www.mystis.gr

Cover Design - Layout: Mystis Editions

Edited by Jean Hannah

First Edition 2015
Second Edition 2016

ISBN 978-618-5024-41-3

Front cover drawing of Sfakia by Marco Boschini, Venetian painter and engraver, published in "Il regno tutto di Candia" in 1651

SFAKIA

A history of the region in its Cretan context

by

George K. Dalidakis and Peter Trudgill

Second Edition 2016

To all of our Sfakian friends, who have over the years always shown us the unsurpassed hospitality for which Sfakia is so famous, and who have demonstrated a degree of friendship which we can only hope we deserve

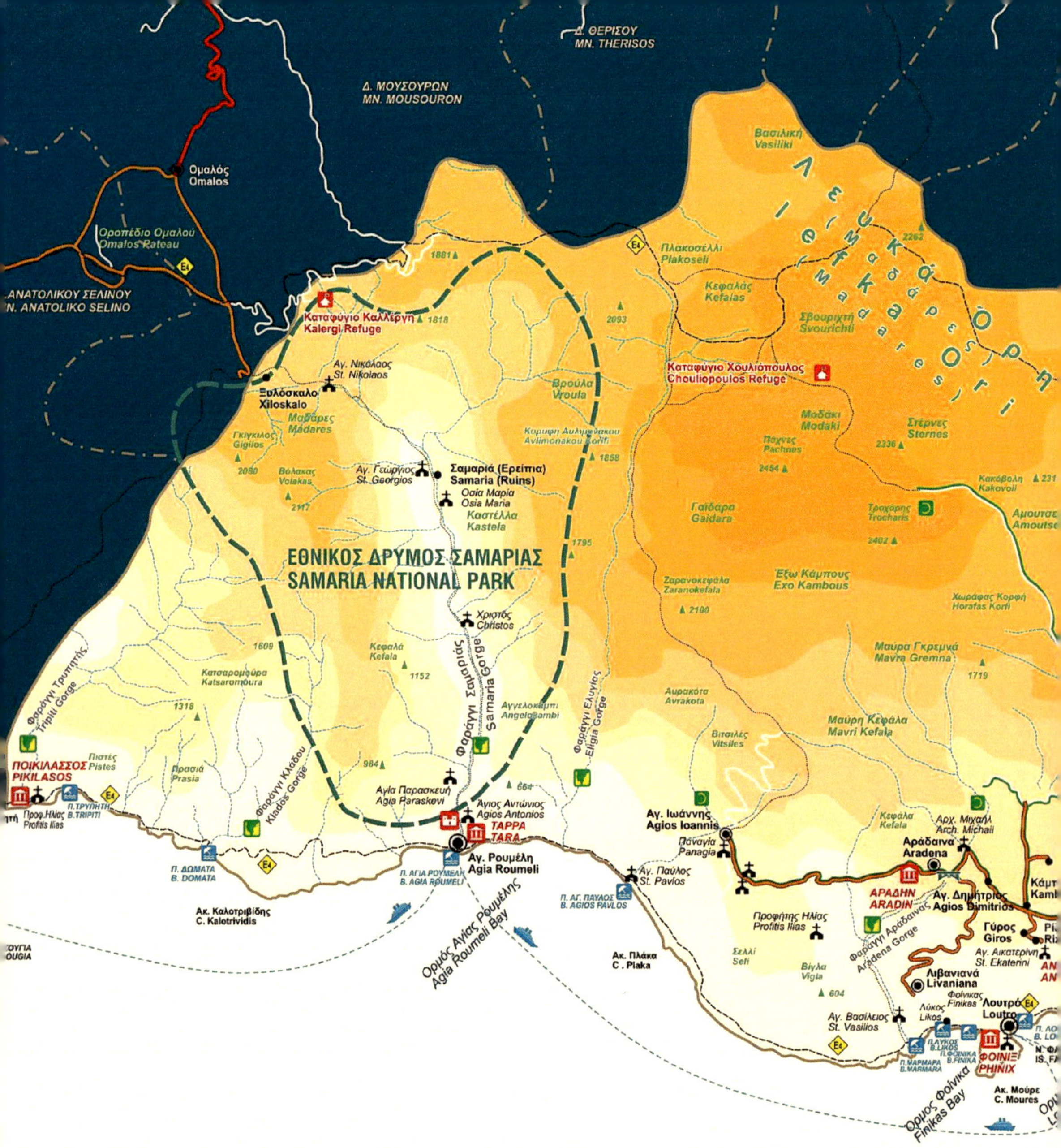
Δ. ΘΕΡΙΣΟΥ
MN. THERISOS
Δ. ΜΟΥΣΟΥΡΩΝ
MN. MOUSOURON
Ομαλός
Omalos
Οροπέδιο Ομαλού
Omalos Plateau
ΑΝΑΤΟΛΙΚΟΥ ΣΕΛΙΝΟΥ
N. ANATOLIKO SELINO
Καταφύγιο Καλλέργη
Kalergi Refuge
Ξυλόσκαλο
Xiloskalo
Αγ. Νικόλαος
St. Nikolaos
Μαδάρες
Madares
Γκιγκιλος
Gigilos
Βόλακας
Volakas
Αγ. Γεώργιος
St. Georgios
Σαμαριά (Ερείπια)
Samaria (Ruins)
Οσία Μαρία
Osia Maria
Καστέλλα
Kastela
Βρούλα
Vroula
ΕΘΝΙΚΟΣ ΔΡΥΜΟΣ ΣΑΜΑΡΙΑΣ
SAMARIA NATIONAL PARK
Χριστός
Christos
Κεφαλά
Kefala
Φαράγγι Σαμαριάς
Samaria Gorge
Αγγελόκαμπι
Angelokambi
Κατσαρομούρα
Katsaromoura
Φαράγγι Τρυπητής
Tripiti Gorge
Πιστές
Pistes
Πρασιά
Prasia
Φαράγγι Κλάδου
Klados Gorge
ΠΟΙΚΙΛΑΣΣΟΣ
PIKILASOS
Προφ. Ηλίας
Profitis Ilias
Π. ΤΡΥΠΗΤΗ
B. TRIPITI
Αγία Παρασκευή
Agia Paraskevi
Άγιος Αντώνιος
Agios Antonios
ΤΑΡΡΑ
TARA
Αγ. Ρουμέλη
Agia Roumeli
Π. ΑΓΙΑ ΡΟΥΜΕΛΗ
B. AGIA ROUMELI
Π. ΔΟΜΑΤΑ
B. DOMATA
Ακ. Καλοτριβίδης
C. Kalotrividis
Όρμος Αγίας Ρουμέλης
Agia Roumeli Bay
Φαράγγι Ελυγιάς
Eligia Gorge
Πλακοσέλλι
Plakoseli
Κεφαλάς
Kefalas
Σβουριχτή
Svourichti
Βασιλική
Vasiliki
Λευκά Όρη
Lefka Ori
Μαδάρες
Madares
Καταφύγιο Χουλιόπουλος
Chouliopoulos Refuge
Μοδάκι
Modaki
Πάχνες
Pachnes
Στέρνες
Sternes
Κακόβολη
Kakovoli
Τροχάρης
Trocharis
Γαϊδάρα
Gaidara
Αμουτσέ
Amoutse
Ζαρανοκεφάλα
Zaranokefala
Έξω Κάμπους
Exo Kambous
Χωράφας Κορφή
Horafas Korfi
Μαύρα Γκρεμνά
Mavra Gremna
Αυρακότα
Avrakota
Μαύρη Κεφάλα
Mavri Kefala
Βιτσιλές
Vitsiles
Αγ. Ιωάννης
Agios Ioannis
Παναγία
Panagia
Αγ. Παύλος
St. Pavlos
Π. ΑΓ. ΠΑΥΛΟΣ
B. AGIOS PAVLOS
Ακ. Πλάκα
C. Plaka
Κεφάλα
Kefala
Αρχ. Μιχαήλ
Arch. Michail
Αράδαινα
Aradena
ΑΡΑΔΗΝ
ARADIN
Αγ. Δημήτριος
Agios Dimitrios
Προφήτης Ηλίας
Profitis Ilias
Φαράγγι Αράδαινας
Aradena Gorge
Σελλί
Seli
Βίγλα
Vigla
Γύρος
Giros
Αγ. Αικατερίνη
St. Ekaterini
Λιβανιανά
Livaniana
Φοίνικας
Finikas
Λύκος
Likos
Λουτρό
Loutro
Αγ. Βασίλειος
St. Vasilios
Π. ΜΑΡΜΑΡΑ
B. MARMARA
ΦΟΙΝΙΞ
PHINIX
Ακ. Μούρε
C. Moures
Όρμος Φοίνικα
Finikas Bay
1881
1818
2093
2263
2080
2117
1858
1795
1609
1318
1152
984
664
2336
2454
2402
2100
1719
604
E4

CRETE
Chania
Rethymno
Heraklio
Agios Nikolaos
Sfakia

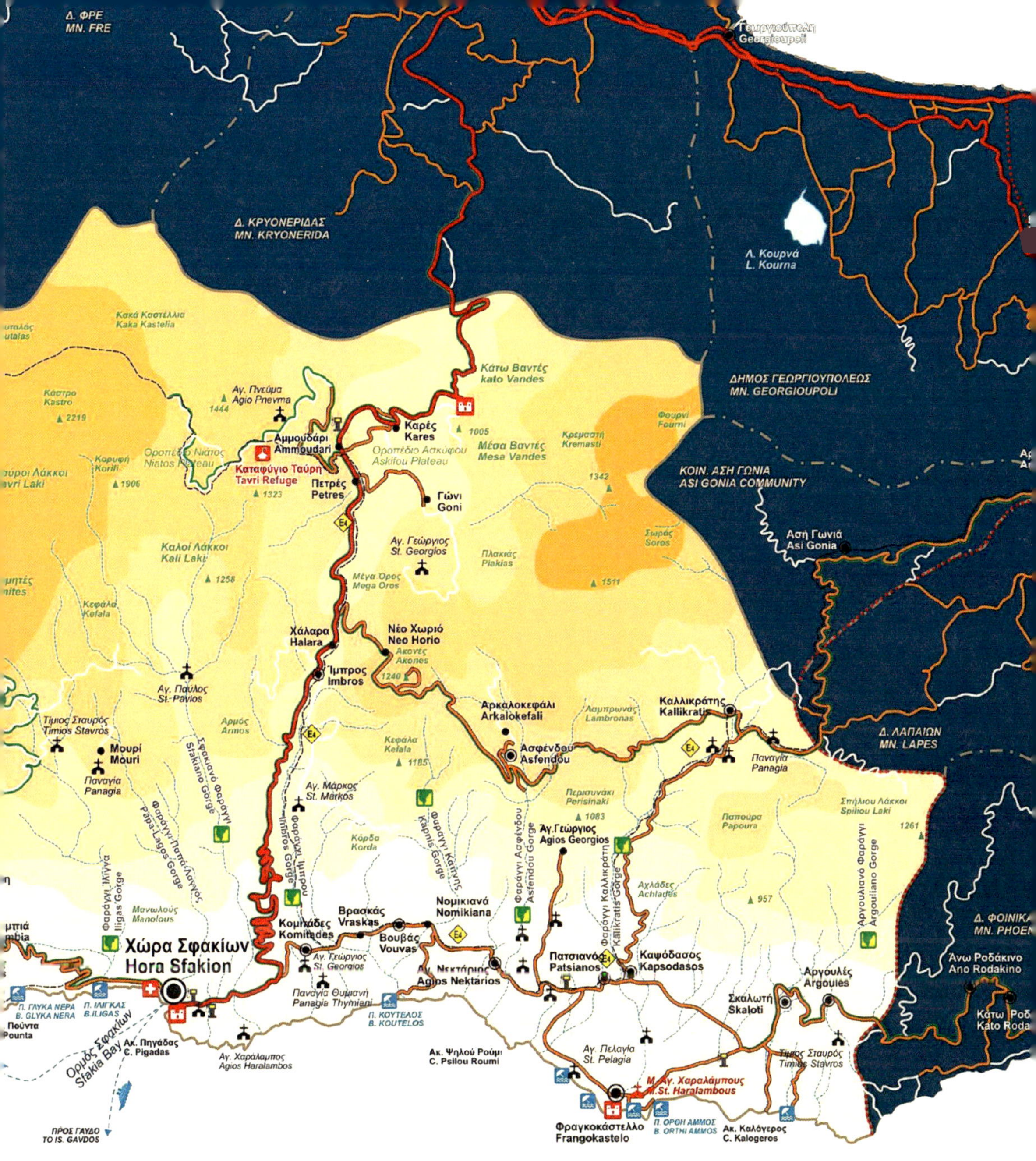

ΥΠΟΜΝΗΜΑ - KEY TO MAP

- ΕΘΝΙΚΗ ΟΔΟΣ / NATIONAL ROAD
- ΚΥΡΙΟΣ ΔΡΟΜΟΣ / MAJOR SURFACED ROAD
- ΔΕΥΤΕΡΕΥΟΥΣΑ ΟΔΟΣ / SURFACED ROAD
- E4
- ΜΟΝΟΠΑΤΙ / FOOTPATH
- ΓΡΑΦΙΚΗ ΔΙΑΔΡΟΜΗ / SCENIC ROUTE
- ΡΕΜΑ / GULLY
- ΟΡΙΑ ΔΗΜΟΥ / MUNICIPALITY BOUNDARIES
- ΟΡΙΑ ΕΘΝΙΚΟΥ ΔΡΥΜΟΥ / NATIONAL PARK BOUNDARIES
- ΠΡΩΤΕΥΟΥΣΑ / ΧΩΡΙΟ / ΟΙΚΙΣΜΟΣ / CAPITAL CITY / VILLAGE / SETTLEMENT
- ΑΚΤΟΠΛΟΪΚΗ ΓΡΑΜΜΗ / SHIPPING ROUTE
- ΒΕΝΖΙΝΑΔΙΟ / FUEL STATION
- ΛΙΜΑΝΙ / PORT
- ΓΕΦΥΡΑ / BRIDGE
- ΦΑΡΑΓΓΙ / GORGE
- ΣΠΗΛΑΙΟ / CAVE
- ΥΨΟΜΕΤΡΟ / ALTITUDE
- ΑΡΧΑΙΟΛΟΓΙΚΟΣ ΤΟΠΟΣ / ARCHAEOLOGICAL SITE
- ΕΚΚΛΗΣΙΑ / ΜΟΝΑΣΤΗΡΙ / CHURCH / MONASTERY
- ΚΑΣΤΡΟ / CASTLE
- ΚΑΤΑΦΥΓΙΟ / SHELTER
- ΠΑΡΑΛΙΑ / BEACH
- ΑΓΡΟΤΙΚΟ ΙΑΤΡΕΙΟ ΧΩΡΑΣ ΣΦΑΚΙΩΝ / HEALTH CENTER of HORA SFAKION

ΣΥΝΤΟΜΟΓΡΑΦΙΕΣ
ABBREVIATIONS

Π.: ΠΑΡΑΛΙΑ
Ακ.: ΑΚΡΩΤΗΡΙΟ
Μ.: ΜΟΝΗ
Αγ.: ΑΓΙΟΣ
Δ.: ΔΗΜΟΣ

B.: BEACH
C.: CAPE
M.: MONASTERY
ST.: SAINT
MN.: MUNICIPALITY

Acknowledgements

Very many people from Sfakia have been extremely helpful to us by offering their personal stories, knowledge and advice. We are particularly grateful to †Giannis Douroundous, Andreas Fasoulis, Kanakis Geronymakis, †Nikos Gialedakis, †Manoussos Korkakas, †Angeliki Mangelaki, Damoulis Perrakis, †Stelios Stamatakis, †Giannis Tzardis, Stelios Tsirintanis, and Pavlos Votzakis.

from George Dalidakis

A special mention should be made about the help and encouragement I received from the late Paris Kelaidis, the Sfakian historian whose contribution to preserving and promoting the history of Sfakia spans 50 years and 42 books, the last being his *History of Sfakia and its mythology*, which was published in 2009, a couple of years before his death. I first met him almost 10 years ago, and received a great deal of invaluable encouragement and advice from him about completing my own work on a history of Sfakia in English, addressed to different readers from those which his own books in Greek were aimed at. And at our meetings once or twice a year, he always gave me another of his books as a present. Without his assistance, this book would have been much poorer in content.

Two other people kindly provided me with access to their libraries of Cretan history books, and I owe them a debt of gratitude for this. They are my Melbourne Cretan friend Socrates Tsourdalakis, originally from Melambes in Crete, who, to my knowledge, has the largest private book collection on Cretan history in the Greek language in Australia; and Dr Alfred Vincent, of Sydney, who also provided me with advice on various related matters.

Special thanks to Mrs Theano Boraki and other staff at the Chania Municipal Library – they were always most helpful with my research and the lending of books.

And without our editor, Jean Hannah, this book would never had been finished: she was the one person who encouraged and prodded me at times when I suffered from writer's block, or was overwhelmed by the amount of material that needed to be studied, just to get through to the next chapter. For her assistance in getting through these difficult times, I am eternally grateful to her.

I also want to thank Peter for joining me in this fascinating adventure of preparing this book, something that neither of us thought was going to take us this long to complete.

from Peter Trudgill

I have been the grateful recipient of invaluable help and advice from very many people over the years of writing this book, but I would particularly like to single out for my thanks Enam Al-Wer, Sean Damer, Colin Janes, Maria Sifianou, and Yvonne Trimmer, who have generously supplied important and insightful information, modifications and corrections.

We also owe a truly enormous debt of gratitude to Jean Hannah, who has genuinely contributed as much to this book as we have. She has painstakingly edited our writing, and spent an enormous number of hours taking our sometimes formless text and beating it into a coherent shape. Without her, as George says, this book would never have happened; and without her, it would have been a greatly inferior volume. Any errors, though, are obviously ours alone.

I also want to thank George very warmly indeed for involving me in this project. The idea for this book was his; most of the vast amounts of research was carried out by him; and the majority of the chapters were written by him. Thank you George!

July 2014

The White Mountains as seen from Aradena (by West-Crete.com)

Contents

Prologue

Knossos, the major city of ancient Minoan civilisation, lies just inland from the north coast of Crete and from the major modern city of Heraklion. At the archaeological site of Knossos, tourists today can walk along Europe's oldest roadway, carefully exposed by excavations. The Royal Road is about eight feet wide, smooth and even, and paved with limestone slabs. We know that the Minoans built wheeled carts and chariots, and that they had a system of roadways which linked their different settlements together, so we can imagine such wheeled vehicles heading down this road towards the Minoan Royal Palace. The roadway is about 4,000 years old, and it is not entirely inconceivable that it was constructed during the 1950s BC.

Not far away, on the south coast of Crete, about 60 miles to the southwest of Knossos as the crow flies though considerably further on the ground, lies Chora Sfakion,[1] the major settlement of the historic region of Sfakia. During the Minoan period, and for thousands of years after the disappearance of Minoan culture, the Sfakia area remained entirely without roadways. Such was the isolation of the area, and the difficulty of the terrain in which it lies, that there was no access at all to wheeled vehicles from the outside world. During World War II when the retreating Allied forces of Britons, Australians, New Zealanders, and Greeks were evacuated from the little harbour at Chora Sfakion in 1941, all 30,000 of the weary and dispirited troops had arrived over the mountains from the north coast on foot following mule tracks and footpaths. The 15,000 or so who could not be evacuated by the Royal Navy then had to trek all the way back to the north coast again, as prisoners of the Germans, once more on foot. The first road to Chora Sfakion, and so the first wheeled traffic from the outside world, did not arrive in the village until 1952 AD.

[1] *Chora Sfakion* means 'the main village of Sfakia'.

Preface: Sfakia today

Of all the countries of Europe, Greece is the one which lies furthest to the south. Crete, Greece's largest island, is also its southernmost region. And on the south coast of this most southerly of the islands of Greece, with nothing between it and Africa except for the small island of Gavdos and its even smaller partner Gavdopoula, lies the famous region of Sfakia. The island of Crete has played a vital role in European history and remains to this day a very special part of Greece. But some parts of Crete are more special than others, and none is more so than the remote south coast outpost of Sfakia.

The Sfakian people, too, are rather special. The writer Adam Hopkins speaks of their "majestic courtesy", and even today visitors can note their remarkable dignity and quiet self-esteem. Other writers have described the indomitable spirit of the Sfakians who, it was once said, are "hospitable to the point of insanity". Today Sfakians sometimes profess to be surprised, although surely they are not, that tourists should come to Sfakia at all – "this land is only stones", they claim. But they say this with a pride which indicates their satisfaction with their historical ability to survive in a landscape that others could not have endured. And it is probably not too fanciful to suppose that it is the arid, rocky terrain of the area which has helped to lead to their strong feeling of otherness; and that it is their isolation which has led over the ages to the fierce spirit of independence, the anarchic love of freedom, and the hatred of officialdom for which they are known – Sfakia was the only region of Crete which was never totally subjugated by the Venetian and Turkish overlords who ruled the rest of the island.

Modern Sfakia is an administrative region of the western Cretan prefecture of Chania. It has 25 miles of coastline on the Libyan Sea, stretching from Cape Tripiti at the bottom of the Tripiti Gorge in the west to Cape Kastellos below the village of Argoules in the east. In earlier times, Sfakia's eastern border varied: during certain periods it was considered to extend further east to include the village of Rodakino; and at other times it ran no further than the bottom of the Kallikratis Gorge, between the villages of Patsianos and Kapsodasos which lie above the Venetian fort of Frangokastello.

At Frangokastello, there is a coastal alluvial plain not much more than five miles long. But everywhere else along the Sfakian coast, mountains rise precipitously and forbiddingly from the shoreline. These are the Lefka Ori or White Mountains, one of the wildest parts of Europe, all of whose highest peaks are located in Sfakia. Pachnes ('frosts') is the highest at 2,453 metres (8,048 feet) above sea level, and it is a measure of the steepness of the terrain that this peak is only 6 miles from the sea. But there are also many other peaks in the Lefka Ori that are higher than 2,000 metres, including Trocharis (2,401m / 7,877 ft), Svourichti (2,356m / 7,730ft), Grias Soros (2,331m / 7,648ft), Kastro (2,219m / 7,280ft), Kakovoli (2,214m / 7,264ft), Melintaou (2,133m / 6,932ft), Volakas (2,116m / 6,942ft), and Zaranokefala (2,099m / 6,591ft). The name of the mountain range is generally said to come from the fact that the bare limestone rocks of the highest peaks glint and shimmer white in the summer sun, and not because the summits of the mountains are covered in snow in the winter. Beneath the barren moonlike desert landscape of these highest peaks, but above the tree-line at heights between 1,700 and 2,000 metres, lies an area known locally as the *madara*, plural *madares*, which is used for the summer pasturing of sheep and goats.

The mountain range is split at intervals by remote, deep gorges that run southwards into the Libyan Sea, many of them dotted with oleander, for which the local word is *sfaka*, perhaps the source of the region's name. The gorges are generally very dry in the summer but can become raging torrents after rain storms. The main gorges, from west to east, are: Tripiti, Kladou, Samaria, Eligia, Aradena, Kavis or Ilingas, Sfakia, Imbros, Kapnis, Asfendou, Kallikratis, and Argoules. But there are very many other minor ones, such as the Priest's Gorge, which comes down into the village square in Chora Sfakion. Of these gorges, the Samaria is the most famous, being Europe's longest and deepest. These days, this gorge provides a long but popular day's hike for tourists, but in times gone by, as we shall see, the Samaria Gorge was variously a religious sanctuary, a place of refuge, and a haunt of outlaws.

The White Mountains are generally very arid and inhospitable. Much of the rainfall drains through the limestone and eventually emerges near the southern shore line. At many points along the south coast, there are places where digging in the sand or stones reveals fresh water just below the surface, most famously at Ghlika Nera or Sweet Water Beach between Chora Sfakion and Loutro. Swimmers encounter sudden cold patches in the sea where fresh mountain water rises up, and Sfakian fisherman know of places out to sea where they can scoop fresh water off the surface and drink it.

The rugged mountainous terrain means that very little of Sfakia is suitable for agriculture. Apart from the Frangokastello plain, the main exceptions are the fertile plateau of Anopoli, and the large upland basin at Askifou, into which water drains from the surrounding hills and can leave again only by means of swallow-holes. There are also smaller upland basins at Asfendou and Kallikratis, as well as at Krapi, the only part of Sfakia to lie on the northern slopes of the White Mountains. Krapi is today the main gateway into Sfakia for travellers entering the region from the north coast via the town of Vrises. At earlier times, however, it is likely that most newcomers entered by other routes.

I. Prehistoric Sfakia – before 500 BC

We do not know who the first human beings to visit Sfakia were. But they may have arrived there a very long time ago indeed. Archaeological finds of stone tools beside the path from Loutro up to Anopoli at about 200 metres (650 feet) above sea-level have been interpreted as being signs of human presence in the area during the transition period from the Lower to the Middle Palaeolithic (Old Stone Age) era, so about 300,000 years ago. And they "might suggest that the first humans reached the island across the sea from Libya",[2] perhaps, we might add, via Gavdos.[3] This interpretation is strengthened by similar and more extensive findings along the coast to the east of Sfakia in the region of Plakias.[4]

Neolithic Sfakia

The first solid archaeological evidence we have of permanent settlement on Crete comes from the Neolithic (New Stone Age) era, from around 6000 BC (see e.g. Rackham & Moody, 1996). It is obvious that the bearers of the initial Neolithic farming culture to which this evidence testifies must have arrived from Greece, Asia Minor, Africa or the Middle East, but the most likely routes are from southern Greece or, more probably, from southwestern Asia Minor via the Dodecanese.

From Libya in northern Africa to the shores of southern Crete there is as much as 200 nautical miles of open sea, with no intervening islands until one reaches Gavdos, which is only about 17 nautical miles from Crete; although, of course, if Palaeolithic people had come that way, Neolithic people could certainly have done the same.

On the other hand, on a clear day the tips of the White Mountains are

[2] Mortensen (2008).

[3] Kopaka & Matzanas (2009).

[4] http://www.ascsa.edu.gr/index.php/news/newsDetails/plakias-survey-finds-stone-age-tools-on-crete.

actually visible from the Greek mainland at Cape Malea in the south of the Peloponnese. From the nearby harbour of modern Neapoli, it is a sea journey of about 10 nautical miles to Agia Pelagia harbour on the island of Kithera. From the south of Kithera to the island of Antikithera the distance is about 22 sea miles. And from Cape Apolitaris at the southern end of Antikithera, there are roughly 16 miles of open sea before the lee of Cape Vouksa is reached at the northwest end of Crete. Alternatively, the distance from the Asia Minor/Anatolian mainland to Rhodes is not more than 10 miles or so. Between Rhodes and Karpathos lie about 26 miles of open sea, and from Karpathos to the smaller island of Kasos, to the southwest, another 6 miles. Finally, from Kasos to the eastern tip of Crete the sea journey is a further 22 miles.

There is a certain amount of physical-anthropological evidence from skeletal remains which suggests a link between Crete and Anatolia. And according to the distinguished archaeologist J.D.S. Pendlebury's book *The archaeology of Crete*, the earliest Neolithic settlers, who were rather few in number, did indeed settle originally in the part of Crete nearest to Kasos – the rocky uplands at the eastern end of the island, the isthmus of Ierapetra, and the Lasithi plateau, all well away from the sea. There was also settlement further west on the Messara plain.

The best known of the early Neolithic settlements in Crete was at Knossos, where there is evidence of post holes made for the construction of wooden houses dating from around 6000 BC, as well as of walls made from mud bricks from about 5700 BC. Remains of a Neolithic house have also been found at Phaistos.[5]

As far as the arrival of Neolithic settlers in Sfakia is concerned, it will be no surprise to people familiar with the area that they seem to have been in no hurry to leave the more hospitable areas of Crete and venture into the rugged mountains of the region. Indeed, it seems that for many hundreds of years after the arrival of the first settlers on the island, habitation was mostly confined to the centre and east of Crete. The entire west of the island, including Sfakia, was densely forested at that time and, as Pendlebury says of this area, "probably the country was too wild" to be especially welcoming – which is something which is often still said of the Sfakian region some 8,000 years later.

[5] Pendlebury was a brilliant young scholar, who students of Cretan history owe a great deal to (Grundon, 2007). He was an athlete who represented Cambridge University and England at the high jump, and who worked in Cretan archaeology from the 1920s until 1939. He spoke fluent Greek, and his fitness and athleticism enabled him to traverse most of Crete, most often on foot. His knowledge of the island was unparalleled. The first chapter of his book, published when he was 34, contains a description of the entire island, together with routes between major ancient centres, with details based on his own experience of how long each journey would take. He fought in the battle of Crete (see Chapter XVI) and, badly injured, was killed by German paratroopers in cold blood in May 1941, aged 36.

It is true that the archaeologists of the Oxford University Sphakia Survey[6] have found considerable evidence of Neolithic habitation in many parts of Sfakia, but the datable material is nearly all pottery, and it goes back only to the Final Neolithic period – that is, to 3500 BC or later – a period which apparently saw a considerable expansion of the island's population. Material consisting mainly of red and black burnished pottery fragments has been found in Kambia, the area of the upland village of Anopoli where the modern road enters from Chora Sfakion; and in Riza, the part of Anopoli between the modern village centre and the road leading up to Agia Ekaterini church.

Minoan Sfakia

Not many centuries after the beginning of this Final Neolithic period, important changes began to take place in Crete. From around 3000 BC, a new Bronze Age culture – referred to by historians as the Minoan Age, after the legendary King Minos of Crete – begins to appear in the archaeological record. For example, there was a radical change in pottery styles at about this time.

It is likely that this new culture coincided with the arrival of a new group of people, again most likely from Anatolia, who gradually became dominant in the main inhabited areas of the island. Their arrival was not necessarily a peaceful one, as the indigenous Cretans seem to have started taking refuge in caves at this time, a sign of social upheaval and disruption. And it is noticeable that new Bronze Age settlements from this period tend to be located on hills which would provide good defensive positions. We can imagine that the arrival of newcomers with a superior, metal-working technology might have been resisted by the local Neolithic population, but that in the end this resistance was in vain.

The new Minoan culture of Crete, which lasted for an astonishingly long period of 1,500 years, gave rise to the flowering of the earliest advanced civilisation in Europe. This civilisation traded with Egypt, which influenced it considerably, and with the Middle East and Greece. Its people came to dominate a region comprising many areas of the nearby Mediterranean world, including parts of the Greek mainland. There were Minoan colonies on Thira, Milos, and Rhodes, for instance, and there may also have been colonies in what is now Libya – Minoans seem to have been familiar with monkeys and antelopes, and may have employed black Africans as mercenary soldiers.

The centre of this culture was the town of Knossos, and the apogee of its civilisation was reached between 2000 and 1500 BC, with a marked prosperity

[6] http://sphakia.classics.ox.ac.uk.

and a flowering of the arts. It was a peaceful and probably matriarchal society in which women enjoyed a privileged position; a mother-goddess played an important role, and the inhabitants referred to their motherland rather than fatherland.[7]

Who the Minoans were we do not know, but one way to approach this question is to ask what sort of language they spoke. It is from Knossos during the period between 2000 and 1500 BC that we find writing on clay tablets in a syllabary[8] that is known as Linear A, which has not yet been deciphered with any degree of assurance. If we were able to tell what sort of language these tablets were written in, we might have a better idea of where the Minoans came from originally and who they were exactly.

It is widely agreed that their language was not Greek, which descends, like English, from the Indo-European proto-language that was probably spoken on the northern shores of the Black Sea around 4000 BC. The Greeks themselves arrived in what is now Greece only in about 2500-2000 BC, travelling down the Balkan peninsula from the north and most likely arriving through what is now Albania or via the area around Florina and Kastoria. Did the Minoans speak a Semitic language, related to Phoenician? Or perhaps it was something akin to Ancient Egyptian, an Afro-Asiatic language related to Semitic and to the modern Berber languages of North Africa? Or was it a pre-Indo-European language like the extinct Etruscan of Italy or modern Basque? Perhaps it was actually Indo-European, like most of the languages of modern Europe, Iran, Afghanistan, northern India, and Sri Lanka? All of these are possible.

The distinguished philologist L.R. Palmer argued on detailed linguistic grounds that the language of the Minoans was likely to be an Indo-European language closely related to Luvian, if not Luvian/Luwian itself.[9] This extinct language was a member of the Anatolian language sub-family which also includes Hittite, and was the ancestor of the Lycian language which was known in classical times. Luvian was spoken in more or less the whole of southern Asia Minor – modern Turkey – including the coastal districts, which as we have already seen were within relatively easy reach of Crete. There are also clear archaeological links between the Minoan sites of Crete and the important Luvian centre of Beycesultan (modern Denizli in southwest Turkey). Palmer also argues for place-name similarities between Minoan Crete and southwest Anatolia.

Of course, even if we could establish what the language of the Linear

[7] R.W. Hutchinson (1962) has suggested that the reason that male Cretans to this day swear by the name of the Virgin, the *Panagia*, whereas elsewhere in Greece it is traditionally only women who do so, may be an inheritance from this time.

[8] Whereas an alphabet has letters which represent individual vowel and consonant sounds, such as *p, k, a, e ,i, o,* a syllabary has symbols which represent syllables, such as *pa, pe, ki, ko.*

[9] L.R. Palmer (1965); Younger & Rehak (2008), p. 176.

A tablets was, there is no guarantee that this was the same language that had been brought by the original newcomers; it may have been only one of a number of languages spoken on Crete. But there is also religious evidence of Minoan origins in Anatolia. Minoan religion was focussed on the worship of a mother-goddess, as we have noted, and in representations she appears together with many symbols which the early Bronze Age inhabitants probably brought with them from Asia Minor. These symbols include birds, snakes, poppies, lilies, double axes, and the horns of a bull, which are known to have been associated with Anatolia.

There are also clear archaeological links between the Minoans and the people of Caria, which was on the Anatolian coast close to the islands of Kos and Kalimnos. They too had a mother-goddess cult which was very similar to that of the Minoans. The tradition of the later Greek goddess Leto (Lato in Dorian Greek), who was the mother of Apollo and is associated with Crete, may represent a survival of the Minoan mother-goddess, and there is a suggestion that her name comes from the Carian word *lada* 'woman'. Carian was an Anatolian language related to Luvian.

The Minoans were Europe's first construction engineers, but none of their paved roads, aqueducts, viaducts or harbours have been found in Sfakia. Minoan civilisation did not exactly pass Sfakia by, but it is clear that the centre of this culture for most of its 1,500 years was in eastern and central Crete, mainly focussed on Knossos and Phaistos. Most of western Crete was probably still virgin forest, covered in cypress, lentisk, juniper, oak, myrtle, mulberry, almond, quince and other trees and shrubs. The Akrotiri peninsula, however, does seem to have been rather densely populated at least in Late Minoan times. There was also a Late Minoan settlement in Kydonia (Chania) on the north coast, and it is believed that there was a Minoan palace nearby, though this has not yet been found.

The Sphakia Survey team have discovered signs of Minoans in the Sfakia area which, significantly, are by no means confined to coastal areas, although they are more common nearer the sea. For example, pottery fragments from the Early Minoan period 3000-2100 BC have been found in Anopoli – once again in the Kambia area – and there have been other finds in Aradena and Mouri. It is especially fascinating that pottery fragments have also been found in the *madares*, the summer pasture areas which lie above the tree line but below the high desert of the White Mountains. These finds could simply be the result of people travelling across the White Mountains between the north and south. But they might also indicate temporary summer occupation by shepherds pasturing their flocks at high altitudes, as they still do today – since agriculture was not much of an option in most of Sfakia, we have to assume that, in addition to fishing and hunting, the pastoral way of life was very important. Later Minoan pottery fragments from the period 2100-1450 BC have also been found in the Samaria Gorge, and there were Minoan sites on the Frangokastello plain as well.

The fact that pottery found in Sfakia resembles the pottery also found on the north coast of Crete indicates that the region was not isolated from the rest of the island. And the fact that obsidian cutting tools have been discovered at very many sites also indicates that Sfakia was not even cut off from the outside world, since this naturally occurring glass can be shown geologically to have been brought or traded from the island of Milos in the southern Cyclades.

The Greek invaders I: Mycenean Sfakia

Around 1400 BC, another very major change took place in Crete. The archaeological record shows clear signs of havoc and upheaval on a very large scale. There was widespread destruction of Minoan cities and palaces, often by fire. This was accompanied by signs of the arrival of another group of people from elsewhere, bringing with them a culture different from that of the Minoans. For example, clay tablets have been discovered from this period which employ a different writing system and language from that used by the Minoans.

Our best understanding of what happened is that there were two large series of earthquakes which occurred some time before 1700 BC. These were soon followed by a truly colossal volcanic eruption on the island of Thera (Santorini) in the southern Cyclades, about 70 miles to the north of Crete.[10] (Some people have suggested that it was this event which gave rise to the myth of the destruction of Atlantis.) Thera itself was fractured into three separate islands, with its colonial Minoan city buried under pumice; and massive tidal waves bore down on the Cretan north coast. The earthquakes also caused widespread destruction in Crete of buildings as well as the bridges, harbours and roads that the Minoan civilisation had constructed.

There then seems to have been an invasion, or invasions, of Crete from overseas. The Minoans, probably weakened by the earlier natural disasters, were overrun. The invaders appear to have systematically destroyed all the major Minoan cities of central and eastern Crete, including Zakros at the eastern end of the island, which was never rebuilt. The major centre of Knossos, however, seems to have been spared, perhaps because the invaders wished to preserve it for their own use.

So who were these invaders and destroyers? Their identity was not established until the 1950s, when it was revealed through one of the most impressive intellectual feats of modern times. The invaders' new writing system, which dates from the period after 1400 BC, was known to scholars as Linear B, to distinguish it from the earlier Minoan Linear A, of which

[10] Papadopoulos (2011), p. 69.

it was probably an adaptation. Linear B had defied all earlier efforts at decipherment, although some scholars had supposed that the language might be Etruscan. However, in 1951 a brilliant young English amateur linguist, Michael Ventris, succeeded in deciphering the script, and in 1953 he published a paper together with the established and erudite classical philologist John Chadwick, showing that the language was in fact an early form of Greek. Linear B tablets had also been found on the Greek mainland, and their later analysis confirmed Ventris' electrifying discovery.

What had happened was that, from about 2000 BC onwards, the first wave of Greek-speaking peoples, who had arrived from the north, began to establish a civilisation of some importance on the mainland of Greece. One of the main focal points for this Greek culture was at Mycenae, in the northeast of the Peloponnese between modern Corinth and Nafplio, so the culture is often referred to as Mycenean. There were other major centres in Boeotia, Attica and the Peloponnese: at Athens, Thebes, Pylos in the southwestern Peloponnese (where Linear B tablets were found), and the port for Mycenae at Tiryns near modern Nafplio.

Mycenean society and culture appear to have been very different from the Minoan. The society was patriarchal and given to "male conceptions of deity", as R.F. Willetts puts it.[11] It was also militaristic, hierarchical, centralising, and authoritarian. The defensive construction of their settlements signal that, unlike Minoan civilisation, the Myceneans were used to warfare and unrest, and therefore lacked the benefits of trade, but there are signs that they had begun to have some interaction with – and influence on – the Minoans from about 1600 BC onwards.

The invasion of Crete signified that these Greeks had continued their migrations southwards across the Aegean and established control over a wider area. Exactly what happened after the invasion is not certain, but one reasonable conjecture is that the Minoan and Greek populations coexisted on the island for a very long time. Certainly, the Minoan language exercised some influence on the Greek language, with many Greek words being of Minoan origin. For example, the word for olive tree, Archaic Greek *elaiwa*, is of pre-Greek origin, and the linguist Antoine Meillet thought that it was significant that remains of olive presses had been discovered which date back to Minoan Crete. The Archaic Greek words for king (*basileus*), wine (*woinos*), fig (*sykon*), mint (*minthe*), rose (*wrodon*), and lily (*leirion*, a flower which was also found in Minoan Crete) are also all of pre-Greek origin. And the word *labyrinth*, which now occurs in English and very many other languages, is of Minoan origin too.

Perhaps, then, some Minoans remained as fellow citizens – or as an underclass – in Knossos and other central areas of the island; but there seem to be many other areas of the island which did not immediately fall

[11] Willetts (1977). Willetts was Professor of Greek at University College, London.

under total Mycenean control. The original Minoan population remained in these areas, perhaps augmented by refugees from the Greek-dominated regions.

Pendlebury argues that the natural disasters, and the invasion by an alien people, led to the dispersal of the original population to previously uninhabited areas in the west of Crete. This relocation was perhaps partly done in search of safety, but he also suggests that, since the Minoans were now cut off from trading with their most important partner, Egypt, they were forced to try and cultivate the wilder land in the west where before there had been only outposts of Minoan civilisation. For example, he supposes that some of the people from Phaistos and elsewhere on the Messara plain headed westwards along the south coast, and that the Late Minoan cemetery at Atsipades, northeast of Plakias, indicates movement in the direction of Sfakia. Late Minoan pottery fragments from the period around 1400 BC have certainly been found by the Sphakia Survey on the Frangokastello plain.

As far as Sfakia itself is concerned, there is a suggestion that the name of Asfendou, the village in the White Mountains above Patsianos, like the name of Knossos itself, cannot be Greek on philological grounds. (Rethymnon, Phaistos, Praesos and Phalasarna are also pre-Greek names.) If that is so, and this is by no means certain, then it is of course likely that the name goes back to Minoan times. As we have seen, there are not nearly so many traces of Minoan civilisation in the White Mountains as compared to the more easterly areas. But if after 1400 BC Minoans were seeking refuge from the invaders, then Asfendou, tucked away high in the mountains, protected on all sides by the towering hills which surrounded it, would have made an ideal place to escape to from the Greeks.

In fact, members of the original Minoan population appear to have remained culturally and linguistically unassimilated on Crete for a very long time indeed. In Mycenean Crete as described by Homer, the settlement of Praesos, located in the far east of Crete in the Sitia mountains, is described as being inhabited by Eteocretans ('original Cretans'); and Kydonia (Chania) is cited as being inhabited by Kydonians, who were not Greek speakers either. The legendary founder of this city, Kydas, was said to be Minos' grandson. It is therefore probable that total Mycenean Greek control did not ever extend beyond the central areas of Crete.

The Greek invaders II: Dorian Sfakia

The Mycenean domination of Crete was relatively short-lived, and although we are not entirely clear about what happened – this was a period of unrest and insecurity throughout the eastern Mediterranean – it seems that between 1100 and 900 BC, control of the island gradually passed to another group of Greek invaders who we know as the Dorians. Dorians appear to have reached Greece from the north many hundreds of years later than the earliest Helladic arrivals. Their original Greek homeland was probably in the northwest, in Epirus and western Macedonia, where they seem to have been living around 1200 BC; and their dialect was distinctively different. By the time we find them in Crete, they had brought with them an important innovation – weapons made of iron, which no doubt helped them to subjugate the previous Greek and Minoan inhabitants.

In Sfakia, there is a small cave outside Asfendou, at the top of the Asfendou Gorge, with rock engravings which have been interpreted as representing animals, weapons and ships. Although some investigators have thought that the carvings on the floor of the cave date from the Mesolithic era, it has been argued that in fact they date from this early Dorian period, and that they "offer a rare glimpse at the religious or magical practices of the earliest Dorian Greek settlers in Crete and their expression in art"[12] before they came under the influence of the more sophisticated, albeit Bronze Age, civilisation which they ended up dominating.

Of course, the Bronze Age did not give way to the Iron Age overnight, and the total replacement of bronze by iron took several centuries. But the early military use of iron would have given any group of fighting men a distinct advantage over their adversaries, which would have been particularly important if, as is thought to be the case, the Dorians were relatively few in number at the time of their invasion of Crete, where they probably originally formed a minority ruling aristocracy.

What evidence we have for the Greek dialect spoken by the Dorians in Crete shows clear signs that, while it did eventually replace the Mycenean dialect, it was subjected to considerable Mycenean influence, suggesting close contact between the conquering minority and the subjugated but initially majority Myceneans. And the fact that this linguistic influence was more noticeable in the centre of the island than in the east or west is further evidence that the Myceneans had tended to remain concentrated in that central area.

The arrival of the Dorians was again accompanied by massive social upheaval. The historian Detorakis tells us that there was a miserable period of perhaps 200 years which was characterised by intense struggle between the invaders and the native Mycenean and Minoan Cretans. The population of the island declined considerably during this time, in spite of further waves of immigration from Greece. Dorian society in Crete, like other Dorian societies, notably Sparta, was conservative and inflexible, and Crete became something of an autocratic backwater, isolated from the rest of the Greek world. For several hundred years, according to Detorakis,

[12] Hood (1974).

Crete was in an "almost permanent state of civil war".

The Dorians established themselves in strongly fortified citadels, including one in southwest Crete at Hyrtakina in the hills to the northeast of modern Paleochora, and "a new warlike order was established". Coastal villages were abandoned, and surviving Minoans and/or Myceneans constructed new upland settlements of refuge. In Sfakia, there is a defensible site of this type, known as Kolokasia Kastri, on the slopes of Mount Kastri above the now abandoned village of Kolokasia/Agios Georgos, to the north of Agios Nektarios.[13] Other refuges have been found at Vrokastro, a naturally fortified coastal peak west of Gournia on the Gulf of Mirabello; at Kavousi in the Sitia mountains to the east of Gournia, about 2,500 feet above sea level; and at Karfi. Karfi has been described by many writers as an "eyrie" and is situated at a height of over 3,000 feet in the Dikti mountains in the east of Crete. Here, extraordinarily, remains have been found of an apparently Minoan culture dating from as late as 700 BC.

Even more remarkably, there is evidence from elsewhere that the Minoan culture and language survived even longer than that. Inscriptions in the undeciphered Eteocretan language, which is widely believed to be the descendant of the classical Minoan Linear A language, have been found, some dating from later than 300 BC, more than a thousand years after the initial arrival of the Mycenean Greeks, and 800 years after the Dorian invasion. These inscriptions were found in Praesos, as well as in Driros near Neapoli, both in the eastern province of Lasithi. An indigenous population, possibly speaking the same language as the Eteocretans, also survived on the island of Karpathos, east of Crete, into classical times.

It is probably significant that Praesos, Driros, Karfi, Vrokastro and Kavousi are all located in Lasithi, the easternmost province of Crete. In our western region, Sfakia, according to the Sphakia Survey there is little sign of human occupation in the immediate post-Dorian invasion period, nor for the following centuries up until about 500 BC. However, we have already noted the existence of sites close to Asfendou and at Kolokasia Kastri; and some graves from this era have been found at Tarra, at the southern end of the Samaria Gorge. Some pottery fragments which may perhaps also be from this time have been found in the same area, and in Anopoli.

There is a tradition in Crete that modern Sfakians are the direct descendants of the Dorians. There is no particular reason to believe that this is the case, and indeed, as we have just seen, the original Dorians seem to have penetrated less far into Sfakia than into other areas. On the other hand, it is perfectly possible that, as Crete became more and more influenced by Athens, Macedon, Rome and Byzantium, Sfakia was the area of the island that was most insulated from these external influences. Because of its isolation and the relative inhospitableness of the White

[13] Nowicki (2011).

Mountains, Sfakia may have retained more of the ancient Mycenean and Dorian culture, and retained it for longer, than other areas of the island.[14]

[14] It has also been claimed that the Sfakian dialect of Modern Greek retains many elements of Ancient Dorian. This is not the case. Although Crete was Dorian speaking up until at least 400 BC, all modern dialects of Cretan Greek are derived from the Ancient Athenian dialect, via the Attic *koiné* which emerged after 300 BC, to the same extent as all other modern Greek dialects.

II. Greek and Roman Sfakia – 500 BC to 395 AD

Classical and Hellenistic Sfakia

As historians generally use these terms, the Classical Greek period lasted from approximately 500 BC until 323 BC, which marked the death of Alexander the Great of Macedon. The Hellenistic period from 323 BC onwards was characterised by the development of Greek colonies in Africa and Asia as the result of Alexander's conquests; after his death, the empire split up into separate Hellenistic states. In Crete, the Hellenistic era lasted until 67 BC, which was when the Romans gained total control of the island. During this 500-year period, Sfakia began to emerge into the historical spotlight again, although during the Classical period, which saw the flowering of Athenian democracy, Crete still remained outside the mainstream of important events in Greek history and culture. And the island was still not entirely Greek – the Eteocretan city of Praesos continued to maintain its independence and, we can assume, its language.

In Crete as elsewhere in Greece, this was the period of semi-independent city-states. Once again, however, especially in the earlier Classical period, the most important of these were in the centre of Crete – notably Knossos and Gortyn (east of Phaistos in the Messara plain). Nevertheless, there were four city-states in Sfakia: Anopolis (modern Anopoli), Araden (or Heraden, now Aradena), Poikilasion (above the southern end of the Tripiti gorge), and Tarra (or Tarrha, on the coast at the southern end of the Samaria Gorge – more or less where modern Agia Roumeli stands today). Tarra became important enough to mint its own coinage, which had an image of an *agrimi* – the large wild goat found in the White Mountains – on one side, and a bee on the other, no doubt signifying the production of honey. The city must have been enormously dependent on trade for its wealth, however, because it had no agricultural land worth speaking of. Anopolis and Tarra seem to have become important centres earlier than Araden and Poikilasion. The name Poikilasion survives into modern Greek as Pikilassos, but there is no longer any settlement there. One of the major achievements of the Oxford University Sphakia Survey has been to locate the precise position where the city once stood.

Ruins of Classical Period Anopoli

In Greek mythology, Tarra was the place where the god Apollo met and fell in love with Acacallis, the daughter of King Minos and sister of Ariadne and Phaedra. Apollo was the son of Zeus and Lato (Leto). Apollo was in Tarra, together with his twin sister Artemis, to undergo a purification ceremony conducted by Carmanor in connection with his killing of the fearsome snake (or dragon) of Delphi, called Python. The cult of Apollo is thought to have come originally from the Luvians in Asia Minor, where he was called Aplu.

His sister Artemis came to be associated or identified with the Cretan goddess from Minoan times, Britomartis (Vritomartis in Modern Greek), the goddess of hunting, nature and wild animals, who was also identified with Diktynna (the goddess of Mount Dikte, Zeus' birthplace). According to the late Latin author Solinus, who was writing in about 250 AD, Britomartis meant 'sweet virgin' in Minoan. This is confirmed in part by the lexicon of non-Greek words written by Hesychios of Alexandria in the 400s AD, where *britu* is given as a Cretan word meaning 'sweet'. It is most likely that in Tarra the goddess was actually known by the Greek name Diktynna, as the Minoan name survived longest in the east, where of course the Eteocretans also survived longest. Acacallis is probably also a Minoan name.

There were many shrines to Apollo and Britomartis in ancient Tarra, and Britomartis' birthplace is supposed to have been in the Samaria Gorge. The 19th century English traveller and scholar Robert Pashley suggested that the church of St Nikolas, towards the top end of the gorge, which is built on the ruins of an ancient temple to Apollo, was the site of the ancient settlement of Kaino where Artemis/Diktynna/Britomartis was supposed to have been born. Tarra was also the home of Lucillus of Tarra ("the Tarrhaean"), who wrote a work on the city of Thessalonica, a very influential collection of proverbs, and a commentary on the *Argonautica* – the only surviving Greek epic poem from the Hellenistic period. The *Argonautica* was written in the 200s BC by Apollonius Rhodius and tells the story of Jason and the Argonauts.

The four Sfakian cities were probably rather modest in terms of size and prosperity in comparison with cities in the more fertile areas of the north coast and the centre and east of the island. The Sphakia Survey has found no evidence in any of them of the impressive statuary, theatres, odeons, covered walkways, or agoras (market places-cum-forums) that have been found elsewhere. The probable relative unimportance of Sfakia is also indicated by the fact that the island of Gavdos, which was nearer to Anopolis than to any other city, nevertheless had a special relationship with the more distant Gortyn: Gavdos had to pay certain taxes to Gortyn and to supply this major city with salt and juniper berries.

Of course, these cities were by no means the only populated areas of Sfakia. We know, for instance, that Patsianos was inhabited at this time. But it is interesting that nothing has so far been found indicating serious habitation of the high inland area of Askifou. Nor has anything of significance been found dating to this period in the upland areas of Asfendou, Kallikratis, or Manikas (above Skaloti), or at Mouri or Kali Lakki. In spite of some evidence of human presence in the *madares* during this period, again probably transitory, most of what was happening in Sfakia occurred on or near the coast. And we can assume that most connections with the rest of Crete were by sea – the most useful form of transport into and out of Sfakia up to and including the 1940s.

Civil wars continued to plague the island, and the instability of the period is reflected in the sites of three of the Sfakian cities. Tarra seems to have had external walls which served as sea defenses rather than protection from attacks. (Tarra was located about 4 metres, or more than 12 feet, lower than where the site is today – the Early Byzantine Paroxysm, or earthquake, tilted Crete up at its western end and raised the entire Sfakia coastline by that amount.) But Poikilasion was sited defensively: it was on high ground above the bottom end of the Tripiti gorge, just to the east of Cape Tripiti, on the far western edge of the Sfakia region. It would in any case have been readily accessible only by sea – an obvious example of how sea transport was paramount – but the city "occupied a site of some physical inconvenience", as the Sphakia survey has it, about 400 metres / 1,300 feet above sea level, and higher than all the possible agricultural land, testifying to a fear of piracy and other attacks from the sea.

Araden and the large and fertile upland plain of Anopolis, while also near the coast, were also very defensible. They are not visible from the sea and were apparently well out of harm's way at around 600 metres / 2,000 feet above sea level. Araden was only about 3 kilometres west of Anopolis, but it was located in a very secure position on the western edge of the very deep Aradena Gorge, which separates the two settlements. Anopolis was also protected by defensive walls. Anopolis and Araden were served by the port of Phoenix, modern Finikas, on the west side of the Cape Moures peninsula, which has modern Loutro (which means 'bath') on its eastern side. (The Early Byzantine Paroxysm resulted in Loutro later on supplanting Phoenix as the deeper and better harbour).

The Anopoli Plateau, with the ruins of the ancient city on the left

The unstable situation in Crete during these centuries also led to the establishment of various alliances between the Cretan city-states, as well as between them and states elsewhere. One of these Cretan alliances was known as the Mountain League, and it appears to have come into being before or around 300 BC. It consisted of the Sfakian cities of Tarra and Poikilasion plus three city-states to the west, in modern Selino province: Hyrtakina, Elyros (inland from modern Sougia), and Lissos (on the coast to the west of Sougia).

It is also notable that between 280 and 250 BC or so, this south coast league formed an alliance across the Mediterranean with the King of Cyrene, a Greek colony and city-state in what is now Libya. Pottery from Africa has been found at Anopolis, a sign that other cities in Sfakia also had connections across the 200 miles of the Libyan Sea. The Hellenisation of the North African coast, and of the Middle East, now meant that Sfakia and the rest of the south coast of Crete were no longer on the far periphery of the Greek world, but much closer to its centre.

Some time not long before 200 BC, Anopolis was attacked and defeated, quite possibly by its near neighbour Araden. Interestingly, it was later liberated by a citizen of Anopolis named Charmadas, who had probably been away serving as a mercenary. We know that he later served in the army of the Ptolomaic Hellenistic kingdom of Egypt, which was very influential in Crete at this time (and whose last ruler was Cleopatra). He served in Coele Syria, the territory of Palestine and southern Syria which was disputed between the kingdom of the Egyptian Ptolomies and the Hellenistic Seleucid empire. We can suppose that he had taken his family with him to Egypt, because his daughter married one of his fellow soldiers who was from Aetolia in western mainland Greece. It is sad to think that Charmadas is known to have died in Gaza without returning to his native Sfakian city that he helped liberate.

This military life-style was probably quite typical for many Sfakians. The unrest on the island, and in particular the poverty and weakness of the Cretan economy compared to many other Greek areas, led many of the men to find employment in this way. Crete supplied Alexander with many soldiers, and Cretans commonly fought with foreign Hellenistic armies as skilled archers and guerrilla fighters. We can imagine that at least some of these would have been Sfakians, the terrain of this region lending itself to the development of guerrilla fighting techniques, as the Turks were to find out to their cost many centuries later. We know, too, that Cretan archers fought in the armies of Julius Caesar.

Peace must soon have been made between Anopolis and Araden, because they jointly had good connections with the Greek world beyond the island. Together with Tarra and many other Cretan city-states, they were parties to a treaty with Eumenes II of Pergamon, a Hellenistic kingdom in Asia Minor, in 183 BC.

Contact with North Africa and the influence of the Graeco-Egyptian Ptolemaic kingdom, transmitted via trade, is also seen in the adoption in Crete of the Egyptian religious cult of Isis and Serapis (Egyptian Osiris). Isis was the goddess of fertility and motherhood, and Osiris, her husband/ brother, was the god who judged the dead. There was a temple dedicated to them in Sfakian Poikilassos.

The long and continuing period of unrest also had one very poignant consequence in that, after 3,000 years, the last vestiges of Minoan civilisation on Crete were finally destroyed. In 140 BC, some 1,300 years after the first arrival of the Greek invaders, the independent Eteocretan city of Praesos in the east of the island was wiped out by a coalition of forces from the Dorian cities of Hieraptyna (modern Ierapetra) and Itanos.

Sfakia and the Phoenicians

From about 1000 BC, the Phoenicians, a Semitic-speaking people whose original homeland was in modern Lebanon, gradually came to dominate trade in much of the Mediterranean – the Greek word *chrysos* 'gold' is of Phoenician origin. Their influence spread further and further westwards, and they established trading posts and colonies all along the north African coast, in Cyprus, Malta, Sardinia, Sicily, Ibiza, and in southern Spain. It is known that they even made voyages as far as southern England. Voyages westwards from Lebanon would most usually have taken them past Crete; and the Phoenicians have a number of historical connections to Sfakia and the rest of Crete. The Cretan goddess Europa was, according to legend, a Phoenican princess who was carried off by Zeus, disguised as a bull.

The use by the Phoenicians of the south coast of Crete as a staging post on their trading voyages westwards may help to explain the location of the four ancient cities of Anopolis, Araden, Poikilasion and Tarra near the Sfakian coast, remote from the rest of Crete and readily accessible only by sea. Phoenix and Tarra would have been very desirable stopping-off places for Phoenician sailors in need of water, provisions and rest. Elsewhere on the south coast, there is a shrine which is probably Phoenician at Kommos (Komo), the port for Phaistos and Gortyn, dating from about 800 BC. The name Gortyn itself is also sometimes said to be of Phoenician origin.

The Phoenicians may have even played a role in the development of the four Sfakian settlements. It is possible that the name Tarra comes from a Phoenican word *tar* meaning 'gorge with river'. There is also a tradition that Araden was founded by the Phoenicians, with the name deriving from the Phoenician word *aruad* meaning 'shelter'. And the name of the port for Araden – Phoenix – may not be a coincidence, although the more obvious explanation is that it means 'date palm', as does its modern name, Finikas, in Modern Greek. On the other hand, the Phoenicians did not call themselves by that name; the word is Greek, and it is probable that both it and the word for palm tree go back to the same Greek root *phoinix* meaning 'dark red/brown colour'. The association of the colour with the Phoenicians would have been because of the famous purple or crimson dye associated with the Phoenican (now Lebanese) city of Tyre.

For Crete generally, the word Phoenician is of some considerable interest in terms of the development of alphabetic writing. An archaic Cretan text dating from about 500 BC contains the word *poinikastas,* which has been interpreted as meaning 'scribe', as well as the verb *poinikazen,* which appears to mean 'to write'. Scholars are not entirely sure how this word arose, but one theory is that it derives from the same root we have just discussed. If that is really so, then the verb could either mean something like 'to do what Phoenicians do', i.e. write; or 'to make red', implying that writing was done with red paint, and/or that engraved letters were typically filled in with red.

We do know that it was the Greeks who developed the first ever truly alphabetic writing system, with each consonant and vowel sound being represented by a letter (as opposed to a syllabary). And it is known that this was derived historically from the Phoenician writing system, which represented only consonants. Indeed, Herodotos says that the Phoenicians wrote Greek before anybody else, including Greeks. It is therefore possible that it was Phoenicans, instead of or as well as Greeks, who first converted their original system to a true alphabet by adding symbols for Greek vowels. The impetus for this would have been a linguistic one. Semitic languages like Phoenician lend themselves very readily to being written without vowels, and both modern Arabic and Hebrew most usually still are. This is because these languages typically have only three vowels, and their grammar makes extensive use of roots typically consisting of three consonants, with vowel changes indicating more precise meanings, rather like English does in an extremely limited way with *sing, sang, sung, song*. In Modern Arabic, from *ktb* we find *kataba* 'to write', *kitab* 'book', *katib* 'writer', *kutubi* 'bookseller', and so on. This would have worked much less well with an Indo-European language like Greek, where a lot of guess-work would have been needed in order to decipher exactly what was meant from consonants alone, just as it would be difficult to work out in modern English whether *stt* was intended to represent *astute, estate, satiate, situate, statue,* or *stoat,* words which are not at all connected in meaning with each other. In any case, the presence of the Phoenicians in Crete means that it is not surprising the island seems to have been one of the first places in the world where the first true alphabet was used, and that it played a vital role in the wider diffusion of this alphabet.

In time, the most significant Phoenician settlement in the Mediterranean came to be the one located well to the west of Crete at the city-state of Carthage, in modern Tunisia. Its name in Phoenician was something like Qart Hadasht, meaning 'new town'. Carthage eventually eclipsed in importance all of the Phoenician settlements back in their Middle East homeland and became the centre of an empire that rivalled Greece and Rome in terms of power and influence.

Conflict between Rome and Carthage eventually led to warfare, and in 218 BC, the Carthaginian general Hannibal famously crossed the Alps from north to south, with elephants, on his way to attack Rome. Hannibal remained in Italy for many years, but eventually returned to Carthage. Rome then invaded Carthaginian territory in North Africa, and in 202 BC Hannibal was defeated and eventually forced out. He arrived in Syria, where he had already been cultivating an anti-Roman alliance with King Antiochus III. However, in spite of Hannibal's aid, Antiochus was defeated by Rome at a series of battles, mostly on mainland Greek territory, and Hannibal fled again, this time to Crete, where he arrived in 190 BC, 28 years after his legendary crossing of the Alps.

The years that Hannibal spent in Gortyn, at this time one of the major cities of Crete, rivalled only by Knossos, attracted the attention of the Romans. During this period, a number of important Roman emissaries arrived in Crete, supposedly to mediate in one of the many Cretan civil wars, but probably their major concern was to keep an eye on Hannibal and to organise his arrest. Roman influence eventually led once again to Hannibal fleeing, this time to Bithynia, now the Izmit region in northern Turkey.

Sfakia under the Romans

There were a number of other reasons why Rome, a growing power, was getting more and more interested in Crete. Romans were increasingly being involved in genuine mediation between different Cretan and Greek states. And various states in Crete also had alliances with, and were supplying military help to, a number of anti-Roman polities, such as the tyrant King Nabis' Sparta and Philip V's Macedon. The island, especially the western end, had also for a long time been a base for piracy, which disrupted Roman trade and control; and perhaps as many as a few thousand Romans were being held captive by Cretan privateers. Indeed, mercenary soldiering and piracy, including the taking and trading of slaves, seem to have been a major source of income for many Cretans. We can guess that men from the not very prosperous or fertile area of Sfakia would have been heavily involved in this.

Eventually, Nabis, Philip and the other rulers of Greece were subdued by the Romans, and Crete was left as the only area of Greece which remained independent. It was then obvious that control of the island would be a very desirable goal for Rome. Not only would this mean an end to piracy, but Crete would also represent an excellent basis for Roman expansion projects in the Middle East and North Africa.

In 85 BC Mithridates VI, who was of Persian origin and who ruled the Hellenistic kingdom of Pontus on the shores of the Black Sea in northern

Anatolia, sought help from Crete in his defensive struggle against the Romans, and Cretan mercenaries took part in the second Mithridatic war against the Romans which started in 74 BC. This gave the Romans the pretext they needed, and in 71 BC Marcus Antonius, the father of the more famous Mark Antony, invaded Crete. However, the Cretans under Lasthenes were ready for him and defeated him in a naval battle off Heraklion, where many Romans were taken prisoner.

A second and ultimately successful Roman campaign then started in 69 BC, but the conquest of Crete was not a question of one simple, glorious victory. It was the outcome of a messy civil war, with Cretans and Romans fighting on both sides. The Romans were now under a different commander, Metellus, who arrived with three legions. His army probably embarked for Crete from Gythion in the southern Peloponnese and arrived at Kissamos, the port for the northwestern city-state of Polyrrenia, which seems to have welcomed him. Its support for the Romans was likely to have been the result of enmity between Polyrrenia and neighbouring Kydonia (Chania), which Metellus now proceeded to attack – the first battle, at which Metellus defeated Lasthenes, certainly took place somewhere near Kydonia, which then fell under Roman control.

In 68 BC Metellus again landed in Crete, on the north coast close to Knossos. After subduing this city, he then attacked Lappa, where he defeated Cretans fighting under the leadership of Octavius, a legate of Pompey, the Roman general who had been nominated independently to be commander of a special naval task force campaigning against pirates. In 67 BC the Cretans under Octavius were defeated a final time by Metellus at Hierapytna (modern Ierapetra) on the southeast coast. Metellus then made Gortyn the capital of Roman Crete, leading us to suppose that this was some kind of reward for the city's support of the Romans, or at least for its failure to give active support against him to any of their rival city-states. Crete was then governed as part of a province which also included Cyrene, modern Libya.

This was the first time that Greek Crete had been conquered by a foreign power. Sadly, though, it was by no means the last. As we shall see, various invasions of the island by alien forces were later to have important and usually unpleasant consequences for Sfakia: invasions by the Arabs, the Genoese, the Venetians, the Turks – and finally the Germans, who began their battle for Crete by landing close to where the Romans had begun their first land battle 2000 years before, near Chania.

After the Roman invasion, perhaps because Roman control was more or less total from very early on, there does not seem to have been much of an attempt by Greeks to escape this alien control and seek refuge. However, there is some indication that the remoteness of Sfakia, as would be the case so often in the future, made it an attractive place for people fleeing from the conquerors in order to maintain their independence. There is a local tradition that, high in the Samaria Gorge about an hour's walk north of Samaria Village, there was a settlement called Ellenais, the 'City of the Greeks', described by Pashley as the "last refuge of the Greeks".

After the conquest, it was obviously beneficial that Roman rule led to the end of civil war and instability on the island, and there was little actual opposition to Roman control. Communications also improved. One of the most lasting artifacts of the Roman occupation that can still be seen today is what are called in the Sfakian dialect the *kadirimia* (*kalderimia* in Standard Greek). This modern word is of Turkish origin, but many of these stone-paved mule tracks that run between the most important Sfakian centres, such as from Anopolis down to Chora Sfakion, are probably of Roman origin. Sadly, having lasted for perhaps as many as two thousand years, they are now falling into disuse and therefore into disrepair. The two most spectacular paths are the one that descends into the depths of the Aradena Gorge between Anopolis and Araden and then back up the other side, and the one that descends the two thousand feet from the cliff edge below Agios Ioannis at Selouda to just above the shoreline east of Agios Pavlos.

A couple of decades after the Roman conquest, some famous historical names appear on the scene. In 44 BC, ten years after his second expedition to England, Julius Caesar separated Crete from Cyrene administratively. After his murder, Brutus was placed in charge of Crete, and Cassius was in control of Cyrene, probably in an attempt to get them out of Rome. Then in 37 BC Mark Antony granted part of Crete to Cleopatra, probably the eastern city of Itanos where a Ptolemaic garrison had been stationed. Finally, under Octavian, Crete and Cyrene were once again reunited in 27 BC, an administrative union which lasted for 300 years.

One consequence of the new feeling of security under the Romans was that many coastal port communities again flourished without fear of attack from the sea, at the expense of their inland counterparts. Polyrrenia gave way to Kissamos, and Knossos to Heraklion (Iraklio). In Sfakia, however, this did not occur – Araden and Anopolis continued to flourish alongside Phoenix, where the Loutro peninsula became the site of a major Roman city. It is true, however, that Poikilasion was eventually abandoned, perhaps because its inconvenient defensive position was no longer necessary.

Initially, Tarra also maintained its importance and must have continued to benefit from trade, particularly from vessels which travelled the important trade route from Egypt and Syria along the south coast of Crete to Rome itself. The south coast cities of Hieraptyna (Ierapetra) and Suia (Sougia) became very large settlements indeed, by the standards of the time, as a result of the route that vessels were forced to follow because of the prevailing winds, hugging the coast on their voyage from Egypt to Italy via the shores of Syria and the south coast of Asia Minor.

Generally, too, although villages and farmsteads which were dependent on towns and cities seem to have begun to flourish under the security of Roman rule much more than they did during the Hellenistic period (when not only civil unrest but also the Dorian urban-centred culture remained influential), in Sfakia this did not occur. The terrain of the White Mountains led to the maintenance of a pattern of isolated towns and cities, with hardly any satellite villages, though some Roman remains have been found in Asfendou.

Crete remained very Greek during the whole of the Roman occupation, with the Romans constituting a relatively small and unopposed overclass, although Knossos was settled by Roman soldiers and turned into a Roman colony. Greeks remained in control of nearly all the land; and there were probably as few Romans in Sfakia as there were Turks during the later Turkish occupation. Gortyn remained the capital of the island, but Kydonia (Chania) increased in importance.

Late in the Roman period, Tarra was relocated to the other side of the mouth of the Samaria Gorge, on the western side of the river, near to where modern Agia Roumeli is sited today. The name Agia Roumeli is itself very interesting and puzzling, but it may date from this Roman period. *Agia*, from Ancient Greek *hagia*, is the feminine form of the Greek word for 'saint' or 'holy', the masculine form being *Agios*. The problem is that there is no Christian saint called Roumeli, so where does the name come from? One theory is that when the Romans arrived in Crete they identified the goddess Britomartis, whose temples stood at the end of the gorge, with their own goddess Rumilia (who was said to have breast-fed Romulus and Remus), and renamed the temple after her, in Latin.

The Cretan historian Spanakis presents another theory, which would place the name a few hundred years later. This was proposed by Papagrigorakis, who suggested that the name has nothing to do with 'saint' or 'holy', but is actually from Arabic. In modern Greek *Agia* is pronounced 'aya'. Papagrigorakis claims that in Arabic *rumeli* meant 'Greek' and that *aya* meant 'water', the implication being that Arab sailors knew that this was a location in Greece where they could obtain supplies of fresh water. Crete experienced quite a lengthy period of Arab control (see Chapter IV), and prior to that it had a lot of contact with Arabs from North Africa and Spain; and *rum* or *rumi* does mean 'Greek' or 'Greek Orthodox' in Arabic. Unfortunately, there is no Arabic word *aya* meaning 'water'. However, there is an Egyptian Arabic word *mayya* which does mean 'water', and another word *ayn* which means 'spring'. So the name could perhaps be derived from Arabic *mayya rumi* 'Greek water', or *ayn rumi* 'Greek spring', although it is not clear where the *-eli* could have come from.

A third possibility is that *Rum Eyli* is Turkish for 'the province of the Rum [Greeks]'. The term *rum* was used by the Turks to refer to areas of Greece, and it occurs in many other European languages as Rumeli or Rumelia. So another explanation is that the name is much more recent, coming after the Ottoman invasion, and that it is due to someone from these areas of Greece owning land in the Agia Roumeli area – but then we would have no explanation for the *Agia* element of the name.

While Tarra eventually declined under the Romans, Anopolis and Araden continued to increase in importance, as did Phoenix. Although, like all the other coastal areas of Sfakia, it had no cultivable land, Phoenix thrived not only because of its importance as a port, which we have already noted, but because it was the only viable winter harbour on the entire south coast of Crete. Evidence that it played an important role in trans-Mediterranean trade comes from the North African and Italian pottery which has been found in Sfakia from this era.

Evidence for the importance of the trade with Africa for Phoenix/Loutro is also to be found in an inscription[15] from Phoenix which was made as an offering of thanks by shipwreck survivors. It was dedicated by the Alexandrian captain of the *Isopharia*, probably a corn ship, to Serapis (Osiris), who had clearly become identified with Jupiter, and to other gods and the Emperor Trajan. We can date the inscription quite accurately because it was not until the end of 102 AD that Trajan acquired the title Dacicus, so the plaque must have been written some time between then and his death in 117 AD.

Under the Romans, Christianity came to Crete early on. During the Hellenistic period there had been a certain amount of Jewish settlement on Crete, particularly from Alexandria, and notably in Gortyn, where the community is said to have been rich and peaceful. It is reported that a number of Cretan-based Jews were present in Jerusalem at the original Pentecost in 31 AD and were persuaded by the experience to convert to Christianity. Back in Crete, they formed the kernel of the new religious movement, as Christianity took hold amongst both the Jewish and the Greek communities on the island.

One of the first missionaries to Crete was St Paul himself, who made at least two visits to the island. His first was in 61 AD, when he was being taken as a prisoner to Rome in a vessel which was sailing from Palestine via Cyprus and Rhodes to the Cretan south coast and "came to a place called

[15] The inscription runs: IOVI SOLI OPTIMO MAXIMO / SARAPIDI ET OMNIBUS DIIS ET / IMPERATORI CAESARI NERVAE / TRAIANO AUG[usto] GERMANICO DACICO N[ostro] / EPICTETUS LIBERTUS TABELLARIUS [= tabularius] / CURAM AGENTE OPERIS DIONYSIO SOSTRA- / TI FILIO ALEXANDRINO GUBERNATORE / NAVIS PARASEMO ISOPHARIA T[iberii] C[laudii] THEONIS [To Jupiter Sol Optimus Maximus Sarapis and all the gods, and our Emperor Caesar Nerva Trajan Augustus, victor over the Germans, victor over the Dacians, Epictetus, freedman and painter of votive tablets, at the command of Dionysius, son of Sostratus and helmsman from Alexandria of the ship called Isopharia of Tiberius Claudius Theon].

Fair Havens". (This village, still bearing the same name – Kali Limenes – survives to this day on the south coast west of Lendas.) There was then some discussion about what to do because of the impending winter – the sailing season ended in September – and in the *Acts of the Apostles*, written by St Luke, who was also on the journey, we find:

> because the harbour was not suitable to winter in, the majority advised to put to sea from there, on the chance that somehow they could reach Phoenix, a harbour of Crete, looking northeast and southeast, and winter there. And when the south wind blew gently, supposing that they had obtained their purpose, they weighed anchor and sailed along Crete, close inshore. But soon a tempestuous wind struck down from the land; and when the ship was caught and could not face the wind, we gave way to it and were driven. And running under the lee of a small island called Clauda, we managed with difficulty to secure the [ship's] boat.

Clauda is modern Gavdos, and anyone who has seen the katabatic winds which roar down without warning from the Sfakian mountains and out to sea, turning it from blue to white in a matter of minutes, can understand how "a tempestuous wind" could cause such havoc. Eventually leaving Gavdos, and after enduring a terrible storm for several days, they were shipwrecked on Malta, and Paul was taken to Rome, where he was placed under house arrest for two years. After his release in 63 AD, Paul travelled widely, and during his journeyings he returned to Crete. He is said to have landed at the Sfakian beach to the east of Agia Roumeli where the 10th century church of Agios Pavlos (St Paul) now stands. There, below the steep cliffs which descend to the sea from Agios Ioannis, he baptised people using the fresh water spring that still bubbles to the surface of the beach there.

Paul's chief Cretan disciple was Titus, who was a Cretan himself and who is credited with the initial spread of Christianity on the island. Paul sent him a letter after departing from Crete for the second time, leaving Titus in charge, and it is thought that Paul wrote this in approximately 66 AD in Epirus, in northwestern Greece. In this letter (the New Testament *Epistle to Titus*), Paul wrote:

> "this is why I left you in Crete, that you might amend what is defective", because there are in Crete "many insubordinate men, empty talkers and deceivers". It has been said that "Cretans are always liars, evil beasts, lazy gluttons", and "this testimony", confirms St Paul, "is true".

Those wishing to defend the honour of Cretans might want to point out that St Paul appears to be quoting from Epimenides, a seer and poet from Knossos, writing in the 500s BC, who is credited with the following lines in which Minos says to Zeus:

> They fashioned a tomb for thee, O holy and high one –
> The Cretans, always liars, evil beasts, idle bellies!
> But thou art not dead: thou livest and abidest forever,
> For in thee we live and move and have our being.

The assertion that Cretans were liars refers to the fact that it was traditionally and widely believed on the island that Zeus was mortal, whereas Epimenides himself, like most other Greeks elsewhere, considered Zeus to be immortal.

Titus is believed to have died in about 105 AD. Not long after his death, it is quite probable that the anti-Christian Emperor Hadrian visited Crete. He seems to have been very popular on the island, and perhaps this is because he actually landed there. It is known that Hadrian made a grand tour of his empire, and by 123 AD this had taken him to Cyrene, Roman North Africa; he travelled on from Libya to Syria – so Crete could have been on the route. After arriving in Syria, he is said to have planted a grove of trees in Bethlehem in honour of the god Adonis as a deliberate insult to Christianity. The position of Christianity in Crete remained uncertain for many generations, and as late as 250 AD official Roman victimisation led to the martyrdom of ten Cretans near Gortyn at Aulonion, which is the site of the present-day village of Agioi Deka, 'Ten Saints', in southern Heraklion province.

This may have been an uneasy time altogether for the eastern part of the Roman Empire. In 264 AD, the Goths, a pagan Germanic people who invaded the Balkans from the north, reached Galatia and Cappadocia in Asia Minor; and Gothic pirates landed on Cyprus and Crete. In the process, the Goths seized enormous amounts of booty and took thousands of people into captivity. Then in 268 AD, another massive raid was made on the Balkans by the Goths; they sacked Athens, Corinth and Sparta, and even launched a further attack on Crete before they were eventually defeated by Emperor Claudius II. Even then the troubles of the Christians were not quite over – the Bishop of Gortyn was martyred in 304 AD.

One lasting effect in Sfakia of the arrival of Christianity is the name of the Samaria Gorge, which seems to be due to one of Titus' successors. It is named after the small village of Samaria, situated half-way up the gorge, which is said to take its name from its church, dedicated to the *Ossia Maria*. This may well be true. What is not true is that this means 'the bones of Mary', as is often claimed, implying that the church contained relics of a St Mary. The Mary in question was an Egyptian prostitute in Alexandria who saw the error of her ways after an epiphany during a visit to Jerusalem, and then spent 47 years living as a hermit in the Jordanian desert. She was born in about 344 AD and died about 421. The tradition has it that her entire body was buried there in the desert. *Ossia* in any case has nothing to do with bones. It comes from the Ancient Greek word *hosios,* which meant 'sanctioned or approved by the law of nature' (and was often opposed to *hieros,* 'sacred, reserved for the gods'). It gradually took on the meaning of 'pious, devout, religious, pure' when applied to people, and in modern Greek *osios,* feminine *osia,* means 'sacred, venerable, blessed'. So *Ossia Maria* simply means 'The Blessed Mary'.

It is not surprising that a church should have been dedicated to her in Sfakia. St Andrew of Crete, who was born in Damascus in about 660 and who became a monk in a monastery near Jerusalem, later became Bishop of Gortyn in Crete. He wrote the massive Great Canon of St Andrew, which is performed in Orthodox churches during Lent. The story of St Mary of Egypt was very well liked in Jerusalem, and it is thought that it was popularised by St Andrew. Certainly, the chanting of his Canon is generally accompanied by the reading of the story of St Mary. So if the name Samaria really is derived from *Ossia Maria,* which is by no means certain, we can suppose that the name can date from no earlier than the 700s.

III. The First Byzantine Period – 395 to 824

The history of the Byzantine Empire began with the founding of Constantinople in 330 by the Roman Emperor Constantine I the Great. This was to be his new capital, the "New Rome", located in the eastern provinces of the Roman Empire on the site of the ancient Greek town of Byzantium. Crete at that time was a Roman province governed as part of the imperial administrative unit of Illyricum, as the southern part of the Balkan Peninsula was then known.

Following Constantine's death in 337, the Empire entered a volatile period that saw its western areas coming under frequent attacks from strong emerging nations to the north – we have already noted attacks by the Goths. After the death of Emperor Theodosius in 395, the Roman Empire was divided and governed by his two young sons. Illyricum together with Crete became part of the Eastern Roman Empire, known later as the Byzantine Empire. Thus the first period of Byzantine rule of Crete started in 395, and was to last almost 430 years.

The administrative structure established by the Romans survived until Emperor Justinian's reforms in the middle of the 6th century, which saw the gradual concentration of power in the hands of the Empire's 64 provincial governors. The capital of Crete remained at Gortyn.

New administrative units called *themes* were put into place throughout the Empire early in the 7th century; their heads were directly responsible for both military and political matters. This led to autonomy for the provinces, but at the same time it resulted in further concentration of power in the hands of the governors, whose titles changed over time from *Consularis* to *Proconsul* to *Archon* or *Archon Protospatharios*. There is debate amongst academics as to whether Crete did actually become a *theme* before the Arab conquest, and whether, if it did not, this could have contributed to Crete being unprepared and unable to defend itself from the Arab invasions (see the next chapter).[16]

[16] Tsougarakis (1988), pp. 170-178; Detorakis (1994), pp. 110, 111.

The population of the island was about 250,000 by the end of this era.[17] The Cretans were mainly engaged in agriculture (producing grain and wine for the most part, and olives and olive oil to a lesser extent) and pastoral activities as well as trade. Mining and processing of iron ore and copper also occurred, but in quantities that satisfied only local needs. The large number of settlements on the northern and southern coasts suggest that the island was experiencing a period of relative prosperity. Crete was self-sufficient for most of its needs, importing only marble, pottery and some luxury items. Its exports included timber, whetstones, cheese and glass, and its main export markets were Egypt to the south and the Mediterranean regions to the west. Changes in social and economic policies saw the introduction of restrictions on changes in occupation, forcing families to remain farmers, traders or even administrators from generation to generation. At the same time, land ownership became concentrated in the hands of fewer people, as farmers with small-holdings were forced to become tenant farmers.

The first three centuries of this period were quite unusual for Crete in that they were peaceful, although the island experienced a number of natural disasters. Several severe earthquakes hit the island, one in 415 destroying most towns, including Gortyn, which was then rebuilt by Emperor Theodosius II. The plague also affected the island a number of times, the worst being the epidemic of 542 that started in Egypt and spread to Constantinople and throughout the Mediterranean.

During this period, Christianity was also spreading rapidly throughout the eastern and western parts of the old Roman Empire. Despite the fact that Crete was administered from Constantinople, control of its archdiocese remained under the Holy See of Rome until 754 (except for a short period after 476 when Rome was controlled by the Visigoths), when it was finally brought under the control of Constantinople. Many churches were built on the island during this time; more than 70 early Christian basilicas have been discovered by archaeologists so far. Some of the largest basilicas were at Gortyn (Agios Titos), Panormos near Mylopotamos, and Almyrida in Apokoronas.

Sfakia during the first Byzantine period

Unfortunately, there is only limited historical information available about Crete for this period, and even less relating to Sfakia. In the administrative and ecclesiastical records, only Phoenix and Araden are mentioned – as a single location, Phoenix being the harbour for Araden – and the island of Gavdos, which at the time was called Klaudos (Clauda). Both must have had substantial populations at the time, as they are included in the

[17] Detorakis (1994), p. 112.

list of the largest 22 Cretan population centres. These 22 urban areas were allowed to have a degree of self-government through the operation of local councils (*vouli*). Phoenix-Araden is also mentioned as a bishopric,[18] one of only twelve on Crete.

Further evidence that the district of Sfakia was experiencing a prosperous and peaceful period is found in the number of relatively large basilicas built during the 5th and 6th centuries in the area, especially on the coast. Evidence of such churches can be found at Frangokastello underneath the church of Agios Nikitas (300 meters east of the Frangokastello fort); and the ruins of an earlier church from this era can also be seen 2 km further west, at the site of Astratigos, named after the ruined church of Archangel Michael on the same site (Astratigos derives from *Archistratigos* 'chief general', as the Sfakians refer to Archangel Michael). At Aradena today there stands another church dedicated to Astratigos, which was built on top of a much larger old basilica, whose lower components can still be seen. There are also ruins of basilicas at Loutro on the site of Theotokos; at Phoenix; at the ancient town of Tarra; and at Tripiti.[19] The fact that the centre of Cretan glass production during that time was at Tarra provides more evidence for the area's prosperity. As we saw above, in view of Tarra's isolated location, this glass must have been destined for export by sea.

The church of Archangel Michael in Aradena

[18] Kelaidis (1982), pp. 151-153. Another view is that Phoenix and Araden were the seats of two separate bishoprics.
[19] Andrianakis (1982), pp. 33-38.

Piracy and the emerging Arab threat

Piracy started to become a menace again throughout the Mediterranean in the early centuries of the first millennium. Crete's first recorded experience of piracy in the Byzantine era was an attack in 623 by Slav pirates who were threatening the Byzantines further north.

Also in the 7th century, the lands around the Mediterranean started to feel the impact of a new and expanding power – the Arabs. The Byzantine Empire suffered a series of humiliating defeats against the Arabs in 634 and 636, resulting in the permanent loss of Damascus and Jerusalem, followed in rapid succession by Alexandria, Cyprus and Rhodes, as the Arab expansion continued. The Arabs had become a permanent threat to Byzantium, and from 650 onwards they possessed a formidable fleet that constantly imperilled all Byzantine possessions. By the end of the century they had conquered Egypt, Armenia and large parts of Persia, and by 711 they controlled the entire North African coast and had invaded Spain, soon moving into France. They besieged Constantinople twice, first in 673 for five years and again in 717.

The Arabs first attacked Crete in 654, and further raids probably took place in 656 and 671. There is evidence that Arab forces invaded and spent some time on Crete in 674.[20] The Byzantine fleet proved to be quite ineffective in protecting its coastal territories, being preoccupied with defending Constantinople. These raids against Byzantine territories intensified during the 8th century, with Crete being attacked again in 705 and a number of times from 713 to 716.

From then on Crete suffered a continuously deteriorating situation. The army was unable to prevent Arab incursions or even sieges of fortified towns. The plague affected the island's population in 746, while Constantinople was being decimated by the same epidemic. Another strong earthquake hit the island in 796, causing considerable damage. There is evidence that most of the towns on the southern coast of Crete were being abandoned as the population tried to escape from the frequent Arab raids. The prosperity and trade previously enjoyed during the earlier years of the Byzantine era was disappearing fast. By the end of the 8th century, Crete and the rest of the Byzantine Empire found themselves in a very weak, if not desperate, situation. During the same period the Arabs were also experiencing problems of their own, but these would contribute eventually to their conquest of Crete in 824.

[20] Tsougarakis (1987), p. 340.

IV. Arab Rule – 824 to 961

Background: Byzantium and the Arab world

The Arabs were not a unified nation but consisted of a number of independent tribes. Although they shared the same religion, had certain common objectives and at times cooperated against a common target, on many occasions they fought against each other. Following the death of the Prophet Muhammad in 632, the Islamic community was ruled by a rapid succession of four caliphs until 661. During this brief span of time, the Arabs brought under their control Iraq, Persia, Armenia, Syria, Palestine, Egypt and North Africa as far west as Libya. At the end of this period differences between the various Arab tribes emerged, mainly because of issues surrounding the succession to the Prophet, which resulted in divisions into Sunnis, Shiites and other sects.

Muawiyah, the governor of Syria who became Caliph in 661, was the first of the rulers from the Umayyad dynasty, a Sunni clan from the same Quraish tribe in Mecca that the Prophet Muhammad belonged to. The Umayyads ruled until 750 when the Abbasids, descendants of one of Muhammad's uncles who regarded themselves as the rightful heirs of the Prophet, attacked and defeated them, killing all of the ruling family except for one man who managed to escape, Abd al-Rahman (see below). During the 90 years of the Umayyad dynasty, Arab rule expanded east into today's Central Asia and the borders of China, west through Tunisia to the Atlantic Ocean, and north into the Iberian Peninsula. This expansion strained the centralised governing structure, and local rulers started asserting their independence.

Since the beginning of the 7th century, the Arabs had been threatening Byzantium on a number of fronts. Their naval power had improved to the point where it was a serious challenge to the Byzantines in the number and quality of its vessels, the level of technology and expertise in its use.

Although the various emirates[21] were semi-independent and would often not cooperate with each other, all of them were a cause for concern to the Byzantines, as they all shared the aim of spreading the Islamic religion, by force if necessary. Their early successes in imposing their rule on others was partially due to the fact that they permitted both Christians and Jews to continue practicing their own faiths, although these subjects were treated differently from Muslims in terms of taxes and other freedoms. Many people readily converted to Islam in order to gain the same rights and privileges that Muslims enjoyed. This posed a serious threat to Byzantium, which was facing internal turmoil because of numerous religious disputes involving iconoclasts, Monophysites, Copts and other Christian sects.

During this same period Byzantium was experiencing another internal conflict, this time a rebellion by a Byzantine army general, Thomas of Gaziura, also known as Thomas the Slav. Leading a large force of 80,000 mercenaries, Thomas arrived in December 821 outside Constantinople and attacked the city.[22] This obliged Emperor Michael II to recall all available forces from other parts of the Empire that were still loyal to him, and the two armies fought one another for more than 12 months. In March 823, to the surprise of the two fighting forces, the Bulgars arrived from the north and attacked Thomas' forces, defeating them and taking significant spoils with them. The Emperor set out in pursuit of Thomas, whose forces continued to be hunted down and eliminated until early 824. By that time the Arabs had landed in Crete, which had been left virtually undefended.

Abu Hafs and his followers' long search for a new home

The Arabs' expansion westward, following the North African coast, stopped for a while once it reached the Atlantic. After absorbing the indigenous nomadic Berbers, who readily converted to Islam, the Arabs turned their attention to the north, and in 711 crossed the Straits of Gibraltar. These Arabs were of the Umayyad tribe, which as we saw would be forced out of power in the east later on by the Abbasids. But the new emirate established in the Iberian Peninsula was to remain under the Umayyad dynasty for nearly 800 years. Starting in 756, it was headed by the only Umayyad leader to escape the massacre by the Abbasids a few years earlier, Abd al-Rahman, who created a civilization there unequal to anything that existed at that time in Europe. This was the beginning of a long and prosperous

[21] Syria-Iraq was ruled by the Abbasids, Egypt was governed by a Turk nominally loyal to the Abbasids of Baghdad, and Ifriqiya (Arabic for Africa, covering the areas of Tunisia, Algeria and Morocco) was controlled by the Aghlabids and the Islamized and Arabized Berbers.

[22] Norwich (1993), p. 33.

period for the Arab state in the Iberian Peninsula, which they called al-Andalus. Over time, large numbers of locals with Roman, Celtic and Gothic ancestry converted to Islam and became Arabized. Cordoba became one of the outstanding cities of the medieval world and was the centre of skilled craftsmanship and scholarly pursuits.

With the accession of Emir Hakam in 796 at the age of 26, the emirate entered a turbulent period as the young emir became paranoid about conspiracies against him. In 797 he ordered the arrest and execution of the distinguished indigenous citizens of Toledo – some say the victims of this bloodbath numbered in the thousands. A few years later a violent uprising of the indigenous population of Cordoba was put down, but Hakam was prevented from massacring everyone involved by his advisers, who recommended that he follow due legal process. The judges, after deliberation, called for the crucifixion of three hundred of the rebel leaders and the expulsion of all others involved in the uprising.[23] These people were predominately skilled artisans and tradesmen, mainly descendants of Arabised converts.[24] The exiles were divided into two groups, both of which were referred to by other Arabs wherever they went as the "Andalusians".[25] The first group, consisting of about 8,000 men, women and children, settled in Fez, Morocco. The second, of a similar size, was led by Abu Hafs; this group eventually arrived in Crete in 824 and conquered the island.

Abu Hafs' "Andalusians" initially travelled to the shores of North Africa; from there they raided settlements on the Aegean islands and Crete. They eventually reached Egypt in about 814, and in 818 took over Alexandria unopposed due to the disorder that existed there at the time.[26] The Egyptians, under new leadership, sought to negotiate the Andalusians' departure from Alexandria. They convinced Abu Hafs that Crete offered more attractive settlement prospects for his group, and that they would be able to conquer the island easily because the Byzantines' preoccupation with Thomas' uprising meant they had withdrawn most of their forces from the island. Furthermore, the Egyptians would provide Abu Hafs with boats to transfer his people to Crete. This proposal suited both parties. The Egyptians would get rid of the unwanted new arrivals; in addition, through the Andalusians they would gain access to Crete, which was a key location for their longer-term plans to extend their territory at the expense of the Byzantine Empire. For Abu Hafs, the proposal was attractive as he had already seen the riches of Crete during his earlier raids on the island.[27]

[23] Bendiner (1983), p. 83.
[24] Ibid., p. 82; Christides (1984), pp. 81 and 82.
[25] Christides (1984), p. 82.
[26] Ibid., p. 84.
[27] Ibid., pp. 88, 89 and 103.

The conquest of Crete by the Arabs[28]

Abu Hafs and his people, about 10,000 men, women and children travelling in 40 boats, probably landed in 824 on the south coast of Crete in an area that was totally unprotected. There are no records of any strong resistance against these invaders by Byzantine troops – if there were still any stationed on the island – or by the local inhabitants. Their progress towards the north of the island must have been easy, and once they reached the north coast they decided to build a new fortified town. For this purpose they chose the location of today's Heraklion, which was the ancient port for Knossos, called Herakleia. They surrounded the town and its fortifications with a deep trench from which the town took its name: Rabd-el-Khandak, 'the town of the trench'.[29] The conquest of the island continued at a rather slow pace over a period of some years. The Arabs progressively captured a number of well-defended fortified towns, but their occupation covered mainly the eastern and central parts of the island. Exact records of which areas they controlled are not available, but discoveries of Arab coins from that period indicate their presence in the area east of Rethymnon as far as the Lasithi plateau and south down to the coast.[30]

Sfakia during Arab rule

One of the areas that was never occupied by the Arabs was Sfakia. The mountainous tracts of Sfakia provided safety for those on the coastal plains who needed to escape from the regular harassment by Arab raiders. The level of economic activity that existed in the coastal population centres

[28] Historical information about the conquest of the island is sketchy and has been derived through analysis of both Byzantine and Arab texts, many containing contradictory information. This section is broadly based on the work of Professor Vassilios Christides (1984).

[29] When the Byzantines recaptured Crete from the Arabs, they kept this name, which in Greek was pronounced 'handax' (the Arabic *kh* sound corresponded to Greek χ, transliterated in English as *ch* here: *Chandax*). The Venetians two and a half centuries later also used this name, although it was transformed in Italian into Candia. The entire island of Crete became known as Candia under the Venetians, and the new state was called Regno di Candia ('Kingdom of Candia'). During the subsequent Turkish occupation, the town was known by its Greek name, Megalo Kastro ('big fortress'). The name Heraklion was used for the first time in 1822 by the Commander in Chief of the 1821 revolutionary government of Crete. The Greeks then started using the name Heraklion in their commercial dealings with each other, and its use became so widespread that by 1869 the Turkish government adopted Heraklion as the town's official name.

[30] Christides (1984), map on p. 96.

The Arabs heading to Crete, from a 12th century manuscript of Byzantine History by John Skylitzes

of Sfakia during the earlier Byzantine period (see previous chapter) had diminished or totally disappeared by the time the Arabs occupied large parts of the island. In view of their complete isolation from the rest of the island and the dangers of seeking supplies and trade by sea, the Sfakians had to become totally self-sufficient.

They organised their own form of self-government to ensure the security and stability that was required in such difficult times. Although details of this governing system have come to us though local tradition, it appears that this system reflected some ancient Greek democratic principles and operated at both the village and district level. The most senior members of each community, called *prokritoi, gerontes* or *dimogerontes*, formed the community's governing council, called the *gerousia*. Although these men were not elected by a public vote and were strongly influenced by the local clans, they were accepted as members of the *gerousia* by their peers on the basis of their influence, experience and wisdom in public matters. They passed judgements about disputes amongst members of the community and took decisions on matters affecting the whole community after holding public meetings. A district council consisting of senior members of each local community operated in a similar fashion.[31] This form of self-government appears to have continued in Sfakia through the centuries, even during the subsequent Byzantine, Venetian and Turkish occupations, though the influence of the *gerousia* today is considerably reduced.

[31] Papadopetrakis (1971 [1888]), pp. 92-95.

Crete under Arab rule

Historians have long debated the conditions under which the local population lived following the arrival of the Arabs on the island. One position is that the Muslim invasion resulted in the complete annihilation or forced conversion of the Cretan population, and that the island became a nest of pirates and the centre of the slave trade in the eastern Mediterranean. This view was primarily based on contemporary reports by Byzantine historians who took an extremely biased view of the Muslim threat to Christian Orthodoxy, and produced numerous reports of events that subsequent examination has revealed to have no foundation.[32] A recent thorough and extensive study of that period by Professor Vassilios Christides provides ample evidence that the situation was nothing like that.[33] The invading Arabs, who consisted primarily of skilled artisans and tradesmen of Roman, Celtic and Gothic ancestry, as we have already noted, arrived on the island with their families and were accompanied by a small number of Christians, Jews, and Egyptians. They settled mainly in urban centres, where they engaged in their own trades and occupations, relying on the indigenous population for agricultural products. As happened in other places that Arabs occupied, they were tolerant of the Christian religion, and there are no records of forced conversions or of the destruction of churches.

When the Arabs arrived, Crete was suffering from economic recession and urban decay similar to that being experienced in other parts of the Byzantine Empire. However, its agriculture, livestock and dairy production were fairly strong, and the emergence of new export markets via the Arabs increased demand for those products, improving the economic wellbeing of the rural population. The Arabs were concentrated in the towns, and their increased craftwork and trade activity contributed to the revival of the urban centres. Prior to the Arab invasion, the local population had been suffering from the turmoil brought about by religious iconoclasm, and there was also a high degree of discontent with the Byzantine administrators and tax collectors. Under Arab rule most of these problems diminished, with taxes probably remaining at acceptable levels, as there are no reports of dissatisfaction with the Arab administration and no records of any

[32] Here are two examples of stories that had no foundation: 1) It was claimed that Abu Hafs burned all his boats when he arrived in Crete so that his men would not try to go back, and that he told them they could take local women to replace the wives they had left behind. Both statements are incorrect: no boats were burned – most belonged to the Egyptian navy anyway – and the Arabs arrived with their own women, as Arabs always travelled with their families. 2) It was claimed that the Arabs killed Cyril, the Bishop of Gortyn, when he refused to convert to Islam and sacked the town of Gortyn. Cyril died four centuries earlier at the hands of the Romans, and there is no evidence that Gortyn was destroyed at that time.

[33] Christides (1984), pp. 104 to 121.

uprisings by the local population. In summary, the change in rule from the Byzantines to the "Andalusian" Arabs must have provided some relief to the local population, with the exception of the Byzantine administrators, landed gentry and other officials.

The Arabs' gradual occupation of Crete was concurrent with intense efforts to fortify the urban centres in anticipation of an attempt by the Byzantines to recapture the island. In addition to the urban population's normal activities , their life therefore consisted of ongoing preparations for military conflict, together with raids on nearby Byzantine settlements in the Peloponnese and the coast of Asia Minor.

These attacks by the Arabs of Crete were part of the larger conflict between Arabs and Byzantium which was to last till the middle of the 10th century, by which time the Byzantine naval forces had improved considerably. Byzantine sources of the time speak of the "piratical activities" of the Arabs, a term picked up by some contemporary historians, when in fact these were part of the Arab *jihad* – holy war – for the expansion of Islam, and not raids solely aimed at looting and destruction. Many of these incursions were carried out by substantial naval fleets manned by Arabs from Syria, Egypt and North Africa, and the Arabs of Crete participated in only a very few of them. One of the largest raids was the sacking of Thessalonica in 904, carried out by Leo of Tripoli with some co-operation from the Arabs of Egypt.[34] Such activities of course were not an Arab monopoly; the Byzantines also carried out similar raids, such as the sacking of the Egyptian port of Damietta in 853.[35] Attacks by naval forces, either state-sponsored or by privateers, were to become a familiar phenomenon over the next 1,000 years in the eastern Mediterranean.

Attempts by the Byzantines to recapture Crete

When news of the capture of Crete in 824 reached Constantinople, Emperor Michael II immediately sent an army under General Photinos to Crete, followed by additional troops under Count Damianos. The Byzantine forces were defeated and the survivors returned to Constantinople. Another expedition was soon mounted under General Krateros which managed to defeat the Arabs in initial engagements, but later they were surprised in a night-time attack and defeated. A further attempt to retake Crete two years later was again unsuccessful.

In March 843, early in the reign of the young Emperor Michael III, a new expedition to reconquer Crete was organised under the leadership of one of his regents, Theoktistos. The forces did not meet any resistance, having

[34] Tsougarakis (1987), Vol. I, p. 350; Christides (1984), p. 6.
[35] Christides (1984), pp. 164 and 165.

landed in an area that at the time was not occupied by Arabs. Events did not progress favourably for the Byzantines, however. Rumours of an attempt to depose the Emperor reached Crete, and Theoktistos returned immediately with part of his force to Constantinople, leaving behind the balance of the troops under Sergios Nikitiatis. The Arabs soon attacked and destroyed this force, killing Nikitiatis.[36]

In 866, Emperor Michael III made a further attempt to recapture the island following some successful battles against the Arabs on other fronts. This expedition was to be headed by the Emperor's uncle, Caesar Vardas, but before it could leave the shores of Asia Minor, Vardas was assassinated by the High Chamberlain, Basil, in front of Michael III.[37] The young Emperor was apparently aware of the plot, since he soon promoted Basil to the rank of Emperor and shared the throne with him. This was to last only sixteen months before Michael himself was assassinated by Basil's supporters, resulting in Basil becoming the next Byzantine Emperor.

Over the next 45 years, Arab attacks continued against Byzantine locations, many of them by Arabs from Crete, at times in cooperation with Arabs from other emirates. At the same time, Byzantium was reinforcing its naval fleet and trying to contain the Arab threat, achieving some significant victories along the way. In 911 a large Byzantine force of 177 boats with more than 50,000 men, 19,000 of them under Admiral Himerios, reached Crete but was defeated. The remnants of the defeated Byzantine fleet fled Crete for Constantinople, but they were attacked and totally destroyed by an Arab fleet from Syria near the island of Chios.[38] Another expedition against the Arabs of Crete was organised by Emperor Constantine VII Porphyrogennetos in 949, but under the inexperienced leadership of Patrician Constantine Gongylis, the Byzantines were once again defeated by the more experienced Arabs soon after landing on Crete.

The reconquest of Crete from the Arabs

After so many unsuccessful attempts to retake Crete, the Byzantines had reached the point of believing that only a miracle could deliver the island back to the Christian fold. One of the more widespread beliefs at the time was a prophecy that the man who liberated Crete would become Emperor.

In 960, early in the reign of Emperor Romanos II, it was decided that a new expedition should be launched. The young Emperor was convinced by arguments put to him by the High Chamberlain, Joseph Vringas, that it was the moral responsibility of Byzantium to liberate their fellow Christians in

[36] Tsougarakis (1987), pp. 347 and 348.
[37] Ibid., Vol. I, p. 348.
[38] Ibid., p. 351.

Crete, and that the economic benefits of eliminating the ongoing threat of the Arabs were worth the risks involved in undertaking such expensive and perilous action.[39] The leadership of the expedition was entrusted to General Nikiforos Fokas, an experienced fighter against the Arabs. The forces that gathered at Phygela on the coast of Asia Minor, south of Ephesos, consisted of Byzantine troops and Russian and other Slav mercenaries. There are conflicting and exaggerated claims about the size of the expedition, but a reasonable estimate would be that it comprised about 250 boats of all sizes and close to 70,000 men, including cavalry and support personnel.

Fokas' army landed on the sandy beach a few kilometres to the west of Chandax (Heraklion). The Arabs, although prepared for another Byzantine invasion, were surprised by the size of the force. Unable to contain such a large army, they barricaded themselves into the fortified town and prepared for a long siege. Realising that the siege was going to be quite a difficult and lengthy one, Fokas set up a permanent camp on the beach and secured it by drawing the heavier boats onto the beach, encircling the camp with them, and digging a deep trench around them. He also ordered part of his forces to pursue any Arabs who remained in the countryside outside Chandax.

The siege of Chandax lasted for nine months. Finally the Byzantine troops, after undermining a section of the Arab fortifications, set fire to the timber supports, causing part of the wall to collapse. Through that opening the Byzantine troops entered Chandax in March 961, and a massacre of the Arab fighters and population began. The conquerors' lust for revenge was so strong that only General Fokas' personal intervention prevented his troops from killing those who had surrendered.[40] The campaign in the countryside was also successful for the Byzantines; although they suffered some setbacks, they eventually managed to defeat the Arab forces that they encountered.

According to Sfakian historian Papadopetrakis, large numbers of Sfakian fighters joined General Fokas; they were entrusted with guarding his troop's rear flank from possible attacks from the south, but many also joined the siege. The general showed his gratitude and admiration for their fighting prowess and contribution to the campaign's success by presenting the Sfakian fighters with weapons and ammunition, and the Sfakian *gerontes* with lavish gifts of clothing. He also awarded the Sfakians the right to continue with their own form of self-government and exempted them from all taxes. When Fokas became Emperor a couple of years later, he reconfirmed these privileges.[41]

After taking Chandax, the Byzantines were surprised at the wealth that had been amassed by the Arabs which now came into their possession. In

[39] Ibid., p. 356.
[40] Ibid., p. 358.
[41] Papadopetrakis (1971 [1888]), pp. 95-97, but unconfirmed by other historical sources.

addition to the spoils of war, they also captured the Emir of Crete, Abd Al-Aziz El Qurtubi, his family and a number of his senior officials. Fokas took most of the captured wealth and the important prisoners, including the Emir, with him to Constantinople. The amount of treasure was so large that, according to records from that time, 300 boats were needed to transport the spoils to Constantinople, although this seems to be an exaggeration given that the entire Byzantine fleet which had arrived in Crete was only of approximately this size.

In Constantinople, Fokas was not feted with the traditional triumphal procession that usually welcomed back victorious generals. The Emperor was afraid of the prophecy that the liberator of Crete was to become Emperor. But Fokas did become the Emperor two years later, thus fulfilling the prophecy!

As for the defeated Arabs, those who managed to escape the slaughter in Chandax left the island on ships which were based on the south coast of the island, thus avoiding a direct confrontation with Fokas' much larger fleet. They headed mainly to Spain, Sicily and Egypt. Other Arabs did not come to their assistance because of conflicts between the various emirates – none of them were interested in the fate of the Arabs of Crete.

The impact of the Arab occupation on the Cretan population

Although historians refer to the Arab occupation as one of the darkest eras in Cretan history, the 140 years of Arab rule did not leave the same mark on Crete as the subsequent occupations by the Venetians and Turks. There were many exaggerated claims made by contemporary Byzantine writers about the activities of the Arabs and their impact on the Cretan population, which quite a few current historians have repeated without confirming their validity. There are many indications that the impact of Arab occupation was less significant than claimed. Most of the Cretan population lived in the countryside, while the Arabs mainly occupied the few fortified urban centres on the north coast, so there was little interaction between the two peoples. There were very few known forced conversions of Cretans to Islam; most Christian churches escaped destruction; and there are no documented uprisings by the local population against the Arab occupiers. Today's Cretan Greek has very few words that can be traced back to the Arabic language of the time, other than a few place names that might have originated from that period.[42] The only thing that can be said with certainty about this period is that, although there was no drift towards Islamization by the locals, there was a drift away from Byzantine traditions because of the isolation of the Cretan population from their traditional cultural and

[42] For example Ατσιπάδες, Ατσιπόπουλο, Spanakis S. (1991), p. 165.

spiritual links with Byzantium. This was one of the first matters that Fokas would address prior to his return to Constantinople.

V. The Second Byzantine Period – 961 to 1204

The second Byzantine period began with the liberation of Crete by General Fokas on the 7th of March 961, after 137 years of Arab rule.

The island was in a state of economic, social and moral decline by the time Fokas wrested control of it from the Arabs. Many factors had contributed to this situation, amongst them the Arabs' failure to set up proper governmental and administrative structures for the indigenous population, and the effects of the Cretan population's isolation from the rest of the world. Fokas' immediate attention went into fortifying the island against possible future attacks by the Arabs, and arranging for a permanent army and navy to be stationed on the island. In order to establish internal social controls and re-establish links with Constantinople, he arranged for many of the war veterans to stay on the island on a permanent basis by granting them property, thus creating a new landed social class. Some of the new settlers were mercenaries who had fought with the Byzantine army in the siege of Chandax. This led to the introduction of Russians, Slavs and Armenians into the Cretan population, something which is reflected today in a number of place names such as Rousochoria ('Russian village'), Armenoi ('Armenians'), and Varvaroi ('barbarians').

Fokas was also concerned about the impact of Arab rule on the spiritual decline of the Cretan population: in his eyes they did not demonstrate an appropriate degree of dedication to the Christian Orthodox faith. He converted all Arab mosques into churches, constructed new churches and monasteries, and invited monasteries from around the Byzantine Empire to send clerics to teach the true faith. One of the most famous of these recruits was a monk known as Nikon the Metanoite (so named because he called on the Cretans to repent – from Greek *metanoó* 'to repent'), who stayed on the island for five years. These endeavours must have been successful – or else the situation was never really so desperate, since *The Life of St John Xenos*[43]

[43] Saints' lives are a major resource for anyone concerned with the history of the late ancient world, Byzantium, or the Christian Middle Ages. At a time when whole genres of ancient literature were vanishing or on the wane, the genre of hagiography became a major literary form. Such saint's lives – or *synaxaria* – survive in astonishing numbers.

talks of the pious Cretan flock which 50 years later provided the saint with everything that he required.[44]

Government

Soon after Crete was liberated from the Arabs, Byzantine governmental structures were re-introduced. Crete became a *theme* with a governor who had both administrative and military authority and who thus held the titles *Stratigos* and *Protospatharios*. Chandax was selected as its capital. The Cretan *theme*, like all others, was further divided into a number of regions called *tourma*. Legal matters and the collection of taxes were administered by officials called *Krites* ('judge'), who often had authority over more than one *theme*. This function became obsolete towards the end of the 11th century, when governors of *themes* were given more power and their title changed to *Doukas* or *Katepano*, reflecting the higher status of the position.

By the 12th century, the position of *Doukas* (Duke) of Crete had became quite prestigious within the Empire, and a number of prominent Byzantines, close relatives of the Emperor or of other very senior court officials, were appointed to that role. But their authority over military matters diminished as the size of forces stationed on the island was reduced significantly. Like many other heads of provinces, the Duke of Crete became dependant for military support on the Grand Domestic and the Grand Duke in Constantinople, who respectively commanded all of the Empire's army and navy.[45]

Economic, social and cultural renewal

Once the Arabs were expelled from Crete in 961 and from Cyprus in 965, and the threat of Arab pirates was diminished, trade with other parts of the Empire and nations in the Mediterranean was re-established. Economic recovery was slow, but all sectors of the Cretan economy appear to have recovered – records of trade with Venetian merchants indicate substantial exports of grains, livestock, cheese, wine and honey, though there is no mention of oil or olives. Some earlier Arab records indicate that oil and olives were imported into Crete during Arab rule, but it appears that cultivation of olive trees did not gain any importance in Crete until much later, at the instigation of the Venetians.

As mentioned earlier, land ownership was becoming concentrated in the hands of the privileged few; in addition, monasteries received large amounts of property as gifts from the government and private individuals.

[44] Tsougarakis (1988), p. 76.
[45] Ibid., p. 192.

More rural people were thus forced to become tenant farmers, but small land holdings continued to exist, although in reduced numbers. Various goods were produced at the time on the island, many for external trade (e.g. timber, metals, cotton, flax), with Byzantium being the major destination.

The religious and educational renewal that Fokas believed was needed on the island was slow to come. The only centres of knowledge, learning and art were the monasteries, but access to these was confined to the very few. The decline in the urban centres that occurred during Arab rule was not reversed, and Chandax remained the only major town on the island. The cultural and educational opportunities that larger urban areas could have provided were thus not available.

Rebellion and the arrival of the new Byzantine aristocracy

It is unclear from the very few records that exist for this period why the recovery following the liberation of Crete was so slow. Close links had been established between the island and the Empire in most spheres, including trade, administration, defence and religion. There must have been some serious problems, however, because in 1090 the Duke of Crete, Karykes, declared independence from Byzantine rule. Emperor Alexios I Comnenos did not respond immediately, as he was preoccupied with two other threats facing the Empire.[46]

It was not until 1092 that the Emperor was able to take measures to quell the rebellion in Crete. The commander of the Byzantine navy, Ioannis Doukas, was assigned the task of dealing with the rebels. When news of the approaching fleet reached Crete, the local population, fearing reprisals from the Byzantine forces, rose up against Karykes, who was arrested and executed, delivering the island to Doukas. After restoring order on the island, he reinforced the local armed forces and sailed to Cyprus, where with some difficulty he managed to put down a rebellion that had erupted there. From the way the Cretan population turned on Karykes when the Byzantine fleet was approaching the island, it appears that this rebellion was not a mass popular uprising but was fomented by senior provincial officials who were dissatisfied with the Emperor. The fact that a number of similar uprisings took place during that period in other parts of the Empire supports this view.

After the Emperor re-established control over Crete, he sent a number of Byzantine families from Constantinople to settle on the island. They were granted significant land rights and important administrative

[46] During this time, the Turkish emir of Smyrna was extending his power along the Aegean coast, taking over some Byzantine islands and controlling the entrance to the Sea of Marmara; and further north, the Pechenegs, a semi-nomadic Turkic tribe, were becoming a danger to Constantinople.

responsibilities, bolstering the Emperor's control over the provinces. Crete in the 12th century appears to have been improving economically, according to the few available sources. Trade with Venice again increased significantly, a number of prominent Byzantine visitors frequented the island, and many churches with impressive murals were constructed. But the most significant impetus to growth and development on the island must have been the arrival of another large group of Byzantine settlers at the end of the century. This event has been the subject of some controversy amongst historians over recent years.

The twelve archondopoula

The leaders of this second wave of Byzantine settlers have been known for centuries as the twelve *archondopoula* ('young aristocrats'). Their story, or myth according to some, is detailed below.

Emperor Alexios II Comnenos, concerned by the continuing unrest in Crete, dispatched twelve prominent Byzantine families to Crete to re-establish strong links with Constantinople and improve the religious, moral and economic standing of the community. Like his great-grandfather Alexios I a century earlier, he allocated large tracts of property to the settlers and granted them administrative positions with significant authority over the local population. In a document known as *Chrysoboulo*, ('sealed with gold', to authenticate it), the Emperor threatened the Cretans with severe punishment if they did not fully submit to his will, and he stated that he was sending his son, Isaakios, as king and trustee, together with twelve *archondes* ('noblemen') and their families, to reign over the island. The current historical debate mainly revolves around the document's authenticity and the date it was issued, although there are other issues involved.

They were accompanied by their wives, children and other dependents, as well as several branches of their extended families, so the total number of incomers was quite substantial. The twelve *archondopoula* were: Ioannis Fokas (the family's name changed during the Venetian era to Kallergis), Philippos Gavalas, Marinos Skordilis (nephew of the Emperor), Thomas Arkholeos, Eustathios Chortatsis, Leon Mousouros, Constantine Varouchas, Andreas Melissinos, Loukas Lithinos, Nikiphoros Argyropoulos, Dimitios Vlastos, and Mattheos Kalafatis.[47] Their family names are reflected today as place names in numerous locations in Crete, and their family crests can be found on churches and monuments. The same names will appear again in subsequent chapters of this book, as many of them played important roles over the centuries, and families with these names are still prominent in the Greek community today.

[47] V. Psilakis (1970 [1906]), Vol. 2, pp. 144-147.

There are no original documents relating to this settlement. All we have are Venetian records supposedly of translated Greek documents, and Greek translations of Venetian documents, and errors may well have been made in these. One current hypothesis is that the original document and its associated story were fabricated by members of the families. They could have created this history in order to convince the Venetians who arrived on the island a century later of their aristocratic status and right to their lands, thus securing for themselves a place within the new political elite.[48]

What is not disputed, though, is that these and other prominent Byzantine families did settle in Crete after the Karykes rebellion of 1090 and later in the 12th century; that they were awarded substantial privileges and property; and that they formed a new elite group which was to play a prominent role in Crete from then onwards, especially during the Venetian era.[49]

The archondopoula in Sfakia

Today's area of Sfakia was allocated to Marinos Skordilis, who was accompanied by nine other branches of his family. The Skordilises, according to a number of sources, had emigrated to Constantinople from France, where they were known as Pegolino.[50] They were a renowned military family; it was claimed that Marinos was the nephew of the Emperor and held the rank of *Strategos* ('commander of the army').

It appears that some time after the original *archondopoula* settled in Crete, some or possibly all of them had their land allocations withdrawn by the Emperor, for reasons that are not known. In 1183 the Skordilis family were reallocated their land by the Duke of Crete, as attested in a land grant document, three versions of which exist today, two in Greek and one in Italian. These are copies of what a number of experts believe to be a genuine document, possibly the only genuine one related to the story of the twelve *archondopoula*.[51]

This document provides some interesting information relating to the history of Sfakia. It was issued to Constantinos Skordilis Kapsokalyvas, as head of the family, and his eight brothers; all of them have a second surname after Skordilis, reflecting the branches of the family, many of which still exist today. These were Kapsokalyvas, Finokalis, Sarakinos,

[48] Detorakis (1994), p. 136.

[49] For a more comprehensive discussion of the authenticity of the documents and other matters related to the settlement and claims of these elite families, see Tsougarakis (1988), pp. 81-87 and 124-127.

[50] V. Psilakis (1970 [1906]), Vol. 2, p. 147.

[51] Tsougarakis (1987), p. 364.

Pateros, Lignos, Psaromelingos, Kontis, Pardiotis, and Tarchinos Kalivitis.[52] Although the document states that they were brothers, the existence of the second surname suggests otherwise, probably indicating descent from the original group related to Marinos Skordilis. The area granted to them was called *cavallaria kai eparchia Anopolis (cavallaria* from Latin *caballārius*, 'horseman', and *eparchia* from the Greek επαρχία 'province'). What is most interesting, though, is that it was not called Sfakia at the time, and the name of Sfakia does not appear in the more than 40 toponyms that are listed in the document specifying the borders of the area. The earliest references to the name Sfakia are in a 1323 Venetian document referring to a Cretan called Nichiforus Sfachioti, suggesting that he came "from Sfakia"; and in a book by the Florentine priest Buondelmonte who toured Crete in 1417 and referred to Chora Sfakion as *Sfichium*.

The document specifies the boundaries of the allotted area as starting at the sea west of Frangokastello and south of the village of Vouvas, at a small cove known as Rousolimionari, then heading northwest towards the village of Agios Nektarios, up the gorge towards the village of Asfendou, continuing in a northwesterly direction towards Askifou, and across the Lefka Ori towards Livada, just below the mountain peak Agio Pnevma, probably following today's E4 footpath. From there the boundary of the district continues in a westerly direction to the southern edge of the Omalos plateau, across towards Linoseli, down into the Samaria gorge, and then along the gorge to Agia Roumeli and the sea. To the east of this territory were the lands of the Kallergis family.

The Skordilis clan led and participated in a number of uprisings against the Venetians starting in the early years of their rule, continuing the proud history of the fighting prowess of the Sfakians. The name appears today in place names in many areas of Crete, such as Skordilo in Milopotamos and Sitia, demonstrating the extent of their land ownership as well as their contribution to Cretan history.

The large size of the Skordilis clan of Sfakia has resulted, after the passage of many centuries, in a considerable number of Sfakian families today claiming links to some of the original Skordilis aristocracy. Families which are their descendants include Pateros, Kapsokalyvas, Psaromelingos, Loumbinos, Kyriakopoulos, Lignos, Malafaras, Papadopoulos, Kontos, Foumis, Fotinos, Nomikos, and Vasilopoulos.[53] Most of them played a leading role in uprisings against the Venetians and Turks over the following six centuries, and their names will also feature in subsequent chapters of this book.

No other information regarding Sfakia during the second Byzantine period appears in any surviving documents except for a mention of the

[52] Xanthoudides (1939b), p. 302.

[53] Pandelakis (2006), p. 175.

bishopric of Loutro-Aradena, which continued to function during this period.

The Fourth Crusade, the fall of Constantinople, and the sale of Crete to the Venetians

While the new order under the latest ruling elite to come out of Byzantium was settling in, two separate events were unfolding to the north of Crete that would eventually result in the island being wrenched from Byzantium forever.

With the death of Emperor Manuel I Comnenos in 1180, the Byzantine Empire entered one of its most turbulent periods, with a series of emperors being deposed; some were executed, some imprisoned. Manuel's successor was his young son, Alexius II Comnenos, but as he was only 10 years old, his mother governed as Regent. Her poor management of state affairs, coupled with the young Emperor's frequently odd and at times offensive behaviour, caused a great deal of disquiet amongst the population of Constantinople. This provided an opportunity for the Emperor's first cousin, Andronikos Comnenos, to march on the capital and arrest Alexios and his mother. He soon assassinated both of them and became Emperor in 1183. Andronikos' reign was very short, however, as his cousin, Isaakios Angelos, overthrew him in 1185. Isaakios II Angelos reigned until 1195, when he was in his turn deposed by his brother, Alexios, who arrested him, blinded him and threw him into prison together with his son, also called Alexios. A couple of years later, the son escaped from prison and sought help from his sister Irene and his brother-in-law, the German King Philip of Swabia.

During this same period, Pope Innocent III called for another Crusade. The plan was to attack Egypt first, as it was considered the weakest entry point into Muslim territory, and that required a large fleet. The Venetian Republic agreed to supply 50 fully manned galleys at a cost of 84,000 silver marks, on the condition that it received one half of the territories conquered.[54] When the leader of the Crusade, Marquis Boniface of Montferrat, reached Venice, the entire enterprise became at risk since the Crusaders did not have the agreed sum to pay the Venetians, who were not prepared to supply any ships unless payment was made in advance.

The Venetians then came up with a proposal which the Crusaders could not refuse: that they should help the Venetians retake the town of Zara (now Zadar) on the Dalmatian coast in exchange for deferring the payment until a later date. The joint forces soon recaptured Zara, but the Crusaders and the Venetians started fighting amongst themselves over the spoils. While in Zara, Boniface received a letter from Philip of Swabia proposing that

[54] Norwich (1996), p. 166.

if the Crusaders transported young Alexios to Constantinople, overthrew his uncle and reinstated the deposed Emperor Isaakios II Angelos, Alexios would fund the conquest of Egypt and supply 10,000 troops of his own. In addition, Alexios would place the Church of Constantinople under papal authority in Rome. Both the Crusaders and the Venetians stood to gain a great deal from this proposal, and they readily agreed to it.

The siege of Constantinople started on the 5th of July, and by the 17th of July 1203, the city was in the hands of the Crusaders and Venetians. Emperor Alexios III Angelos fled the city, and his blind brother Isaakios was freed from prison and regained the throne, to be joined on the 1st of August by his son Alexios as joint Emperor. Unfortunately, young Alexios found the treasury empty and was unable to pay the Crusaders what they had been promised. Tensions intensified and fighting erupted. The Byzantine population also revolted, and the Emperor and his son were removed, a new ruler was elected, and the two Angelos Emperors were put to death.

For the Crusaders and Venetians, there was only one option left – to seize the city – and an agreement was soon reached on how to share the spoils once Constantinople was theirs. The Emperor, who was to be a Frank (a Western European), would receive a quarter of the Empire and the city; the remaining three quarters would be divided equally between the Venetians and the Crusaders. Their attack began on the 9th of April 1204, and within three days the invaders were inside the city. The looting and carnage that followed was unprecedented. "Never, since the barbarian invasions some centuries before, had Europe witnessed such an orgy of brutality and vandalism; never in history had so much beauty, so much superb craftsmanship, been wantonly destroyed in so short a space of time", wrote historian John Julius Norwich in his account of the fall of Constantinople.

The crusader Count Baldwin of Flanders was crowned the new Emperor and was allocated a quarter of the territory previously controlled by his predecessor, as previously agreed. Boniface was allocated Asia Minor and Morea (the Peloponnese) as his share of the Empire. However, his dream was to control Thessalonica, so he offered to exchange Asia Minor for it. Baldwin objected to this and marched on Thessalonica. Boniface rebelled but others, including the Venetian Doge Enrico Dandolo, stepped in to negotiate a solution to the dispute. Boniface had been awarded the title to Crete by Alexios IV Comnenos for helping to depose his uncle,[55] and Dandolo knew that Boniface was willing to sell this title – the island was of little practical value to him as he did not have the military resources to conquer and occupy it. So Dandolo offered to buy Crete from Boniface for 1,000 silver marks plus a guarantee of receiving either Thessalonica or

[55] It is interesting to note that Crete does not appear in the treaty partitioning the Empire amongst the conquerors, since Alexios IV had already awarded Crete to Boniface. Madden (2003), p. 188.

lands in Greece of equivalent value in exchange for lands that he had in Asia Minor.

This famous transaction, whereby Crete was sold for a ridiculously low sum to the Venetians, was signed in Adrianopole on the 12th of August 1204.[56] It marked the beginning of the longest and probably the most brutal occupation ever experienced by large parts of the Cretan population.

[56] Madden (2003), pp. 183-185.

VI. Venetian conquest and the first years of occupation – 1204 to 1210

The sacking of Constantinople, the conquest of large parts of the Byzantine Empire by forces participating in the Fourth Crusade, and the expansion of Venice's control and influence in the Aegean were to have a tremendous impact on the future development of Crete. For the Venetians, Crete – together with their other new possessions in the Aegean and around the Sea of Marmara – would deliver control of sea routes and trade in the eastern Mediterranean and into the Black Sea. Crete's future over the next few centuries would be tied to these events and to the power-play between the three major forces that came to dominate this area: victorious Venice, the temporarily defeated but not totally extinguished Byzantium, and the Ottoman threat that was emerging from the east.

The Genoese attempt to control Crete

For the Genoese, Boniface's selling of Crete to Venice, their enemy for centuries, was an outrage, because he had first offered to sell Crete to them. This sparked off a new undeclared war between Genoa and Venice in which Crete would become involved.

Venice was slow to take possession of Crete. The Venetians were preoccupied with securing their new possessions in the Peloponnese and the islands in the Aegean. This provided the Genoese with the opportunity to attempt to capture Crete. They employed the services of Enrico de Castro, better known by his nickname Pescatore, formerly one of the most notorious pirates in the Mediterranean.[57] Pescatore arrived in Crete with his troops early in 1206 and, without meeting any resistance, quickly occupied

[57] Pescatore had inherited the title of Count of Malta from his father-in-law, who had been granted Malta by the Normans for his assistance in capturing large parts of southern Italy and establishing the kingdom of Sicily.

Chandax. From there he started fortifying a number of castles on the north coast in anticipation of a Venetian reaction, which occurred as soon as the Venetians became aware of the Genoese activities.

The Venetians dispatched a fleet of 30 boats to Crete in the summer of 1206, but they were unable to take control of the island and returned to Venice. Early the next year the Venetian fleet returned to Crete, and this time they managed to capture a fortified castle near Chandax. Pescatore sought additional help from Genoa, who sent a small naval force and money for hiring more mercenaries. In 1209, Venice dispatched additional boats together with the first Venetian governor for the island, Giacomo Tiepolo. Pescatore managed to retain control of his areas, but in 1210 he once more sought assistance from Genoa, which again supplied boats, armaments and money. By 1212, however, the Genoese had entered into peace treaties with Venice and Pisa, who they were also fighting at the time. This brought an end to Pescatore's long drawn-out battle for Crete, and he abandoned his objective of controlling the island. Another mercenary, Alamanno da Costa, who had joined Pescatore on his expedition to Crete, remained on the island and continued fighting the Venetians, but he finally gave up and left in 1217.

What is remarkable is that there is no historical record of what the local population did during this period of protracted fighting. One historian suggests that the Cretans, unwilling to accept the Venetians as their new rulers, fought on the side of Pescatore and the Genoese, and even speculated that Pescatore came to Crete at the invitation of some of the prominent Cretan families.[58] Another historian hypothesizes that the ease with which the Genoese took control of the island was due to the absence of any Byzantine military presence, and that the local population had been paralysed by the catastrophe that had hit the Byzantine Empire through the loss of Constantinople and large parts of the Empire to the crusaders.[59] Unfortunately, there is no evidence corroborating either of these views.

Government and social structure under Venetian rule

Upon establishing control over the island, Venice took immediate action to introduce a government structure that reflected the centralised Venetian model. It introduced tight internal military controls in anticipation of resistance from the Greek population and embarked on fortifying the island against attacks from pirates and other potential enemies, such as the Genoese. Venice realised that they needed a large and permanent presence on Crete in order to control such a vast area from a great distance. The Doge

[58] V. Psilakis (1970 [1906]), Vol. 2, p. 207.
[59] Xanthoudides (1939a), pp. 6-7.

of Venice, Pietro Ziani, issued an edict in September 1211 granting large tracts of land to Venetian settlers in return for them undertaking military duties for the state.

Crete was divided into six provinces; each of these was further subdivided into fiefdoms. This system was later simplified to only four provinces, which coincide with today's four administrative districts, the *nomoi* of Chania, Rethymnon, Heraklion and Lasithi. These were subdivided into a number of *castellanie*.

The governor of the island was given the title *Duca* (Duke); he and two other senior officials called *Consiliarii* (advisors) formed the central government. They were appointed for a two-year period only, after which they were required to submit a report to Venice on their administration and make recommendations for future improvements. Crete was declared a 'kingdom' – *Regno di Candia*, reflecting the Italianised name of Chandax, which became the capital of the island. Responsibility for the armed forces lay with the *Capitano General* of Candia. Below him were *Castellani*, who had political and limited military responsibility for their *castellanie* and the fortified castle in their assigned territory. The navy remained under the control of the Admiral of the fleet of Venice, the *Capitano General da Mar*. A large number of Venetian boats were stationed in Crete, where significant facilities known as the *arsenali* were built, some of which are still in existence today in Chania and Heraklion. In times of external threat or serious internal unrest, Venice would appoint a person with supreme authority over all military matters in Crete called the *Provveditor General*. From the middle of the 16th century, this position became permanent as the threat from the Ottoman Empire grew serious. This was one of the most prestigious positions that Venice could allocate, and a number of *Provveditors* later became Doges of Venice.

There were also three councils of an advisory nature, the *Consilium Feudatorum* for all feudal landowners, the *Consilium Maius* or *Maggior Consiglio* (the Large Council), and the *Consilium Rogatorum* or *Consiglio dei Pregadi*, which had the authority to formulate requests and submissions to the governing council in Venice. Although the governmental structure in Crete involved establishing a number of tiers of responsibility, actual authority still remained with Venice, and this was to create a number of problems for Venice and those governed by its centralised authoritarian system in Crete in the years to come.

The first Venetian settlers arrived on the island early in 1212, consisting of 132 *milites* (knights) and 48 *pedites* (infantrymen) and their families.[60] Many more were to follow over the next few years. By the end of the century, it is estimated that about 10,000 new Venetian settlers had arrived and settled on the island, a significant number given that Venice's population was

[60] There is a suggestion that the correct number is only 93 and 42 respectively.

only 60,000 in 1252. Nevertheless, this represented less than 5% of the total population of Crete, which was reported to be just over 200,000. These new settlers were given land rights in exchange for an obligation to maintain a specified military force that was to be made available to the state when required.

The population was divided into four hierarchical divisions or classes, as in other areas of Greece under the control of Venice. The upper class consisted of the Venetian nobles, the *Nobili Veneti,* who had rights to the best, most productive feudal lands, which were allocated to them by the state along with full inheritance rights. It was their duty to be available to fight for Venice when required and to maintain war horses for this purpose. Next were the Cretan nobles, the *Nobili Cretensi.* This title was granted by the Doge of Venice in recognition of services to the state, and was mainly awarded to ordinary untitled Venetians who had previously settled in Crete, although it was also over time given to members of the Orthodox population.

The third class comprised professional people and tradesmen from the cities. They were the *cittadini* or the *burgenses,* the bourgeoisie, and included public servants, military officers, lawyers and notaries, merchants and boat owners, doctors, painters and craftsmen. These were mainly the better-off Greeks. The lowest class consisted of the poorer inhabitants of the urban settlements and rural dwellers (mostly farmers), known variously as *villani, plebe, populani,* or *contadini.* Rural people were sometimes known as *agrafi,* 'illiterate'; some were free, *franchi,* while others were serfs, *villain parici,* who belonged to the estates where they worked, either private (the *villain militum*) or public (the *villain comunis*).[61] The *contadini* were free citizens and were obliged to pay only minimal taxes and provide housing for the state's mercenaries. However, most of the *villani* were the property of their feudal masters. They were subject to various taxes, and were obliged to provide compulsory labour for the state and serve on the galleys as rowers.

This social structure changed over the centuries as more and more Venetian settlers became Hellenised, some converting to the Orthodox faith, and as land holdings changed hands, with some going over to local Greek ownership. The rise of the middle classes in the towns and a burgeoning in the ranks of professionals and tradesmen saw a significant increase in the *cittadini*'s numbers, influence and wealth. Finally, the numerous uprisings resulted in some concessions being given to the population, including certain exemptions from compulsory labour for the state and service on Venetian galleys.

Land holdings were initially divided between state, church and private ownership. The number of fiefdoms varied over time, but a recent study suggests the initial allocation was 25 feudal holdings as church properties,

[61] Maltezou, C. (1988), p.115.

25 owned by the state and rented out, 394 granted to *Nobili Veneti, Nobili Cretensi* and untitled Venetians, and 35 given to Cretan nobles of Byzantine ancestry following their early uprisings.[62] The best and largest private tracts were allocated to the *Nobili Veneti,* while untitled Venetians, the *pedites,* received land of lesser value. Certain Cretans were able to reclaim some of their previous land rights following successful uprisings, but they were in the minority. This situation changed over the centuries of Venetian rule, with land ownership shifting away from *Nobili Veneti* to *Nobili Cretensi.* This land ownership pattern was not unlike the feudal system which existed in other parts of Europe.

Sfakia during the early period of Venetian occupation

Sfakia was something of an anomaly in this tightly structured Venetian system. The Venetians never tried to occupy it and bring it under their control, since it was viewed as difficult of access, inhospitable, and unsuitable for any of the productive enterprises that the Venetians intended to pursue. The area was not allocated to new settlers under the feudal system and did not become subject to the exploitation that other parts of Crete experienced. Sfakia remained the only part of Crete to maintain semi-independence from the new rulers and continue with its own system of self-government.[63]

It did however become a separate district under the *territorio* of Chania; and responsibility for its control was allocated to a *Provveditor,* who was usually a Venetian noble from Chania or Venice. Population records from later periods indicate that about 2,500 people lived in the area, comprising 600 households in 20 villages.[64] The names of the Sfakian villages cited by Spanakis from the 1644 chronicle by Trivan are:

Castel Sfachia – Χώρα Σφακιών – Chora Sfakion
Giorgici – Γιωργίτσι – Giorgitsi (now a deserted upper part of Chora Sfakion)
Comittadhes – Κομιτάδες – Komitades
Paciano – Πατσιανός – Patsianos
Anopoli – Ανώπολη – Anopoli
Limgnia – Λιμνιά – Limnia
Cabia – Καμπιά – Kambia
Cabo – Κάμπος – Kambos
Scalla – Σκάλα – Skala
Agio Dimitri – Άγιος Δημήτριος – Agios Dimitrios

[62] Giannopoulos (1978), p. 39.
[63] Detorakis (1994), p. 149, and Maltezou (1988), p. 112.
[64] Spanakis (1958), p. 74 and footnote 23.

(the previous five villages are all on the Anopoli plateau)
Vura – possibly Βουβάς – Vouvas
Frasca – Βρασκάς – Vraskas
Francocastelo – Φραγκοκάστελλο – Frangokastello
Callocasia– Κολοκάσια – Kolokasia, the winter village for
Asfendou near the coast, renamed Agios Georgios in 1940
Aschifu – Ασκύφου – Askifou
Aradhena – Αράδαινα – Aradena
Agiogiani – Άγιος Ιωάννης – Agios Ioannis
Agia Rumeli – Αγιά Ρουμέλη – Agia Roumeli
Samargia – Σαμαριά – Samaria
Tripites – Τρυπητή – Tripiti (no longer occupied).

It is interesting that Phoenix, Loutro, Livaniana, Asfendou and Kallikratis are not mentioned. Kapsodasos, Skaloti and Argoules were not included either, because the Venetian-defined territory of Sfakia ended at Patsianos.

The *Provveditor* and ten soldiers maintained a Venetian presence in Sfakia but in reality had no effective control. It was not until some centuries later that the Venetians built a more substantial fort in Chora Sfakion at an elevated location overlooking the village, where the ruins of the old Turkish fort are sited today. The *Provveditor General* of Candia, Lorenzo da Mulla, complained in his report to Venice in 1569 that to his knowledge there had been no *Provveditor* in Sfakia who, at the end of his two-year service, did not leave there better off by one thousand ducats, which represented the proceeds of bribes and a share of the spoils from the illegal activities of the Sfakians.[65] This situation was to cause significant problems for the Sfakians and the Venetians later on in the 16th century.

The Sfakians did not pay any taxes, nor did they provide labour for state projects or the galleys, since all of them claimed privileges as descendants of the Byzantine aristocracy.[66] The Venetians accepted this claim of ancestry from the Sfakiot clans as an alternative to trying to enforce the collection of taxes and compulsory labour from the few but ferocious inhabitants of the district. The Sfakians primarily worked with their flocks and produced cheese which, together with meat and skins, supplied the local and export markets, where in addition they sold honey and timber from the densely forested mountains. Sfakians were also involved in processing timber for shipbuilding, activities in which they were experienced.

Because of its inaccessibility and the fierce reputation of its inhabitants, Sfakia's Lefka Ori (White Mountains) became the refuge for many of those

[65] Giannopoulos (1978), p. 141.
[66] Report by the Provveditor General del Regno di Candia, Benetto Moro, 1602, as per Spanakis (1958), p. 76.

involved in failed uprisings against the Venetians. A number of Sfakians also participated in and led these early uprisings, including many from the expanded Skordilis clan, as we will see.

VII. Resistance to Venetian rule – 1210 to 1453

The arrival of the Venetians and their imposition of a new governmental structure was immediately resisted by the Cretans when it became clear that the Venetians intended to confiscate the holdings of the wealthy landowners. At the forefront of this movement were the prominent Byzantine families who would lose their property rights, their wealth and their privileged position on the island. A large proportion of the population were serfs in the service of those large landowners, and they also felt endangered by the uncertainty surrounding their status, as well as the threat to their religion.

During the more than 400 years of Venetian rule, the Cretan population rebelled against the Venetians no fewer than 27 times – and that is without counting any of the smaller local uprisings. Some of these revolts lasted for years and were suppressed by the Venetians with great brutality. Many of them were led by members of the *archondopoula* families, and members of the Sfakian-based Skordilis clan played a leading role in most of these rebellions. Some of the uprisings originated in the White Mountains of Sfakia.

The reasons that the Cretans took up arms against the Venetian rulers so many times varied. Initially the Cretan aristocracy led a number of uprisings to restore the loss of their property and privileges, and some of these succeeded. These rebellions were followed by clashes arising from property disputes between Cretan landowners and newcomers from Venice, which soon escalated into broader conflicts that affected even the poorer people in the countryside. Many of the rebellions in the later period of Venetian rule were the result of the brutal oppression of the native population by the feudal landowners and the Venetian administrative and military officials. We will concentrate here on the major revolts and those involving Sfakians, Sfakia and the Skordilis clan.

1211 – The revolt led by the Agiostephanites family

Just a few months after the Venetians had taken control of Crete, the first clashes erupted in the eastern part of the island. Cretans took up arms in protest over land confiscations by the newcomers. Under the leadership of the Agiostephanites (or Argyropoulos) family, the rebels seized the castles of Mirabello and Sitia and soon occupied the whole of eastern Crete. The Duke of Candia, Giacomo Tiepolo, lacking adequate resources to fight the rebels, sought assistance from the Duke of the Archipelago, Marco Sanudo.[67] Drawn by promises of rich rewards, Sanudo arrived with a powerful military force and, following protracted fighting, managed to put down the insurrection. But when Tiepolo refused to hand over the promised rewards, Sanudo, in cooperation with the Cretans Sevastos Skordilis and Theotokis Agiostephanitis, attacked Tiepolo, who fled, and captured Candia. Venetian forces eventually arrived on the island and assisted Tiepolo in recapturing some of the castles held by Sanudo, but during the early fighting Skordilis and Agiostephanitis were killed.[68] In 1213, Sanudo eventually entered into a treaty with Tiepolo, who handed over some of the promised rewards. As part of this treaty, 20 of the Cretan elite who participated in this uprising were allowed to leave the island with Sanudo.

What is interesting about this event is that the Cretan elite were prepared to enter into an alliance with an adventurer such as Sanudo in order to fight the Venetians, in spite of the unpredictable outcome of such a venture.

1217 – The revolt led by the Skordilis and Melissinos families

Another uprising soon started, sparked by an incident in which a Venetian noble stole horses and other livestock from a property held by the Skordilis family near Rethymnon. The Duke of Candia refused to resolve the dispute and punish the culprit, and this led to a widespread insurrection. The Skordilises were joined by the Melissinos family (also descendants of one of the twelve *archondopoula*) and soon, after defeating the Venetians on a number of occasions, they controlled significant parts of western Crete. A new Duke of Candia decided that negotiation was a better option than

[67] The Duchy of the Archipelago was created in 1207 by Marco Sanudo, nephew of the Doge of Venice, Enrico Dandolo. Sanudo, having participated in the sacking of Constantinople, borrowed eight galleys from the Venetian arsenal and, together with a group of privateers, captured a number of the Byzantine islands, including Naxos, Paros, and Melos. Together with his co-adventurers, he established the Duchy, paying tribute to Venice and the Latin Emperor of Constantinople but retaining the Duchy's independence.

[68] Maltezou (1988), pp. 116-117.

war with the rebels, and by September 1219 a treaty had been signed. This granted significant privileges and fiefdoms to the Cretan elite, made free citizens of 70 *villani* chosen by them, and established laws that imposed penalties on Venetians who abused Cretan peasants. Furthermore, a general amnesty was granted to all those who had participated in the uprising. This was to be the first of many revolts that gained land rights and privileges for the Cretans, mainly for the elite but also for some townspeople and villagers.

1228 – Another revolt led by the Skordilis and Melissinos families

Ten years later, in 1228, another uprising was instigated by the same two families. What lay behind this uprising appears to have been dissatisfaction with the granting of new fiefdoms to Venetians, some involving land previously belonging to Cretans.[69] The Duke of Candia was unprepared for this insurrection and sought assistance, as one of his predecessors had done in 1211, from the Duke of the Archipelago, Angelo Sanudo, son of Marco Sanudo. The Cretan aristocracy asked for help from the Byzantine Emperor Ioannis III Vatatzis, who sent 33 galleys with troops to assist the Cretans. Sanudo was unwilling to join battle with the Byzantine fleet and withdrew, leaving the Venetians to their own devices.[70]

The rebels, together with the Byzantine army, captured Rethymnon and a number of other places. The Duke of Candia tried to enter into a treaty with the admiral in charge of the Byzantine forces, and they agreed to a withdrawal of the Byzantine fleet after further negotiations. The Byzantine fleet ran into trouble on the way back, and most of it sank. The Byzantine troops that were left behind continued to fight the Venetians alongside the Cretan rebels. Eventually, in 1233 the Duke of Candia signed a treaty with the most prominent rebels, the Melissinos and Skordilis families. New fiefdoms were granted to them, as well as privileges and guarantees of protection for their people. Some Cretans were unwilling to enter into a treaty with the Venetians and continued fighting alongside the Byzantine troops in the east of the island. Soon another fleet of twelve Byzantine galleys arrived to provide assistance but was eventually driven away. In the end, an agreement was reached and the remaining rebels and Byzantine forces were allowed to leave Crete for Asia Minor, bringing this uprising to a close in 1235.

The years between 1235 and 1261 were relatively quiet for Crete, with the exception of occasional localised clashes between Cretans and Venetian nobles, which successive Dukes of Candia managed to keep from flaring up

[69] V. Psilakis (1970 [1906]), Vol. 2, p. 223.
[70] Maltezou (1988), pp. 117-118.

into full-blown uprisings.

Constantinople becomes the capital of Byzantium again

The year 1261 was very significant in the history of the Byzantine Empire, as its forces in exile in Nicaea managed to free Constantinople from the control of the Latin invaders. The Latin Empire, ruled at the time by young Baldwin II, the grandson of the first Emperor, had been slowly falling apart as its Frankish knights gradually returned to their homes in the west, taking with them anything of value. It had also been facing a chronic shortage of funds. Baldwin II was getting desperate, having to pawn or sell anything that had been left behind by the crusaders, including the city's most holy possession, the crown of thorns that Christ had worn on the cross, which was pawned to the Venetians.[71]

The Byzantine Empire, under the more than 30-year reign of Ioannis III Vatatzis, had consolidated its position in Asia Minor, reconquered large parts of the Balkan Peninsula and the Aegean Sea, and strengthened its finances. Vatatzis died in 1254 before achieving his objective of liberating Constantinople. During the last years of his reign a strong and popular general, Michael Palaeologos, had emerged, who was appointed co-Emperor to Vatatzis' very young grandson by popular demand of the army and the clergy. He entered Constantinople on the 15th of August 1261 through the city's Golden Gate as its new ruler, Emperor Michael VIII Palaeologos, after the city had been freed by one of his generals three weeks earlier while Palaeologos was fighting a campaign on another front in Asia Minor. The Latin troops defending the city had sailed off to attack an island held by the Byzantines which guarded the approach to the Bosphorus from the Black Sea, leaving the city without proper defences. Local Greeks informed the Byzantine General Alexius Strategopoulos, who was advancing on Constantinople with a small army on his journey back to Nicaea, that the city was almost undefended and suggested ways of sneaking into it under the cover of darkness. On the night of July 24th 1261, a small detachment entered the city and opened the gates to the Byzantine troops. Constantinople was taken without any resistance.

This was a humiliating end to one of the darkest chapters of Western civilisation. The historian John Julius Norwich quite appropriately summarises the Latin Empire of the East as being "the miserable offspring of treachery and greed, in the fifty-seven years of its existence it achieved nothing, contributed nothing, enjoyed not a single moment of distinction or glory".[72] Byzantium, along with Constantinople, recovered, but not to its

[71] Norwich (1996), p. 201.

[72] Ibid., p. 212.

previous strength and glory.

For Cretans, the freeing of Constantinople brought the hope of their own liberation from the Venetians. The Byzantine Emperor also viewed Crete as one of the areas he needed to free from the clutches of the Venetians in order to regain control of the eastern Mediterranean. But unfortunately for Crete, and for Byzantium, he had too many enemies to deal with.

1262 – The Chortatsis, Melissinos and Skordilis uprising

The freeing of Constantinople created a new impetus amongst the Byzantine elite families of Crete for the overthrow of the Venetians. The Emperor, too, wanted to free Crete as soon as possible, and to achieve this he dispatched to Crete a man (possibly Genoese) named Stengo with letters for the Cretans Giorgos Chortatsis and Michael Skordilis-Psaromelingos, encouraging them to revolt. The Cretan elite rose up immediately against the Venetians, led by these two families and the Melissinos clan, descendants of one of the *archondopoula* families. The revolt was enthusiastically supported by the Orthodox clergy, who saw the return of the Byzantine Emperor in Constantinople as a precursor to the Cretan Orthodox Church being freed from the restrictions imposed on it by the Church of Rome and being reunited with the Church of Constantinople.

Unfortunately for the Cretans, the Emperor was preoccupied with freeing the Peloponnese from its Latin occupiers and sorting out problems with his allies, the Genoese, who were not upholding their side of the treaty signed in March 1261 when he had sought their support in freeing Constantinople.[73] The Cretans, without any external assistance, continued their struggle for liberation, but they did not have any support in this from one of the most prominent Cretans, Alexios Kallergis. This was mainly due to Kallergis' doubts about the chances of success for this uprising, his concern about losing his privileges if they were defeated, and the uncertainty surrounding the intentions of Emperor Palaeologos. In 1265, the powerful Cretan elite decided to negotiate a peace treaty with the Venetians, receiving in return an amnesty, reconfirmation of previously held privileges, and a number of additional fiefdoms.[74]

The Byzantine Emperor also realised that his chances of taking Crete had diminished significantly now that the local Cretans were showing reluctance to take up arms. He signed a treaty with the Venetians in June 1265 recognising Venice's rights over Crete, which was further confirmed in a subsequent treaty in 1268.

[73] Ibid., pp. 220-221.

[74] Detorakis (1994), p. 157; also Xanthoudides (1939), pp. 46-48.

1272 – The Chortatsis revolt

Some minor unrest continued after the end of the 1262 revolt and new uprisings were talked about, but nothing significant occurred until 1272. That year, a new insurrection started which was of a totally different character and which resulted in a change in the way the Venetians resolved such uprisings.

The initial causes of the revolt are unclear, as various historians have given different accounts of how it started. Psilakis in his *History of Crete* suggests that the uprising began in the mountain areas of Sfakia, Selino and Rethymnon when the villagers raised the Byzantine flag with the double-headed eagle, attacked Venetian settlers, and surrounded the fortified towns on the south coast.[75] Xanthoudides attributes the rebellion to a desire for freedom from the Venetians, with the possible encouragement of Byzantium, given the Chortatsis family's wealth and privileged position amongst the elite of Crete.[76] Others have referred to Venetian reports from the time which imply that it began with the murder of a Cretan who was a Venetian sympathiser.[77] Whatever the initial cause, the uprising involved large numbers of Cretans, aristocrats and villagers, all inspired by the freeing of Constantinople, the efforts of the Emperor Palaeologos to liberate previously lost territories, and the more aggressive and barbarous treatment of the local population by the Venetians. The leaders of the revolt were the brothers Giorgos and Theodoros Chortatsis, from one of the *archondopoula* families. They brought discipline and planning into the fight, and the insurrection would have progressed favourably but for the intervention of Alexios Kallergis, who chose to help the Venetians put down the rebellion instead of joining in.

Psilakis suggests that Kallergis resented those who thought that they could lead a rebellion without him, since he considered himself the rightful leader of all Cretans. So he joined the Duke of Candia in fighting against them. Initially, the Venetians and Kallergis appeared to be winning a battle near the river Aposelemis, east of Candia, but the rebel forces retreated towards the Lasithi area, where they regrouped and counter-attacked, forcing the Venetians all the way back to Candia and behind the town's fortifications. There is some uncertainty as to whether Kallergis continued assisting the Venetians in their struggle, but reinforcements soon arrived from Venice together with a new Duke of Candia, and they marched towards the Messara plain, where the rebel forces were camped. The Cretans initially retreated, thus drawing the Venetians into a trap; the rebels then decimated

75 V. Psilakis (1970 [1906]), Vol. 2, p. 239.

76 Xanthoudides, (1939) p.50.

77 Maltezou (1988), p. 122.

their troops, killing the Duke and many of the Venetian nobles. There are no reports of Alexios Kallergis participating at this stage, but he was well versed in the Cretan tactic of drawing enemies into a trap in locations which were difficult to defend.

This disaster shook Venice, which was concerned about the expansion of the revived Byzantine Empire and the possible intervention of Emperor Palaeologos in the conflict. Further reinforcements were sent with a new Duke, who attempted to negotiate a treaty, offering amnesty and rewards, but this time unsuccessfully. Candia came under siege a number of times, but the rebels were unable to defeat the Venetians. Nor could the Venetians quell the uprising. The end finally came with the arrival of a new Duke in 1278. He broke the siege by pushing back the rebels and then reorganised his forces, combining them with foreign mercenaries he brought to the island. He promised vast rewards for those who won their battles, and he declared all the Chortatsis family members outlaws and offered bounties for their capture.

The rebels decided to attack the Venetian forces once more, and advanced on Candia, preparing to lay siege to the town again. This time the Duke introduced a new tactic: he assembled fresh and better-trained forces outside in front of the town walls and waited. The Cretans, who saw the Venetian troops waiting for them, were initially uncertain about how to deal with this situation. Their leaders preferred to hold their forces back to deal with the enemy under more familiar conditions, but some Cretans broke rank and attacked. Many more joined them, but the Venetians held their position, unable to retreat. Some Cretans were wounded or killed, and this gave the Venetians the opportunity to advance. One of the Chortatsis brothers, Giorgos, was wounded and tumbled from his horse but was rescued by two of his brothers. The Cretan troops, seeing one of their leaders fall, began to retreat, and this soon became a full-scale flight from the pursuing Venetian troops. It was a total disaster for the Cretans who, until that day, had experienced only success. The revolt was totally quashed in one fateful day. And there was worse to come.

Whereas, in the past, treaties and amnesties had been agreed after an insurrection, this time there would not be any pardons for the rebels. For months, entire families were tracked down and killed without mercy, villages were destroyed, and whole areas were denuded of their populations, their flocks and their possessions. Chortatsis family members were pursued throughout the island, but they managed to escape by boat to the island of Chios and from there to Constantinople. Eventually they moved to properties given to them by the Emperor on the coast of Asia Minor, where many Cretans who were forced to flee the island joined them, although some returned to Crete later on.

This revolt differed from previous uprisings in that it had a broader political aim: to free Crete from the Venetians and reunite it with the Byzantine Empire. The Venetian response was also different: this time they responded with bloodshed, reprisals and horrific punishments aimed at setting an example to any others who might consider similar schemes in the future.

1283 – Alexios Kallergis' rebellion

The behaviour of Alexios Kallergis during the 1272 revolt must have perplexed the Cretans then just as much as it has more recent historians. Was he an opportunistic traitor trying to win favours from the Venetians at the expense of the other members of the Cretan elite? Or was he playing a double game, waiting for the right opportunity when he would be certain of outright victory? There is no consensus amongst historians on this issue. He has been described as a person of great personal talent, valour, astuteness in martial matters, fine judgement, intelligence, and eloquence; but at the same time he was egoistic, vain, with a thirst for power and pre-eminence that diminished the purity of his patriotic sentiments, and he was flattered by the high honours and privileges conferred on him by the Venetian rulers.[78]

The Cretan historian Psilakis is kinder to Kallergis, describing him variously as admirable and the most illustrious of the Cretan aristocrats; and, although he exhibited the Byzantine weakness of lust for power, he had a heart that remained purely Greek which compensated for this. Psilakis is quite sympathetic about this flaw, but he is very critical of Kallergis' irresolute and changeable character, which he states is inappropriate in a rebel leader.[79] Psilakis also quotes a contemporary Italian historian, Capeletti, who wrote that Kallergis hated the Venetians deeply, firstly because he loved his country and secondly because the Venetians had become the masters of Crete by buying it instead of conquering it. Capeletti also says that Kallergis rarely associated with Venetians, only occasionally approaching any of them.[80]

More recently, the historian Maltezou has explained Kallergis' activities as being based on a longer-term plan to establish a state within a state. Kallergis realised that it would have been almost impossible to overthrow the Venetian occupation and that there was also the worse threat of an occupation by the Catalans or Genoese; he opted for a compromise that would have resulted in him becoming the most powerful force within a

[78] Detorakis (1994), p. 159, quoting the Greek historian Xanthoudides.
[79] V. Psilakis (1970 [1906]), Vol. 2, pp. 250, 251.
[80] Ibid., p. 249.

Venetian-controlled Crete.[81] It is obvious that Kallergis was quite a complex character who enjoyed a high standing amongst the elite of Crete and was well respected by both Cretans and Venetians. One should judge him only after examining the events surrounding the revolt he led that started in 1283 and lasted for 16 years, and not by the events of the previous Chortatsis uprising.

What prompted Kallergis to foment another revolt is again unclear. Some historians attribute the rebellion to ambition and lust for power; others ascribe his action to his remorse about the Venetians' brutal suppression of the Chortatsis revolt, despite assurances of leniency that were given to him. Whatever the reason, Kallergis left Candia (or fled, according to one source, because he knew that the Venetians were about to arrest him) for the Lasithi plateau, from where he invited all the prominent Byzantine families to join him in an uprising. Leadership positions were allocated to the Melissinos, Gavalas, Vlastos, Mousouros, Skordilis, and Arkholeos families, as well as to the Kantanolas and Kavasilas clans, who were also related to the *archondopoula* families. Michalis Chortatsis, nephew of one of the leaders of the previous revolt, was included as well, which suggests that Kallergis' activities during the previous insurrection were now forgiven. Historians again speculate as to whether the flag under which Kallergis' rebels marched was the double-headed eagle of Byzantium, or the Cretan flag of St Titus, or the banner of the house of Kallergis, each of which would have signified a different aim for the revolt.

The Venetians reacted immediately, charging Kallergis with treason, confiscating all his properties and posting a reward for his capture. Massive arrests of nearby village leaders, priests and abbots took place with the intention of holding them hostage as a bargaining ploy. These moves frightened the local Greek population, who fled Candia in panic, heading for the mountains or the Greek settlements in the Peloponnese and Asia Minor; soon only a few Venetian sympathisers who stayed there for their own protection remained in the town.

These events strengthened the resolve amongst the rebels to be prepared to fight until the end. Cretans from all over the island joined the uprising at the Amari plateau and marched down to the Messara plain, where they soon captured Gortyn. There Kallergis organised the men into detachments, which were despatched throughout the island to try to isolate the Venetians and restrict their movements outside their fortified towns and castles. He also instituted a governing structure of ministers and generals, introduced laws, and made provisions for safeguarding personal and property rights. Soon virtually the whole island, with the exception of the fortified towns and castles on the coast, was under the control of the rebel Cretan forces.

The two major powers that could have intervened in this conflict were

[81] Maltezou (1988), pp. 122-123.

themselves deeply involved in other crises. Venice had been caught up in several wars for control of the Adriatic, which had depleted her naval resources.[82] Venice was also experiencing internal unrest as the public became dissatisfied with the way in which the new mercantile aristocracy, who had benefited from the conquest of Constantinople, were governing the state. Massive public demonstrations diverted the government's attention from external threats. And relations with Genoa were strained because of tensions related to trade out of Constantinople.

The Byzantine Empire, on the other hand, had gone through a difficult period under Emperor Michael VIII Palaeologos, who had had to deal with threats from both the West and the East. The main threat from the West was Charles of Anjou, the most powerful ruler in the West,[83] who was determined to recapture Constantinople with the help of the monarchs of Hungary, Serbia and Bulgaria and the support of Venice. The Emperor's diplomatic manoeuvring prevented this, although in the process he had to accept papal primacy in order to secure the Pope's intervention. To the East, Turks and Mongols had a virtually free rein in Anatolia, with only a few strongholds still under the control of the Byzantines.

The Byzantine Empire was also in deep financial straits and was split internally by the Emperor's decision to acknowledge papal primacy and adopt the Catholic creed.[84] On the 11th of December 1282, just a few months before Alexios Kallergis raised the flag of rebellion on the Lasithi plateau, Michael VIII Palaeologos died. His son and co-Emperor, Andronicos, succeeded him to the throne. Andronicos, a deeply religious person, immediately proclaimed the full independence of the Orthodox Church and abrogated the union with Rome that had been agreed to by his father. Over the next few years, he became preoccupied with ecclesiastical affairs, trying to repair the damage caused by his father's betrayal of the Orthodox faith.

With no decisive intervention from outside, the Venetian forces on Crete tried to suppress Kallergis' uprising through brutal attacks against the population in the countryside, as well as against monasteries, which usually provided support to the Orthodox rebels. The fighting went on for years, the rebels employing guerrilla tactics against the better-armed Venetian forces, drawing them into ambushes in areas difficult to access, a tactic that was to

---

[82] Norwich (2003), pp. 170-173.

[83] Charles held the titles of Count of Anjou, Maine, Forcalquier and Provence, King of Sicily, Naples and Albania, Prince of Achaia, and overlord of Tunis.

[84] In addition to the recognition of papal supremacy, Palaeologos agreed to alterations to the Orthodox creed, although he was not authorised to do this by an Ecumenical Council as would be required. These changes in the creed included accepting the *filioque* (the Western church's belief that the Holy Ghost proceeded from the Father and the Son rather than directly and exclusively from God), the doctrine of purgatory, the seven sacraments as maintained by Rome, and the use of unleavened bread in the Mass.

be followed by the Cretans over the next few centuries against the Turks as well as the Venetians. The situation remained unresolved, as neither side had the strength to force the other side to capitulate.

It was more than ten years after the start of this uprising that the Genoese made their appearance on the coast of Crete. A truce had existed between Venice and Genoa since their treaty of 1270, which had been renewed twice but had expired in 1291 with neither party offering a further renewal. Venice made the first move in October 1294, when its naval forces attacked the smaller Genoese fleet near the Gulf of Alexandretta.[85] Although outnumbering the Genoese, the Venetians were defeated, losing a third of their fleet. The Genoese decided to strike back by attacking the Venetian-held fortified town of Chania, which they managed to capture.

The Genoese admiral Doria invited Kallergis to join forces with him to fight against and expel the Venetians from Crete. Kallergis refused on the basis that this would only achieve a change of masters for the Cretans, from the Venetians to the worse and much stronger Genoese.[86] Psilakis describes in his *History of Crete* how Kallergis insisted that the negotiations should take place between only himself and Doria. Kallergis' refusal to provide support to the Genoese together with his exclusion of any of the other Cretan leaders from the discussions created a serious split amongst the Cretan leaders. A number of them suspected that Kallergis had continued to favour a deal with the Venetians which would benefit him personally, and that this was the reason he had rejected the Genoese proposal. And so rumours started that Kallergis was once again going to betray the Cretans. The leadership and the Cretan population divided into factions, each supporting a different option – entering into a treaty with the Venetians, joining forces with the Genoese, fighting to rejoin Byzantium,[87] fighting for autonomy and independence, or calling for the removal of all privileges from the Cretan elite!

In the meantime, the Venetians became aware that disagreements amongst the Cretan rebels had resulted in their loss of impetus and leadership. Seeing this as an opportunity to force the Genoese off the island, the Duke marched his army from Candia to Chania, where he easily recaptured the city, with most of the Genoese fleeing to their boats. The Venetian army then indiscriminately attacked any Greeks they came across, the most brutal massacre being committed at the Monastery of Agia Triada at Akrotiri. Psilakis also mentions an attack by the Venetian forces against a band of Cretan rebels, supporters of the independence and autonomy

[85] Alexandretta, modern İskenderun, Turkey, was a trading port for Venetians and Genoese.

[86] V. Psilakis (1970 [1906]), Vol.2, p. 257.

[87] A contemporary Venetian chronicle reports that the Byzantine Emperor Andronicos II, who was an ally of the Genoese, had written to the Cretan leaders encouraging them to join the Genoese in their fight against the Venetians. Maltezou (1988), p. 123.

option, near Anopoli in Sfakia.[88] The rebel forces were defeated; some of the Cretans who had not escaped or been killed were hanged there, while others were taken away to serve on the galleys.[89]

The revolt, although it had lost its momentum, continued in a fragmented and disjointed way. The Venetians had bigger problems to deal with, and they wanted an end to this long, drawn-out conflict. Kallergis, although disappointed by the turn of events, also wanted to conclude the hostilities, but only after negotiating the best terms that he could extract from the Venetians. Early in 1299, a new Duke arrived from Venice with full authorisation to negotiate a peace treaty with Kallergis. Negotiations were lengthy and were kept secret from many of the other Cretan leaders to avoid any reactions that would have jeopardised the difficult and tense process.

1299 – The treaty with Alexios Kallergis

The treaty agreed between the two parties was to have a significant long-term impact on relations between Cretans and the Venetians on the island, although it is unclear whether anyone realised this at the time. The treaty was signed in April 1299, sixteen years after the start of the revolt. Most of its provisions related to Kallergis directly or indirectly. He was to be given back all his privileges and properties that he owned prior to the rebellion. He was also to be given four new fiefdoms, the right to buy two fiefdoms previously owned by Giorgos Chortatsis (the fugitive leader of the previous uprising), and an additional two fiefdoms, one of which he could grant to another rebel. Further benefits accruing to him were the right to buy 15 war horses every year, a privilege exclusive to Venetian nobles up to that time, and the right to allocate war horses and fiefdoms to whoever he wanted. He was also allowed to lease a large number of properties which belonged to monasteries in central and western Crete on very favourable terms. Kallergis and his descendants were permitted to live outside the fortified towns, provided that a family representative was always left in the town. He was also authorised to appoint a Greek bishop to any vacancy without reference to the Latin Church representative or the people.

One could be forgiven for thinking that the treaty only involved benefits and privileges for Kallergis. But there were a number of provisions that would benefit others. Some of the main ones were: all participants in the revolt received an amnesty and the return of their confiscated properties; all those who were free citizens prior to the uprising were to remain so; in addition, Kallergis was given the right to emancipate 100 of his followers

[88] V. Psilakis (1970 [1906]), Vol. 2, p. 261.
[89] Xanthoudidis (1939), p. 62.

who were not free citizens; and marriages between Greeks and Venetians would now be permitted.

In return for all the above, Kallergis and his followers were to swear obedience to the Doge of Venice. It is obvious that the major beneficiary of the treaty was Kallergis himself, who on top of his rewards was also recognised by everyone, and especially by Venice, as being the most important leader in Crete.[90] A large number of Cretans, though, saw him as traitor to their cause. Kallergis lived for 22 years after the treaty was signed, enjoying the privileges and the status gained after 16 years of struggle against the Venetians.

The rest of the island's inhabitants profited indirectly from the treaty's stipulations in the longer term. The rights given to Kallergis over certain church and monastic matters resulted in weakening the Latin Church's hold over Christianity on the island and helped the Orthodox faith survive. Similarly, permission for marriages between Greeks and Venetians helped assimilate many of the Venetians into Greek culture. These two changes contributed to the Hellenisation of the island to some degree in the later part of the Venetian era and resulted in a more peaceful period of coexistence and cultural advancement prior to the Ottoman invasion.

1319 – A Sfakian uprising: the Chrysomallousa revolt

During the 20 years following the treaty with Alexios Kallergis, Crete experienced a period of unrest with occasional minor local clashes that were mostly put down through the intervention of Kallergis and, following his death, his sons and the Venetian authorities. Sfakia, which had no significant fertile land available for Venetian newcomers, was left undisturbed and untouched by the Venetians, enjoying its own form of self-government and autonomy without paying taxes or experiencing any other form of pressure from the Venetians. Its population must have been rather small; census records for this earlier period do not exist, but it would have been in the order of about 3,000. As mentioned previously, the only Venetian presence in the district was a small detachment of ten soldiers and their commander stationed in Chora Sfakion; they mostly kept to themselves rather than risk any contact with the Sfakians, who had a fearsome reputation.

There are only a few references to Sfakia in records from the first 100 years of Venetian rule: one is about the area's participation in the 1272 Chortatsis revolt; and the other occurs in reports about the end of the

[90] His four sons obeyed their father's wish to strictly follow their obligations under the treaty. The elder son, Giorgios, was honoured by the Venetians by being awarded the Venetian rank of *Nobilitas Veneta* and having his name inserted in Venice's *Libro d'Oro* ('Golden Book') of Venetian nobility. This was the only time during the entire period of the Venetian occupation that a Greek was given equal status with Venetian nobility.

Kallergis revolt. Members of the Skordilis family, who by that time had expanded their land holdings further north and east on the island, were frequent participants in the revolts and played leading roles in them during this period. It is quite obvious that Sfakians had been active all along in the struggle against the Venetians, but in view of their small numbers, and since most of the fighting took place away from their territory, their relative level of involvement was rather modest.

The first truly Sfakian revolt is said to have been sparked by an incident in Chora Sfakion which would have been considered merely an unfortunate part of everyday life under an occupying force in other parts of the island – but not in Sfakia! The event, described in detail by the Sfakian historian Bishop Grigorios Papadopetrakis in his 1888 book *The History of Sfakia,* is summarised below.[91]

One day the commander of the Venetian guard, Capeletto, chanced upon a beautiful young village girl named Chrysi, who was known by all as Chrysomallousa ('the golden haired one') because of her long blond hair. Attracted by her beauty, he grabbed the girl and kissed her. She reacted angrily, slapping him across the face, while her two servants swore and threw stones at him. Capeletto, enraged by this response, grabbed the girl's hair and sliced off her golden plaits with one swipe of his dagger. Chrysi ran home in tears to her father, Stratis Skordilis of the famous Skordilis clan. He and others from the family, together with her fiancé, Polos Psaromelingos, caught up with Capeletto and killed him on the spot, also slaying some of the soldiers who came to assist their commander. The rest of the soldiers escaped back into their barracks, but they too were attacked and killed soon afterwards. The Venetians in Chania soon learned what had happened and sent an army detachment to Sfakia by boat to hunt down the culprits. By that time, the Skordilises had fled to the safety of the Samaria Gorge, and the Venetians sailed off to Agia Roumeli in pursuit. Fellow Sfakians rose up in support of the Skordilis family. They attacked the soldiers in the Samaria Gorge, decimating their troops; a few managed to escape onto their boats and sailed away to safety.

Thus what would have been a minor incident to some, but which was a mortal insult to the Sfakians, became a full-blown uprising.The Venetians sent more troops, Sfakians from the entire district joined in the fight, and even the Byzantine Emperor Andronicos II Palaeologos dispatched troops to assist the Sfakians, according to the Cretan historian Psilakis.[92] But the Emperor was soon obliged to withdraw his forces to fulfil a condition of his agreement with the Venetians for the return of previously captured Byzantine troops from earlier clashes with them elsewhere. The fighting dragged on, but the Venetians were not able to suppress the rebellion until

[91] Papadopetrakis (1971 [1888]), pp. 106-107.
[92] V. Psilakis (1970 [1906]), Vol. 2, p. 275.

Alexios Kallergis[93] intervened and put an end to it. Unfortunately, details about his intervention and the treaty that was entered into, if there was one, are not available, although another Sfakian historian, Paris Kelaidis, claims that the Sfakians gained certain benefits from this settlement.[94]

Those members of the Skordilis family who survived remained in the gorge – according to local tradition, at a location known as Chora, high above the village of Samaria about half an hour's walk to the southwest. The Venetians soon gave up their pursuit in the extremely difficult terrain and left the gorge. After that, the family moved down to today's Samaria village, and many returned to Chora Sfakion. Chrysi stayed behind but, filled with despair by the events and the subsequent massacre of many of her relatives, she died soon afterwards and was buried next to the small chapel of Ossia Maria on the slopes of the gorge, near Samaria village.[95] Her fiancé, Polos, also died before long. Next to Chrysi's grave, where Polos sat mourning her loss, he had planted asphodels. The location was known by the locals for a long time as *tou Polou i Asphentili* ('Polo's asphodel').[96]

The story of the Chrysomallousa uprising has been passed down through the generations in Sfakia, and it is hard today to sort out history from legend. But that is the case for a great deal of Sfakian history.

1333 to 1347 – Kallergis against Kallergis

Many Cretans, including members of a number of the elite Cretan families, remained quite uneasy about the close relationship that Alexios Kallergis, and his four sons after his death, had with the Venetians, seeing this collaboration as a betrayal of the oppressed Cretans and their political aspirations. There were also a number of members of the broader Kallergis family who were unhappy with this situation. Their discontent finally resulted in a series of uprisings over a 14-year period between 1333 and 1347.

The first revolt erupted as a result of new taxes imposed by the Duke of Candia for the construction of new galleys to pursue the pirates, who

[93] It is unclear whether this was the by now very old Alexios or his grandson, also named Alexios.

[94] Kelaidis (2004), p. 88.

[95] Some believe that the chapel was built after Chrysi's death by her family to commemorate her death, based on frescoes in the chapel which bear the year 1379. In the 1960s some work was carried out to stabilise the chapel; the grave outside the chapel was opened and its remains removed. Locals claim that the remains were of a female with cropped hair dyed a dark colour. This confirmed in their minds that this was Chrysi's remains, as local women do not cut their hair short or dye it, and tradition has it that when Chrysi was in mourning she cut and dyed her blond hair with natural pigments that occur in the area.

[96] Plymakis (2010), pp. 182-186.

were turning up more frequently along the shores of the island. The local population in the western districts of Apokoronas, Selino, Kissamos and Sfakia resented this levy and put up resistance to the demands of the tax collectors, who they saw as behaving like pirates and thieves themselves. The uprising started at the villge of Margarites in the Mylopotamos district, about 20km/12 miles east of Rethymnon, led by the renowned fighter Nikolaos Prikosyridis. The Venetians reacted by sending troops to arrest the culprits, but the uprising spread, and soon a force of more than 5,000 armed men attacked Chania and the Paleochora fort in Selino; the latter, after being stormed and its garrison killed, was razed to the ground.[97] A well-known and respected Cretan elder was elected as leader of the rebellion: Vardas Kallergis, a relative of Alexios, who was by then dead. Vardas, from the Kissamos area, was chosen as leader because of his well-known anti-Venetian feelings, his fervent belief in a free Crete, and the strong position he had taken against Alexios over the previous decades.

The Cretan forces, encouraged by their early successes, advanced on Candia with the intention of attacking the fortified town. Vardas sent a letter to the Duke of Candia demanding his surrender but allowing him and all Venetians free passage to leave the island. The Duke waited for the Cretan forces to draw near to Candia and then sprang an attack with a well-armed and trained cavalry force headed by Georgios Kallergis, Alexios' eldest son. The Cretans, who were on foot, had no chance of defending themselves against such an attack on flat ground and were comprehensively defeated. Vardas Kallergis was captured and put to death by Georgios Kallergis himself, while Prikosyridis was tortured before being hanged. The victorious Venetian troops, assisted by some pro-Venetian Cretans, pursued the fleeing rebels and flattened Margarites, killing all those they encountered. A number of the rebel leaders' families were sent into exile, while Vardas' children and brothers were imprisoned for life. The destruction and killing went on for quite some time, devastating the countryside in an attempt to intimidate the population and prevent further uprisings.

Seven years later, in 1341, another rebellion erupted, this time fomented by Leo Kallergis, the nephew of Alexios, who was the grandson of the great Alexios Kallergis. Leo had been adopted by his uncle Alexios and educated in Latin ways, then had been sent to Venice to further his education. But this exposure had the opposite impact upon Leo: having observed how Venetians regarded his fellow Cretans, and how his uncle aligned himself with the Venetians for his own personal gain, he began to despise both the Venetians and Alexios. Leo soon made friends with Cretan aristocrats throughout the island who shared his feelings and secretly incited them to rebel. Amongst them were members of the Melissinos, Skordilis, Sevastos

[97] V. Psilakis (1970 [1906]), Vol. 2, p. 277.

and Psaromelingos families, as well as Costas Smyrilios and his sons from Apokoronas. Smyrilios hated the Venetians deeply, having witnessed his father and uncle being hanged at the end of the previous uprising.

Action against the rebels was led by Alexios Kallergis, who wanted to strengthen his leadership amongst the Cretans of Byzantine descent. Having superior armed forces, Alexios soon defeated the rebels and arrested Smyrilios and his sons. Under torture, Smyrilios betrayed Leo Kallergis' role by revealing the existence of secret correspondence written between them as they plotted to overthrow the Venetians. Smyrilios and his sons were executed. The Duke of Candia, pretending that he did not know of Leo's role in organising the uprising, invited him to Candia to thank him for not participating in the rebellion and then arrested him. Leo was tortured and forced to sign confessions, then was sewn into a sack and thrown alive into the sea and left to drown.[98] His murder occurred in 1341, but the revolt was rekindled soon afterwards and continued for another six years.

The tragic death of Leo Kallergis had an enormous impact on all Cretans. He was declared a martyr, and regular requiem masses were performed in churches throughout the island in memory of his life and his sacrifices. Local poets and minstrels wrote songs about his heroic martyrdom, singing them throughout the island even though the Venetians had banned such songs; some of these have survived to this day.[99] His death strengthened the hatred that Cretans felt towards the Venetians, and they cried out for revenge.

This call was taken up by three Sfakians who were well known at the time, all from the Skordilis extended family: Leo Kallergis' father-in-law, Skordilis Kapsokalyvas, and his two sons Michalis and Emmanuel Skordilis Psaromelingos from Anopoli. Others who joined included another Alexios Kallergis, also known as Souleas, from the Kissamos branch of the family. The new revolt spread from Sfakia across the island – within a few months the Cretans had taken control of the areas surrounding Rethymnon, Chania, Ierapetra, Mirabello and Sitia. This uprising was far more widespread than any of those before it, with people from all over the island taking up whatever arms they could find and joining in the fight, after being blessed by priests.

The Venetians called for assistance from Alexios Kallergis who, together with the Venetian General Gradenigo and the Venetian fleet, attacked the rebels and set fire to a number of the areas that had participated in the uprising. These actions soon provoked other areas to join the uprising, and soon most of the island was in the hands of the rebels. However, they were unable to capture the well-fortified city of Candia and a number of

[98] Xanthoudides (1939), pp. 77-78.
[99] Kelaidis (2004), p. 42.

other fortified towns, and they were incapable of defeating the Venetian cavalry and troops when they did venture out of the few towns and castles that they still controlled. Battles raged occasionally in different parts of the island; during one, Michalis Psaromelingos, wounded and trapped by the Venetians, ordered his lieutenant to cut off his head rather than let him be taken alive.[100]

The situation remained in a stalemate for a number of years, with neither side able to defeat the other. The two external powers that could have intervened to end this protracted conflict were themselves once again preoccupied with their own more immediate problems. Venice was facing strong competition from the Genoese for control of commerce in the Black Sea, which often led to local clashes in far-away places like the Crimean peninsula. In the Mediterranean, Venetian dominance over trade was being threatened by a strong Ottoman armada of more than 230 ships; in addition, Venice had given an undertaking to the Pope to protect all Christian shipping from any Ottoman threat in return for significant financial gains. And closer to home, Venice was fighting an insurrection in Zara on the Adriatic coast which had been going on since 1343 and was to last close to two years, thus further stretching its fighting resources.

Byzantium was also facing its own problems. Since the death of Emperor Andronicos III Palaeologos in 1341, Byzantium had been torn apart by a civil war between the supporters of his nine-year-old son and those of General Cantacuzenos, both of whom claimed to be the successor to the Emperor. Fighting and intrigue between the two Byzantine camps went on for a number of years. One night in February 1347, Cantacuzenos managed to enter Constantinople secretly with 1000 troops and surround the palace. Negotiations led to an agreement stating that for the next ten years, the two Emperors would reign jointly, with Canatacuzinos as the senior ruler, and after ten years the two would share equal status.[101]

During the same period, the Empire was being threatened externally from all sides – by Serbs in the west, by Bulgars in the north, and by Ottomans who were plundering Thrace while occupying most of Asia Minor as far as Bursa, where the Sultan had established his capital, only 100 kilometres from Constantinople.

Early in 1347, a better-resourced Venice sent a strong military force to assist their besieged compatriots in Crete under a new Duke with three new *Provveditors*. The Venetians divided their troops into three armies: one moved west towards Chania and the Kissamos district; a second, including forces under the leadership of Alexos Kallergis, advanced towards the areas around Rethymnon; and the third headed south towards the Messara plains in pursuit of the rebels. The two remaining leaders of the uprising,

[100] Xanthoudides (1939), p. 80.
[101] Norwich (1996), pp. 293-305.

Kapsokalyvas and his son Emmanuel Psaromelingos, were both killed during fierce battles in the south, the former at the hand of his lieutenant in circumstances similar to those of his son, Michalis. The Venetians, having put down the uprising in most of the island, turned their attention towards the east, and soon the rebels who had taken over the forts at Sitia, Ierapetra and Mirabello surrendered.

By the end of 1347 the revolt had ended, but retributions and further killings of Cretans continued for some time. It was during this period that Alexios Kallergis, the grandson of the first Alexios Kallergis, died.[102]

Social changes in Crete following the first 150 years of Venetian rule

These various rebellions and treaties were the outcome of changes within Cretan society, some of which Venice had not anticipated. As we noted above, the new Venetian settlers began adopting aspects of Greek culture, including its language, customs, and names, and became tolerant of the Orthodox Church. They started intermarrying with Greeks, as some of the Venetian commoners wanted to establish bonds with the Cretan families of Byzantine aristocratic descent. Similar cultural changes occurred on the Greek side; in particular, some Greek elite families sought links with the new Venetian aristocracy on the island. Prominent amongst those was, of course, the Kallergis family.

In the towns, the *cittadini* – both the Greeks, who were the majority, and the Venetians, who were becoming Hellenised – enjoyed closer relations. Venice's policy of lightly taxing the *cittadini* and exempting them from any compulsory labour encouraged the rapid growth of this middle class, which led to a significant increase in the numbers, output, influence and wealth of these professionals, artisans and tradesmen.

In the countryside the situation was totally different. The vast majority of the population were at the mercy of the feudal landowners, mostly Venetians but increasingly also members of the Cretan aristocracy of Byzantine descent. The exploitation of rural people had worsened during the first century and a half of Venetian rule, and there were no close bonds between the *contadini* and *villani* and their Venetian feudal landowners. In addition, many of those who remained in traditional subservient positions now had to endure additional compulsory labour reconstructing fortifications and serving on Venetian galleys, from which many never returned.

Because of Venice's policy of maintaining a central power structure, with the government in Crete having only an implementational role, the Venetian nobility in Crete felt increasingly disenfranchised. Many of the *Nobili Veneti* and *Nobili Cretensi* considered themselves more Cretan than

[102] Other sources indicate that his death took place well before these events, in 1343.

Venetian and resented the treatment meted out by Venice. Society on the island was evolving into distinct groups with common interests and objectives which were to have a significant impact on the direction that Crete's history would take.

One group comprised the great landowners, mostly Venetians but increasingly including some of the old Byzantine aristocracy; they had vast feudal interests to protect and exploit, and many resented Venice's control, although some Venetian nobles were still loyal to Venice, and some powerful Greek clans who came from the old Byzantine elite continued to secretly long for the return of Byzantine rule. The *cittadini* in the towns were happy with the way the new order was developing but despised the elite, especially those from old Venetian families, and the government administrators who arrived every two years to oversee the implementation of the dictates from Venice. The largest group consisted of the *contadini* and *villani* from the countryside, who suffered under feudal rule. They were not familiar with the notions of freedom and Cretan independence, so their only dream was for a more considerate feudal master and escape from the state's demands for labour. They feared and hated the landed aristocracy and were jealous of the townspeople. The restrictions imposed upon the Orthodox Church were also seen as a threat, and the Orthodox priests would have fuelled this fear since their own existence was threatened. So this group was willing to follow anybody who offered them the opportunity to remove the Venetians from control and hasten a return to Greek Orthodox rule.

This goal was shared by the *privilegiati,* who were exempted from compulsory labour. This group consisted partly of the *archondopoula* families who had not had their feudal properties returned to them, and the *archondoromei,* other Cretans of Byzantine descent with no feudal claims, both of whom longed for the return of Byzantine rule and their lost possessions and status. It also included Orthodox priests, whose main objective was liberation from the dictates of the Latin Church. The final faction within the *privilegiati* were the Sfakians: the Venetians accepted their claim that they were all descendants of the Skordilis family and, as such, were all *privilegiati archondoromei!* Little is known about their aspirations as a group, but one would expect that they wanted to continue their independent way of life. The only indication that we have of their goals comes from the Cretan historian Psilakis, who in his *History of Crete*[103] states that Anopoli had been the centre of the military leadership of the "autonomy" group which the Venetians had attacked towards the end of Alexios Kallergis' 1298 rebellion.

[103] V. Psilakis, (1970 [1906]), Vol. 2, p. 277.

1363 – The St Titus uprising by the Venetian nobles

The first 150 years of Venetian rule had also proved to be quite difficult for Venice. The Venetians often needed to bring in additional armed forces to suppress the frequent uprisings, keep the population under control, and maintain their general readiness on the island. Furthermore, external threats were becoming more frequent as pirates – Arabs, Christians, and Ottoman raiding parties – increased their forays to the island, which meant that continuous improvements to the island's fortifications were required. Crop failures, together with the devastation wrought by the plague of 1348 that hit most of the Mediterranean,[104] put additional pressure on Venetians and Cretans alike.

The Venetian nobles living in Crete had been complaining to Venice about ever-increasing tax demands and lack of recognition of their status amongst the noble families of Venice, which was an affront to their honour.[105] Some of these families had lived on the island continuously for over 100 years and, as we have noted, felt more Cretan than Venetian. Venice, noting these changes from afar, was at the same time concerned about their loyalty to Venice and to the Latin Church.

In 1363, new taxes were imposed for the repair and improvement of the port of Candia. The Venetian nobles refused to pay this and started organising an uprising against the rule of Venice. Two of the most prominent Venetian families in Crete, the Veniers and the Gradenigos, assumed leadership of the movement; they were joined and supported by many prominent Cretan families, the Kallergis clan being the most important. The uprising erupted on the 9th of August 1363 when the rebels stormed the Duke's fortified castle, arrested him and his advisors, and threw them in jail.

The rebels declared the formation of a new independent state, called the Republic of St Titus in honour of the patron saint of Crete,[106] and elected Mark Gradonigo as the governor, supported by four advisors and a General Council comprised of Venetians plus some Greeks. The governmental system that was introduced reflected the Venetian pattern of the time – an oligarchy of the aristocracy. One of the government's first decisions was to proclaim equality between the Catholic and Orthodox churches on the island, allowing Orthodox services to be conducted in all churches, including Catholic ones (this was also to apply to the cathedral of St Titus in Candia), and removing the restriction against ordaining Orthodox priests. In this way the Venetian-dominated government tried to win support from

[104] The plague came to Venice on its trading ships from Crimea and spread from there all over Europe. Venice was hit extremely hard – more than half of its population perished within a year. Norwich (2003), p. 216.

[105] Detorakis (1994), p. 166.

[106] The name was modelled after the Republic of St Mark, as Venice was known at the time.

all Cretans for a state which would be independent of both Venice and Byzantium. The new order took hold very quickly throughout the island; those who remained pro-Venice kept their opinions to themselves.

Venice was shocked by the events in Crete and was unsure how to deal with the situation. Initially they tried to persuade the Venetian nobles that this move was against their own best interests, expecting them to repent this foolish act and seek forgiveness. Venice sent a delegation of five representatives to Crete to address the full council of the rebel government. But after listening to these representatives, the Council of the new Republic of St Titus sent them back with the message that they were determined to live in an autonomous state and were ready to protect Crete from any invasion. Venice realised that the only avenue available to them was to invade the island. Since the army at their disposal was insufficient for the task, they embarked on hiring mercenaries and preparing for the invasion. The Doge wrote to the heads of all allied states, including Genoa, and to the Pope, asking them not to provide any assistance to the rebels.

The new government, while preparing for the inevitable attack by Venice, sought assistance from possible allies, but none of them were willing to provide help on acceptable terms. Byzantium was unable to offer any aid, as it was defending its ever-shrinking borders and had no financial resources to spare; the Emperor was also very reluctant to do anything that would antagonise the Pope, whose help he needed. The Ottomans were very willing to give assistance, but on their own terms – they demanded to be given the city of Chania and large tracts of land around it in return. The new rulers realised that once the Ottomans had gained control over part of Crete, there would be nothing to stop them from attempting to capture the whole island. The other potential source of help was Genoa. Although Genoa had signed a peace treaty with Venice, the new government of Crete knew that the Genoese were always prepared to consider a deal that would provide them with an advantage over Venice. So they sent a delegation of three *Nobili Veneti* to try to reach a deal about assistance on terms that they could live with. Negotiations went on for quite some time, but the Genoese were too insistent on gaining control over the way the island was to be governed. By the time the three representatives returned from Genoa without an agreement, Crete was already back in the hands of Venice.

Early in 1364, just over six months after the rebels had declared independence, Venice reached an agreement with a well-known Italian mercenary from Verona, Luchino dal Verme, who was to assemble a troop of mercenaries largely made up of Italians, Dalmatians and Illyrians. The force of 1,000 cavalry and 2,000 foot soldiers departed from Venice on 40 ships. The fleet arrived near Candia on the 7th of May 1364; the cavalry and most of the soldiers disembarked at the bay of Fraskia, near Paleocastro, northwest of Candia, while the Venetian fleet blocked Candia harbour. The first and most decisive battle took place on the 9th of May at the pass near the river Almyros, just west of Candia, where the rebel forces tried to stop the mercenaries advancing towards the town. The rebels were eventually defeated after fighting valiantly all day, but both sides suffered enormous losses. By the next morning Candia was surrounded on land and at sea. Dal Verme and his mercenaries advanced towards the town and plundered the area outside the city walls. Within the city walls, the rebels surrendered to the Venetian Admiral, seeking forgiveness and protection from the mercenaries who had gathered outside. With some difficulty, dal Verme eventually managed to restrain his mercenaries, who wanted to enter Candia and pillage the city.

Soon the Venetian *Provveditors* who had arrived with the fleet tried and executed the ten most senior instigators of the uprising, including Mark Gradenigo. Over the next three months, most of the leaders of the uprising were arrested and executed, their properties were confiscated by the state, and many members of their families were thrown into jail or sent into exile. As for those who managed to escape, significant rewards were offered for their capture, including three members of the Kallergis family who were to play a leading role in the next uprising.

1365 – The Kallergis brothers' rebellion

Soon after the Venetian forces and the mercenaries had left Crete, the rebels started to regroup and prepare to continue their struggle against the reinstated Venetian administration. Leadership of the rebellion was assumed by the three Kallergis brothers, Ioannis, Alexios and Georgios, who were from the Kissamos branch of the family. In contact with them were some of the other fugitives and members of noble Venetian families, such as the Veniers and Gradenigos, who were also on the run. The Kallergis brothers' uprising differed from the previous St Titus revolt in that the leadership was clearly Cretan, although it also included some men of Venetian stock; and their declared objective was to reunite Crete with the Byzantine Empire.

Unfortunately for the Cretans, the Byzantine Emperor was still struggling to ensure his Empire's survival. Palaeologos, needing protection against the Ottomans who were occupying Gallipoli, just 200 kilometres southwest of Constantinople, sailed across the Black Sea and up the Danube to Buda to ask the King of Hungary, Louis the Great, for help. In Buda, Palaeologos was pressured to submit his church to the authority of the Pope before any assistance would be provided, something he was not prepared to do. While returning to Constantinople, he was detained for six months by the Bulgarians before being freed, an event that demonstrated the desperate situation that the Byzantine Empire had reached. In the end, the only assistance that he was able to give the Cretans was to send them an Orthodox bishop to provide guidance to the rebels during their struggle![107]

Ioannis Kallergis proclaimed the start of this uprising in August 1364 at Mylopotamos, in western Crete. He raised the Byzantine flag bearing the double-headed eagle and declared that he was fighting to free the island from Venice and rejoin Byzantium. The Venetian authorities responded immediately: forces under *Provveditor* Giustiniani poured out of Candia and pushed back the rebels, destroying those villages that had helped them. After regrouping, the rebels attacked and forced the Venetian troops back into Candia, burning Venetian properties in retaliation. The rebels then turned their attention on Rethymnon, forcing the Venetians to abandon the fortified town and sail to Candia; again, they destroyed Venetian properties that lay outside the fortifications. Soon the whole of western Crete, other than the fortified towns, was under their control. The rebels then advanced on the eastern part of the island, taking over the Messara plains, and from there headed towards Lasithi. Battles were fought as they progressed, and losses were sustained by both sides.

Venice soon gave its approval for hiring mercenaries, Ottomans from Asia Minor this time, and for purchasing horses for the cavalry. In March 1365, five new *Provveditors*, bearing full authority to deal with the insurrection, arrived in Crete with the Ottoman troops. A by now familiar stalemate had developed, with the rebels controlling the countryside and withdrawing to more secure positions whenever the Venetians ventured outside their fortresess. Unfortunately for the Cretans, they also suffered serious losses on the battlefield, as well as through the execution of those who were captured.

A year later, five more new *Provveditors* arrived with more troops, as Venice was becoming impatient with this unresolved situation. The reinforced Venetian troops were now able to take the battle to the insurgents' strongholds. The rebels' food supplies were becoming desperately short as a result of the Venetian campaign of destroying all crops, combined with lower than usual harvests since fields had been left unattended during the fighting. Starvation soon resulted in criticism of the uprising, and many rebels became willing to negotiate a treaty with the Venetians. Early in 1367, disgruntled Cretans in the Lasithi district managed to arrest some of the rebel leaders, including two of the Gradenigo brothers and Theodore Venier, and handed them over to the Venetians, who executed the men immediately.

This incident frightened the rebels in the eastern districts, so they retreated westwards. A large Venetian contingent from Candia headed for the area south of Rethymnon, where rebels led by the brothers Ioannis and

[107] Detorakis (1994), p. 169.

Georgios Kallergis had taken refuge; the rebels were defeated, but the two brothers managed to escape to what is now Argyroupoli. Another force advanced on the Mylopotamos area, where the locals in Eleutherna had already arrested the Venetian rebel leader Molino, who they handed over to the Venetians. The Venetians then captured the fort of Kastri where Alexios Kallergis and his family had taken refuge. All the rebels sheltering there were brought to Candia and publicly executed, as were their wives and children. The Cretans and the few Venetian nobles who were still fighting alongside them withdrew to the centre of resistance in the Lefka Ori at Anopoli.

By April 1367, the Venetian forces had invaded Sfakia. Desperate battles were fought around Anopoli and the Aradena Gorge, but eventually the rebels were defeated. Georgios Kallergis, Ioannis Kallergis and Tito Venier escaped and were hiding in a nearby cave but were betrayed, and after fierce resistance they were taken prisoner. Locals claim that the cave where the three were eventually captured is opposite Timios Stavros chapel in the Kavis/ Ilingas Gorge, below Mouri. Georgios Kallergis was publicly executed in Chania; Ioannis Kallergis and Tito Venier were executed in Candia. Ioannis' wife and two sons were captured in Anopoli, and sent to Venice, where they were imprisoned for life.

This was the tragic end of the Kallergis brothers' rebellion, which was suppressed with great brutality in the closing stages. The damage to the countryside from the three years of burning and destruction by both sides was enormous. But it was not to end there. The Venetian authorities ordered the complete destruction of the three areas that had become the centres of uprisings in Crete: the Lasithi plateau, the Margarites/Eleutherna area east of Rethymnon, and Anopoli in Sfakia. All the buildings in these areas were razed to the ground, and large parts of the countryside were put to the torch. Venice prohibited all habitation and grazing in these areas for more than 100 years. Some 50 years later, in 1415, the Florentine priest Cristoforo Buondelmonti commented on the devastation of the village of Sfakia and wrote that the locals were grazing their flocks on the fertile Anopoli plateau but were afraid of planting crops or living there because of the Venetians' ban.

This was not just the end of another uprising against the Venetians; it was the end of a long struggle lasting more than 160 years against an oppressor who had tried to deprive them of their personal freedom and their Orthodox church, which in the past had provided them with the moral support they needed to get through difficult times. The surviving Cretans were left with no further power or will to fight the Venetians. And seeing the desperate situation that the Byzantine Empire was in by then, they knew that there was no longer anyone who could come to their rescue. Crete would not experience another rebellion for close to 100 years.

1371 to 1374 – The Venetians' struggle to build a fort in Sfakia

A few years after the destruction of Anopoli and all the nearby villages in Sfakia, the Venetians decided to erect a castle on the plain east of Sfakia where fertile land had been allocated to Venetian nobles. The objective was to protect them from pirates[108] who frequently raided the coast, but it would also serve as protection against attacks by Sfakians living in the mountains to the north and west who harassed the Venetians from time to time. Candia had requested such a castle as early as 1340, but funding had not been available. With the end of the uprisings, finances were finally allocated, and in 1371 a Venetian fleet carrying soldiers, builders and materials arrived at the site, south of the Kallikratis Gorge, to start constructing a castle near the church of Agios Nikitas.

The Sfakians were against the construction of a castle so close to their district and decided to sabotage the project. Under the leadership of the six Patsos brothers from nearby Patsianos, the Sfakians would come down from their mountain hideouts every night and destroy what the Venetians had built during the day.[109] They were able to do this because the Venetians, fearing attacks by the Sfakians, slept on board their ships. Eventually the Venetians were obliged to bring additional troops to surround the whole area day and night while the castle was being built. Unfortunately for the Sfakians, the Patsos brothers were betrayed to the Venetians, and were arrested and hanged at the castle site.

The castle was eventually completed in 1374, but the Sfakians were never threatened by the Venetian troops stationed there, who preferred to stay inside the fortress watching for pirates rather than trying to bring the unruly Sfakians under control. It was initially called the Castle of St Nikitas after the Byzantine-era church that existed nearby, but soon it became known derisively as Frangokastello ('Castle of the Franks'). Frangokastello was the site of a number of battles involving Sfakians during the Ottoman occupation, as we shall see.

The years leading up to the last siege of Constantinople

By the end of the 14th century, the Cretans had given up their struggle against Venetian rule, at least for the time being. Byzantium was also facing its final capitulation to the Ottomans. Emperor John V Palaeologos, endeavouring

[108] Some of these pirates included Sfakians who were known to attack coastal Venetian settlements by boat.

[109] Papadopetrakis (1971 [1888]), pp. 108-109.

to save what was left of the Empire, travelled to Rome in 1369, where he signed a humiliating declaration of his acceptance of the Catholic faith in the hope that this desperate act would gain him assistance in saving Constantinople. However, Rome would provide no assistance until the two churches were united, something that the clergy in Constantinople were refusing to accept. In 1394 the Ottomans again attempted to conquer Constantinople, and this siege continued for eight years. During this time, conditions became intolerable for the citizens of Constantinople, and many of them fled the city. In December 1399, Emperor Manuel II Palaeologos followed the course that his father had taken 30 years earlier in seeking help from the West, but he also returned to Constantinople empty-handed three and a half years later.

Constantinople was given a reprieve from the Ottoman threat when the Mongols, led by the fearsome Tamburlain, defeated the Ottoman army in July 1402. Over a very brief period of time, the Mongols managed to wreak an unprecedented level of devastation on the Ottoman Empire, and this gave Constantinople a new lease of life. Soon, though, the Mongols lost interest in Asia Minor. However, it took ten years of fratricidal conflict between the four sons of Sultan Bayezit before the Ottomans were once again unified under the command of Sultan Mehmed, who was replaced by his son Murad II a few years later.

Murad II laid siege to Constantinople in 1422 but was unable to capture the city, despite using a more aggressive strategy of attack. The Byzantine Emperor Manuel II, who by then was old and sick, allowed his eldest son, John, to take over the reins of the crumbling Empire. John sailed to Venice in November 1423 to seek help, and from there travelled to other parts of Italy and finally Hungary on this mission, but no assistance was forthcoming as long as the two churches remained apart. Six months later, in July 1425, his father died and John VIII Palaeologos became Emperor of a hugely diminished Byzantium which was now contained within the old crumbling walls of Constantinople.[110] Its citizenry, numbering only about 50,000 by this time, was demoralised, chronically undernourished, and had been decimated on a number of occasions by the plague; its buildings, churches and palaces were in serious disrepair; its treasury was virtually empty; and its trade network had been taken over by the Venetians and Genoese.[111]

In 1437, Pope Eugenius IV invited the Emperor to attend the Council of Ferrara to negotiate the union of the two churches, and it took more than a year for the two parties to reach an agreement. They signed the Decree of Union on the 5th of July 1439, in which the Emperor was forced to concede

[110] There were still two other isolated and by now very small parts of the Empire in existance that could offer no assistance to Constantinople. They were in Morea, today's Peloponnese, and at Trebizond, in northeast Turkey, which were to last until 1460 and 1461 respectively.

[111] Norwich (1996), pp. 388, 389.

on all ecclesiastical differences that had kept the two churches apart for so many centuries. On his return to Constantinople, the Emperor faced a public and clerical revolt for caving in to Rome and for recognising Papal supremacy over the Orthodox Church. The Pope's part of the agreement was to encourage the Hungarians and the Serbs to embark on a new crusade to rescue Constantinople, which set off in 1443, but again it was unsuccessful as they were defeated by the Sultan at Varna on the Bulgarian Black Sea coast. For the Emperor this was a bitter outcome to all his long and frustrating negotiations with the West and his betrayal of his church, for which he had incurred the hatred and contempt of his subjects. A few years later, in October 1448, Emperor John VIII Palaeologos died, sad and bitter about the West not coming to the rescue of Constantinople.

The last Emperor of Byzantium, and the new Sultan of the Ottoman Empire

John VIII had nominated one of his brothers, Constantine, as his successor. He had to face a divided church, with the majority of the population and clergy vehemently rejecting the union and expecting the new Emperor to do likewise. The Pope, Nicholas V, immediately demanded that Constantine ensure compliance with the Union Decree, which was not being adhered to in Constantinople. In response, Constantine sent a detailed explanation to the Pope of why it was unwise for him to enforce the agreement.

The situation continued unchanged until February 1451 when Murad II suddenly died, leaving as his successor his 19-year-old son Mehmed. From a very young age, the young Sultan had shown that he was very ambitious, energetic, and strong willed; he was also well educated.[112] He immediately started preparations to lay siege to Constantinople, including blocking its sea access from the north by building a massive fort across from the existing one on the Asian side of the Bosporus; this was completed within a few months.

This panicked the people of Constantinople, who tried to renovate their crumbling fortifications, and they sent pleas for assistance to the West again. The Emperor asked permission from Venice to recruit archers from Crete to defend Constantinople, which was soon granted.[113] That November, eight boats arrived from Crete with supplies for the citizens of

[112] It is claimed that he was well trained in the sciences and in philosophy, well read in Islamic and Greek literature, and as well as his native Turkish spoke fluent Greek, Arabic, Latin, Persian and Hebrew. Runciman (2005), p. 56.

[113] Ibid., pp. 63, 67. There are numerous descriptions of the fall of Constantinople, some by contemporary observers and historians as well as by modern-day historians. This section will follow the events as described by the British historian Sir Steven Runciman in his book *The Fall of Constantinople 1453*.

Constantinople. Six of these vessels left again in late February, taking with them 600 Venetians who were abandoning the city. A month later there were 26 boats in the city's Golden Horn harbour ready to defend the city, amongst them three from Crete.[114] The crews from those three Cretan boats were to play a remarkable role during this tragic event.

The siege and fall of Constantinople

The siege began on the 5th of April 1453. Ottoman troops, supplied with cannons and large siege towers, had been amassing in front of the city walls since Easter Monday, three days beforehand. The month before, a large Ottoman fleet had sailed from Gallipoli and arrived outside Constantinople's sea walls at the same time as the Sultan's 100,000 troops[115] were gathering on the landward side. The Emperor's forces inside the city consisted of only 4,937 men who were able to bear arms, including priests and monks, and just under 2,000 foreigners,[116] mainly Genoese and Venetians. The Sultan concentrated all his efforts on the landward face of the city, a double wall approximately seven kilometres long punctuated with towers at regular intervals and surrounded by a moat. His troops bombarded the walls with their cannons and soon turned parts of it to rubble, but the walls were not breached. During the night, the city's defenders repaired the damage as well as they could.

This scenario of continuous cannon bombardment and overnight repairs lasted for the entire 54-day period of the siege. Waves of Ottoman troops attempted to scale the walls but were repelled, their siege towers were toppled over and destroyed, and those caught tunnelling under the walls were killed. But it was a war of attrition for the Byzantines and their allies as their numbers dwindled; exhaustion was also their enemy, food supplies were running out, and the effects of long-term malnutrition were taking their toll. Most of the city's defenders realized that the end was approaching

The only outside assistance that the besieged city received during this period was the arrival of three Genoese boats which had been hired by the Pope to bring arms and provisions, and one Byzantine boat bringing corn from Sicily. The four vessels arrived together at the Sea of Marmara, but while approaching the city walls they were intercepted by a large Ottoman fleet. A fierce battle ensued until the wind changed, allowing the four

---

[114] Ibid., p. 85.

[115] The strength of the Sultan's forces differs in the various reports, but a reasonable estimate puts it at about 100,000, including irregulars and support staff.

[116] From the report to the Emperor at the end of March, as given in the diary of events kept by Georgios Sphrantzes, the Emperor's trusted secretary. Sphrantzes & Barbaro (1993), p. 26.

boats to escape to the security of Golden Horn harbour, joining the other defensive vessels there, including the three Cretan boats.[117]

To the superstitious people of Byzantium, all the omens portending the fall of the city were present on the night of the 24th of May. There was an eclipse of the moon, and a procession of the holiest of the icons of the Mother of God went badly when the icon fell off its platform, and then a thunderstorm caused the procession to be abandoned. The next morning the city was covered in a thick blanket of fog which hung there all day; in the evening when the fog lifted, a strange light hovered over the dome of the church of Hagia Sophia.[118] The 28th was the strangest day for all inside the city, as very little activity was taking place outside the walls, and there was no noise. That evening all the citizens not on watch duty congregated for one last mass in Hagia Sophia.

The final assault on the city started with a horrifying intensity at 1:30 on the morning of the 29th of May. By daybreak Constantinople had fallen, as the Ottomans had managed to enter the city through a small gate that had been left unlocked by Byzantine troops returning from an earlier attack on their besiegers. The Ottoman troops streamed into the city, and the tragic destruction of Constantinople and the massacre of its people began.

The invading troops only met resistance at three towers by Horaia Gate, on the north wall of the city overlooking Golden Horn harbour. The men from the three Cretan boats in the harbour had barricaded themselves in these towers and continued to fight, refusing to surrender. It was not until late in the afternoon that they negotiated terms with the Sultan's officers under which they were willing to leave their positions.[119] They were allowed to walk away with their weapons and other possessions, board their boats, and sail away unmolested while the sailors from the Ottoman fleet all scrambled towards the city to participate in the pillage and destruction. On the 9th of June, the three Cretan boats arrived in Candia with the horrific news that Constantinople had fallen. For all Greeks in Crete, this was a severe blow to their dreams of freeing themselves from the Venetians and the Latin Church, and of rekindling what had once been the glory of Byzantium.

The events surrounding the death of the Emperor are uncertain, although it is firmly believed that he was killed during the fighting. One legend tells of the Emperor being surrounded by Turks and, while fighting bravely, calling out: "Is there a Christian around to cut off my head?" According to another legend, which has been memorialised in a traditional song, the Emperor called out: "Cut off my head, Christian Romans, take it good Cretans, and carry it to Crete, for the Cretans to see it and be sad at heart".

[117] Runciman (2005), pp. 100-103.

[118] Ibid., p. 121.

[119] Ibid., p. 143.

This latter legend commemorates the Cretans who fought side-by-side with the Emperor and indicates that he trusted the Cretans and wished them to carry on the Byzantine tradition in Crete.

The legend of the five Cretan boats which sailed to help the Emperor

There are many legends about the fall of Constantinople and its aftermath,[120] but one relates specifically to Sfakia. It is based on a manuscript discovered by I.A. Kontos in 1919 at Vatopedion monastery on Mount Athos, which he used to compose an epic story in verse entitled "The Cretan boats in 1453". The manuscript tells of a Venetian emissary arriving in Sfakia early in 1453 with a request from Emperor Constantine XI for assistance in defending Constantinople. Responding to this appeal, a Sfakian leader, Manousos Kallikratis, gathered together 1,500 Cretans, sailors and soldiers, and in that March they set off in five boats from Souda Bay to Constantinople. Three of the boats were Sfakian, owned by Manousos Kallikratis himself, and many of those aboard were Sfakians. When they arrived at the Sea of Marmara, they were attacked by the Ottoman fleet; after a long battle, during which they lost two of their boats, they managed to break through into Golden Horn harbour. The 600 surviving Cretans fought alongside the Byzantines throughout the siege, and the manuscript claims that it was 170 of those men who refused to surrender in the towers near Horaia Gate. Following negotiations with the Sultan's officers, they were allowed to leave with their weapons on one of their boats. Because the one surviving Cretan leader, Captain Petros the Grammatikos, was seriously wounded, they sailed to Mount Athos, where they left him at Vatopedion monastery before returning to Crete. He was cared for by the monks, joined their holy order and lived at the monastery for another eight years. Just before dying, he dictated these events to another monk.

There are certain inconsistencies between the events presented in the manuscript and those described by other chroniclers of the fall of Constantinople, but the main one relates to the naval battle between the five Cretan boats and the Ottoman fleet. All historians and contemporary witnesses describe this sea battle as taking place between one Byzantine and three Genoese boats and the Ottoman fleet.[121] All historians also inform us that no other outside help arrived during the siege period other than these four boats. However, the manuscript does contain certain information that is consistent with the events of the siege, such as the fact that a number

[120] An interesting article on this topic is Papayianni (2010).

[121] Moniou (2007), pp. 69-71, 203-209, 309-313; Sphrantzes & Barbaro (1993), pp. 32-35, 134-136; Runciman (2005), pp. 100-104; and Norwich (2006), Vol. III, p. 424.

of Cretans who were defending Horaia Gate did not surrender and were allowed to leave in their three boats (the manuscript says one). The document also mentions the Genoese General Giustiniani and states that he was wounded in the battle and died two days later; in fact, he died rather later than that, when the Genoese boats arrived in Chios.

Obviously, the manuscript was based on some of the events as described by contemporary witnesses and historians of the time, but it outlines a story that in part cannot be substantiated by historical evidence. The names of the Sfakian leaders mentioned are not useful in researching the veracity of this story as they are fairly common, and we are unable to relate them to any known personages of that time.[122]

A book about Kontos' life[123] indicates that he indeed was at the monastery of Vatopedion in Agion Oros for two days in 1903, and that he had opportunities to visit the monastery later on while he was working in Thessaloniki in 1914 and 1939. He claimed that he found the manuscript in the monastery's library in 1919. The first volume of his book, which included this epic tale, was published in 1948, almost 30 years after his alleged discovery of the manuscript.

---

[122] E.g. Manousos Kallikratis can be Manousos from Kallikratis, the well-known Sfakian village. Some names cannot be found today (Karchas). One name purportedly from Askifou, that of Sifis Maniakis, can be found in western Crete as Manias (Pashley's guide was Manias from Askifou) but not as Maniakis; note that surnames ending in –akis did not emerge in western Crete until after the 16th century.

[123] Pissanos (1971).

VIII. The 15th and 16th centuries and the rebellions in Sfakia – 1453 to 1610

The plots by Sifis Vlastos (1453) and Ioannis Gavalas (1462)

The mass influx of refugees into Crete after the fall of Constantinople made Venice quite concerned; they suspected that the pro-Byzantine prominent Greek families and the local population might attempt another uprising aimed at re-establishing the Byzantine state in Crete. Their suspicions were not wrong. A few months after the city fell, a group of Greeks in Rethymnon started devising precisely such a plan. Encouraged by the Orthodox clergy who had recently arrived from Constantinople and were very much against the religious compromises agreed with Rome, they believed that the Byzantine Empire could be revived in Crete if they overthrew the Venetians. Their main leader was Sifis Vlastos, a descendant of one of the *archondopoula* families. But their secret activities and intentions were betrayed to the Venetians, and the entire Vlastos family was arrested, interrogated, tortured and eventually executed.

The Venetians had developed an effective network of informers by using a system of significant rewards for information about plots against them, and they gained a horrific reputation for unprecedented levels of violence and torture against those suspected of inciting rebellion. In such an environment, none of the prominent Greek families were prepared to take the risks involved in initiating another uprising for purely ideological reasons now that most of their grievances about personal property had been settled.

Despite this oppressive situation, one more plot aimed at overthrowing Venetian rule and the Church of Rome, and re-establishing Byzantium and the Orthodox Church, was hatched in Rethymnon in 1462. Many refugees from Constantinople were involved, as well as some prominent Cretans, including members of the Gavalas and Melissinos *archondopoula* families. This group was also betrayed to the Venetians, who arrested and executed most of them. A small number of participants in this plot managed to escape and, under the leadership of a member of the Skordilis family, fled to the White Mountains of Sfakia. The Venetians pursued them for more than 11 years, according to the Cretan historian Psilakis,[124] until they were all tracked down and killed.

Venice also took measures to quash any further attempts at rebellion being incited by the Orthodox clergy and monks, especially refugees from Constantinople who were vehemently opposed to the union of the two churches. The Venetians provided special allowances to Orthodox priests who actively encouraged their parishioners to accept the union of the churches.

This was the last rebellion in Crete against the Venetians under the leadership of powerful Cretan clans. By the end of the 15th century, most of the old Cretan aristocracy had regained significant parts of their privileges and property, many of the Venetian nobility had intermarried with them, and the Venetians resident in Crete for generations had adapted to Greek customs and culture to the extent that they felt closer to the Cretan elite than to the Venetian high officials who were sent to rule them. All these factors, combined with the prosperity that the Venetian trade network had brought to the island, had resulted in an environment that was comfortable and secure for those with property and wealth, as well as for those living in the larger towns. Further rebellion was seen as futile and counterproductive to their own personal interests.

But the situation in the countryside amongst the rural population, the *villani* and *contadini*, as well as amongst some of the poorer *privilegiati*, especially the Sfakians, had reached a stage where social unrest and the early stages of insurrection started to surface again early in the 16th century. This led a few years later to the last large-scale rebellion against the Venetians that the island was to experience.

The "chicken war"

The Sfakian historian Papadopetrakis relates a story in his *History of Sfakia* about how the Sfakians rebelled against increasing pressure by the Venetian feudal lords to extract additional taxes from the long-suffering Cretans.[125] This centered around a probably illegitimate tax imposed in western Crete, without the sanction of the central authorities in Candia, which required all *villani* families on the first day of every month to provide their Venetian masters with a plump chicken. As time went by and the population increased, so did the number of chickens that were demanded, and

[124] V. Psilakis (1970 [1906]), Vol. 2, p. 360.

[125] Papadopetrakis (1971 [1888]), pp. 104-105. This story is told without historical references or any attribution.

disputes developed about how many chickens each family had to supply to the feudal lord. Some of the poorer families, who could not afford to raise more chickens, instead offered eggs to their master on the basis that he could hatch and raise the chickens himself! Of course, this was considered an affront and serious insubordination.

The Sfakians, who refused to comply with this tax from the beginning, decided to take the matter into their own hands. A delegation of senior Sfakians prepared a submission to the *Provveditor* in Chania seeking the abolition of this illegitimate tax, and demanded that this petition be sent to Venice. The *Provveditor* rejected their claim outright and threw all of them in jail. The Sfakians' reaction was immediate. They took up arms, encouraged others to follow their example, and began a full-blown insurrection which, according to Papadopetrakis, lasted three years. The Venetians eventually acceded to the Sfakians' demands to abolish this tax and withdrew the more than 10,000 outstanding legal cases against those who had not complied with it.

The same story is also related by the Cretan historian Psilakis,[126] but it is unclear from his writings when this event occurred. It probably took place some time during the late 15th or early 16th century, but perhaps earlier than 1608, when Papadopetrakis places it. The incident must have been part of the general unrest that western Crete experienced during that period, and although this tale does not feature in any of the published Venetian reports of the time it has become part of Sfakian folklore since it displays many elements of the Sfakian psyche – disrespect for authority, fighting against injustices inflicted on the downtrodden, and a quirky sense of humour. Many still talk about the *ornithopolemos* ('chicken war'), and the offer of an egg instead of a chicken, an intentional insult disguised as an offer of compromise!

Unrest in Sfakia in the 16th century

The general discontent in Sfakia in the first few years of the 16th century caused some concern to the Venetian authorities in Candia, as described in Professor Papadia-Lala's study of unrest in western Crete at that time.[127] This unrest grew mainly out of complaints by Sfakians about the *Provveditore* appointed from Chania – they claimed that he treated them unfairly and failed to enforce laws, which resulted in unnecessary disputes between families and factions in the district. In addition, there were many

[126] V. Psilakis (1970 [1906]) Vol. 2, pp. 364-366. As with Papadopetrakis, Psilakis does not provide any historical sources for this story, so it is possible that it could have been based on Papadopetrakis' earlier writings.
[127] Papadia-Lala (1983).

Sfakians,16th century sketches by Venetian Cesare Vecellio

grievances about the illegitimate taxing of Sfakians, as well as arbitrary arrests and other punishments. The Sfakians were initially angry only with the local authorities, and the Candia government wrote to the officials in Chania pointing out their failings. But it appears that this was not effective, because these complaints soon increased in magnitude and the Sfakians started to show their displeasure with the central government in Candia as well.

By the second decade of the 16th century, Sfakian families were taking the law onto their own hands, and the more widespread cases of family disputes (vendettas) worried the authorities in Candia. The Venetian authorities sent an official (*avogador*) to Sfakia in mid 1512 specifically to defuse these disputes, but the intervention failed since it was seen by some as taking sides rather than dispensing justice. Candia ordered a sterner approach to be taken and gave special instructions to its officials not to be seen as favouring any parties. By July 1512, new orders forbade carrying arms and using insulting language; the former was to be punished by hanging and the latter by corporal punishment and exile of up to three years. The ineffectiveness of these directives is obvious from the records, as the same orders were issued a number of times over the next several years, naming the families involved in the disputes and putting them on notice to stop their vendettas.[128]

A report from early 1515 indicates that the situation had deteriorated further.[129] By mid 1515 the Venetian authorities had recognized that the

[128] Some of the family names mentioned are: Medikos, Pateros, Nomikos and Kontos, all of them descendants of the Skordilis clan.

[129] Two other families appeared to be creating problems now: Lignos and Psaromelingos.

situation was totally out of control; they threatened to declare all Sfakians enemies of the state and punish the entire district of Sfakia severely, but they were ignored again by the factions who had declared open warfare against each other.

The trouble in Sfakia had been evolving over a long period and was not reflected in other parts of the island. A number of factors contributed to this situation. Although Sfakians were recognised by the Venetians as part of the *privilegiati archondoromei* class, their isolated location and the barrenness of their district led to them being excluded from developments in the rest of Cretan society, where much of the population was settling down to a more peaceful coexistence with the Venetian privileged classes and enjoying the benefits of the wealth that Venetian trade was bringing to the island.

The uprisings over the previous two centuries had also resulted in the Lefka Ori becoming a refuge for many who had fled from other areas. The difficult and infertile landscape that the Sfakians inhabited had kept the Venetian authorities uninterested in this area, so there was no system of law and order there other than the traditional ways of settling disputes, which required compromise and could not be imposed upon any party. The Sfakians' bitterness at seeing nearby areas enjoying a more comfortable standard of living drove them to carry out raids against more prosperous people, and to wage low-level guerrilla warfare against Venetians and Cretan elite families who were trying to protect their land and wealth. Disputes between Sfakian factions about territorial rights over areas that were being raided, and quarrels about their share of these ill-gotten proceeds, also contributed to the chaotic situation. The Venetians were unable to stem this level of lawlessness, partly due to the inaccessibility of the area, but also because of the nature of some of these inter-family clashes.

The insurrection of the villani in western Crete

A number of Sfakian extended families had by now moved away from the mountains to more productive lower-lying areas in the northern foothills of the Lefka Ori, seeking a better life. Because they did not own any land, they had to work for Venetian landowners as *villani*, virtual slaves to their master. The first large-scale insurrection by *villani* in western Crete against their very restrictive working conditions occurred around 1518. It involved about 300 members (some reports talk about 600) of the extended Sfakian Foumis family, descendants of the Skordilises, who toiled for Lorenzo Massolo in the area of Keramia in the Chania district. According to Venetian reports, they refused to hand over to Massolo the compulsory (or unreasonably excessive, according to other reports) share of their production and refused to obey orders from the Venetian authorities.

Their insubordination soon spread to other nearby villages, and *villani* started attacking local Venetian army units and landowners, assisted by related Sfakian clans from the Lefka Ori who looked on this as an opportunity to take revenge for their own grievances. The *villani* continued to demand changes to the conditions of their servitude. The landowners were loath to make any concessions, but at the same time they were afraid of losing their agricultural labourers. The unrest continued for some time, but eventually in 1523 the situation settled down when the Venetian authorities offered an amnesty to all those involved in the uprising and its associated acts of violence and insubordination.

This period was the first occasion when a revolt was instigated by the oppressed agrarian population of Crete, without recourse to the leadership of the *archondopoula,* who by then were enjoying the advantages won over the previous three centuries of fighting. The demands of the *villani* for better conditions was mirrored in other areas of Europe where serfdom were slowly being replaced by different kinds of arrangements between landlords and peasant workers.

The Kantanoleos uprising and the legend of the Cretan wedding

There was soon to be another uprising in western Crete which has become a Cretan legend since the publication in 1872 of *The Cretan Weddings,* a book by the Greek historian Spyridon Zampelios.[130] The events have had a direct impact on Sfakian folklore because many Sfakian families were involved in the activities surrounding this rebellion and its tragic suppression.

According to Zampelios, the main protagonists of this uprising were: Giorgis Kantanoleos, from the small village of Koustogerako,[131] just north of Sougia on the southwestern slopes of the Lefka Ori; his son Petros; Francesco da Molino, a Venetian noble from Chania; and da Molino's only daughter Sophia, of Greek ancestry on her mother's side, who was educated in the Greek language and customs and believed in the aspirations of the Greeks on the island. Kantanoleos was from the Sfakian Skordilis family; some sources claim that his correct surname was Skordilis and that

[130] Zampelios was born on the island of Lefkas, in the Ionian Sea, and was educated in Italy at the Universities of Bologna and Pisa. He wrote extensively on Greek history, and later in his life he became interested in Cretan history. He wrote *The Cretan Weddings* in 1871, with the subtitle *An unpublished event in the history of Crete during the Venetian era (1570).* He also co-authored *The History of the Cretan Revolutions,* published in 1893.

[131] Koustogerako, according to some sources, was on the border of the Skordilis territory allotted to the family by the Emperor Alexios I Comnenos. Venetian records show the name as Christogerako or Cristogeraco, reflecting the earlier Greek name. Pashley, in early 1800, cites the name as Krustogherako, while a century later the Greek writer Zampelios refers to it as Kroustogerako.

Kantanoleos was a name given to him by the Venetians. Finally, a large number of Sfakian families were involved, which is why this is considered to be a predominantly Sfakian-instigated rebellion.

Zampelios writes that some time before 1570, in reaction to unbearable taxes and the brutal treatment of the rural population, a large number of the heads of leading families in western Crete, including the Skordilis, Pateros, Papadopoulos and Psaromelingos families from Sfakia, met at the monastery of Saint John the Hermit (Katholiko) in Akrotiri near Chania and decided to rise up against the Venetian rulers. There they elected Giorgis Kantanoleos as head of a new independent government for western Crete. Zampelios claims that Kantanoleos had ambitions to free all Greeks from the oppressors and that he had secret contacts with the Patriarch in Constantinople, the Tsar of Russia, and a number of powerful people in mainland Greece. Following several successful battles against the Venetians at the Imbros Gorge, Agia Roumeli and the Samaria Gorge, and other locations between Chania and Rethymnon, the Venetians inhabiting the western areas of the island withdrew to Chania, allowing the new Cretan government total freedom to govern all of western Crete. Kantanoleos established his headquarters at Meskla, in the foothills of the Lefka Ori about 15 km south of Chania, and set up proper government processes, including tax collection – although at a more acceptable level than under the Venetians.

According to Zampelios, Petros Kantanoleos, the leader's son, had fallen in love with Sophia, Francesco da Molino's only daughter, who he had met at a jousting competition in Chania where he received the winner's award from her hands. Her father conspired with the Duke of Candia to eliminate all the rebels by arranging for his daughter to marry Kantanoleos' son, then arresting and killing all the rebel guests at their wedding.

A large number of Cretans were invited to the wedding. Following the traditional festivities where vast amounts of wine were consumed (spiked with opium, according to Zampelios), the guests were surrounded by Venetian troops who had arrived secretly from Chania, Rethymnon and Candia; they arrested Kantanoleos and his son and hanged them on the spot, together with more than 30 other Cretan leaders. The rest of the prisoners, numbering in their hundreds, were divided into four groups; one group was hanged at the gates of Chania, one at Koustogerako, one on the road from Chania to Rethymnon, and the fourth at Meskla, the headquarters of the rebel government. But the atrocities did not stop there – whole villages were destroyed, including Koustogerako and Meskla. Acts of violence continued for some time, and quite a few leaders and their families fled up into the mountains until, eventually, an amnesty was arranged.

Zampelios largely based his story on a manuscript written more than 100 years after the events by a Venetian notary, Antonio Trivan, who lived in

Candia until it fell to the Turks. Zampelios claimed that his story also drew on information from a number of other documents that he had examined in Venice, but he did not provide any references to them. Trivan's manuscript presents a brief history of the "Regno di Candia", covering the period from 1182 to 1669. It omits a number of important events while extensively covering others of lesser importance. Trivan discusses the Kantanoleos uprising in a separate section, mixing facts and fiction, and sets the events in 1502; but he wrote that the person who defeated the rebels was *Capitano di Candia* Marino di Cavalli, who we know arrived in Crete in 1570 and who was reported by others as inflicting heavy casualties against Cretan rebels in the western district around 1570-71. Zampelios, drawing on this document which mentions Cavalli's involvement, thus sets his historical novel in 1570.

The main difference between the events as presented by Zampelios and Trivan concerns the respective roles of Francesco da Molino and Giorgis Kantanoleos. Trivan claims that it was Kantanoleos who insisted his son marry da Molino's daughter in an attempt to force a reconciliation between Cretans and the noble Venetian families and establish a new dynasty to govern western Crete, while Zampelios states that the wedding proposal came from da Molino in order to entrap and kill the rebels. Zampelios does not disagree with Trivan's representation of the events that followed the ambush at the wedding, but he presents them in a more melodramatic way. The fate of Kantanoleos and the rebels has inspired Cretans over the generations.

The British writer Robert Pashley gives Trivan's version of events in his book about his travels in Crete[132] without questioning the validity of the story. Early Cretan historians, such as Psilakis, Kondylakis and Kriaris, have opted to follow Zampelios' interpretation, thus contributing to the strong belief amongst Cretans in his version. Later on, historians such as Stephanos Xanthoudides[133] started questioning Zampelios' and Trivan's narratives. The British writer and diplomat Michael Llewellyn Smith's book about Crete[134] outlines clearly the problems with Trivan's account; while he acknowledges that there was an uprising led by Kantanoleos and brutal punishment of locals in western Crete, he suggests that the two events might have been unrelated and could have taken place more than 50 years apart.

Some recent Greek historians have tended to avoid expanding on this subject, given the strong belief amongst Cretans in the events as presented by Zampelios. Detorakis[135] takes a more diplomatic approach by saying that

[132] Pashley (1989 [1837]), Vol. II, pp. 151-155.
[133] Xanthoudides (1939), pp. 119-121.
[134] Llewellyn Smith (1973), pp. 28-32.
[135] Detorakis (1994), pp. 173-175.

there is a "lack of reliable sources for this revolt" and that "Zampelios served to confuse the record"; he then discusses some of the events surrounding this uprising as gleaned from more reliable sources. Chrysa Maltezou[136] in her work on the Venetian era in Crete refers to Zampelios' "historical novel" and says that it interpreted historical events in the "spirit of the times", presenting the hero Kantanoleos as the organizer of a movement aimed at "freeing the whole enslaved Greek nation".

Separating fact from fiction has been a difficult task which was, however, happily achieved in Professor Anastasia Papadia-Lala's[137] 1983 doctoral thesis on the events surrounding the uprising, where she raises three important points. First, there was indeed an uprising in western Crete led by Kantanoleos (Papadia-Lala states that the more correct version of his name is Gadanoleos, Γαδανολέος) which took place in 1527, not in 1502 as Trivan has it or 1570 as per Zampelios. Secondly, it was indeed suppressed brutally, though not by Cavalli but by another Venetian, Hieronymus Corner, who was *Capitano General* of Candia at the time. The violent suppression described by Trivan in part is related to a later Venetian expedition against the Sfakians in 1571 which led to the destruction of Sfakia by Cavalli. Finally, the events surrounding the wedding and the ensuing massacre are not supported by any reports from that time and therefore should be considered a fictional account created by Trivan and further embellished by Zampelios.

Reports by Hieronymus Corner and other contemporary officials provide us with a somewhat different picture from that presented by both Trivan and Zampelios. The Venetians noted down acts of impropriety and insubordination by the locals starting early in 1527 in the districts of Sfakia, Selino and Apokoronas. Soon this discontent grew into an uprising, and Giorgis Gadanoleos, referred to by the Venetians as Lissogiorgi ('Rabid George'), assumed the leadership of a movement which engaged in guerrilla warfare against the Venetians. The authorities granted Corner full power to suppress the uprising and punish all involved. Corner and a large contingent, including support from Andreas Kallergis, made for the mountain villages of Kydonia, Apokoronas and Selino, where the rebels had sought refuge, and suppressed the uprising there. Corner then advanced on the centre of the rebellion in Meskla, Keramia, Lakki and Koustogerako, where he arrested and executed many rebels and destroyed Gadanoleos' village, Koustogerako. Unable to capture Gadanoleos, the Venetians offered a large reward for his arrest. He was soon betrayed, captured and executed. Other captured rebels were sent into exile in Cyprus, as had happened before. Reports at the time put the number of those executed at either 300 or 700. And so ended the last large-scale uprising against the Venetians

[136] Maltezou (1988), p. 128.

[137] Papadia-Lala (1983).

in Crete – but not the continuing unrest in Sfakia, which was to lead to another brutal invasion of Sfakia.

Most Cretans, including Sfakians, still believe in the tragic story of the Venetians' treachery during the wedding, and visitors to Alikianos are shown the ruins of the da Molino house where the terrible events are supposed to have occurred. Some people search, in vain, for the inscription that Zampelios tells us was inscribed above the entrance:

Omnia mundi fumus et umbra
[Everything in the world is smoke and shadows][138]

As indeed, it seems, is the story of Kantanoleos and the Cretan wedding.

Unrest continues in Sfakia

Soon after the suppression of this latest uprising, the authorities had to deal with the many Cretan families who applied for pardons and the return of their confiscated properties, as well as those who requested permission for exiled members of their families to be allowed to return. Furthermore, many exiles came back illegally, creating another permanent problem for the authorities, who had to contend with the ever-increasing threat of a new rebellion. One of Giorgis Gadanoleos' sons was eventually granted permission to return from exile, and other exiled members of the Kontos extended family (part of the Skordilis clan) were allowed to move back to their properties in the Alikampos area.

Agrarian unrest by the *villani* in the west, rebellious Sfakian families, raids by Sfakians on Venetians and other well-off Cretans, and increasing concerns about the activities of the Ottoman fleet in the Mediterranean all combined to make the Venetian authorities extremely worried. They were especially fearful about a consipracy between the Sfakians and the *villani* to overthrow them in favour of the Turks. Numerous Venetian reports speak of the need to pacify the Sfakians and win their cooperation in helping to fend off an invasion by the Turks, while at the same time criticising the local Venetian authorities for not reining in the insubordination and illegal activities of a number of Sfakian clans.

Loredan, the *Rettore* of Chania, wrote in his annual report to Venice[139] about his expedition to Sfakia in 1554 to capture the Sfakian pirates who had attacked a French ship. The authorities sent a large contingent – 10 galleys

[138] Zampelios (2003), p. 383. This inscription is not to be confused with a similar one that can be seen above the door of an old Venetian ruin at Argyroupoli; this confusion has resulted in the claim that da Molino's house and the wedding events took place at Argyroupolis instead of Alikianos.
[139] Ploumidis (1972).

and 600 men – given that the population of the district was about 2,500 people, including women and children. Loredan's force met no resistance. They arrested six and killed a further four of the "assassins", as he describes them, but their leader, Antonios Pateros, escaped; he was captured a year later when he returned to Sfakia to build another boat for his piratical activities and was put to death. Loredan also wrote that he burned down two of the leaders' houses and condemned the Sfakians he had captured, along with Pateros, to galley service, and sentenced the whole community to forced labour on the state's fortifications for disobeying his orders.

Loredan furthermore reported that the source of all these problems was the general neglect by the local Venetian authorities of their governmental duties. He recommended that the *Rettore* of Chania visit Sfakia at least once a year to punish those guilty of insubordination, but also to ensure that the local Venetians were not unlawfully exploiting the native population.

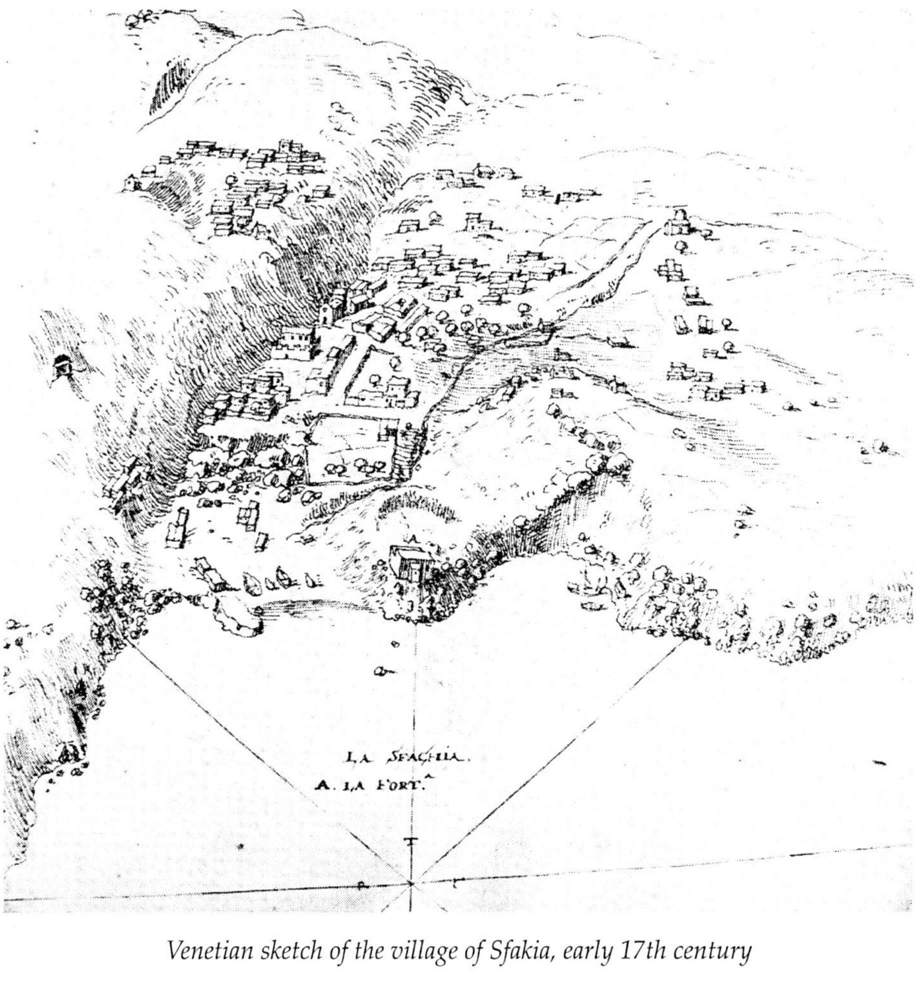

Venetian sketch of the village of Sfakia, early 17th century

Sfakia had by then become an area to which most of the bandits and fugitives sought by the state fled, as they felt safer amongst the Sfakians, who had very clearly demonstrated their disregard for Venetian authority. The Duke of Crete reported in 1561[140] that Sfakia was "inhabited by fugitives and thieves, and the locals disobey all Venetian orders". Reports were filed in Candia in 1568 which similarly recognised that the situation continued to be out of control, blaming it on the behaviour of nobles and officials to the village population and recommending more severe penalties against those breaching the laws.

In 1569, Venice instructed the newly appointed *Provveditor General* to contain the Sfakians within their district and to protect others from them. They also gave him a mandate to take any necessary action to help the Sfakians become better citizens and return to a more peaceful existence.[141] But none of this had any impact at all on what was happening in Sfakia.

The threat of an Ottoman invasion, and events in Sfakia

During this same period, the Venetians faced an emerging threat from the Ottoman fleet which, having captured Tripoli in 1551 from the Knights of St John and having defeated the Spanish fleet which came to free the city nine years later, then attacked Malta in 1565. The Knights managed to defend the island, assisted by the Spanish fleet, and eventually the Ottomans gave up. Next they turned their attention to Cyprus, which had been occupied by Venice since 1490, but its proximity to the Asia Minor mainland made it much easier for them to conquer it. In January 1570, the Grand Vizir advised Venice's representative in Constantinople that the Sultan considered Cyprus to be historically part of the Ottoman Empire and that he was determined to set things right. The next day there were mass arrests of Venetians in Constantinople and seizures of Venetian ships in the harbour. This was the end of a quarter century of peace between Venice and the Ottoman Empire, and the beginning of a series of events that would eventually lead to the capture of Crete by the Turks.

In 1570, the authorities in Crete were given responsibility for preparing and manning a number of galleys that were to join the combined Spanish, Papal and Venetian fleets to fight the Ottoman forces threatening Cyprus. Manning the galleys was especially difficult because epidemics took a disastrous toll on the crews. Thousands of Cretans were conscripted for galley service, but many fled to the mountains rather than accept a fate that in many cases would result in death.

In response to orders from the Admiral of the fleet, the *Provveditor* of

[140] Papadia-Lala (1983), p. 158.
[141] Giannopoulos (1978), p. 141.

Chania, Luca Michiel, travelled to Sfakia to recruit as many volunteers as possible. (Sfakians were not obliged to perform galley service.) Michiel, not known for using high-pressure tactics, proposed that the Sfakians select a third of their suitable men to serve in the war against the Ottomans. The Sfakians agreed, and eventually 170 joined him, but when they saw the devastating effects of the epidemics on the existing crews in Souda harbour, 100 of them fled. Michiel, angry and embarrassed, vilified the Sfakians in front of the Admiral and criticized their unruly nature; he even suggested that this incident gave the authorities an excuse to return to Sfakia and kill all of them.[142] But the time was not right for this since the fleet was getting ready to sail. When the fleet reached Kastellorizo, halfway to Cyprus, they learned that Cyprus had already been captured by the Ottomans, so they turned back without ever having caught sight of the enemy.[143]

The *Provveditor General's* report in early 1571 urged the exemplary destruction of Sfakia and its inhabitants in order to end their continuing piracy, raids and killings, but nobody had the time or interest to pursue this. At the same time, the newly appointed Admiral General proclaimed that any fugitive criminals would be pardoned if they presented themselves for service on the Venetian galleys within a specified period of time. The Venetian authorities needed to deal with the Ottoman fleet, which was now preparing to attack Crete.

In June 1571, a large flotilla of more than 200 Ottoman boats of various types and sizes gathered in Evia (the large island off the eastern coast of mainland Greece, then occupied by the Ottomans) and set sail for Crete. The fleet arrived in Souda Bay on the 16th of June and offloaded troops which attacked the nearby villages, but they did not attempt to lay siege to Chania, which was strongly defended by the Venetians. The Ottomans also sent a small section of the fleet to Rethymnon, which they found almost deserted and defended only by 100 soldiers. They soon overran the town and destroyed it, and then turned to demolishing and pillaging nearby villages. They then rejoined the rest of the fleet in Souda Bay while Ottoman troops continued to burn and plunder the surrounding countryside and capture citizens to be slaves. The defending Venetians and Cretans[144] inflicted serious losses on the attacking forces, but the depletion of the local population and the damage to the countryside was enormous. Contemporary reports talk of 3,700 Ottoman deaths, while it has been claimed that they took 8,000 Cretans as slaves; both figures are probably exaggerated, but they still indicate the magnitude of the losses on both sides. By the end of June, the Ottoman fleet had left without attempting to capture Crete.

---

[142] Giannopoulos (1978), pp. 142, 143.

[143] Norwich (2003), p. 471.

[144] A later report by Foscarini mentioned that Sfakians fought against the Ottoman troops who were destroying and pillaging the countryside.

With the departure of the Ottoman fleet, the new *Provveditor General*, Marino di Cavalli, had to contend with an uprising by villagers outside Rethymnon against their oppressive treatment. Having seen the ease with which the Ottoman army had managed to capture Rethymnon and attack the Venetians in nearby areas, these villagers took up arms against the Venetians. Cavalli authorized Matthaios Kallergis, who wielded great influence in the area, to put down this insurrection. Kallergis decided instead to negotiate with the rebels, and after receiving assurances from them that they would submit peacefully to Venetian rule, he pardoned them all. He then prepared a report to Cavalli in which he took the side of the villagers, claiming that their motives reflected an understandable reaction to the injustices inflicted on them by the feudal lords, but he also emphasized the need for their support in view of the ongoing Ottoman threat. Venice agreed with Kallergis' approach to defusing the situation and asked for the villagers to be informed that Venice wanted them to be treated justly and considered them to be of great value to the state. Cavalli had different ideas, and a few months later he dispatched one of his trusted officers with a large army to Rethymnon, where they captured eight priests and another man who were considered to be the leaders of the uprising and hanged them.

Cavalli was aware of the problems that his predecessors had experienced with the Sfakians and intended to sort out the situation once and for all, but he had to wait until the fleet was manned again and the coastal defenses were reinforced before addressing this issue. In the meantime, the Sfakians appeared to be prepared to assist the Venetians against the Ottoman threat, just as they had participated in the battles against them near Chania. But Cavalli had already made up his mind about their fate.

The destruction of Sfakia by Cavalli

Late in September 1571, Cavalli attacked Sfakia with a large force and completely destroyed the area. His report to Venice is very brief: "I punished the Sfakians for good, and I would have brought them completely under submission if I had not been restrained by some quarters."[145] This last comment refers to those in authority who disagreed with Cavalli's approach to solving the Sfakian problem, and who thought that the Sfakians would have been valuable as allies in fighting the Ottoman army. It is from several reports by *Provveditor General* Giacomo Foscarini, who came to Crete in 1574, that we learn of the extent of Cavalli's destruction of Sfakia. He wrote that all their houses were razed and burned, many were killed or arrested, and the remainder were forced to flee into the mountains. Those who were

[145] Theotokis (1933), p. 332.

arrested were sent into exile in Corfu, many of them dying on the way because of the atrocious conditions aboard the ships. A reward was offered for the capture of those who had escaped, and as a result many had to exist on the run, in gorges or up in the mountains, without food or shelter. All Sfakians were banned from coming within 20 miles of Sfakia, and they were not allowed to rebuild their houses until the authorities gave them permission to do so.

Cavalli's hatred of the Sfakians can be seen from another section of his report to Venice where he says:

> For Crete to become peaceful again it is necessary to eliminate the Pateros and Papadopoulos clans. They are the ones who have been raiding Messara and Psychro, and the entire districts of Chania and of Rethymnon. Messara could have fed the whole of Crete but because of these raids it remains barren. In addition to the damage that these families are causing, they are providing a bad example to others who try to imitate them, as the priests[146] did with the Ottoman fleet. I believe that such animals should not be allowed to run our lives.[147]

In 1573, two years after Cavalli's troops destroyed Sfakia, the *Provveditor General* Luca Michiel (previously *Provveditor* of Chania) was concerned about new reports of preparations by the Ottoman army to invade the island, and he approached the Sfakians for their assistance in return for offering them a pardon. After a long period of service in Crete, he understood them well. He wrote: "The Cretans, whatever they will not do after one talks to them nicely, they will not do even after the biggest threats and the harshest punishment." The Sfakians, having suffered severe adversity over the preceding two years, promised to supply 300 well-armed men if such a danger emerged in exchange for his assurances of a pardon.[148] Unfortunately for them, these negotiations did not result in any significant improvement to their situation, as no need arose for their armed assistance. Another year would pass before the Sfakians' plight was addressed by the Venetians.

Foscarini, the next *Provveditor General,* travelled to Sfakia in 1575 to see the situation for himself. In his report, he talked about finding the people of Sfakia in a sorrowful condition, "suffering because of crimes of their fathers". He also wrote that the Sfakians were a beautiful, war-loving and brave people – "bellisima, bellicosa et brava" – and that the authorities must use them to their own benefit and not listen to the scheming and

[146] He refers to the uprising in Rethymnon following the Ottoman attack in June 1571 described in the previous section.
[147] Theotokis (1933), p. 330.
[148] Giannopoulos (1978), p. 147.

greedy Venetian feudal lords who wanted to exterminate them. When the Sfakians became convinced of Foscarini's peaceful intentions, they met with him. The heads of the Pateros clan expounded the injustices meted out by Cavalli and other Venetians who had indiscriminately punished both the guilty and the innocent; they asked Foscarini to pardon them and grant them permission to rebuild and reinhabit their houses, under the protection of the Venetian central authorities. Foscarini held similar meetings with the heads of the Papadopoulos clan from Frangokastello and Apokoronas, and the Skordilis clan from Sfakia. He entered into an agreement with the Sfakians that pardoned all of them, and he granted them and all the exiles permission to return, rebuild their houses and reside on their land.

For their part, the Sfakians promised to offer their services to the authorities whenever required to do so, to hand over to the authorities anyone guilty of theft or murder, and to be obedient citizens. Furthermore, they would provide eight men, as soldiers, for each galley manned out of Chania, give one week's service to the state (other Cretans were obliged to serve for two weeks), and enlist all Sfakian men in the Civil Guard. The various clan leaders were obliged to present themselves to the authorities in Chania twice a year to confirm the agreement, and were obliged to stay there for eight days each time. Foscarini was so pleased with the outcome of his negotiations that he reported Sfakia had become the quietest part of the island – other than some minor thefts of livestock, nothing else serious had occurred.[149]

But achieving a long-term change in the behaviour of the Sfakians was not going to be that easy.

Further unrest in Sfakia

Ten years later in 1585, Giulio Garzoni (*Sindico* of the East, a functionary of the Venetian justice system) visited Sfakia for four days; he was welcomed at the border of the district (this must have been at Askifou) by 500 armed Sfakians, amongst them 200 members of the Pateros clan. They then proceeded to Chora Sfakion, where he held a meeting with the leaders of the local clans (Skordilis and Peteros), during which he berated them for disobeying the *Provveditor's* orders and for breaking their agreement with Foscarini through their continued thieving and insubordination. Garzoni reported that the Sfakians humbly explained to him about the government imposing illegitimate demands on them, and asked him to address the authorities' failure to capture criminals in the area. Garzoni resolved some of the issues raised and took measures to ensure that whoever was sent there as *Provveditor* applied the laws in a just manner.

[149] Xanthoudides (1939), p. 146.

The Sfakians, pleased with the outcome of their discussions, performed a *giostra* (a military exhibition) in his honour, and Garzoni awarded prizes to the men who excelled in their respective activities.[150] Next Garzoni went to Frangokastello, where the Papadopoulos clan lived, to address the same problems. When Garzoni left Sfakia after four days, he asked the Sfakians to come to Chania to declare their loyalty to the state and receive an amnesty for their alleged crimes, which they did a few days later.

In his report, Garzoni attributed the problems in Sfakia to the Venetian feudal lords' hatred of the Sfakians and their attempts to portray these people as thieves, criminals and murderers. He added, though, that some of the problems also related to the deep hatred between the Pateros and Papadopoulos clans.

The successful diplomacy of Foscarini and Garzoni unfortunately did not result in a lasting change in Sfakia. We learn from the 1589 report by *Provveditore Generale* Zuanne Mocenigo[151] that the long-standing hatred between the Papadopoulos clan and the Pateros, Skordilis and other families had once again led to anarchy and crime in Sfakia. His report states that the Pateros clan numbered about 600 and lived solely from raising flocks and from theft, while the Papadopoulos, Skordilis and other families were seamen, shipbuilders, carpenters, iron forgers, tree fellers and resin gatherers, who thus lived off their own labor and were also beneficial to the state. This second group, being craftsmen and workers, wanted a peaceful existence, but when provoked by the other side they took revenge, resulting in lawlessness and crime. Each faction supported and protected its own perpetrators, and as their numbers grew more such crimes were committed. But when a perpetrator was being pursued by the Venetian authorities, all familes joined into one cohesive group to protect this fugitive. The local guards were unable to arrest the guilty parties, and other fugitives and criminals were unwilling to kill or capture them even in return for their own pardon.[152]

Mocenigo found fault with the justice system, which required decisions made by the *Provveditore* of Sfakia to be submitted to the authorities in Candia for approval. He reported that the Sfakians themselves desired a *Provveditore* with the authority to implement his own rulings, including the death sentence, because this was the only way that peace could be achieved in their district. But even more important was the *Provveditore's* capabilities and impartiality: most of the previous ones had been corrupt and had

[150] When the Admiral visited Chania later the same year to see a *giostra* and inspect the local armed forces, 600 Sfakians travelled to Chania, and he was very pleased with it. Xanthoudides (1939), p. 147.

[151] Spanakis (1940), pp. 8–12.

[152] In order to reduce the number of renegades at large, the Venetians encouraged criminals and fugitives from justice to capture or kill those on the run who had perpetrated a crime similar or worse that theirs in return for receiving a pardon.

sought their own share of the proceeds of crimes rather than punishing the criminals. Dispensing justice had become a commercial activity, benefiting most the corrupt *Provveditori.*

Similar problems were reported in 1594 by Filippo Pasqualigo, *Capitano di Candia* and *Provveditor della Canea.*[153] In the section of his report regarding the problems encountered with the *archondoromei,* the Cretans claiming aristocratic Byzantine status, he wrote:

> The worst of all of them today are the Pateros, who are the largest clan and the strongest one, and if they had not been counterbalanced by the Papadopoulos clan of the district of Chania and Rethymnon, certainly nobody would have been able to tolerate them. Even amongst the Pateros clan there are deathly hatreds, despite the fact that all of them are Skordilises.

The Papadopoulos clan now numbered more than 700, many of them living in fortified villages in the foothills south of Rethymnon. The report states that although the Pateros clan was the less aggressive of the two, they usually were the ones who instigated insulting attacks and thefts against the Papadopoulos clan, thus starting another round of infighting. Pasqualigo believed, on the basis of discussions and written submissions, that both clans wished for the past to be forgotten and the internecine strife to cease, and to this end they petitioned the authorities to appoint an impartial and strong nobleman from Venice who would have the authority to punish all crimes severely, instead of the usual officials who had limited authority and suspect judgement. This written submission[154] was signed by 18 Sfakians, many of them bearing the familiar names of Skordilis, Papadopoulos and Pateros.

However, the situation in Sfakia did not change as the years went by. The new *Provveditor General,* Benetto Moro, complained in his 1602 report to Venice about the myriad problems that the Sfakians continued to create, but he also highlighted the important role that they could perform if they were on the side of the authorities:

> It is in our interests to find a way to bring them on our side because of the qualities that they have. We could base a lot of our hopes on them and expect from them important services once their living conditions have improved, because they are superior to all those from the other districts, not only in that they are more manly, able and agile, with proud and strong bodies, bold yet polite in their manners, but what is most interesting, they possess sharp minds, the highest ethical standards

[153] Spanakis (1953), pp.142-144.
[154] Ibid., pp.164-168.

> and unsurpassed ability in handling weapons, bows and arrows and arquebuses, with which they are superb, because in the end, without any doubt, they are the most daring, brave and courageous of all the men in the kingdom [Regno di Candia, i.e. Crete]. And to this end, there is no better way than finding a government representative of rank, to have the full powers of a judge and strength to protect the good ones and contain the bad ones.[155]

A few years later in 1608, *Provveditor General* Sagredo was preparing to invade Sfakia again and punish the Sfakians for the continuing unrest and crimes that Venetian nobles accused them of. According to Trivan, there were more than 10,000 outstanding criminal prosecutions levied against 3,000 Sfakians, many of them being accused of six, eight or ten crimes.[156] Sagredo mentioned in his reports the continuing infighting between the Papadopoulos and Pateros factions, the latter now divided into the White Pateros and the Black Pateros clans, and he commented that their quarrels mostly derived from the theft of livestock, which escalated as reprisals multiplied. On three occasions Sagredo tried to meditate between the warring families, with no success. Finally he gave up and decided to punish all of them, as Cavalli had done just over 30 years earlier.[157] He gathered an army of 4,300 men and was ready to send them to Sfakia, by land and sea, but the invasion was cancelled at the last minute with the arrival of a new *Provveditor General*, Gerasimo Capello.

Although Capello recognised that stern measures were required, he wrote in his report that "this business needs to be approached calmly and with great circumspection". He initially sent three of his own people, including Michel Kallergis, to take stock of the situation and try to resolve the problems. He also decided to rectify one of the main causes of the unrest, the appointment of an effective *Provveditor* for Sfakia, a position which had been vacant for quite some time as nobody was willing to accept this tough assignment. He eventually chose Zuanne (Yannis) Kallergis (possibly Michel's father), who held some influence with the Sfakians but was willing to please the Venetians.

Kallergis soon achieved results, including the return of a large number of stolen animals to their rightful owners and the burning of a number of boats used in raids. He arrested a number of the criminal ringleaders, but more importantly, he convinced the Sfakians that they themselves should bring to justice those who were accused of the most serious crimes. The Pateros and the Skordilis clan leaders even promised that they would assist in imposing law and order in the region. He also persuaded 50 leading

[155] Spanakis (1958), pp. 77-79.
[156] Xanthoudides (1939), pp.147-148.
[157] Vincent (2001), pp. 225-226.

members of the Pateros clan to go to Chania and declare their loyalty to the Venetians. Kallergis advised Capello of the importance of having the Sfakians as loyal subjects of Venice, given the Ottoman threat at the time.[158]

Capello decided to visit Sfakia himself to achieve this objective, and he assembled a large entourage in order to impress the Sfakians. He reported the encounter with the Sfakians as follows:

> They came to meet me on the little plateau of Askifou, at the edge of the mountains, about 800 in number, under six standards, led by Colonel Mario [Mario Gazzi, assistant to Kallergis], all armed with sword, dagger, bow and long arquebus, which they handled with great agility. When they were close to me, the leaders threw down their standards, laid down their weapons, prostrated themselves on the ground, and began to beg forgiveness in the most humble manner, and the whole band did the same. While they remained prostrate on the ground, the Colonel spoke in their name, at their request, and said in substance that they confessed their shortcomings and crimes, but begged for pity and forgiveness, for their errors were the result of living for many years without a system of justice, which was either non-existent or badly administered by the persons sent as governors from Chania. However, they consoled themselves with the thought that they had never committed any act of infidelity towards their natural Prince [the Doge].

The report has to be read with the understanding that it was written by a Venetian official and addressed to the state's most senior authority, and thus reflects a degree of self-aggrandizement; in addition, the manner in which the Sfakians were presented to him was staged by a Venetian official who wanted to please his superior. This orchestrated encounter displays some quite important characteristics, though. The Sfakians came fully armed, presenting an impressive image of military preparedness, and although they laid down their weapons, there was no indication that they intended to give them up. It was unlikely that they had fully agreed with or even understood much of the address Colonel Gazzi gave in Venetian on their behalf. It is significant that his speech highlighted the claim that their alleged crimes were the result of the lack of proper government, and that they were loyal subjects of the state. This was the line maintained by the Sfakians for most of the previous century in their dealings with the Venetian authorities, and lay at the heart of their problems with the authories all along. This fascinating description of Capello's meeting with the Sfakians echoes the two previous negotiation sessions, with Foscarini in 1575 and Garzoni in 1585, during which the Sfakians also laid down their arms, blamed the authorities, and promised to be law-abiding.

[158] Ibid., pp. 228-231.

After this meeting, Capello proceeded down the Imbros Gorge to Chora Sfakion, where he met Zuanne Kallergi, who handed over to him 14 prisoners; five of them were condemned to death immediately, while he reserved judgment on the others until he could review their cases (which were found to be trivial, so they were released). Trivan reports later that Capello eventually annulled all existing sentences and charges and set up better machinery for the administration of justice in Sfakia. As Foscarini had done earlier, he also organized the Sfakians into military units under the control of their own officers. Capello next sailed to Loutro and then walked up to Anopoli at the invitation of *Kapetanios*[159] Katsoullis Paterozapas (from the Pateros clan), where he was honored with a magnificent dinner during which 300 silver dining pieces were used![160]

Unfortunately for the Sfakians, the situation soon deteriorated again. Kallergis was replaced in 1610 by a new *Provveditor* for Sfakia, in line with the two-year limit for all official positions. Incidents in the district of Chania in which Sfakians played a leading role appear in reports by the Duke of Crete a year later.

[159] A *Kapetanios* (plural *Kapetanioi*) is the leader of a group of armed men, informally promoted to the position on the basis of his leadership skills and proven fighting ability.
[160] Xanthoudides (1939), p. 148.

IX. The last years of Venetian rule – 1610 to 1669

The Cretan Renaissance

From the fall of Constantinople to the Ottomans in 1453 until Crete was captured by them in 1669, the island experienced a remarkable cultural renaissance, with a particular flowering of art and literature from about 1580 onwards. Initially this Cretan Renaissance was inspired by the arrival on the island of Greek refugees fleeing from Constantinople. Many of the aristocrats and scholars who managed to escape found their way to Crete. Some of them arrived on the three Cretan boats that fled from Golden Horn harbour on that fateful day in 1453. Others arrived later, having initially been transported by the Venetian and Genoese boats to the island of Chios. But some had arrived in Crete much earlier, since many people had started leaving Constantinople from the later part of the 14th century onwards, when it was becoming obvious that it was only a matter of time until the Byzantine Empire would fall to the Ottomans.

Crete soon became a microcosm of the Greece that had been eclipsed with the fall of Constantinople, attracting many learned men of letters and the arts, scribes who reproduced old Greek manuscripts that had survived the fall, icon painters who enriched the already advanced Cretan school of painters, and poets and playwrights. All of them found an environment that was ready to nurture and advance Greek culture and tradition. The major population centres in Crete had been fairly peaceful following the end of the long series of uprisings in 1367, and they provided a milieu that was conducive to attracting and retaining people who were searching for a new centre of creativity and learning. (Many also sought refuge in Venice, Genoa and Rome, where they were also welcomed, as the West was once again becoming receptive to Greek culture.)

The new arrivals found themelves in a society where there had been increasing Cretan-Venetian intermarriage over the centuries, accompanied by an increasing mutual respect and tolerance between the Catholic and

Orthodox forms of Christianity. In this Veneto-Cretan society, a new Hellenised identity had developed amongst the originally Venetian families who had made their homes on the island, accompanied by a shift in language.[161] Many, if not most, of the Venetians, especially women, stopped speaking Venetian Italian altogether, while some were bilingual in Venetian and Cretan Greek. By the end of the Venetian period in Crete, virtually nothing took place in the Venetian language other than administration and trade.

The Renaissance in Crete came to be of particular importance because of the synthesis it represented between the Italian Renaissance, as mediated through the Venetians, and the eastern Mediterranean Byzantine culture of the Greeks: it was not a renaissance of earlier Greek culture as such but rather a Greek version of the Italian Renaissance. In Cretan cities, unlike in the Byzantine and Ottoman-occupied areas of the Greek world, familiarity with the Western way of life made Crete a window onto the Renaissance, which led to a remarkable cross-fertilisation. Many hundreds of Cretans studied at the University of Padua – Venice had no university of its own. And the blending of Eastern and Western traditions produced a golden age for literature, painting, music and architecture. Domenicos Theotokopoulos "El Greco" (1541-1614), who was born near Heraklion, is of course the most famous product of this fusion, not only as a painter, but also as a sculptor and architect of the Spanish Renaissance.

But, crucially, Veneto-Cretan culture gradually developed a homogenous character all its own. Crete became more than just a bridge between two cultures – it became a vital and innovative cultural centre in its own right. In literature, during these 200 years of cultural syncretism, Crete "responded to the stimulus of contact with the Renaissance in a body of narrative, personal and dramatic poetry, written in the Cretan dialect, and now regarded as an important influence on Modern Greek literature".[162] The Cretan dialect became a literary language, and was in fact quite often written in the Latin alphabet. Both the eastern and western forms of the Cretan dialect became, in the words of Professor David Holton, "a sophisticated literary vehicle". Spoken Greek, in its written version, came to be of equal or even higher status than the archaising mediaeval Greek of Byzantium. The first demotic text to be printed in the vernacular Greek of the period was the poem *Apokopos* by Bergadis, which was published in Venice in 1509. The most famous literary product of the era was the romantic epic poem *Erotokritos*,

[161] This was not totally unlike the development of a new American identity by people who were originally English. Or perhaps, in view of the cultural mix that developed and the language shift from Italian to Greek that took place, a more accurate comparison would be with the Gaelicisation of the English nobility in Ireland in the mediaeval period; or the gradual Anglicisation of the Norman French population in the centuries after their conquest of England.

[162] Holton (1991).

which was composed some time between 1590 and 1610 by Vitsentzos Kornaros, who was a member of the aristocratic Veneto-Cretan family of Cornaro or Corner. He was born in Sitia but lived in Heraklion as an adult. And Western influence was manifested not only in art and high culture but also in cuisine, fashion, architecture and furniture.

The Veneto-Cretan cultural renaissance was evidenced in Heraklion, and to a lesser extent in Rethymnon and Chania. Heraklion in particular had become an increasingly cosmopolitan centre since the 15th century, with a substantial Jewish community as well as Germans and non-Venetian northern Italians. This renaissance also spread to the countryside through the landowners' mansions and gardens, through the Orthodox monasteries when they were rebuilt and modernised, as at Arkadi, and even through western-influenced Orthodox artists. But in rural areas, Greek peasants continued to labour under the repressive conditions imposed by their feudal overlords. We can suppose, though, that the Sfakian aristocracy would not have remained totally untouched by the cultural currents of the Cretan Renaissance.

The 17th century and the Ottoman conquest of Crete

After Constantinople fell to the Ottomans, relations between Venice and the Ottoman Empire went through alternating periods of truce and conflict, as the Ottomans' expansion into the Aegean and western Europe affected Venice's commercial interests. The Ottoman fleet raided Crete in June 1571, and then attacked the western coast of Greece, destroying Venetian settlements there, and landed in Corfu and further north in Dalmatia. The Venetians feared an attack on Venice itself, and assembled a fleet of Venetian, Spanish and Papal vessels to attack the Ottoman fleet. In the face of this approaching combined Christian fleet, the Ottomans turned back for their bases in Greece. Eventually the two fleets engaged in battle off the western Peloponnese at Lepanto, near modern Nafpactos at the entrance to the Gulf of Patras, where on the 7th of October 1571 the entire Ottoman fleet was destroyed.[163]

A long period of peace followed, almost three quarters of a century, but the Venetians knew that it would not last forever. Orders were issued quite frequently to fortify Crete and prepare for a potential Ottoman invasion; officials were dispatched from Venice to inspect the progress on these measures, but the work proceeded slowly. The defence of Crete had been entrusted to local landowners, who were required to maintain a certain standard of military preparedness, and to local militias from the cities and countryside, but rarely did either fulfil their obligations. Discipline and

[163] Norwich (2006), pp. 322-327.

training were poor to nonexistent, and we have numerous reports of farcical events that occurred during parades and inspections organized for officials from Venice who had been either appointed for the usual two-year period of duty or were visiting the island on an inspection tour. Reports back to Venice by the inspectors expressed concern about the strength and training of the local military forces and about the inadequacy of the fortifications.

Provveditor General Foscarini, who had spent four years on the island, had instituted considerable changes in order to improve the behaviour of the feudal landowners towards the villagers, who he considered indispensable for the defence of the island, and to force the landowners to maintain the military preparedness required by their privileged position. But soon after his departure all this was disregarded. Twenty years later, we see the *Capitano di Candia's* despair in his 1594 report about the situation: he says "not to expect much from these people [feudal landowners and militia] for the defense of Candia" because "if one was to try and select the able ones ... few would [be chosen] out of the 12,000 who are enlisted".[164] A few years later in 1602, the *Provveditor* reported that of the 1,388 horses the landed gentry were obliged to keep for a cavalry force, only 447 met the required standard, nothing could be expected out of another 617 – indeed, they would be an impediment to the others – and the rest of the horses had perished. As for the riders, most had no experience on horseback at all![165] With regard to the local militia, he reported that they accepted their duties and would show courage in times of need, but they had very little fighting experience.[166] Subsequent reports do not show much improvement in the military preparedness of the local forces.

Although Venice was extremely concerned about the situation, it does not appear that the local ruling classes on the island shared these anxieties or were willing to do anything about preparing for the impending invasion. As for the long-suffering Cretans in the villages and on the estates of the rich landowners, they sometimes felt that a change in ruler might bring them some relief from their punishing exploitation.

Then, in October 1644, an incident of common piracy was to spark a series of events that resulted in the capture of Crete by the Ottomans 25 years later.[167] A fleet of six ships from the Knights of St John of Malta seized an Ottoman galleon which was carrying some important pilgrims to Mecca, amongst them the court's Chief Eunuch and thirty ladies from the Sultan's harem.[168] On the journey back to Malta with the captured galleon,

[164] Spanakis (1953), p. 26.
[165] Spanakis (1958), pp. 108-109.
[166] Ibid., pp. 116-117.
[167] Norwich (2006), p. 342.
[168] Early historians claimed that the Sultan's wife was also amongst those captured, but this confusion may stem from the fact that the Turkish ship bore the name *Sultana*, i.e. 'the Sultan's wife'.

they landed on the southern coast of Crete[169] to take on water and release some Greek slaves on board. The Venetian authorities, not wanting to have anything to do with this act of piracy, ordered them to leave, and after a number of unsuccessful attempts to get water, the Knights abandoned the Ottoman ship – which by then was unseaworthy – as well as the captured passengers and sailed back to Malta. The Sultan was enraged by the incident and decided to take revenge – not against the Maltese, as everyone initially presumed, but against the Venetians on Crete, based on the assumption that they had provided support to the Knights and had shared in the seized treasures. The incident had given the Sultan an ideal pretext to take on the Venetians and capture their best land asset in the eastern Mediterranean – Crete.

The Venetians were warned by their representative in Constantinople that the Sultan was preparing to attack Crete but they remained sceptical, still expecting the Sultan would target Malta instead. Nevertheless, Venice sent *Provveditor General da Mar* Andrea Corner to Crete, together with an army of 2,500, a fleet of 30 galleys, and military architects and engineers; but there was not enough time for him to properly prepare the island for the impending invasion.

In April 1645, an Ottoman fleet of 400 ships carrying about 60,000 armed men left Constantinople and entered the Aegean Sea, apparently heading for Malta. The fleet stopped at Navarino in the western Peloponnese to take on supplies and then set sail again. But the fleet quickly changed direction and headed eastwards towards Crete, landing at the western end of the Bay of Chania in June without meeting any resistance. Within a few hours they attacked the fortress on the small island of St Theodoros; its Venetian commander blew up the fort rather than surrender. By that evening the Ottoman army had reached the walls of Chania and laid siege to the town for two months. Chania's garrison of 800 mercenaries and about 1,000 locals were no match for the formidable strength of the Ottoman forces, who bombarded them from both sea and land and attempted to undermine the fortified walls. A Venetian fleet was hastily assembled to help the defending forces, but it did not arrive in time. Another Venetian naval fleet stationed at Souda Bay did not offer any help to the besieged town other than a few supplies; its commander, fearful of the large Ottoman force, soon fled for Candia.

Venice was now preparing for total war against them, not only on Crete but closer to home, in Italy and Dalmatia. Galleys were dispatched daily to Crete and other areas threatened by the Ottoman aggression. The Doge appealed to Christian Europe for help against the common threat of further expansion by the Ottoman Empire, but none was offered. An

[169] According to the Cretan historian Psilakis, this was at Kali Limenes, south of Phaistos, where St Paul had also landed – see Chapter II.

attempt to prevent the Ottoman fleet from bringing reinforcements to Crete by blockading the Dardanelles Straits (the Hellespont) was successful for a short time, but the Ottomans eventually broke through and made it to Chania. The Venetians did manage to further restrict them access to the sea routes leading to Crete, while getting their own fresh supplies and troops in place to assist in the battle for control of Crete.

The Venetian authorities in Crete sent some of their local armed forces from Rethymnon and Candia to offer support to those besieged in Chania, but they were confronted by strong Ottoman forces at Tsikalaria in the Apokoronas district and were obliged to retreat. Others from the nearby mountainous areas of the Lefka Ori joined the fight outside the besieged town, but details of this are rather sketchy. Cretan historian Giannis Tsivis[170] tells us that a small group of "battle-hardened and brave" Sfakians under the leadership of Michalis Kallergis, using Malaxa as their base, attacked the Ottomans who were in the vicinity of Chania by night, inflicting significant casualties on them. Psilakis also mentions Sfakians fighting alongside the Venetian forces outside Chania.[171] Detorakis states that "the Venetians attempted to create a diversionary attack by mobilising Cretans from the districts of Selino and Sphakia, but it came to nothing".[172] He also names Michalis Kallergis as the leader of the Sfakians, but he concludes with the remark that "[they] were crushed by the numerically superior and better equipped Ottoman soldiers". But the strategy adopted by the Sfakians of attacking during the night gave rise to the legend of the *Hainides* (from Turkish *hayin* meaning 'disloyal'); the Ottomans dreaded the night-time raids by these fearless warriors.

Chania surrendered to the Ottoman troops in August 1645. During the two months of the siege the Ottoman army had captured most of western Crete, except for Sfakia, where they did not venture. Only the forts at Souda Bay and Gramvousa in the far northwest of the island remained under Venetian control. Reinforced by 40,000 fresh troops, the Ottoman army next advanced on Rethymnon, killing all who resisted them on the way. Most of the civilian population abandoned Rethymnon and headed for Candia, expecting protection there, but they were turned away from the already overcrowded town. The small Venetian force left behind in Rethymnon, together with some Cretans who had stayed to help protect the town, fought gallantly but eventually surrendered in November 1646. From there the Ottoman army moved eastwards again, aiming to capture the rest of the island before attempting to attack the well-defended and fortified town of Candia.

The situation was tragic everywhere, as the population tried to flee from the advancing Ottoman army. Some Cretans decided to accept the

170 Tsivis (1993), p. 74.

171 V. Psilakis (1970 [1906]), Vol. 2, p. 399.

172 Detorakis (1994), p. 231.

new order and converted to Islam in order to avoid the harsh hand of the new occupier, or the even worse fates of slavery and death. Many more, especially the wealthy and those with links to Venice, left the island for the safety of Venice and other Italian towns. The Venetians, often assisted by Cretans, continued to fight against the Ottoman army from their remaining fortified positions as well as at sea around Crete.

By the spring of 1648, the Ottoman forces had captured most of the island and advanced on the heavily fortified town of Candia for a final offensive. Their first assault was against the fort of Agios Dimitrios outside Candia,[173] but they were repulsed by a strong Venetian contingent. This scenario was repeated on an almost daily basis: the Ottoman army attacked from the land and were driven back by the defenders, who would then spend the night repairing the walls damaged by the Ottoman cannons. The Ottomans also tried to place explosive charges under the walls to bring them down. The Venetians' lifeline was the seaward side of the town, which was successfully protected by the Venetian fleet; this enabled the besieged Venetians and Cretans to acquire the supplies and reinforcements which helped them hold out for 21 years, the longest siege in history.

Events in Sfakia during the siege of Candia

There is some evidence that Sfakians were involved in fighting the Ottoman invaders over the next two years, but the reliability and depth of the available information falls well short of what we find for the Venetian occupation era. One of the main reasons for this is the scarcity of researchers who can translate the Turkish records that are accessible. Information given here about the Sfakians during the early period of the Ottoman invasion is therefore based on our assessment of what is the most reliable and credible information available.

After the Ottoman army laid siege to Candia, Matthaios Kallergis and other Cretans who were fighting alongside the Venetians urged the Sfakians and men from the nearby districts of Agios Vasilios and Kissamos to join them in an attack on the fort of Almyros,[174] which had been captured earlier by Ottoman forces. In the poet Marinos Tzanes Bounialis' 17th century epic poem *The Cretan War*, he wrote that Kallergis had promised the Sfakians "honours, all of them would be given titles and villages as presents; that he would give anyone whatever he asked for".[175] They stormed the fort and gained control of it, but soon Ottoman troops arrived from Chania and

[173] To the east of Candia, at Ak Tambia, today's Chrysopigi neighbourhood.
[174] In the municipality of Georgoupoli at the location known today as Kastellakia or Paliokastella; only the ruins of the fort can be seen today.
[175] Bounialis (1979), p. 376.

Rethymnon and defeated the Cretans. Kallergis and his contingent from Candia headed for Souda Bay, boarded the ship he had arrived on, and sailed back to Candia, abandoning the Sfakians.[176]

The Sfakians retreated to their stronghold of the White Mountains, pursued by the army of Deli Hussein Pasha, but they were eventually obliged to seek peace; they had to pay the Pasha 1,000 silver coins and 1,000 sheep[177] and declare obedience to him. The extent of their defeat is uncertain, but two Turkish historians claim that the two forts in Sfakia – which must have been the ones in Chora Sfakion and Frangokastello – were seized,[178] so the impact on Sfakia must have been significant, given the size of the penalty that they were made to pay. This must have been a humiliating experience for the proud and brave Sfakians, and they would have placed the blame for their predicament squarely on the shoulders of the Venetians. Two years later in 1650, the district of Sfakia was given to Deli Hussein by the Grand Vizier as a reward for suppressing the unruly Sfakians.[179] It appears that the Sfakians' earlier "peace offering" was considered to be an annual contribution or tax payable to the Pasha, because this was later changed to an annual contribution of 5,000 *γρόσια*, the Turkish silver coin known also as a *kurus* (or *piaster*).

Deli Hussein was recalled to Constantinople in 1658,[180] but before leaving Crete he "donated" the district of Sfakia to the holy cities of Mecca and Medina. This followed a Muslim tradition whereby one could donate property, and thus the income generated by that property, to a religious institution or charitable cause. This tradition was called *Vakf hairi* in Turkish and represented an endowment of a distinctly public or religious nature. Thus the whole district of Sfakia became a *Vakf* (which in Greek was known as *Βακούφιον*), and the annual sum of 5,000 *γρόσια* went to Mecca and Medina. Other *Vakf hairi* were created in a similar manner to fund the needs of the newly established mosques in Crete. The people living in the *Vakf* were considered privileged and were not subject to the pressures and exploitation that others had to endure: they did not have to provide compulsory labour for the Turks or pay taxes, and orders were issued by

[176] V. Psilakis (1970 [1906]), Vol. 2, p. 425.

[177] According to Andrea Valiero in *Storia della Guerra di Candia*, as quoted in Stavrinidis (1955), p. 232. These events are also reported by the Sfakian historian Papadopetrakis, again attributed to Andrea Valiero, as written in 1679. See Papadopetrakis (1971 [1888]), p. 120.

[178] One of the two Turkish historians (Naima) even claimed that one of the forts was destroyed.

[179] Papadopetrakis (1971 [1888]), p. 119.

[180] He was executed there, since he was seen as a threat to the Grand Vizier. One story relates that Deli Hussein was graciously received by the Grand Vizier and invested with a robe of honour; but as he left he was arrested and transported to the Seven Towers, where, two days later, he was strangled with a bowstring in his cell; the loyalty of Deli Hussein's troops prevented the Vizier from risking a public execution.

the authorities from time to time clarifying this situation.[181]

There is very little else in histories of this period, until the final fall of Crete to the Ottoman troops in 1669, where Sfakians feature prominently. The Sfakian historian Paris Kelaidis does not provide any specific details of Sfakian participation in the actual siege of Candia in his book about the Cretan war,[182] other than repeating a comment by the Cretan author Kondylakis that amongst those who participated in the defence of Candia were three Sfakian officers: Zympis, Kalamos and Varsamos.[183] One cannot escape the impression that the Sfakians were angry and unwilling to offer the Venetians any help after their defeat and subsequent abandonment at Almyros.

The Venetians had not given up hope of recapturing Crete as they carried out their war against the Ottoman Empire in other parts of the Mediterranean, and they still had superiority on the seas. By 1660 the first substantial promises of help from the other Christian nations in the West materialized. The Venetians also controlled three forts in the north of Crete – Souda Bay and Gramvousa in the west, and Spinalonga[184] in the east – and from these bases they would often harass the Ottoman forces and encourage the Cretans to resist the Ottoman occupation.

A French force arrived at Souda and was joined by Venetian troops as well as Cretans who were prepared to take up arms. Rebels from the Apokoronas district captured the fort at Almyros (where the Sfakians had been defeated twelve years earlier), and together with the French troops advanced westwards with the aim of taking Chania. In the meantime, a large Ottoman army unit from Rethymnon regained Almyros fort and attacked the combined French–Venetian–Cretan forces. The French eventually abandoned their aim of taking Chania, boarded their boats, and headed for Candia to help the besieged Venetians, leaving the rebels behind to deal with the vengeful Ottomans.

A previously unknown incident that explains why the Sfakians were reluctant to assist the Venetians against the Ottomans came to light when some correspondence from the Venetian state archives was published in 1973.[185] These letters, between elders and *Kapetanioi* from Sfakia and other western districts of the island and Venetian officials from August 1660

[181] The situation changed after 1690, when an additional head tax was imposed on the Christian citizens living in a *Vakf*.

[182] Kelaidis (1992), p. 47-66.

[183] Zampelios & Kritovoulidis (2004 [1893]), p. 272.

[184] The fort at Souda Bay as well as those at Gramvousa and Spinalonga remained in Venetian hands for many years after the fall of Crete to the Turks. Gramvousa was surrendered by its commander to the Turks in 1692, following his receipt of a substantial bribe. The forts at Spinalonga and Souda Bay were surrendered by the Venetians in 1715 when they lost interest in the area.

[185] Karathanasis (1973).

to January 1661, concerned possible cooperation between Cretans and Venetians against the Ottoman forces. The correspondence relating to Sfakia was between *Provveditore* Bragadin, commander of the fort at Souda, and some Sfakian *Kapetanioi* from Askifou. Bragadin was seeking the Sfakians' assistance in fighting the Ottoman army in the northwest of the island after the French left, and the *Kapetanioi* stated that they were ready to assist if required, but that they were unhappy the Venetian fleet had departed (referring to the fleet sailing back to Candia with the French troops), and that they needed arms and ammunition. Subsequent correspondence between Bragadin and *Provveditore* Morosini in Candia shows that this was part of an ongoing attempt by Bragadin to gather support against the Ottoman forces, and that Sfakians were reluctant to commit themselves and were sceptical about the Venetians' sincerity and intended level of involvement.

Amongst the documents are copies of orders sent to the Sfakians by the Ottomans demanding their submission and threatening them if they disobeyed. The Ottomans were concerned about the possible involvement of Sfakians against them, so they prepared to approach Sfakia from Rethymnon and attack them via Asi Gonia. About 800 Sfakians and men from nearby districts had gathered at Askifou and headed towards the village of Poli, today's Argyroupolis, to confront the Ottoman forces; a quarter of the men had no weapons but were prepared to fight with their bare hands. The Ottomans were ambushed in a gorge near Argyroupolis and, having suffered heavy casualties, retreated towards Episkopi. The Cretans, who by then had run out of ammunition, headed for Kefala, near the fort at Almyros, to meet Morosini as had previously been arranged with Bragadin, but instead they caught sight of the Venetian fleet sailing away from the fort at Souda.

A bitter letter was sent to Morosini from all the *Kapetanioi* of Sfakia, Agios Vasilios, Roustica, Asi Gonia and Selino as well as the Rethymnon district, relaying their disappointment at watching him depart without meeting them, demanding to know whether he intended to return with his fleet, and asking for weapons and ammunition. The letter finishes by requesting Morosini to "tell us if you have no intention of coming back, so that we will know that we must become the subjects of the children of the Devil!"

The Venetians responded by sending arms and ammunition to the Sfakians, who were facing an attack by the Ottomans brought on by their non-compliance to demands for their submission, according to a letter from the Sfakian *Kapetanioi* thanking Bragadin for the weapons. Bragadin advised Morosini, amongst others, that the Sfakians had paid the Vizier in charge of the Ottoman army 1,000 silver coins and 1,000 sheep not to invade Sfakia.[186] Most of the correspondence from Sfakians to the Venetians concern requests for weapons, with few offers to engage in a full-blown uprising like those

[186] Ibid., p. 99.

that had gained the Sfakians their reputation. Obviously, the small amount of trust that might have existed between the Sfakians and the Venetians since the arrival of the Ottoman forces had entirely evaporated following the events at Almyros in 1648 and 1660.

The fall of Candia and the end of Venetian rule

Candia was able to endure the siege for so many years, and fighting was able to continue throughout Crete, because of the ability of the Venetian fleet to keep breaking the Ottoman naval blockade and bringing in supplies and additional fighting forces. Their seamanship was such that Venice managed to increase its control over the whole Aegean during this period, and the Ottoman fleet tried to avoid any confrontation with them. The Venetian fleet took the battle to the heart of the Ottoman Empire, frequently blockading the Dardanelles and even once, in 1657, entering the Sea of Marmara and approaching Constantinople.[187] But despite the courage of the Venetians, the Ottoman fleet was able to deliver supplies and fresh troops to Crete, sometimes from Egypt or Syria.

The battle for Crete had become the talk of Europe, and amazing stories of carnage and bravery kept coming out of the island. If the Christian European states had responded earlier, the outcome could have been different. However, it was not until 1660, fifteen years after the Ottoman invasion, that the first substantial military contingent from Europe was sent to Crete. Four thousand armed French troops arrived late in August of that year, attacked the Turks in an area that they were unfamiliar with, and were thoroughly defeated; a week later, struck down by dysentery, the French were forced to return home, having accomplished very little. A similar poor result was achieved by the 2,000 Germans sent to Crete by the German Emperor at the same time. Other detachments of Europeans, seeking adventure and glory, turned up in Candia, but they were soon decimated by fighting, disease and hardship, and the survivers returned home to relate the tragedy that was unfolding in Candia.

As the siege of Candia approached its last days, another force of 6,000 French troops arrived in June 1669 on a fleet of 40 ships. During their first attack against the Ottoman forces a few days later, 500 lost their lives while the rest fled in panic. Their further contribution to the fighting was minimal, since they refused to fight the Ottomans outside the city walls again. Soon one of their largest ships was sunk by the Ottoman guns on the shore; a month later the entire French force set sail for home, having lost more than a third of their men through death and injury. This caused further

[187] Norwich (2003), p. 551. A direct hit on the Captain General's ship resulted in his death and the abandonment of this brave adventure.

panic amongst the few outsiders who had remained in Candia, and they also sailed off, abandoning the Venetians and Cretans still in the garrison, who now numbered only 3,600. The Grand Vizier Ahmed Koprulu, who had taken personal charge of the siege, ordered a full-scale attack. Candia had too few defenders to fight with. An honorable treaty was agreed on the 6th of September, 1669, allowing the Venetians and other defenders to leave the town unharmed and take with them the few personal possessions and holy treasures that had survived the 21 years of the siege. On the 26th of September, 1669, the Venetians left Crete forever, after 465 years of occupation.

The cost to both sides was enormous. Turkish reports indicate that the Ottomans lost more than 137,000 men during the 24 years of fighting, many of them from diseases that repeatedly struck both sides (Greek sources claim that this number was closer to 200,000). On the defenders' side, during the siege of Candia alone 31,000 lives were lost amongst the Venetians, Cretans and others who fought against the invaders.[188] The financial impact of such a prolonged war on all parties was inestimable. But the effect on Crete itself was devastating. The towns had been totally destroyed by the fighting and had been abandoned by the Cretan population, who were never to return. The island's infrastructure had also been shattered. But it was the countryside, where most of the Cretan population lived, that suffered the most: it was laid waste by the large number of Ottoman troops who had killed or destroyed all in their wake.

Sfakia's uncertain future in an Ottoman-occupied Crete

Although Crete faced a grim and uncertain future under the new occupier, the situation in Sfakia was better. The Ottomans had no interest in occupying the inhospitable terrain of the Lefka Ori, which was full of dangerous mountain passes where the fearsome Sfakians were known to ambush their enemies. The Sfakians' reputation as formidable warriors also contributed to the Ottomans' lack of interest in a district whose inhabitants lived from their flocks while at the same time fighting against each other as well as fighting for their independence from foreign invaders. The Sfakians were also very able seamen, with surprisingly extensive fleets, given the small size of their population, which travelled far and wide. Exports of Sfakia's agricultural products – mainly cheese, honey and timber – brought in good earnings for these people. And, of course, seamanship and trade in those days went hand-in-hand with piracy; the Sfakians and the Maniots were two of the well-known Greek pirate groups in the Aegean and eastern Mediterranean, and they were on very good terms with the other large

[188] V. Psilakis (1970 [1906]), Vol. 2, p. 457.

group of non-Muslim pirates, the Maltese.

Alongside shipping, other relevant trades had developed in Sfakia, such as cutting and trading timber, ship-building, and biscuit manufacturing (for boat crews), all of which contributed to the accumulation of significant wealth in the district. The Turks, not being seafaring people, were not threatened by or interested in these Sfakian occupations as long as their piratical activities did not affect them.

As a result of this unique situation in Sfakia, its population found itself fairly well off in comparison with the rest of Crete. As long as they paid the required *Vakf* contribution, which was small in comparison to their income and to the taxes required of others, and kept away from the more fertile, densely occupied areas, they were affected very little by the change from Venetian to Ottoman rule. And indeed, that was the situation in Sfakia during the first 100 years of Ottoman occupation. But newly emerging nationalistic movements and the aspirations of other large nations in the later part of the next century were to change the situation in Sfakia very significantly.

X. The Ottoman[189] occupation: the early years – 1669 to 1770

The impact of the war with Venice and the ensuing Ottoman occupation

The Ottoman conquest of Crete had a sudden and significant impact upon the population of the island. The renaissance of Hellenic culture that had blossomed over the previous 100 years of Venetian rule suddenly ended, plunging the island into a period of cultural darkness similar to that experienced by Greeks living under Turkish rule in other parts of the Ottoman Empire. The population numbers had been depleted by the long war, sickness and famine, as well as by the mass exodus of those who could flee to Italy and the Aegean islands. Reliable statistics are not available, but there are claims that the population had been reduced to half of what it was at the beginning of the Venetian era. The urban centres that would have formed the basis for any renewal had been destroyed and lay empty, slowly becoming inhabited by the newly arriving Turks, who were to be the new masters for more than two centuries. Trade had all but ceased, as

[189] This book makes frequent use of the terms Ottoman and Turk/ish in what might seem to be an interchangeable way. Without either oversimplifying or complicating things, the following broad explanation might clarify the issue. The Ottoman Empire emerged in the 13th century under Osman Gazi, who came from one of the many Turkic tribes in Anatolia. A century later, his descendants became known as Osmanli, and his rapidly-expanding state, through transliteration, as Othman or Ottoman. The elite and higher ranks in this Empire referred to themselves as Osmanli, followers of Osman (Ottomans in English) at a time when the Empire's population consisted of Turks from the various Anatolian tribes as well as Arabs, Armenians, Albanians, Bulgarians and many others, including Greeks from the conquered Byzantine Empire. It was only after the collapse of the Ottoman Empire following WWI and under the leadership of Mustafa Kemal Ataturk that the new state was proclaimed as the Republic of Turkey in 1923. Since the Ottoman army had a predominance of Turks in its ranks, the term Turk is used in this book where fighting forces are involved, unless we know that others were involved, such as Egyptians, Albanians or Muslim Cretans. Where we refer to the governmental rule and structures, we have generally used the term Ottoman.

goods for export were no longer being produced, and demand for imports had disappeared.

But there were two positive developments after the end of Venetian rule.[190] The first was rural repopulation: the Turks encouraged Cretans to return to their productive activities in the countryside so that they could generate tax income for the new occupiers. The other was that most restrictions on the Orthodox Church hierarchy were removed. This facilitated the revival of the Orthodox clerical hierarchy and their reattachment to the Ecumenical Patriarchate in Constantinople, joining them once again to the rest of the Greek Orthodox community living under Ottoman rule. It also immediately enabled the Church to assume the leadership role that it had been deprived of throughout the Venetian occupation.

Administration and military control

The Turks retained the Venetian administration system of dividing the island into four areas (Chania, Rethymnon, Candia[191] and Sitia), now called *Pashaliks* or *Sanjaks,* each governed by a Pasha. Candia and Sitia were ruled over together by a single Pasha, who was also in charge of the military forces for the whole island, now known as the *Eyalet* (a large administration unit of the Ottoman Empire) of Crete. The three Pashas, who reported to the Sultan, were responsible for administering Islamic law, maintaining an army to control the domestic situation, and collecting tax revenues.

The most likely threats to the new occupiers would be uprisings by the local population and attempts by the Venetians to recapture the island, perhaps assisted by Cretans. For this reason the Turks maintained a large army on the island, consisting of two separate groups of Janissaries, an imperial corps, who were part of the Ottoman Imperial Army and a local corps of Islamized Cretans, who were much more vicious and were feared by the local Christian population. The main forts used by the Turks were located in Candia and Chania, where the majority of weapons and food supplies for the army were kept and where large numbers of Janissaries were stationed. Control of the Janissaries was to be an on-going problem for the Ottoman authorities until they were disbanded by Sultan Mahmud in 1826.

The justice system was based on Islamic law, sourced from interpretations of the Qur'an. Each capital city of the four districts had its own court headed

[190] Detorakis (1988), pp. 335-6.

[191] Candia kept its Venetian name under the Turks, who referred to it as Kandiye, while the Greeks used the more popular name for it, Kastro or Megalo Kastro ('the fortress' or 'the big fortress'). The name Heraklion was adopted much later when the island gained autonomy (1898-1913) and harks back to Heraklia, the ancient port of Knossos, which was located where today's Heraklion is sited. Spanakis (1981), Vol. 1, p. 211.

by a *Kadi,* appointed by the chief judge of the Ottoman state, and who wielded broad judicial powers. There were also lower courts that handled local cases of minor importance. The courts heard evidence from all parties under oath (Muslims swore on the Qur'an, Christians on the Bible, and Jews on the Torah), and decisions became effective only when published in the records of the courts, which provide us today with a rich source of information about that era.

Land was distributed by the Sultan to the conquerors according to their position and achievements. The largest property holdings, called *timars,* were awarded to the Pashas and Beys[192] in recognition of their services during the war; 17 smaller areas of land, also called *timars* or *ziyamets,* were given to senior military officers who held responsibility for maintaining internal order on the island; and another 2,500 even smaller parcels of land known as *mukats* were granted to ordinary Turks, who were required to provide a number of specified services to the state. Public property previously owned by Venice was confiscated by the Sultan and become Ottoman Imperial property. And as we saw earlier, there was a further category of property, the *Vakf,* the income from which was earmarked for religious and other charitable causes.

All properties other than the *Vakf* were subject to taxes, which were collected by a large number of functionaries and sent to the Sultan at the Sublime Porte in Constantinople. The main official tax consisted of a land levy, equivalent to 20% of its annual yield, double the amount levied in other parts of the Ottoman Empire at the time. Frequently the peasants and former Christian landowners were exploited by the tax collectors, who based the amount on an estimated, and purposely inflated, level of production rather than the actual yield.

In addition to the land tax, all Christians on the island had to pay a poll tax, or head tax. The method of assessing this changed a number of times: initially there were three different tax rates, based on a family's assessed wealth; later on the three rates applied to individuals' assets; and later again there was a single tax rate applied to individuals. Other minor, unofficial taxes and charges were also imposed on the powerless population for the benefit of high-ranking officials. Sometimes this involved supplying goods and services, such as the famous requirement for large amounts of snow to be delivered from Mount Ida and the White Mountains to cool the drinks of Pashas, Beys and Agas during the summer!

Christians were also burdened with certain compulsory contributions, taxes in reality, to the Orthodox Church, which in turn was obliged to make

[192] Ottoman titles at the time, awarded on a personal basis to senior civil officials and military officers, were: Pasha, conferred in several grades; Bey, a title of lesser status, also used as a courtesy title for the sons of a Pasha; and Aga (or Agha), the lowest-ranking title.

a number of payments to the island's treasury as well as to the Imperial Treasury in Constantinople. Additional regular fees (*peskes*) had to be paid to the Pasha and other Turkish functionaries to ensure that no problems arose during religious feasts.

This extensive system of taxes, and the degree to which it was subject to exploitation, soon became difficult for the authorities to manage and was one of the main driving forces behind the uprisings that were to occur throughout the island.

Widespread conversion to Islam

One unexpected outcome of Ottoman rule, not seen in other parts of the Byzantine Empire conquered by the Turks two centuries earlier, was the degree to which large numbers of Christians in Crete were prepared to convert to Islam once the Ottoman forces took control of the island. There were a number of factors contributing to this.

The more than 400 years of Venetian occupation of Crete, accompanied by persecution of the Orthodox clergy, had already undermined the strength of the Orthodox Church. Conversion to Catholicism for political or economic gain had occurred in the past in many instances. Marriages between people of different faiths had blurred the religious divide, and religious differences within families were now tolerated.

The new Islamic state made conversion to the Muslim faith easy, and this offered new opportunities to young men from the countryside, who upon conversion could join the military, be exempt from taxes, and live in a town, all things which had been unattainable to them previously. Mass conversions of whole villages, including their priests, also occurred, sometimes through compulsion. And for the few middle-class people who remained on the island, religious conversion presented financial opportunities in the new state without any significant cost – and many of them continued to practice their Orthodox faith in secret. The Muslim Cretans retained their Greek language and customs, and the only thing that separated them from their fellow Cretans, other than their religion, was a deep-seated hatred. The most tragic consequences of these conversions involved the young converts who joined the ranks of the Janissaries; they became the tormentors of Christians in the countryside, often in their own local areas.

Cretan resistance – the Hainides

During the Ottoman invasion of the island, many Cretans had sided with the Venetians, despite having suffered at their hands over the previous 400 years, in order to defend their Christian island against the Muslim oppressor. We saw earlier that during the siege of Chania, Sfakians swooped down from the White Mountains and attacked the Turks during the night, thus starting the legend of the *Hainides*.[193] The Venetians continued to encourage the locals to fight the Turks even after the surrender of Candia, as they hoped one day to recapture the island. To this end, they provided weapons and refuge to Cretan fighters in the three island fortresses they still occupied: at Gramvousa, Souda, and Spinalonga. The use of the Gramvousa fort as a safe haven for the *Hainides* ended in 1691 when it was surrendered to the Turks by its commander, a Neapolitan, for a substantial fee.[194] The other two forts continued to be used by the *Hainides* as a base from which to attack the Turks, but these were eventually abandoned by the Venetians in 1715.

Cretans conducted raids against Muslims around the island, spreading fear through their surprise attacks on those who committed crimes against the Orthodox Christian inhabitants. Many of them operated from mountain hideouts in the Lefka Ori, Psiloritis and Lasithi regions. They were the first rebels who took it upon themselves to dispense justice against the Muslim oppressors, and they became heroic figures over the next 200 years, with their achievements being immortalized through *rizitika,* traditional Cretan songs.[195] Many of these men suffered hideous deaths at the hands of the Turks who, through the gruesome execution of those captured, aimed to prevent mass uprisings. But the individuals and small bands of resistance fighters who continued to harass the Muslim occupiers throughout the Ottoman occupation provided the nucleus of experienced fighters for the uprisings that were to follow.

The 1692 Venetian invasion

Venice still had aspirations to take Crete back from the Turks and relied on the Cretans, who hated the new occupiers, for help. In the summer of 1692, a Venetian naval force under Domenico Mocenigo landed near Chania and attacked the town and its vicinity. Cretans from the nearby areas, but mainly from Sfakia, joined the Venetian forces and initially captured the fort

[193] They were also known as *Kalisperides* – those who, with irony, wished their enemies 'good evening' (*kalispera*) before killing them in revenge for crimes committed against the Orthodox Cretans.

[194] Detorakis (1994), p. 256.

[195] The word *rizitika* derives from *rizes*, the northern foothills of the Lefka Ori.

at Kissamos from the Turks. But Mocenigo's campaign soon failed in the face of the strong Turkish reinforcements sent from Heraklion. Mocenigo and the Venetian fleet left the island early in September, taking with them about 2,000 Cretans who were forced to flee, for the Ionian islands and the Peloponnese, where the Venetians were preparing for another invasion by the Turks.[196]

The Turkish reprisals in the areas that had assisted the Venetians were severe. An interesting Ottoman court document[197] sets out the terms that the Sfakians agreed to following the defeated uprising, which had been instigated by "the more lively members [of our community]". In addition to repenting their acts and swearing obedience to the Turks, they promised to return all animals and other goods they had stolen during this period, surrender all weapons they had received from the Venetians for this campaign, release all hostages they had captured, and turn over all those accused of inciting the uprising. They also promised to pay the outstanding head tax from the previous year. This document is another example of the long-standing approach of the Sfakians to authority: express remorse, pledge not to repeat the offending behaviour, promise restitution, and then continue as if you hadn't!

Sfakia up to the 1770 uprising

Sfakia's experience of Ottoman rule over the next 70 years or so was very different from that of the rest of Crete. Being a *Vakf*, Sfakia was not subject to the same degree of exploitation and harassment that other parts of the island suffered at the hands of the Pashas, Agas, the multitude of officials, and the Muslim Cretan Janissaries. Sfakians only had to deal with the few functionaries who were responsible for the *Vakf*, and with the relevant tax authorities: the Registrar (*Moutveli*), who collected the Sfakian's annual contribution as well as an amount for his own expenses and upkeep; the Supervisor (*Topotiritis*), whose upkeep they were charged for; and the tax collectors who became active with the change in the tax regime and the introduction of the new head tax in 1690.

The mountainous terrain of Sfakia, and the Sfakians' rough nature and disregard for Turkish authority, made the area undesirable for any Turks to settle in. These same factors resulted in Sfakia being the only district in Crete where no Muslim Cretans ever resided. Sfakians continued to operate the same self-government system that had served them well over the previous 1000 years, with unelected community elders and *Kapetanioi* resolving issues and taking decisions that affected the whole community.

[196] Zampelios & Kritovoulidis (2004 [1893]), p. 281.
[197] Stavrinidis (1955), pp. 244-248.

Sfakians were predominantly occupied with their flocks, cheese and honey production, and subsistence agriculture on the mountain plateaus of Anopoli and Askifou. They also continued processing timber for boats and were involved in shipbuilding, as they were during the Venetian era. Shipping and trade were significant economic activities for them, and a number of ship owners operated out of the Loutro/Anopoli area, trading all over the Mediterranean and the Black Sea.

There is no evidence of any fighting between the Sfakians and the Turks on the island after their participation in the 1692 Venetian invasion of Crete, until the 1770 uprising. From the few documents in the Turkish archives that have been translated by Stavrinidis, it appears that the Sfakians' main dealings with the Turks related to disputes about amounts of tax owed. An early document from 1674 indicates that the Sfakians regularly paid the Turkish authorities an annual contribution of 5,000 *γρόσια*, which was collected by the community from each member, based on a percentage of the value of what they produced. Their disputes with the tax authorities began after the introduction of the head tax in 1690. Court documents set out the accusations and counter-accusations of the Sfakians and the tax collectors, beginning in 1695. A few years later, the Sfakians appealed to the Sultan directly about what they felt were excessive taxes. By 1759 the Turkish authorities claimed that the Sfakians' outstanding tax debt had grown to 40,000 *γρόσια*.[198] Following direct representations by the Sfakians to Fatma Hatoun,[199] the granddaughter of Sultan Ahmet III who had inherited the responsibility for the *Vakf* of Sfakia and was its Registrar and "protector", the Sfakians were officially relieved of this huge accumulated tax burden. An Imperial Order published in a court document dated the 19th of March 1760 recognised the injustice suffered by the Sfakians through the manipulation and dishonesty of past officials in Crete and Constantinople, which had resulted in demands for a 7,500 *γρόσια* head tax in addition to the 5,000 *γρόσια Vakf* contribution. The order specified that the Sfakians' head tax was to be reduced to 2,210 *γρόσια* per annum, and the resulting 5,290 *γρόσια* shortfall in annual tax was to be collected from Greeks in other parts of Crete and the Ottoman Empire.[200]

---

[198] Ibid., p. 291

[199] Fatma Hatoun was the daughter of Vizier Mustafa Pasha, Deli Hussein Pasha's son, and Princess Saliha, daughter of Sultan Ahmed III; she was given the title of Hanum Sultan (Princess). Considerable confusion existed amongst historians, who thought that she was the Sultan's mother, to whom he had given the Sfakia *Vakf* as a present. This issue was clarified in 1955 when Stavrinidis published a series of translated Turkish documents from the archives in Heraklion. Ibid., p. 237.

[200] Ibid., pp. 293-296.

Sfakians as pirates and corsairs

Another activity that the Sfakians engaged in during this period, as in the previous centuries, was piracy, but not much has been written about this. During the 17th and 18th centuries, numerous pirates operated around the eastern Mediterranean, including Arabs, Maltese, Sardinians, Corsicans, Turks, and Greeks from many islands, as well as Cretans. Although pirates were highly feared, piracy was not as disreputable an activity as it is today. In fact, many countries, including England, France, Austria and Russia, considered this an acceptable means of conducting war, and governments hired manned foreign vessels to sail under their flag with the objective of disrupting their enemy's sea trade. These corsairs were allowed to keep the spoils of their adventures. Many Greek pirates were engaged as *Koursaroi*,[201] flying the English, Austrian and later Russian flags. The Sfakians formed a loose alliance with the Maniots from the Peloponnese, considered to be some of the most active Greek pirates, who themselves had an alliance with the Maltese.[202] They mainly attacked the French on behalf of the English, as well as Turks along the coast of the Peloponnese and Crete in acts of revenge, and for loot and hostages, who they held for ransom.

A Turkish report from 1741 highlights certain activities of the Sfakians. It states that they bought large quantities of grain from all over Crete and transported it to the island of Gavdos, where they produced biscuits which they sold to the pirates who stopped there regularly for supplies.[203] One of the most popular bays on Gavdos, Sarakiniko,[204] derives its name from the Arab pirates who often landed there. The historian Nikolaos Stavrinidis comments in a footnote to his translation of the report that not only were the Sfakians suppliers to the pirates, but they also engaged in piracy themselves.

[201] *Koursaroi* comes from the French name for privateers, *corsairs*. The word corsair is derived from the commissioning document issued by the King of France, the *Lettre de Course*. *La course*, 'the chase', was a euphemism for chasing down foreign merchant ships.
[202] Krantonelli (1998), pp. 48, 50, 77.
[203] Stavrinidis (1955), pp. 266-270.
[204] The Greeks used to call the Arabs *Sarakinoi*, from the Arabic *sharqiyyin* ('easterners'), and from this the Europeans adopted the term *Saracen*.

XI. The Daskalogiannis uprising and its tragic aftermath – 1770 to 1821

The uprising of 1770

One of the leading figures from Sfakia in the mid 1700s was Yannis Vlachos[205] from Anopoli, a wealthy ship owner whose four large vessels traded extensively throughout the Mediterranean and the Black Sea. If we are to believe the details in the famous poem about the 1770 uprising, his ships also participated in a bit of piracy as a side-line, most probably under the Russian flag. He was well educated, spoke Italian and Russian, dressed in the European style, and was highly respected by everyone in Sfakia. His educated status earned him the customary title of *Daskalos*, 'teacher', amongst the largely illiterate population of Sfakia, and resulted in him being known as Daskalogiannis, with the usual combining of title and first name. He also held the position of *Kethountas* of Sfakia (*Κετχουντάς του Καστελλίου*), a sort of First Minister of the district,[206] and together with his brother Nikolos Sgouromalis, they represented Sfakia in its dealings with the Turkish authorities on taxation and other matters related to the district's status as a *Vakf*.

Most of what we know today about Daskalogiannis and his tragic uprising comes from an epic poem composed soon after the event but published some 100 years later (see further below), so the accuracy of its details cannot be guaranteed. Recent translations of the Turkish archives

[205] There is uncertainty about the true surname of this Sfakian hero. In Turkish documents from this period, he is referred only as Daskalo Yani (Stavrinidis 1955, p. 284), his customary Sfakian name. It is unclear when and how the surname Vlachos came to be used in Anopoli, and why it was attributed to Daskalogiannis, as earlier histories (e.g. Papadopetrakis 1888) refer to him only as Daskalogiannis. Similarly, the poem of Daskalogiannis, first published in the late 1800s, does not refer to him using the surname Vlachos, just Teacher Yannis. A recently published study suggests that his true surname was Androuloudakis or Androulakakis (N. Psilakis 2009, pp. 42-45).

[206] Stavrinidis (1955), p. 325.

from this period have helped settle some more contentious issues. The story presented below tries, where possible, to merge tradition with the historical record where it exists.

Daskalogiannis, through his travels to Italy and Russia, met many well-connected, influential Greeks and had extensive discussions about political issues. He became aware of the "grand vision" of the Russian Empress, Catherine the Great, that Russia would liberate Constantinople from the Turks and become the leading light of Orthodoxy in the East. He also came into contact with the many educated Greek-speaking Orthodox Christians who lived outside the Ottoman Empire and who aspired to create a new Hellenic state as they watched the Ottoman Empire slowly crumbling. Both groups saw the benefit of supporting the other's aspirations to achieve their own objectives. The Russians and Turks had been fighting each other since 1768 in Ukraine and the Crimea, where the Turks had suffered a number of humiliating defeats. Catherine the Great at the same time attempted to incite the Orthodox Christians in the Balkans to rise up against and overthrow the Turks as part of her strategy for destroying the Ottoman Empire and expanding her own.

To this end, the Russians sent a small fleet of 14 warships from the Baltic into the Mediterranean under the command of Count Aleksey Orlov, with the objective of instigating a Greek uprising and destroying the Ottoman fleet. The Russians arrived in the Mani in February 1770, but the Maniots, although enthusiastic about the fleet's arrival, were somewhat disappointed by its size, especially the very small number of Russian troops on board. Preparations for the insurrection had been going on for some time, with encouragement from Russian agents and representatives of the Russian Orthodox Church. Discussions and agreements had already taken place with Greek leaders in the Peloponnese and Roumeli well before the Russian fleet entered the Mediterranean. Apparently Daskalogiannis had participated in some of these conferences. He had received assurances of Russian support and had agreed to instigate a similar rebellion in Crete once the Russian fleet arrived.

An uprising started in the Mani soon after the Russian fleet's arrival, but things soon went disastrously wrong, mainly due to misunderstandings between the Greeks and the Russians about respective troop strengths and objectives. Their combined forces were unprepared for the Turkish response, which saw the Ottoman governor bring in large numbers of irregular Albanian fighters, who crushed the combined forces and massacred the defenceless population. Orlov and the Russian fleet abandoned the Peloponnese and the unfortunate Greeks in June 1770 and sailed away in pursuit of the Ottoman fleet, with significant success. But from the Greek point of view, the affair was a failure which cost a huge number of lives, both in battle and from the Turkish reprisals that followed. The Greeks were effectively forgotten in the 1774 Treaty of Kuchuk-Kainarji which ended hostilities between the two countries, and they became increasingly distrustful of the Russians as a result. While connections with Russia remained strong because of the influence of prominent Greeks there, many Greek leaders in the future were to look to the West instead for alliances.

In the meantime, Daskalogiannis was bringing weapons and ammunition into Crete at his own expense and preparing the Sfakians for the uprising. He had decided that it was impractical for him to organize such an undertaking throughout Crete (he had approached the elders of nearby districts, but they were unwilling to join in for a number of reasons), and he was confident that a small army of 2,000 Sfakians would be sufficient to start the revolt, since he was certain that enough Russian support troops would soon arrive and that this would precipitate a general uprising throughout the island. There was some scepticism in Sfakia about the wisdom of the entire undertaking, but Daskalogiannis managed to assure the Sfakians that with the help of the Russians they would be successful. The revolt was declared in Anopoli on the 25th of March 1770,[207] and as had previously been agreed with the Russians, the Sfakians advanced towards Chania, camping on the Krapi plateau just north of Askifou. After celebrating Easter on the 4th of April, they attacked the Turks in the Apokoronas, Agios Vasilios and Kydonia districts, but they waited for the Russian fleet to arrive before attempting to lay siege to Chania, where the majority of the Turks had retreated to. Simultaneously, bands of Sfakians were dispatched to surrounding areas to convince other Cretans to join the uprising, but not many responded to the call, other than a few from the Selino district, as they were not convinced that the Russians would come to their assistance.

And they were right. As mentioned earlier, Orlov and his Russian fleet had abandoned the Greek uprising in the Peloponnese. As soon as the Turks realized that the Russians had no intention of helping the rebels in Crete, they sent a huge force of 20,000 troops to attack the Sfakians from two directions, the pass at Krapi and Kallikratis. The Sfakians defended their positions heroically, but the Turks soon overran them at Imbros and invaded the low-lying areas of Sfakia, destroying all the villages and killing anyone they encountered, sparing the lives of only young women and girls, who they captured to be sold in the slave markets of Heraklion. The Turks rushed to Anopoli to stop the Sfakian families who were attempting to escape either to Loutro, where Sfakian ships were waiting to take them to Gavdos, Kythera and the Peloponnese, or to the safety of the Samaria Gorge. Battles raged in the hills between Imbros, Mouri and Anopoli[208] as the Sfakians desperately attempted to keep the Turks from reaching their families.

---

207 Papadopetrakis (1971 [1888]), p. 129.

208 Papadopetrakis (ibid. p. 137) mentions a fierce battle at Skafidia, between Kali Lakki and Mouri, where more than 1,000 Turks were killed.

The Aradena gorge across which many fierce battles were fought between the Sfakians and Turks during the 18th and 19th centuries

Those fleeing towards Samaria had to cross the Aradena Gorge on a steep path and then make for Krousia, just north of the village of Agios Ioannis. Tragically, about 1000 of them did not manage to clear the gorge in time and were surrounded by the Turks. The women and children were being escorted by about 200 armed Sfakians, and they all decided to fight to the death rather than surrender. Very few escaped the ensuing massacre; only about 100 women and children were captured, and then sent to the slave markets. After that, there was no one to stop the Turks from completely destroying Anopoli and the nearby villages.

Daskalogiannis avoided capture, but his two elder daughters were seized by the Turks while trying to flee from Anopoli to Loutro. His two younger daughters managed to reach the boats in Loutro and were taken to the island of Kythera to the northwest of Crete. His wife had been injured by friendly fire while fleeing with her daughters; she became separated from them but managed to avoid capture.[209]

Conscious of the impact of this defeat on the Sfakians, and having received news from the Mani that the Russians had deserted them, Daskalogiannis met with his remaining fellow Sfakians at Krousia and argued that he should surrender in order to end the bloodshed. The other *Kapetanioi* convinced him that the struggle should continue, not because they were expecting to win eventually, but in order to wear the Turks down and thus receive more favourable peace terms.

[209] There is disagreement amongst historians about the fate of Daskalogiannis' wife, Sgouromallini (her first name is not known), with some claiming that she was also captured. Some historians also assert that the younger of the two daughters who did not manage to escape committed suicide rather than be captured.

The Turks soon returned to the Aradena Gorge. Daskalogiannis and his depleted troops were camped on its western edge. For two days the enemies fired at each other across the gorge. The Turks attempted to cross the gorge a few times but were repelled and suffered great losses. Eventually they tried another strategy. They divided their troops into three groups: one remained on the eastern side of the gorge and continued firing at the Sfakians while the other two groups attempted to encircle them, the first by heading north and crossing the gorge at an easier point, and the second by heading south and crossing the gorge at night at Dialiskari ('Marble Beach') and Sterni. The first detachment was noticed quickly and was driven back. But the Sfakians only became aware of the second group approaching from their rear quite late, so they were forced to take flight, leaving a number of their dead behind. The Turks also attempted to storm the Samaria Gorge, where many of the women and children had sought refuge, by attacking from both the southern shore and the northern entrance at Xyloskalo, but after fierce battles with the few armed men stationed there to protect the families, the Turks were eventually repulsed.

Sfakia now lay in ruins; all its villages were destroyed, and the few Sfakians who had survived were hiding in mountain caves, starving and exposed to the cold as summer now gave way to autumn. Those sheltering in Samaria were confronted with the same twin predicaments of cold and starvation. And the thousands who had escaped to Gavdos, Kythera and the Peloponnese, although safe for the time being, were facing a similar situation, as well as wondering what had happened to those they had been separated from.

The Turks had by now set up camp on the Frangokastello plain, and from there they conducted daily operations against fugitive Sfakians. The few armed Sfakians who had escaped into the mountains engaged in guerrilla tactics, harassing the Turks whenever they ventured up into the mountains to search for the rebels. But their most important targets were the desperately needed supplies that the Turks had to bring in by convoy either from Katre in the north or from Skaloti in the south. They also raided Muslim Cretan villages at night to seize the supplies necessary for the survival of the fugitives and fighting men.

Daskalogiannis, bitter and grief-stricken about the outcome of the rebellion, was still considering whether to surrender in order to bring an end to the on-going tragedy that had befallen his people. The winter was approaching; he knew that the situation would only get worse, and that there was no escape from this unfolding catastrophe. The Pasha of Heraklion, having heard that Daskalogiannis wanted to surrender but was being prevented from doing so by the other Sfakians, wrote him a conciliatory letter suggesting that they meet as friends and discuss ways of ending the conflict. To further persuade him, he forced one of Daskalogiannis' brothers, who had been captured by the Turks, to write a letter stating that nothing would happen to him if he surrendered. But this brother endorsed the letter with a capital M,[210] signifying that he was acting under duress and that his brother should not surrender. Daskalogiannis, driven by guilt about the failed uprising and the subsequent suffering of his fellow Sfakians, decided to ignore the warning and convinced the others to let him surrender. He gave himself up to the Turks in Anopoli and was taken first to Frangokastello and then to Heraklion.

There he was brought before the Pasha, who is said to have addressed him thus: "Welcome to the Teacher, the first amongst the pirates." After being briefly reunited with one of his daughters who had been arrested, the Pasha convinced him to write a letter to the Sfakian leaders saying that he had agreed to the terms of a treaty with the Pasha and recommended that they accept it too. The treaty was not overly onerous: it required the Sfakians to acquiesce, in writing, to Ottoman rule and to pay their taxes, but they would be allowed to keep their weapons and maintain their independent customs. Daskalogiannis was to be kept in custody in Heraklion for a three-year period, as was his brother, but he was to be treated with the respect due to someone of his status.[211]

This, at least, is the version of the treaty's terms which has been widely accepted over the years in Crete as accurate; and it is recounted in numerous histories of these events, including those by Papadopetrakis, Psilakis[212] and Aggelis.[213] However, with recent translations of numerous documents from the Turkish Archives in Heraklion, another version has emerged.[214] An Islamic court document dated the 18th of March 1771 sets out much harsher terms to be imposed on the defeated Sfakians, which included relinquishing all weapons, handing over the ring-leaders of the uprising, and paying outstanding head taxes from the previous year. Sfakians were forbidden to supply food to any Christian ships that approached their shores and were obliged to attempt to capture the crews. All judicial matters in Sfakia were to be overseen by a Turkish official appointed by Heraklion. No repairs could be carried out to any churches and no new churches built, nor could any tall buildings such as towers be erected; and religious ceremonies were banned, including the ringing of church bells. Furthermore, all Muslim captives were to be released, tithes were to be paid, and Sfakians had to wear the same clothing prescribed for all Christians throughout the island (which was different from that for Muslims).[215] As we will see, the Turks would have serious problems enforcing many of these terms in the years to come.

[210] The letter M in Greek is pronounced "me", which means 'don't'.
[211] Papadopertakis (1971 [1888]), p. 148.
[212] V. Psilakis (1970 [1906]), pp. 93, 94.
[213] Aggelis (1962), p. 105.
[214] Detorakis (1994), pp. 281, 282.
[215] Laourdas (1947), pp. 286-289.

Whatever the treaty actually stated, the Sfakians agreed to some set of terms, and they dispatched the required letter recognizing the Pasha's rule and promising obedience to him. A group of about 80 Sfakians then travelled to Heraklion to bid farewell to Daskalogiannis before he was incarcerated. But upon their arrival they were immediately arrested and imprisoned. And thus ended the first uprising against the Turks in October 1770.

But Daskalogiannis' end was slow to come. For a number of months the Pasha tried using Daskalogiannis as bait to entice his brothers and others who had escaped from Crete to return so that he could arrest them as well and thus eliminate the danger of any revival of the rebellion. Finally the Pasha gave up this ploy and exacted his revenge on Daskalogiannis in a most savage fashion. On the 17th of June 1771, in the square at the eastern gate of Heraklion, Daskalogiannis was skinned alive. His brother was brought there to witness the gruesome event and lost his mind as a result.

The Cretans never forgot the barbaric treatment meted out to their leader, nor the slaughter of thousands of women, children and old people. The next 100 years were to be the bloodiest that the island had ever experienced.

The Song of Daskalogiannis

The events of the Daskalogiannis uprising have been burned into the memory of all Cretans through "The Song of Daskalogiannis", composed by an illiterate cheese-maker from Mouri, Barba-Pantzelios, who had witnessed the events. The poem consists of 1,034 fifteen-syllable rhyming couplets, which he dictated to a church reader, the son of the priest Sifis Skordilis, in 1786 – fifteen years after Daskalogiannis' tragic death. He composed this epic poem to preserve the memory of these historic events, and to express his own deep sense of pain about the martyrdom of Daskalogiannis and the horrific destruction of the entire district of Sfakia.

The poem shares some of the characteristics of the ancient Homeric style in invoking God to help the poet with his bitter task as he begins his tragic story:

> God give me thought and a mind in my head,
> To sit down and call to mind Daskalogiannis,
> Who was the foremost in Sfakia, the foremost chieftain;
> With his heart he wished Crete to be Greek again.[216]

He goes on to describe the initial doubts about the wisdom of the whole enterprise, the rebels' disappointment when the Russian fleet did not

[216] As translated by Michael Llewellyn Smith (1973), p. 82.

The statue of Daskalogiannis at Anopoli

arrive, the destruction of Sfakia by the Turks, Daskalogiannis' surrender to the Pasha, and his eventual barbaric execution. The poem finishes by describing the return of the Sfakians who had managed to escape from Heraklion after three years in captivity, and their horror at seeing all of the villages of Sfakia destroyed, with so much loss and suffering.

This is a very important literary and historical[217] epic poem, which is considered by Greeks, and Sfakians in particular, to be of enormous national significance, since it describes the sacrifices, pain and misery that Sfakians experienced in their struggle to gain independence for Crete. It was first published in 1877 by the French philhellene, Emile Legrand, who had received the manuscript in Athens from a Sfakian who reported that he had obtained it from a great-grandson of the priest Sifis Skordilis from Mouri. A few years later, in 1888, a new version was published by a Sfakian journalist, and the next year it was included in a book of Cretan poems by Pavlos Fafoutakis. Before the first publication of the full poem, a number of much shorter versions had been seen by researchers and other visitors to Sfakia, some of which were published before the Legrand version.

The poem has been the subject of detailed analysis over the years, and a number of theories have been put forward to explain several of its unusual characteristics: the unlikelihood that a cheese-maker and shepherd from the remote settlement of Mouri would know about certain historical and geographical details included in the account; its style and uniformity of composition; the explanation at the end about the circumstances under which the poem was written; and the prior existence of a number of much shorter verses about Daskalogiannis. One view gaining support is that it was composed almost 100 years after the uprising, drawing on earlier local poems which related these events, and that it was written by the same person who composed the epic poem about the slaying of the Muslim Alidakis in 1774 (see below) – a poem consisting of 530 lines which was published at about the same time.

"The Song of Daskalogiannis" and other local oral reminiscences provided the basis for the first written record of this uprising, which was compiled by Grigorios Papadopetrakis, the Sfakian Abbot and later Bishop of Sitia, and published in his *History of Sfakia* in 1888. If we accept that the poem was composed around the late 1870s, then this historical record is based entirely on recollections by local Sfakians that were passed down orally over a 100-year period. The next Cretan historians who wrote about those events (Psilakis in 1909, Kriaris in 1902, and Mourellos in 1931) all drew from the Papadopetrakis history and the poem as their only sources

[217] Some of the events described in the poem cannot be corroborated by other documentary evidence; it also contains a number of historical errors, but these do not detract from its value as a source for the events surrounding the uprising.

of information. Only during the last 50 years, since the Cretan historian Nikolaos Stavrinidis started translating the Turkish documents left behind when the Ottomans abandoned Crete in 1913, have we been able to gain a more accurate picture of what actually occurred. The fact is that histories of many areas of Greece, as of other parts of the world, are based in part on oral accounts passed down through the generations via traditional epic poems. These are of great anthropological interest but may not altogether tally with documented historical facts, as and when these emerge.

The slaying of Ibrahim Alidakis

Although the Sfakians had been defeated and their villages lay in ruins, their spirit had not been destroyed. They soon proved this by exacting revenge against one of the most feared and hated Muslims in the area.

On the approach to Sfakia from Apokoronas at Embrosneros sat a fort[218] owned by a Muslim Cretan Janissary, Ibrahim Alidakis,[219] who was greatly feared because of atrocities he committed against the Christian population. In 1774, just four years after the bloody suppression of the Daskalogiannis uprising, he was slain by a band of Sfakians in a heroic feat that proved to all, and especially to the Sfakians themselves, that their fighting spirit could not be quashed.

Alidakis was a very wealthy Muslim of Venetian descent who possessed large tracts of grazing land to the north and east of the Lefka Ori; his flocks grazed up to the areas that were owned by the Sfakians of Askifou, Asi Gonia and Kallikratis. Before the 1770 uprising, a dispute over some animals his shepherds had stolen from a powerful and ferocious priest from Kallikratis, Papa-Sifis, ended with Alidakis returning the sheep in order to avoid a confrontation which he was not sure he could win. After the uprising, with the Sfakian population decimated and Papa-Sifis having been killed in battle, Alidakis decided that the time was right for him to invade Sfakia and seize more grazing land and flocks. The Ottoman authorities were unwilling to assist him in this, so he recruited a private army.

News of his intentions soon reached Sfakia. The Sfakians gathered their forces at Kares, at the northern end of the Askifou plateau where the house of *Archondas* Skordilis had once stood, and took the decision to attack Alidakis in his fort at Embrosneros before he could move onto

[218] The ruined fort of Alidakis can still be seen in the village of Embrosneros.

[219] It is claimed that Ibrahim Alidakis was of Venetian descent and that his grandfather had converted to Islam. The fort dates from the Venetian era and was owned by his family.

their territory. Under the leadership of Manousakas (nickname for big Manousos, of the Patakos family of Imbros), a group of men and women[220] received blessings from fourteen priests attending the meeting, then descended on Embrosneros in the middle of the night and surrounded the fort. They attacked at daybreak; a number of Turks attempted to run away, while 120 barricaded themselves within the fort alongside Alidakis. Eventually the Sfakians managed to breech the fort's defences and kill Alidakis and all his troops. More than 200 Turks and Muslim Cretan mercenaries died defending the fort, while the Sfakians lost 18 men and 2 women. Over the next two days the Sfakians carried away all the treasures and possessions that Alidakis had amassed, as well as his animals and anything else they could carry. They then burned down the village of Embrosneros in revenge for the oppression and atrocities committed by the tyrant over such a long period.

The most interesting aspect of these events is that no Muslims from Embrosneros or the nearby villages of Apokoronas came to assist Alidakis; and none of the Muslim Cretan Janissaries in the district, nor the Ottoman authorities, were prepared to punish the Sfakians for their actions.

This heroic event has been enshrined in the memory of all Sfakians through an epic poem known as the "Song of Alidakis". The poet addresses his audience at the start of the poem:

If you want to learn, just listen for a while
how they dealt with the devious Alidakis

He then describes the tragic events of the earlier Daskalogiannis uprising, the preparations by Alidakis to seize the Sfakians' flocks and grazing land, and the gathering where the decision was taken to attack Alidakis:

Fourteen priests dressed in their holy vestments
read their prayer with tears in their eyes
the villagers to their left are crossing themselves,
the Virgin Mary they ask to be their only assistance

The poem was published at the same time as the Song of Daskalogiannis, around 1880. There are several similarities between the two poems, which has given rise to the theory that both poems were created by the same person.

---

[220] This is the first recorded instance where Sfakian women managed to overcome the men's objections to their taking part in an attack against the Turks. The men conceded reluctantly, saying "Let them come ... they will be good company". The two women who were killed in the fighting, and who are named in the song, were Bourpaho-Katsouli and Sgourofellia.

The next 50 years

Although Sfakia had been completely destroyed by the Turks and its population greatly depleted, the region managed to recover quickly, primarily due to its people's expertise in boat-building, shipping and trading, as well as its remoteness from the main population centres. The authorities tolerated the Muslim Cretans persecuting and even killing Sfakians they encountered, who they regarded as rebels and fugitives. So the only option available to the Sfakians was to rely on the sea, where they excelled. Some of the boats that had been used to help families escape the massacres of 1770 soon returned with these refugees, and together with the survivors who had fled into the mountains, they started building boats again and trading throughout the Mediterranean. According to French reports of the time, in 1772 – only a couple of years after the destruction of Sfakia – a boat was under construction in Loutro, and by 1776 a ship with a 100-ton capacity was being built in Chora Sfakion. The Ottoman state allowed Sfakians to trade once again out of northern Cretan ports, often in partnership with influential Agas, as there was a need for shipping capacity; and Sfakians were preferred to the merchant navies of France and Italy, which were viewed with suspicion.

The plateaus of Anopoli and Askifou once again were producing food, and the absence of harassment from Turks and Muslim Cretans allowed the district to recover and grow in numbers again. Houses were built, signs of wealth became evident again, and the locals received formal education for the first time, something that had only been attainable in the largest towns where a few Greek schools had been established. The German botanist Franz Sieber, writing about his visit to Anopoli around 1817,[221] commented on its large, well-built houses and gardens, the fertile well-cultivated plateau, and the well-dressed people who were not afraid of wearing head-coverings made from muslin, something that was forbidden to Christians on the island.

In the rest of Crete, the situation deteriorated considerably following the 1770 uprising as bands of Muslim Cretan Janissaries roamed the countryside and attacked Christian villages indiscriminately on the pretext that they had supported the Sfakians during the rebellion. They also continued to commit atrocities against clerics and monasteries, and women were attacked or abducted for sale at the slave markets on a daily basis throughout the island. The Ottoman authorities were largely unable, and in many cases unwilling, to control the situation.

In the larger towns of Chania, Rethymnon and Heraklion the situation was better for the Christian population, since Ottoman officials and Turkish

[221] As quoted in V. Psilakis (1970 [1906]), Vol. 3, p. 112.

troops under their command were on hand to rein in the unruly behaviour of the Muslim Cretans. It was in these towns that an Orthodox Cretan middle class emerged once again. They were employed in commerce and professions that the largely Turkish population was not traditionally involved in; this was similar to the situation in Constantinople and other centres of the Ottoman Empire, where Greeks were appointed to positions of authority and allowed to expand into commerce and trade. This same Cretan Orthodox middle class re-established contacts with Greeks living in other parts of the Empire, such as Asia Minor, the Black Sea and Greece itself, as well as with Greeks living and working in Russia and other areas of Europe. These contacts both inside and outside the Ottoman state would enable them to plan Crete's liberation from the Turkish yoke.

Sfakians had continued attacking French and Turkish ships after the destruction of Sfakia by using Kythera as a base, which was also home to pirates from the Mani. A number of their ships had been destroyed by the Turks, and their attacks decreased significantly following their treaty with the Turks in 1770. During the 1768-1774 war that Russia waged against Turkey, the Sfakians had no hesitation in raising the Russian flag, often without any encouragement from the Russians, in order to target Turkish and French merchant ships. French reports from the period mention their losses to Sfakian corsairs on the seas between Kythera and Crete, and relate the French navy's attempts to chase down these pirates.[222]

Sfakian pirates widened their raids to the gulf of Chania and Heraklion, aiming to seize cargo and ships to add to their fleet. The looted cargo was usually taken to Loutro, Chora Sfakion or Kythera, where there were depots to store the goods until they could be sold to various markets, including Chania! The Ottoman fleet pursued the pirates, but the fear of attack drove many merchants to form convoys and travel under the protection of naval ships from Crete. Some Turks living in Crete chose to employ Sfakian ships to transport their goods out of Chania and Souda, secure in the thought that their cargo would not fall prey to other Sfakian pirates.

One celebrated Sfakian pirate was Nikolas Saviolakis from Anopoli, who was active between 1765 and 1795. Following the 1770 uprising, he carried out even fiercer attacks against Turkish ships, so much so that the Ottoman fleet was instructed in 1792 to capture him and destroy his fleet. They did catch up with him and wrecked one of his three ships, but Saviolakis escaped. The next year he again avoided capture. One night he became aware that Turkish ships were moored at an Aegean island; he towed a small boat filled with explosives up to one of the larger ships, tied it fast and set fire to it, engulfing the entire Ottoman fleet in flames. His achievements have since been celebrated in Sfakian *rizitika*. But the Turks finally managed to outwit Saviolakis. He valiantly rescued three foreigners

[222] Krantonelli (1998), pp. 98-101 and 298.

in open water, but after his boat had tied up in a nearby harbour, the three men – who were Turkish agents – set fire to his vessel, which exploded and killed Saviolakis, as he slept onboard.[223] A poet mourns Saviolakis' untimely death:

The mountains shook and lighting filled the sky
Thunder echoed amongst the mountains and waves crashed over the
    headlands
The seas foamed and fish jumped out of the water
And the little birds sat down and lamented:
Saviolakis has died!

In the 1800s, two Englishmen who spent a considerable amount of time travelling around Crete both wrote with great admiration about their guide, the Sfakian *Kapetan* Manias from Askifou. They seemed unconcerned about his activities as a pirate, treating this as something quite acceptable and understandable under the circumstances. Robert Pashley referred to Manias as having "armed a kaik, and made descents upon the coast of Crete, chiefly in the province of Sitia, where he made prisoners... sixty-four Mohammedans... The prisoners he sold as slaves...".[224] Captain Spratt wrote: "Now Manias was a Sfakiot chieftain; and they have the reputation of having been all more or less pirates as well as patriots in their time... But their pirate deeds must die in their own breast: I shall not record them here...".[225] Sfakians, we can say, seem to have kept on making a living from the sea in a variety of ingenious ways.

Emperor Napoleon Bonaparte in Sfakia in 1798

One of the many legends that is well known throughout Crete concerns Napoleon Bonaparte's visit to Sfakia. A similar tale is also told in the southeast town of Ierapetra, where the house that Napoleon supposedly stayed in overnight has been restored and is proudly shown off. Napoleon is claimed to have stopped over in these two locations in 1798 when he and his fleet were on their way to conquer Egypt, then a province of the Ottoman Empire. Napoleon had just captured Malta from the Knights of St John and, according to legend, stopped off in Crete on the 9th of June before continuing to Alexandria, which he reached on the 1st of July.

The story, as told by Papadopetrakis,[226] begins with the French fleet's unplanned landing at Loutro (due to a severe storm, according to Paris

[223] Kelaidis (1984), p. 92-99.
[224] Pashley (1989 [1837]), Vol. I, p. 76.
[225] Spratt (1865), Vol. I , pp. 249-250.
[226] Papadopetrakis (1971 [1888]), p. 174.

The Sfakian Kapetanios Manias from Askifou

Kelaidis[227]). The Sfakians, as usual, laid on their traditional hospitality for the French Emperor. Napoleon, having heard about the Sfakians' courage and expertise in the use of weapons, asked for a demonstration of their shooting ability. He was so impressed by their skill and physical stature that he invited any interested Sfakians to join him in his expedition to Egypt. In view of their bitter disappointment with the Russians a few years earlier, 80 Sfakians joined him under the leadership of Ioannis (Vergas)

[227] Kelaidis (1983), p. 74.

Daskalogiannis,[228] grandson of the hero of the 1770 uprising. When the French forces returned to France, many of the Sfakians remained there as permanent members of Napoleon's army. Papadopetrakis, in passing, mentions that Napoleon stayed overnight in Ierapetra prior to continuing on to Egypt.

Professor Andreas Vourdoumbakis[229] reported hearing about Napoleon's arrival in Ierapetra 100 years after the event from the townspeople. According to them, one day two ships approached the shore and sent ashore a rowing boat manned by five crew in search of drinking water. Amongst them was an officer, who was shown around by a local man, Andreas Petroulios; at the end of the tour he invited the officer to his house, where he had dinner and slept the night. In the morning when Petroulios arose, his guest was gone, and so were the two ships. A message had been left behind by the guest: "If you want to know who the stranger was that stayed with you last night, you should know that he was Napoleon."

There has been much debate about this tale for some time, as no corroborating evidence about this visit can be found, and it is rather unlikely that Napoleon's fleet would have come anywhere near Crete, a Turkish-occupied island, at a time when France was at war with the Ottoman Empire and Napoleon was on his way to attack one of its provinces. In 1961 the French Professor Paul-Faure published a letter[230] stating that he had checked the archives of the French Ministry of the Navy, as well as the archives in Toulon which hold all French ship logs, and he could find no evidence that any of Napoleon's ships landed on Crete. The closest the fleet came to Crete was 40 miles south of the island of Gavdos.

So how did the legend come into being? What event provided the basis for these stories to crop up in two different regions of Crete? It is unlikely that we will ever uncover the answers to these questions. Papadopetrakis' version has been downplayed in the 1971 reprint of his *History of Sfakia* through the insertion of a footnote stating that recent research has shown the tale to be incorrect; but Ierapetra still proudly lists the "house of Napoleon" amongst its tourist attractions.

---

[228] Psilakis mentions that Ioannis Daskalogiannis had been hired by Napoleon for his expedition to Egypt because of his shooting skills. Elsewhere, V. Psilakis (1970 [1906], Vol. 3, p. 73 and pp. 112-113) repeats a summary of Papadopertakis' story about Napoleon's visit to Crete in 1798.

[229] As summarized in Markopoulos (1981), p. 117.

[230] As reported in Markopoulos (1981), p. 115. Further details of the fleet's movements are provided in Stavrinidis (1981), p. 188.

XII. The 1821 Uprising – 1821 to 1830

The national awakening

The Greek national awakening, which culminated in the 1821 uprising in mainland Greece and Crete, was a complex movement that evolved slowly during the late 18th and early 19th centuries. The objectives and aspirations of the uprising were much broader than was the case with earlier insurrections. Whereas in 1770 the long-suffering people of the Peloponnese and Sfakia had sought to free themselves from Ottoman rule with the help of the Russians, this time the Greek-speaking inhabitants of the wider Ottoman Empire, influenced by the social upheavals transforming Western nations which had reached a climax with the French and the American revolutions, were themselves awakening to the new age of enlightenment. As in the West, the cultured professionals and merchants yearned for self-government and individual rights, and the concept of nationalism, which would unite all Greek-speaking people into a single self-governing free state, began to emerge as their ultimate objective.

This goal was driven forward by two separate groups. One was an influential and powerful collection of Christian Orthodox Greeks who had achieved promotion within the Ottoman Empire's administration to positions in foreign affairs, local government and trade, and who through their financial resources could significantly influence the Orthodox Patriarchate in Constantinople. They were known as the Phanariots, after the neighbourhood called Phanar where they and the Patriarchate lived. Their relationship with the church provided them with the power and influence to become, as the historian Stavrianos says, "one of the principal pillars of the Ottoman imperial structure". The other group consisted of the many prosperous Greek merchants who had established themselves outside the Ottoman Empire – in Vienna, Venice, Trieste, Bucharest, Odessa and many other large cities in the West and on the Black Sea – and who eventually dominated trade between the Balkans and central and western Europe.

The growing influence of these Greeks had a beneficial effect on Greek craftsmen in the Ottoman territories. Their goods – woollen and cotton thread, materials, clothes, carpets, silk and furs, and many other such items – were shipped and marketed by Greek merchants. The economic revival which went along with this created a new middle class in Ottoman-controlled lands, as well as in the larger cities of Europe and Russia. It was this new class of Greeks who would provide the stimulus for a further uprising.

Greek merchants and traders could see for themselves the huge differences between life in these wealthy, prosperous cities and life under Ottoman rule. They understood the benefits to the economy and to society at large of upholding the rule of law and safeguarding individual rights and freedoms. They soon reached the conclusion that Ottoman rule had to end if this prosperity was to spread to the Greeks who were struggling under deplorable conditions in the Ottoman Empire. A secret revolutionary organisation, *Philike Hetairia* ('The Society of Friends'), was founded by three Greek merchants in Odessa in 1814, and gradually expanded its membership through careful recruitment amongst the merchant class in the Odessa Greek community. By 1819 this society had more than 400 members.

Cretans soon became aware of *Philike Hetairia* through their travels to the Greek towns in the Black Sea region, and through their connections with émigré Cretans. The society's first Cretan member, who joined it in Moldavia in 1816, was the scholar Emmanuel Vernardos, who became their representative in Crete. Soon after joining, he travelled to Sfakia to assess the potential for an uprising there and to enlist members. The first to be recruited in Crete was Anagnostis Manousogiannakis[231] from Imbros. Soon afterwards, many Cretans who had joined the society outside Crete returned to the island to recruit others, including some high-ranking clergy. A list of 17 Sfakians[232] who joined the society appears in Paris Kelaidis' *Encyclopedia of Sfakia*; they are amongst the 85 Cretans who are believed to have become members of *Philike Hetairia*.

In 1820 the society elected as their leader[233] Alexander Ypsilantis, a general in the Russian Army and a member of a well-known Phanariot family who had fled to Russia at the outbreak of the Russo–Turkish

[231] Grandson of Manousakas, the leader of the Sfakians who killed Ibrahim Alidakis in 1774.

[232] Kelaidis (2007), p. 342.

[233] Ioannis Capodistrias, another prominent Greek in the service of Russia, was the Russian foreign minister at the time; although he was in contact with the society's members and in favor of the uprising, he rejected an offer to become their leader.

War in 1805. Under his leadership, *Philike Hetairia* developed a plan to incite rebellion in two different areas – the Turkish-occupied Danubian Principalities (Moldavia and Wallachia, in modern Romania), and the Peloponnese – since Ypsilantis believed that a revolt by all Christians in the Balkans would draw Russia into the ensuing battles in their support. Crete did not feature in their initial plans, as they felt the island was not ready for an uprising due to the presence of the Muslim Cretan Janissaries and the tight control exercised by the Ottoman authorities, as well as the Cretans' lack of arms and ammunition.

Ypsilantis, together with a small number of Greeks who were also serving in the Russian Army, crossed from Russia into Moldavia and Wallachia in February 1821 and encouraged the local Romanian Christians to join him, stating that he had the support of a "great power", the implication being that Russia backed the insurrection. Ypsilantis' troops marched towards Bucharest, on the way attempting to enlist volunteers from the Greek towns along the Black Sea[234] for his *Ιερός Λόχος* ('sacred company'), whose number grew from an initial 500 to about 2000. The Russian Tsar Alexander, however, disassociated himself from Ypsilantis and dismissed him from the Russian army. This reassured the Ottomans that the Russians were not going to support an uprising, and they gathered a large military force to deal with the threat. The local Romanian leaders and peasants did not show any great enthusiasm for the rebellion. Following a number of battles, Ypsilantis' forces were defeated in June 1821 at the battle at Dragashani (Drăgăşani).[235]

As soon as the news of Ypsilantis' arrival in the Balkans reached the Peloponnese, a number of *Kapetanioi* and church leaders who were waiting there to take up arms launched attacks against the local Turks. On the 17th of March 1821, the Maniots declared war[236] against the Turks in Areopolis, the capital of the district, and an army of 2,000 marched north to Kalamata, which after a two-day siege fell into the hands of the Greeks. Over the next few days they seized several other towns, and by the end of March they controlled the countryside, while the Turks retreated into their fortresses around the Peloponnese. Central Greece joined in the uprising a few days

[234] V. Psilakis (1970 [1906]), Vol. 3, p. 244. Psilakis reports that 13 Cretan sailors who were in Odessa at the time volunteered to join Ypsilantis; two of them were Sfakians. Papadopetrakis (1971), pp. 202-203, tells us that 150 Sfakians joined Ypsilantis at the port of Galatz, where they were crewing some Sfakian ships. He furthermore states that they were part of the 600 Cretans who joined Ypsilantis' failed campaign. We have been unable to corroborate this information from other sources.

[235] Ypsilantis and a small number of his volunteers managed to escape to Austria, where he was confined for seven years. Ypsilantis died in Vienna soon after his release; his remains are buried in Athens.

[236] The declaration of this revolution is celebrated on the 25th of March, which coincides with the feast of the Annunciation of the Virgin Mary.

later, with a number of towns falling to the Greeks by the end of the month.

The uprising in Crete

The Cretan members of *Philike Hetairia,* all prominent and influential figures of the Orthodox community, were active in promoting and supporting the uprising. However, they faced two significant problems. The first was the large number of Turks and Muslim Cretans who lived amongst them, and who had been terrorizing Christians since the failed 1770 rebellion. Estimates put the Muslim population on the island at 125,000 as against 140,000 Christians.[237] The other problem was the serious shortage of weapons in the face of a well-armed Muslim population.

News of the uprisings in the Balkans and Peloponnese soon reached Sfakia, where a hastily arranged meeting took place on the 7th of April[238] at Ghlika Nera (Sweet Water Beach), between Chora Sfakion and Loutro, attended by the elders of the nearby Sfakian villages. It was agreed that Crete should also join in the uprising, but the Sfakians, fearing a repeat of the 1770 events when they were left to deal with the Turks alone, arranged to meet with representatives from all parts of Crete in order to reach a wider consensus. This conference took place in Loutro on the 15th of April and was attended by 30 Sfakians and about 30 Cretans from areas as far away as Amari, Preveli and Messara. Given the secrecy surrounding the gathering, and the speed with which it had been called, representation from the entire island was not possible. Although the assembled elders felt that their people were ill-prepared to launch an insurrection immediately, they agreed to declare a revolution in Crete. The gathering also decided to form a governing body, which was to be called the *Kangelaria* (Chancellery) of Sfakia and be based in Loutro.

An assessment of available weaponry was quite sobering: they realized that there were only 1,200 guns at their disposal, two-thirds of them owned by Sfakians and the rest by Cretans in the nearby Lefka Ori. Sfakian ship owners present at the meeting were asked to acquire arms and ammunition, at their own expense, as soon as possible. They immediately donated whatever ammunition they had on their ships or stored in Loutro's arsenal, but this did not amount to much.[239] They also set about raising funds, with some contributions coming in the form of goods such as honey, oil, soap

[237] V. Psilakis (1970 [1906]), Vol. 3, p. 242.

[238] All dates here are based on the old Julian calendar, as Greece did not adopt the Gregorian calendar until 1923. While some recent history books have attempted to convert these dates to the Gregorian system by adding 11 days to the date, we will adhere to the Julian dates as quoted in the older reference books.

[239] Andreas Fasoulis, a ship owner from Anopoli who was to play a leading role during this uprising, donated 40 barrels of gunpowder. Mourellos (1931-4), p. 403.

and cheese; donations of embroideries and jewellery were dispatched for sale at European markets to raise money for weapons.

A further meeting was arranged for the 21st of May in Loutro to choose the members of the *Kangelaria*. The six men elected as founding members were all prominent Sfakian elders:[240] Protopapas Sfakion Giorgios (Giorgios Morakis from Askifou, the head priest of Sfakia and a member of the *Philike Hetairia*), Hatzis Polios (Hatzi Ioannis Polioudakis from Anopoli, a doctor and member of the *Philike Hetairia*), Sifis Papadakis (from Kallikratis), Stratis Vourdoumbas (from Chora Sfakion), Andreas Kriaras (a ship owner from Anopoli), and Anagnostis Psaroudakis (from Askifou); the secretary was from Heraklion. The committee took charge of managing funds and acquiring weapons, as well as decision-making processes, judicial matters and general discipline. They decided that all available elders, *Kapetanioi* and other willing participants would gather on Sunday, the 27th of May, at Panagia Thymiani monastery near Komitades to officially proclaim the start of the uprising, bless the weapons and flags, and elect their military leaders.

Following a solemn liturgy, the gathering elected ten *Kapetanioi* to lead the uprising: Anagnostis Manouselis from Kallikratis; Giorgos Deligiannakis from Asfendou; Anagnostis Protopapadakis from Askifou; Kostopoulos from Imbros; Pologiorgakis from Komitades; Roussos Vourdoumbas from Ombrosgialos; and from Anopoli, Anagnostis Panagiotou, Giorgakis Tselepis (Giorgos Daskalakis, grandson of Daskalogiannis, known as Tselepis for his handsome appearance), Andreas Fasoulis and Vourdoulomanousos (Manousos Vourdoulakis).[241] It should come as no surprise that all were Sfakians, as they were the only men with the required fighting experience, leadership qualities, and willingness to endure the sacrifices to come. A number of other *Kapetanioi* from Sfakia and various regions were assigned operational responsibility for specific districts.

Rumours that the Sfakians were preparing for an uprising soon reached the Turks in the nearby Ambadia area.[242] They sent a threatening message to the Sfakians ordering them to surrender their weapons immediately, and informed the Pasha of Rethymnon of these developments.[243] The Sfakians of course rejected demands from both parties to give up their weapons, but an armed battle was avoided when the Turks from Ambadia, who had come

[240] Papadopetrakis (1971 [1888]) p. 194. The information in parentheses comes from sources other than Papadopetrakis.

[241] Papadopetrakis (1971 [1888]), p. 200. Information in parenthesis comes from sources other than Papadopetrakis. The Cretan historian Mourellos adds three more names to this list: G. Tsouderos from Agios Vasilios, Sifakas (Sifis Kostandoudakis) from Apokoronas, and Mihail Kourmoulis from Messara. Mourellos (1931-4), p. 433.

[242] Ambadia was the name during the Turkish occupation era of an area south of Amari where a large number of Turks had settled.

[243] V. Psilakis (1970 [1906]), Vol. 3, pp. 252-255.

to confront the Sfakians, retreated. Instead they attacked the monastery at Preveli, where they killed some of the monks and workers and ransacked the monastery and its nearby farm. The Abbot escaped to Kallikratis and sought help, but by the time the Sfakians were able to reach the monastery it was getting dark, and they only managed to kill two Turks and recover the stolen flocks of sheep.

News of the impending uprising had also reached Chania, and the Muslim Cretans there attacked the few Christians living within the town's walls, killing those they could find and looting their properties. The public hanging of Bishop Melchisedek and Deacon Kallinikos on the 19th of May was the climax of the Muslim Cretans' violent reaction brought on by fear of a full-blown insurrection like the one they heard was already taking place in the Peloponnese. Soon their violence spread outside Chania, where they terrorized Christian villages to discourage them from joining the uprising that they feared would start in Sfakia.

In the meantime, the deployment of Sfakians and Cretans from nearby districts was slow, as they were waiting for more weapons. Their first engagement with the Ottoman troops took place after an incident at Theriso, in the foothills of the Lefka Ori just south of Chania. The Turk in charge of this village, and other Turks from Chania, were increasingly making unreasonable demands on the local peasants, who refused to comply. The local *Kapetanioi* had been instructed not to take any action until they received instructions from the *Kangelaria* in Loutro, but armed Christians from nearby regions were already heading to Theriso, having heard that Muslim Cretan reinforcements were to arrive there soon from Chania.

On the 14th of June, a group of about 60 Turkish soldiers left Chania for Theriso. But along the way they were attacked by Cretans who had rushed there to cut them off; one of the leaders was the Sfakian Tselepis. The Turks were unprepared for an ambush and retreated to the village of Loulos (about 10 km south of Chania), where they dug in to fight the Cretans. The battle carried on until dusk, when reinforcements arrived from Sfakia, led by *Kapetanios* Vourdoulomanousos from Anopoli, who attacked them from the rear. The Turks fled to Chania, leaving 18 of their dead behind; the Cretans suffered only one fatality. This was the first battle of the uprising in Crete, and the rebels' victory resulted in a much needed boost to morale, as well as to the seizure of weapons that would prove vital over the next few years.

The Turks' revenge was immediate and savage. The gates of Chania remained shut the next the morning as they carried out a merciless massacre of the Christians inside the walls; more than 300 were killed that day, including women and children. Priests and monks were a main target, as were churches and monasteries. The killing spread out of Chania into nearby villages and monasteries, but the local Christians fought back wherever they could lay their hands on weapons; there were tales of daring and heroism by men who would feature in future campaigns against the Turks. Over the next few days the Turks and Muslim Cretans fought the rebels at Embrosneros, Tsivaras near Kalives, Almyros, Malaxa and many other locations in the Apokoronas, Chania, Kissamos and Selino districts.

News of the battle at Loulos and the massacres in Chania reached Rethymnon within a day, and on the 17th of June, more than 100 clerics and Christians were massacred within the walls of that city. Ottoman troops then fanned out westwards into the countryside to disperse the advancing Cretan rebels, attacking fleeing Christians on their way. Their plan was to head to Sfakia and confront the uprising at its source. The rebels who had gathered near the village of Roustika, about 20 km southwest of Rethymnon, included men from Kallikratis and Asfendou as well as local villagers. They intercepted the enemy at Zouridi, just a short distance away, and routed them. The same day a detachment of 200 Turks from Ambadia advanced on Roustika, intending to surround the rebels and then join the Rethymnon forces' invasion of Sfakia from the southeast. But the rebels, including some of the Sfakia *Kapetanioi* (Vourdoumbas, Pologiorgakis, Tsirintanis, Deligiannakis), fought them off at the village of Ai-Giannis o Kaimenos, killing more than 20 Turks including their leader, Ismail Kountouri.

Reports of the uprising had also reached Heraklion, where the immediate reaction of the enraged Turks and Muslim Cretans was to slaughter priests and other defenceless civilians, again including women and children. When news arrived from Constantinople that the Orthodox Patriarch had been hanged a few weeks earlier, and that widespread massacres of Christians had occurred both there and in Smyrna, this unleashed an unprecedented reaction by the Ottomans which remains one of the most brutal events in the island's history. On the 24th of June, more than 800 Christians were slain, including the Metropolitan Bishop of Crete and five bishops who were in Heraklion on that fateful day.[244] Strong protests from the British and French Vice-Consuls prevented a total massacre of all Cretans in the town and nearby districts.

Similar carnage was carried out in the eastern part of the island, where entire Christian villages were destroyed, monasteries burned down, and untold numbers of defenceless Cretans killed while running away. Families fled from the districts of Heraklion and Chania to the high mountains and gorges of western Crete; many of them reached Sfakia, where the population doubled within a few weeks, creating problems with providing food for all

[244] A few days earlier, the Pasha of Heraklion had asked the Metropolitan Bishop of Crete to call a meeting of bishops from all over Crete. Suspecting his motives, the Bishop sent secret messages with the letters telling them not to come. Only five bishops travelled to Heraklion in response to the summons, disregarding the warning for unknown reasons.

the refugees. Sfakian boats played an important role once again by firing cannons at the enemy troops who were pursuing fleeing civilians along the coast, and by rescuing families and transporting them to Sfakia.

Many more battles took place in the west of the island during June. By the end of the month, virtually all of western Crete was under rebel control, and the Turks and Muslim Cretans had taken refuge in the large fortified towns. The central and eastern districts of the island were slower to join in the uprising, mainly because they lacked weapons and experience in guerrilla warfare.

However, the Christians of the Amari valley, having received some of the captured weapons, were preparing themselves and waiting for the right opportunity to strike. The Ambadia Turks, following their defeat at Ai-Giannis o Kaimenos, barricaded themselves in the village Vathiako, about 5 km northeast of Agia Galini. The rebels attacked them on the 28th of June; the Sfakian contingent was led by Roussos Vourdoumbas, the *Kapetanios* from Ombrosgialos, and the Amari valley men fought under *Kapetanios* Antonis Melidonis. Towards the end of the second day of battle, the Turks fled to the mountains, leaving the rebels to plunder the Turkish villages of Ambadia for supplies that the refugees in Sfakia badly needed.

Some of the rebels headed north to Mylopotamos, while others pursued the enemy, who were now travelling eastwards towards the plains of Messara. But many Christian families from the districts of Amari, Agios Vasilios and Messara fled to the coast, fearful of revenge attacks. Two Sfakian ships were waiting at Agia Galini and Plakias to take them to the safety of Sfakia. The families had to scramble aboard while the Sfakian ships fired their cannons at the Turks, but there were thousands of refugees and not enough space on the ships for all of them. Luckily, two more ships arrived, sent by the *Kangelaria* from Loutro. There are estimates that 30,000 people awaited evacuation, but this could be an exaggeration. The situation in Sfakia was getting desperate, as the district could not support such a large influx of refugees. Luckily the Sfakians were able to trade the goods captured from the enemy for food, as well as for desperately needed weapons and ammunition.

Because of the small number of Cretan fighters available and the difficult nature of the terrain, the rebels usually launched ambushes against the Turks in isolated locations rather than carrying out frontal attacks. By the end of the month, the Ottoman forces in the western district had suffered numerous defeats, lost more than 1,000 troops through death or injury, and abandoned significant quantities of weapons and ammunition to the Cretans as they retreated. Enemy troops would venture out of their fortifications during the daytime to pursue the rebels; and the Cretans would retreat towards more advantageous locations from which they would attack the Turks, chasing them back behind their walls by night time.

One such confrontation took place at the entrance to the Theriso Gorge at Kambia. A large detachment of some 5,000 men led by Latif Pasha of Chania advanced on Theriso on the 4th of July. Waiting for them there were 300 fighters from Lakki and Sfakia, under Ioannis Chalis and Andreas Fasoulis, who attacked the Turks as soon as they entered the gorge. Other Cretans quickly arrived from nearby Keramia, followed later in the day by Tselepis and his band of Sfakians, reinforced by more rebels from Lakki. The battle was difficult for the small Cretan fighting force, but by the end of the day the enemy began to retreat. When the rebels saw this, they attacked with greater fervour, and soon the Turks fled for their lives, dropping their weapons and supplies as they ran. This was a major victory for the rebels, as they had managed to defeat a vastly superior Ottoman force. The enemy lost more than 500 men, but more importantly for the rebels, they abandoned significant quantities of guns, ammunition, pack-horses and other supplies that would be of enormous assistance to the rebels in the struggles ahead.

The same day, a large detachment of Muslim Cretans from the western districts of Selino and Kissamos attempted to ambush the rebels at Theriso from the rear by advancing up the Tripiti Gorge to the west of Samaria. However, a band of rebels from Anopoli, Livaniana, Agia Roumeli and northern Chania district were waiting for them and pinned them down all day, blocking their progress. That evening when the Muslim Cretans heard about the defeat of Latif's troops, they dispersed.

Ottoman troops then attempted to attack Sfakia from the southeast; they sent 1,500 armed men from Rethymnon to Agios Vasilios, and the plan was to advance from there to Kallikratis. But on the 4th of July, at the village of Gallos (5 km southwest of Rethymnon), they were attacked by rebels led by the Sfakians Manouselis and Deligiannakis, whose men were laying in wait. The battle soon attracted other rebels returning from Vathiako, and fighting continued for days. In the meantime, a small group of 150 Turks skirted the battle at Gallos, and on the 6th of July approached Kallikratis from the direction of Roumpado; but when they arrived, the village was empty, as all the men had joined the rebels and the women, children and old people had moved up into higher country. After burning some houses on the outskirts of Kallikratis, they turned back, as they did not have sufficient numbers to take on the Sfakians in their stronghold of the Lefka Ori. The rebels managed to ambush them from the rear. After four days of fighting, the enemy abandoned their positions and retreated to Rethymnon. Although they left quite a few dead behind, the Turks had discovered a strategy for attacking Sfakia when the next opportunity arose.

The Ottoman invasion of Sfakia

The Ottomans now realized that the only way of suppressing the uprising in the west of the island was to destroy Sfakia, as most of the rebels and their supplies were based there. The overall military commander of the Ottoman troops in Crete, Sherif Pasha of Heraklion, gathered a large expedition to attack the rebels in Sfakia via Kallikratis. Led by the head of the Janissaries, Kaounis Aga, these troops consisted of 3,500 men from Heraklion, including cavalry and artillery, 1,500 from the eastern districts sent by Omer Pasha of Sitia, and another 3,000 provided by Osman Pasha of Rethymnon.[245] The forces in Chania were kept in reserve to deal with any rebel actions emanating from the *rizes* – the northern foothills of the Lefka Ori.

The Ottoman troops left Rethymnon on the 14th of July, camping overnight near the village of Agouseliana. The Sfakian rebels were aware of their movements and objective, but since they did not have sufficient men in place to stop them, they shadowed them and notified Sfakia of the impending danger. The next morning, a small band of Sfakians led by *Kapetanios* Pologiorgakis attacked the Turks at a place known as Amygdaloporos, intending to slow them down in order to give Sfakian villagers time to flee to more secure locations. After another skirmish, the Turks succeeded in reaching Kallikratis, but they found it abandoned and burned it to the ground. The next day they headed for nearby Asfendou, but were again ambushed by the Sfakians and suffered many casualties. However, nothing could stop them; they soon reached Asfendou and set the village on fire, then headed north to Askifou, where again they found the whole plateau abandoned.

The enemy forces camped at Askifou and, perplexed by the absence of any further resistance from the rebels, waited to see what the Sfakians' next move would be. Once the rebels had removed their families to safer locations, they descended on the Askifou plateau from the mountains that surrounded the massed Ottoman troops. The Sfakians fired the first gunshots on the 18th of July from the high ground at Stravorachi, and soon rebels from the nearby areas joined them. The Turks responded by shooting wildly at targets that they could not see and firing their cannons blindly at the mountainsides. The noise must have been extraordinary in this small enclosed plateau: the combined echoes of gun shots, cannon fire, shouts of the confused Turks, and screams of those felled by bullets from an enemy that they could not see created panic amongst the troops.

Some Turks fled towards the pass at the northern entrance to the plateau

[245] Other historians claim the Ottoman army was much larger, numbering 12,000. Mourellos (1931-4), p. 489.

to escape the mayhem. The Sfakians, seeing the direction that their panic-stricken enemy was heading, quickly positioned themselves along the western edge of the Katre pass and shot down at these easy targets crowded along the narrow two-kilometre track. The fallen bodies of men, horses and pack animals made escape much more difficult for the Turks who were trying to reach the small Krapi plateau.

As the Turks approached what they thought was safety at the end of the pass, further adversity was waiting for them. Tselepis, Daskalogiannis' grandson, had heard that the Turkish army was in Askifou, and arrived from Malaxa with his band of 200 rebels just in time to block the exit of the Katre pass. This provided their chance to exact revenge for everything the Sfakians had suffered since the fateful 1770 uprising. The Turks tried to scramble up the cliffs on either side of the pass, but the rebels picked off these easy targets until it grew dark. It is hard to imagine the enormity of the Turks' defeat: more than 8,000 well-armed Ottoman troops were routed by about 500 Sfakian rebels .[246]

Robert Pashley, an English traveller who passed through this area some thirteen years later, provides graphic descriptions of those events in his book *Travels in Crete*.[247] He relates that Sfakians had been unable to use the narrow pass for weeks after the ambush because of the intolerable stench from bodies decomposing in the hot summer sun, and that one could still see sun-bleached bones in the pass. The Turks lost 900 men on this occasion, according to Pashley, although other writers put the number much higher.

Those Turks who escaped from Krapi were pursued by Sfakians all the way to the plains of Apokorona and the fort of Almyros. The rebels also tracked down and killed bands of Turks who had fled up into the mountains. Many Turkish troops headed east through the mountains for Rethymnon, but at Asi Gonia their fate was sealed because the locals were waiting for them. The same destiny lay in store for those who fled south towards Skaloti, where Sfakians from Kallikratis and Asfendou were on the lookout for them. Again from Pashley's account:[248]

> their numerous stragglers had other horrors to endure. Those of them who were wounded were unable long to continue flight; and with no friend to aid them, sunk down and died. ...for most of them lost their way in the mountains, or were intercepted by parties of Sfakians, who, for the next two or three days, according to their own accounts, hunted these unhappy stragglers like so many wild-goats.

---

[246] Papadopetrakis and Psilakis give their number as 500, the French traveler G. Perrot quotes 700, while Pashley puts it at 900.
[247] Pashley (1989 [1837]), Vol. 2, pp. 170-175.
[248] Ibid., p. 173.

The horrors that befell the Turks reflected the Sfakians' hatred of those who had inflicted misery on them for half a century.

The Sfakians returned to Askifou and celebrated their victory. Meanwhile, another group of about 1,000 Turks under the leadership of Omer Agas from Sitia had arrived in Kallikratis to join up with the rest of the Turkish army for the planned destruction of Sfakia. They passed through the burnt and deserted villages of Kallikratis and Asfendou and reached the southeastern outskirts of Askifou, where they surprised the celebrating Sfakians. The rebels rushed to higher ground, surrounding the Turks at a location known as Ambelos, and a new battle commenced. Only about 50 Turks were still alive by the end of the second day of fighting; the Sfakians decided to spare their lives in order to exchange them for Christians held captive in other parts of the island. But word came that more Turks were approaching from Asfendou, so the Sfakians, fearing that their prisoners would be a problem during the next encounters, executed them all. The Turkish troop movements proved to be a false alarm, but the consequence was that the entire army of Omer Agas was wiped out. This was the second incredible rebel victory within the space of a few days for a relatively small number of Sfakian fighters against an extremely large Turkish force.

The Turks who had escaped earlier withdrew to Rethymnon and other towns further to the east through Apokoronas, attacking Christian villages along the way. Tselepis and his band of Sfakians returned to Malaxa to join the rebels who were harassing the Turks sheltering in Chania. Others surrounded Rethymnon and kept the Turks confined inside the town walls. However, the rebels were frustrated because they could not breach these fortifications, and because the Turks could easily obtain supplies and reinforcements by sea, since their fleet could operate freely. Sfakian ships were occupied at the time with transporting supplies for the tens of thousands of needy refugees in Sfakia, as well as bringing in arms and ammunition for the increasing number of Christians, especially from the east, who now were willing to join the uprising.

The second Ottoman invasion of Sfakia

At the end of July 1821, Sherif Pasha organized another expedition to attack Sfakia and the northern foothills of the Lefka Ori. His troops in Heraklion were joined by those from Sitia and Rethymnon, and the combined army, estimated at about 8,000 men,[249] plus horses and artillery, made for Episkopi, where they camped for the night. Sherif sent instructions for Latif's Chania troops to join them at Apokoronas. A few kilometres to the

[249] There are conflicting estimates of the size of this army; cf. Zampelios & Kritovoulidis (2004 [1893]), p. 344; Christakis & Paterakis (1995), p. 187.

west, 2,000 rebels had gathered near the villages of Kournas, Kastelos and Patima, intent on stopping them.

On the 1st of August, the rebels crossed the river Mouselas just west of Episkopi and attacked the Turks, who were still waiting for Latif's troops to arrive. At the head of a force of 1,000 rebels was Papa-Yiannis Skordilis, the Sfakian priest who was commander of the Mouri contingent. The battle raged throughout the day, but the rebels were unable to prevail. Papa-Yannis, surrounded by Turkish cavalry, was killed, along with many other rebels. This frontal attack, which went against the Sfakian strategy of drawing the enemy onto disadvantageous territory, proved to be a vital error for which they would pay dearly. Over the next few days, the rebels defended their positions against repeated assaults by the Turks, who had been reinforced by the Chania troops. Eventually the rebels were forced to retreat, leaving the Turks free to overrun the area. Their destruction of Apokoronas, one of the most fertile and well-populated districts of western Crete, was unprecedented; entire villages were razed, and hundreds of old people, women and children who were hiding in caves were either suffocated by the smoke from fires lit at the cave mouths or were dragged out and murdered. Historians estimate that the Turks murdered about 3,000 civilians over six days in Apokoronas.[250]

The Turks cleared the rebels from the higher ground in the northern approaches to Sfakia, then from the northern foothills of the Lefka Ori. An army of 2,000 Turks from Chania and Rethymnon was dispatched from Souda, led by Kaounis Aga – the commander of the unsuccessful invasion of Sfakia the month before – to clear the rebels from the Malaxa, Theriso and Lakki areas. In the meantime, the Sfakian rebel *Kapetanioi* Tselepis and Panagiotou together with the three Chalis brothers from Theriso organised the evacuation of families and the elderly to the Lefka Ori, so that when Kaounis' troops arrived they found Theriso abandoned. The Turks razed Theriso, Lakki and other nearby villages, then headed into the mountains in search of the rebels.

A few kilometres south of Theriso, on a difficult path winding up to the *madares*, the rebels had prepared an ambush near Aliakes spring. The Turks found themselves trapped as the rebels fired at them from both sides of the path and they soon retreated, leaving behind their dead and, more importantly for the rebels, their weapons and 150 mules loaded with ammunition and other supplies. More than 200 Turks died that day; their leader Kaounis Aga was also killed. Twenty-six rebels lost their lives, including Stephanos Chalis, the youngest of the three brothers, one of the brightest of the rebels, a poet and hero of Theriso, whose song about the

250 Detorakis (1994), p. 298; V. Psilakis (1970 [1906]) Vol. 3, p. 289.

uprising,[251] *"Pote tha kanei xasteria"*, is still the most popular revolutionary song in Crete:

> When will there be a clear, starry night, when will February arrive,
> so that I can pick up my gun and my cartridge belt, and
> come down to Omalos…[252]

By the 29th of August the Turkish army, reinforced by Muslim Cretans from Selino and Kissamos and now about 20,000 strong,[253] advanced to the Krapi plateau and the Katre pass with the intent of ridding Sfakia and the Lefka Ori of the rebels who had taken refuge there. The stench of rotting bodies and dead animals that had lain in the open for more than one month hit them as soon as they reached higher ground, and they were forced to march over the gory remains of their fellow soldiers on the path to Askifou. The Turks were expecting the Sfakians to attack at any minute, but to their surprise nothing happened. When they reached Askifou they found the entire plateau abandoned, as was the next village, Imbros. Papadopetrakis mentions that there was one encounter with some rebels in the mountains north of Askifou, but no other action.[254]

The Turks continued on to Ombrosgialos, Komitades, Mouri, Anopoli and Loutro, and likewise found all of them empty. They destroyed everything in their path, and the very few civilians they discovered were murdered on the spot. Thus, 51 years after the 1770 Daskalogiannis uprising, Sfakia was once again razed to the ground. The Sfakians had fled with their families and flocks to higher ground, to secret caves and inaccessible gorges; many of them had escaped by boat with other refugees to Gavdos. But why hadn't they attacked the Turks on the home ground that they knew so well? Why did they let the opportunity pass and not wreak revenge on their enemy, as they had the month before?

[251] V. Psilakis (1970 [1906]), Vol. 3, p. 293. There is some evidence that the song was based on an similar older song from the Byzantine or Venetian era.

[252] Our translation, from one of the many Greek versions that exist today. The rest of the verses are too gory to include here, but they reflect the Cretans' deep hatred of the Turks, stemming from the great suffering inflicted on them during the 150 years of the Turkish occupation of Crete. A translation of the rest of the song can be found in Xan Fielding's book *The Stronghold*, p. 103. It is interesting to note that during the grim period of the junta in Greece (1967-1974), the renowned Cretan singer Nikos Xilouris was at the forefront of an inspired subversive act. He and thousands of others publically sang *"Pote tha kanei xasteria"*, clearly meaning when would the dictatorship end, but the colonels could not ban this song about the heroic Greek rebels fighting the Turks!

[253] Detorakis (1994, p. 299) provides an estimate of 25,000 Turkish troops, while Papadopetrakis (1971 [1888], p. 255) says that there were 30,000. Both estimates appear inflated; a figure of somewhere between 15,000 and 20,000 might be more accurate.

[254] Papadopetrakis (1971 [1888]), p. 252.

Historians cite various explanations for this strange lack of action, but none of them are very satisfactory. Papadopetrakis[255] talks about the Sfakians being incensed by the attitude of the other Cretans, who were happy for the Sfakians to come to their rescue and shelter their families but were unwilling to help the Sfakians when needed. He also quotes some Cretans as saying: "The Sfakians were the cause of our houses being burned and our lives being destroyed, and we should now go and help them? Let them burn now!" Kritovoulidis[256] attributes their inaction to lack of leadership; if they had been prepared to ask for help from the rebels in the *rizes*, the Sfakians would have received assistance. Psilakis,[257] writing 80 years after the uprising, attributes this unusual behaviour by the Sfakians to poor leadership and disobedience amongst the various rebel bands. In his summary of earlier accounts,[258] Detorakis states that the other Cretans "openly accused the Sphakians of bringing disaster on the revolution because of their arrogant indifference, their inertness at the crucial moment and their meanness of spirit and petty quarrelling". Rather than blaming everything on the Sfakians, the absence of a central objective must be seen as one of the causes of this disunity amongst the Cretans. Subsequent events that resulted in the appointment of a military leader over all the Cretan resistance forces support this view.

After the Turks destroyed Loutro, instead of pursuing the Sfakians and refugees who had gathered in the Samaria Gorge, they returned to Rethymnon via Frangokastello, claiming in their report to Constantinople that they had achieved their objective of destroying Sfakia and suppressing the uprising.[259] Their hasty departure from Sfakia has been attributed by Psilakis[260] to the lack of a suitable water supply during the very hot August weather – the Sfakians had thrown pieces of pork into all the wells, thus rendering the water unclean for the Muslim troops. Papadopetrakis' often cited explanation of the Turks' departure is as follows.[261] The Pasha in command of the Turkish troops asked an old lady in Anopoli where all the Sfakian men were. She replied that they had taken their families to the safety of Gavdos and other locations and would return soon to slaughter the Turks as they had done at Katre, Ambelos and elsewhere in the *rizes*; they would arrive by ship, burn down the Turks' villages, and carry off their wives and flocks. While she was telling them this, a number of Sfakian ships appeared from the direction of Gavdos, some making directly for

[255] Ibid., pp. 251-253.

[256] Zampelios & Kritovoulidis (2004 [1893]), p. 354

[257] V. Psilakis (1970 [1906]) ,Vol. 3, p. 294.

[258] Detorakis (1994), p. 299.

[259] Ibid., p. 299.

[260] V. Psilakis (1970 [1906]), Vol. 3, p. 296.

[261] Papadopetrakis (1971 [1888]), pp. 253-254.

Loutro and for Selino. The Muslim Cretans from Selino and Kissamos fled home immediately, while the rest of the Turks departed for Frangokastello and Rethymnon. How much truth is there in this story? All we know is that the Turks left Sfakia without taking any measures to ensure that the rebels would not return.

While the Turks were passing through Frangokastello, 300 rebels led by Ioannis Chalis arrived in Sfakia from Theriso, having walked over the Lefka Ori to help the Sfakians.[262] This was the only aid that the Sfakians received from other Cretans at this most critical moment in their struggle for survival.

Although the region of Sfakia was destroyed, including all the supplies and ammunition stored in Loutro, the Sfakian fighting spirit remained intact, and so the uprising continued unabated. But their relationship with low-land Cretans, who the Sfakians contemptuously referred to as *katomerites*,[263] became more circumspect.

As soon as the Turkish troops returned to their fortified towns, the rebels took control of the evacuated areas and began harassing any Muslim Cretans who ventured outside the town walls. The northwest coastal area as far as Rethymnon came under rebel control. The plains of Messara also joined in the uprising, under the leadership of Michael Kourmoulis, who had been a crypto-Christian until the start of the insurrection. Rebel activity spread to the region around Heraklion, but this was more restrained, since the rebels there were afraid of Sherif's large number of troops. In Sfakia, the *Kangelaria* returned to the ruins of Loutro and began raising funds; they imposed a 5% levy on products that were not subject to Turkish taxes, and sent letters to the nearby Greek islands asking for arms and ammunition.

The rebel forces were now under the command of the original ten Sfakian *Kapetanioi*, plus a few from other regions of Crete. Numerous bands of rebels from other areas with their own commanders served under the Sfakian *Kapetanioi*, an arrangement that sometimes created tensions. Disagreements about objectives and actions in the field resulted in an uncoordinated struggle against a much better organized and disciplined enemy. They all realized the need to appoint an overall leader, but the *Kapetanioi* were unable to reach agreement on which of them it should be. So the *Kangelaria*, with the consent of the *Kapetanioi* and various elders, decided to seek a suitable person from outside Crete to be supreme commander of the resistance.

Two *Kangelaria* representatives were sent to the Peloponnese in

[262] V. Psilakis (1970 [1906]), Vol. 3, p. 296.

[263] *Katomerites* ('down-place people') were from the low-lying areas of the island, as opposed to the the *panomerites* ('up-place people') from the mountains. Those living in the mountains were always perceived as being free and strong, while the plains dwellers had been subjugated by the Turks and were considered weak.

September to ask Dimitrios Ypsilantis,[264] the commander of the regular military forces in Greece, for his advice about an appropriate man for such a position. They first offered the role to Ypsilantis' lieutenant, Prince Alexandros Kantakouzenos, but he turned it down. However, a Greek who had accompanied Ypsilantis from Russia, Michael Afendoulief, accepted the position. Not much was known about Afendoulief, but the representatives respected Ypsilantis' recommendation.

Afendoulief arrived in Loutro at the end of October on a Greek ship which was carrying some supplies and a small quantity of ammunition, as well as a number of Cretans who had escaped to the Greek islands and wanted to rejoin the struggle. Although most Cretans were very happy to welcome a prominent Greek to lead them in ousting the Turks, the Sfakian *Kapetanioi* were not very impressed. Afendoulief was small in stature and looked weak; he wore a European military uniform embellished with golden epaulettes and sported a number of medals; and he insisted on using his double-barrelled surname Comnenos Afendoulis (the first element signified descent from the Byzantine Emperors, while the second was the Greek form of the Russified surname). He took the title General Eparch, to which he later demanded the addition of Commander-in-Chief of Crete, a pompous title that did not go down well with the rough and proud Sfakian *Kapetanioi.*[265] Afendoulis remained in Crete for just one year, and during this period he oversaw some valuable changes. But he did not understand the antagonisms that existed between the various rebel factions and managed to exacerbate the situation.

Afendoulis' first act was to appoint the six members of the *Kangelaria* as his advisors, forming what he called "The 1821 General Directorate of Crete". Following discussions with some of the more influential *Kapetanioi,* he awarded the most prominent rebels from the uprising military titles which reflected the number of men under their command: the highest rank was *Pentakosiarxoi,* with 500 men; lesser ranks were in charge of 400, 300, 200, and down to ten or five men.[266] Although his intention was to officially recognise all those who had fought gallantly, as well as give some structure to the rebel forces, this system created more antagonisms and jealousy, and it contributed to a further loss of cohesion. His first *Pentakosiarchoi* were Vourdoumbas, Tselepis, Panagiotou and Protopapadakis, soon followed by

[264] Brother of Alexander Ypsilantis, who started the uprising in the Danubian Principalities. He was also a Russian officer before joining the Greek uprising in the Peloponnese in 1821.

[265] Papadopetrakis (1970 [1888], p. 263) refers to him as a *tychodioktis* ('fortune seeker') and says that Afendoulis relied on the stupidity and gullibility of the Cretans in accepting him for this position, and that he eventually hoped to be appointed Emperor of Crete!

[266] Zampelios & Kritovoulidis (2004 [1893]), p. 364.

Manouselis from Kallikratis and Deligiannakis from Asfendou – all from the ten original *Kapetanioi* – and three men from outside Sfakia: Kourmoulis from Messara, Vasilis Chalis from Theriso, and Giorgos Tsouderos from Agios Vasilios. The fact that four of the original ten Sfakian *Kapetanioi* received a lesser rank certainly would have created some friction. But giving six of the top positions to Sfakians immediately provoked the rebels from other areas.

Next on Afendoulis' agenda was military action against the Turks. The rebels carried out widespread attacks, focussing on the areas around Chania and Rethymnon. At the beginning of December, Turkish troops managed to reach Varipetro, a village about 8 kilometres southwest of Chania, intending to use it as a staging post to strike at their main target, the village of Lakki, which was a rebel base for attacks against the Muslim Cretans of Kissamos and Selino. After several days of fighting, the Turks retreated, only to return two days later with double the number of men. They planned to attack Tselepis, whose base was a few kilometres away at Malaxa, but Tselepis' men managed to repel them. Soon the rebels from Lakki and Malaxa again controlled all the *rizes* south of Chania.

But in Selino in the southwest, a large concentration of Muslim Cretans continued to harass the local Christians and also posed a threat to the rebels who controlled the area south of Chania. Afendoulis ordered Panagiotou and Tselepis to launch an attack against them, taking a combined force of about 1,500 rebels from Sfakia and Kydonia, together with the few men from Selino who were willing to join the uprising. Panagiotou and Tselepis' men advanced on Selino from the direction of Agia Roumeli while another group of rebels under the command of Vasilis Chalis approached from the northeast to ensure that no Turkish reinforcements from Chania or Kissamos could come to their assistance.

Clashes at the village of Moni, west of Koustogerako, eventually led to the Muslim Cretans retreating to the largest town in the district, Kandanos (10 km north of Paleochora), where they had fortified a number of houses.[267] The rebels laid siege to Kandanos for some time, during which several of them were killed, but the enemy were well protected and had stockpiled ample supplies. Tselepis, incensed by their inability to dislodge the Muslim Cretans, joined two rebels on top of a fortified house who were attempting to make a hole in the earthen roof with their large knifes and push burning oil-soaked rags through it in order to smoke out the occupants. Before they could complete this task, a bullet fired from inside the building penetrated the roof and killed Tselepis instantly.

When the rebels realized that Tselepis was dead, they immediately abandoned the siege and carried his body, together with those of another

[267] These fortified houses were located between the settlements of Stavros and Vambakadou.

twelve dead rebels, in a sombre procession to Loutro, were the men were buried. Historians[268] have criticized Tselepis for taking unnecessary risks, claiming that as one of the leading *Kapetanioi* of the uprising, he should have concentrated on directing the battle rather than exposing himself to such danger. But they were forgetting that he was a Sfakian *Kapetanios*, always leading his troops by example and from the front, not from a position of safety.

Tselepis died on the 6th of December, 1821, at the age of 30; he was the first *Kapetanios* to die fighting the Turks in the 1821 uprising. His loss has been immortalized in *rizitika* that describe his bravery and his tragic death:

> And they took his body for burial in Sfakia,
> and as they passed by the Tridiana stream,
> the young men cried bitter tears.[269]

The second year of the uprising

Rebel operations against the Turks continued unabated and spread into eastern Crete. The rebels made preparations to attack Mylopotamos and Messara, but in January 1822 the Janissary leader Getim Ali from Rethymnon blocked their advance by posting 70 armed men in the key location of Arkadi Monastery, about 10 km southeast of Rethymnon. The rebels, led by the three Sfakian *Kapetanioi,* Giorgos Deligiannakis, Pologiorgakis and Anagnostis Manouselis, and *Kapetanioi* Antonis Melidonis from Mylopotamos and Alexandros Mavrothalassitis,[270] surrounded the monastery. Deligiannakis and 60 of his Sfakians managed to sneak into the compound undetected via an underground passage and hid around the yard in strategic locations, waiting for an opportunity to strike.[271] When the Turks opened the monastery gates in the morning and ventured out, the rebels surrounding the buildings attacked them. As the enemy retreated into what they thought was the safety of the monastery, they faced an ambush from inside the compound. All the Turks were quickly killed, except for one, who escaped and fled to Rethymnon to tell of their bitter defeat. There were 15 rebel casualties, including Giorgos Deligiannakis' brother, the heroic Sfakian *Kapetanios* Ioannis Deligiannakis. A week later 2,000 Turks were sent from Rethymnon to retaliate, but they were again

[268] V. Psilakis (1970 [1906]), Vol. 3, p. 307; Zampelios & Kritovoulidis (2004 [1893]), p. 367.
[269] Our translation of an excerpt from "The song of Tselepis", as published in Kelaidis (1983), Vol 1, pp. 88, 89.
[270] Alexandros Mavrothalasitis (his surname is based on his family originating in the Mavri Thalassa – Black Sea – area) arrived in Crete from the Pontos region of the Black Sea with a number of volunteers to help fight the Turks.
[271] V. Psilakis (1970 [1906]), Vol. 3, p. 308.

defeated by the rebels, who killed more than 100 of them – including their leader, the much hated and feared Janissary Glymid Ali. His slaying has been immortalized in the "Song of Glymid Ali":

> And lo! a Sfakian's right arm struck off Glemedhi's head.
> The Sfakian struck off the head of Glemedhaki true,
> and, like a standard, in his hand he held it up to view.[272]

There was nothing to stop the rebels now, and they continued their attacks in the Mylopotamos district. Towards the end of the month, the Turks from Heraklion, led by Sherif, advanced towards the Messara plains to suppress the uprising there. After reaching Timbaki, they turned northwest up the Amari valley, attempting to coordinate their operations with the troops from Rethymnon who were working their way south. In the ensuing battles near Monastiraki, just east of Amari, the Turks suffered significant losses and retreated to their fortified towns, ceding control of the countryside to the rebels once more.

One of the bravest fighters in these encounters was Antonis Melidonis, the *Kapetanios* from Mylopotamos who Afendoulis awarded with the highest military rank (*Pentakosiarchos*). Roussos Vourdoumbas, the Sfakian *Kapetanios* who was in overall command of the rebel forces, was unhappy about Melidonis' promotion and got into an argument with him about the wisdom of his strategy at Monastiraki. In the ensuing exchanges, Vourdoumbas became enraged by Melidonis' arrogance and lack of respect towards him, and killed Melidonis. This was the first of several occasions where differences between rebel *Kapetanioi* led to open conflict, one of the reasons the uprising failed in the end. The non-Sfakians were furious about the death of their hero, and an armed confrontation between the two groups looked inevitable. To defuse the situation, Afendoulis removed Vourdoumbas from his overall leadership position. This in turn angered the Sfakians, who subsequently tried to undermine Afendoulis' position at every opportunity.

The next month Afendoulis, uncomfortable among the Sfakians in Loutro who by now were quite hostile towards him, travelled to Argyroupoli, saying that he wanted to be closer to the fighting and inspect the nearby areas that were now under firm rebel control. Towards the end of March, a young French army officer, Valestra, who had served in Greece under Ypsilantis and been made a colonel, arrived to provide advice to Afendoulis and assist the rebels. Valestra was the son of a French merchant, and had lived in Chania for many years. He could speak Greek, knew Crete

[272] Pashley (1989 [1837]), Vol. 1, p. 113. Pashley's book contains one of the many versions that exist of the poem; it is given in full, both in Greek and in his own translation, on pages 110-114.

well, and had received military training in the French army, where he had gained the rank of Captain prior to joining Ypsilantis to organize and train the Greek rebel forces in the Peloponnese. Afendoulis was quite uneasy about Valestra's arrival, since he saw him as a threat to his own position and authority.

During discussions with Afendoulis, Valestra argued that the rebels needed to establish a well-fortified base in the north of the island, and that the ideal place was Rethymnon. Afendoulis agreed to the proposal to capture the town and ordered the Cretan *Kapetanioi* to coordinate their forces along the lines of Valestra's plan. The largest rebel contingent, to be positioned in the centre of the attack, was to retreat when the Turks first engaged them, allowing the other rebel contingents to circle behind the advancing enemy and entrap them. Valestra would be in charge of a small force on one flank, which would try to breech the town's defences and seize control of Rethymnon.

The battle for Rethymnon, which took place on the 15th of April, did not go according to plan because the Sfakian *Kapetanios* in charge of the central forces, Protopapadakis, did not order his troops to pull back as agreed. Valestra, the Sfakians Stratis Deligiannakis and Manouselis, and their band of men tried to move in from one side, expecting the Turks to advance into the space left by the retreating rebel contingent, but this did not happen. Soon the Turks launched a counterattack against Valestra's forces, and in the ensuing fierce battle Valestra and 125 of his men were killed. Many have blamed the death of the young French officer and the lost opportunity to capture Rethymnon on Afendoulis,[273] who they believe persuaded Protopapadakis to ignore Valestra's strategy and instead hold his position and fight the Turks. The Sfakian *Kapetanioi*, who had their own views about the events and the loss of many of their own men, decided not to take any action at the time so as to avoid open confrontation with the other rebel leaders who still supported Afendoulis.

Formation of a provisional government in Crete

Afendoulis had been promoting the idea amongst his closest confidants that Crete should become independent from Greece, with him as the head of state. Word of this soon reached the provisional government in mainland

[273] The historians Papadopetrakis, Psilakis, Kritovoulidis, Mourellos and Kelaidis all believe that Afendoulis was behind Protopapadakis' unexpected failure to follow the agreed plan, as he feared that Valestra would threaten his position as Supreme Commander in Crete. Papadopetrakis (1971, p. 276) and Mourellos (1931-4, p. 583) write that when Protopapadakis was confronted about this by the other Sfakian leaders, he said that he had firm orders not to follow Valestra's badly thought-out plan and risk losing many of his men.

Greece, who had received many conflicting reports about leadership problems in Crete. They sent Petros Skylitsis Omiridis to Crete to establish a provisional administration that would address the issue.[274] Afendoulis was unhappy about Skylitsis' arrival and immediately raised with him the idea of securing Crete's independence from the mainland, pointing out that Crete had never been linked politically to Greece.

Omiridis convened a conference in Armeni of representatives from all districts of Crete. He presented a proposal to set up a governing structure similar to the provisional government on the mainland. On the 20th of May, this general assembly adopted a constitution that addressed citizens' rights and obligations, regional administration, and electoral and appointment processes for positions at all levels of government. The highest office was to be called General Eparch, and the assembly proposed that Afendoulis fill that role; Omiridis offered him the position the next day. Afendoulis had no option but to accept the constitution and the appointment, which fell well short of his dream of becoming the supreme ruler of a new "Regno di Candia". This decision represented a compromise for everyone, as the assembly members wanted to avoid any further rifts amongst the various factions. The assembly had also elected 16 members of the provisional government, who, together with Afendoulis, were sworn in on the 21st of May.

This intervention by the provisional Greek government at such a critical moment was quite welcome in Crete and helped to temporarily defuse tensions between the Afendoulis and the Sfakian camp. But everyone in Crete was very bitter that no offer of weapons or funding was forthcoming from the mainland – which of course had its own problems to deal with. Although the mainland Greeks had been successful in their campaign against the Turks in the Peloponnese and managed to withstand Turkish attacks from the north, they lacked strong central leadership and were fragmented because of infighting between politicians and *Kapetanioi*, so they were unable to see beyond their own battle fronts.

Arrival of Egyptian forces in Crete

The Turks' problems dealing with the uprisings in Crete and the Greek mainland forced Sultan Mahmud II to seek help from his vassal Mehmed Ali, the Governor of Egypt. The Sultan promised to hand over Crete to him if he succeeded in suppressing the rebellion there. So while the Armeni conference was taking place to establish the first provisional government of Crete, a fleet of more than 100 ships, many of them having been chartered by the Egyptians and flying the flags of European nations, arrived in Souda

[274] Mourellos (1931-4), pp. 583-586.

Bay on the 28th of May carrying more than 10,000 troops, including many Albanian mercenaries and some European officers,[275] under the command of Mehmed Ali's son-in-law Hassan Pasha.[276] The rebels were unprepared for this, but nevertheless they attacked the Turks who had come to welcome the Egyptian forces and fired on the disembarking troops. However, they soon had to retreat in the face of the enemy's superior numbers and firepower. The rebels regrouped and attacked the encamped enemy troops during the night, killing more than 300 of them, but this did little to alleviate their predicament.

Once the Turks from the nearby areas had joined the Egyptian forces at Souda Bay, Hassan's men advanced towards the rebels' bases at Tsikalaria and Malaxa. On the 5th of July, a large Turkish contingent from Heraklion made for Anogia, 15 kilometres to the southwest and home to many heroic fighters of the uprising. They found the town abandoned: its 2,000 women and children had fled to the nearby mountains while their men trekked south to the Messara region and readied themselves for battle. Small bands of rebels inflicted heavy casualties on the Turks forcing them to withdraw to Heraklion.

Hassan understood that his task was not going to be easy. On the 1st of August, his troops set out from Chania for Lakki and Theriso, forcing the rebels to retreat. But pursuing the insurgents did not prove to be worthwhile, so he returned to Apokoronas, where over a six-day period his troops destroyed everything in their path. The entire population of the area fled into the mountains towards Askifou. Hassan's troops pushed on eastwards, destroying villages where they encountered opposition. They soon reached Rethymnon and then continued on to the Mylopotamos district. By the 30th of August they had reached Haleppa Monastery, about 5 kilometres northwest of Anogia, where they camped. The rebels, reinforced by local insurgents, engaged them in battle and eventually forced Hassan's troops to abandon their supplies and seek refuge in Heraklion.

The rebels took heart from their successes and surrounded Heraklion, cutting off the town's water supply during one of the hottest months of the year. But they realised they couldn't capture the well-fortified town, and that the Turks were not going to surrender, since the large number of Egyptian troops to the west would come to their rescue. Hassan called for the fighters who had been kept in reserve in Souda Bay to disembark and form a second front in order to split the rebel forces and alleviate the situation in Heraklion. On the 24th of September, battles raged around Kalives, east of Chania at the entrance of Souda Bay, between more than 1,000 Egyptian troops and a few hundred rebels from Apokoronas and

[275] V. Psilakis (1970 [1906]) Vol. 3, p. 341.

[276] Both Hassan Pasha and Mehmed Ali were Albanians, as were many other notable leaders in the Ottoman army.

Kydonia, plus Sfakians under the leadership of Andreas Fasoulis. Although they managed to prevent the rest of the Egyptians landing, another enemy fleet of 50 vessels arrived carrying 1,500 Turkish soldiers from Asia Minor. The Turkish and Egyptian forces did not manage to penetrate very far into the countryside, and the battle ended in a stalemate, but they did achieve the desired result of pinning down a substantial number of rebel forces.

Further to the east, the combined Turkish and Egyptian forces left Heraklion early in October to attack the rebels who were taking refuge on the Lasithi plateau. Another contingent headed for the Messara region to confront the rebels under the command of the well-respected *Kapetanios* Kourmoulis, who had cleared the area of Turks over a two-week period and had appropriated a large number of weapons and supplies.

Replacement of Afendoulis

The Cretans faced a leadership crisis due to continuing clashes between Afendoulis, members of the provisional government, and the Sfakian *Kapetanioi*. The situation had reached the point where, on the 15th of November, the government had Afendoulis arrested and issued a public statement[277] accusing him, among other things, of acting without proper authority, granting valuable commercial rights to individuals for his own personal gain, keeping taxes and money intended for the uprising, undermining the authority of elected officials by spreading unsubstantiated accusations about them, making disparaging remarks to foreign dignitaries about the provisional government, and stating that he was going to appoint himself monarch of Crete. A governmental committee visiting mainland Greece at the time to discuss Afendoulis' problematic behaviour recommended appointing Emmanuel Tombazis, a well-known Greek sea captain from the island of Hydra, as head of the government in Crete. It took six months for Tombazis to arrive, and during that time Crete remained leaderless.

Most historians, both at the time and subsequently, have been critical of Afendoulis. Some charge him with incompetence, while others attribute his failure to his ambition to become the permanent head of an independent Crete, coupled with his divisive means of achieving that goal. The present-day historian Detorakis' assessment is that Afendoulis did achieve some success during his period as head of the government,[278] but this view is not shared by many. Afendoulis' most strident critic is the Sfakian historian Papadopetrakis, who accuses him of being a traitor to the cause in order to fulfil his own personal ambitions.

[277] Mourellos (1931-4), pp. 685-689.
[278] Detorakis (1994), p. 302.

The third year of the uprising

Hassan's troops pressed eastwards along two fronts, intending to eliminate the rebel forces based in the Lasithi plateau. The detachment whose task it was to clear the Messara district heard that large numbers of rebels were advancing towards Lasithi, so they made their way instead to the southern pass at Vianos which leads to the plateau. There they encountered strong resistance and were forced to retreat. They then tried to approach the plateau from the east via Kritsa, and on the 25th of January 1823 they invaded Lasithi through the pass at Katharo. The vastly outnumbered rebels could not stop them, and the inhabitants fled in order to escape enslavement or slaughter.

One of the most tragic events of the uprising occurred at Milatos Cave, to the east of Malia, where 3,700 women and children had taken refuge, protected by 150 armed men. The Egyptian and Turkish troops surrounded the cave and bombarded its entrance with cannon fire. The fugitives held out for a fortnight, although they were starving and many died of thirst. The Sfakian *Kapetanios* Roussos Vourdoumbas and 300 of his rebels attempted to break the siege, but there were too few of them to succeed. Eventually, after being promised they would not be harmed, those sheltering in the cave surrendered. But what actually awaited them was a brutal massacre of the men, while the women were captured and sold as slaves.

A few days later, not far from where these tragic events had taken place, Hassan fell off his horse and died from his injuries. The strategy of clearing the east of rebels suddenly halted with his death, and his deputy, Hussein Bey,[279] was appointed the new leader of the combined Turko-Egyptian forces.

While most of the enemy forces were still engaged in the east, the provisional Cretan government, prompted by pleas from Christians in the western districts, took the initiative of liberating the Kissamos and Selino areas, which were still under tight Turkish control. *Kapetanios* Nikiforos Hatzidakis from Anopoli had failed to accomplish this task in 1822 and had been killed in the attempt. Five thousand experienced rebel fighters from Rethymnon and western Crete gathered at Agia Marina, to the west of Chania, and began their attack on the 3rd of February. They soon controlled all the northwest; the Turks fled to Chania or barricaded themselves into Kasteli Kissamos and the fort on the islet of Gramvousa at the northwest tip of Crete.

On the 21st of May, Emmanuel Tombazis arrived at Kissamos Bay, where large numbers of rebel forces had already laid siege to Kasteli. His

[279] Hussein Bey was a brother-in-law of Mehmed Ali of Egypt, as was the deceased Hassan Pasha.

ship was escorted by five naval vessels and three cargo ships from Hydra, carrying 600 fighters as well as distinguished political figures, including the philhellene Englishman Frank Abney Hastings, who was in charge of the artillery company on board. On arrival, Tombazis made his first political mistake as a result of bad advice: he welcomed the Sfakian *Kapetanioi* who had come to meet him with a cannon salute, while the rest of the Cretan military leadership were received in a very formal way.[280] This did nothing to alleviate the existing tensions between the Sfakians and other Cretans, who were already suspicious of Tombazis since he had been chosen by a Sfakian-dominated committee.

Tombazis' first task was to negotiate the surrender of the Turks who had been under siege in Kasteli for almost three months. He offered them unusually generous terms, which they accepted; they were then taken to Chania aboard two Greek vessels, along with all their possessions and weapons. The impact of the siege, from both the fighting and a plague that had struck the town, was devastating: of the 1,800 people within the walls of Kasteli, only 600 came out alive.

Tombazis decided to call off the siege of Gramvousa, which upset some of the local rebels, and set off for the Selino district with his troops, their numbers swelled by the rebel army, now including some men from the eastern districts. The Turks retreated to the fortified buildings around Kandanos and tried to negotiate a settlement, but they also sent for help from Chania. Tombazis gave in to their pleas to be allowed to leave for Chania, but confusion in the rebels' ranks and disagreement with Tombazis' decision resulted in the rebels attacking the fleeing Turks and their families and massacring close to half of them. The rebels did not launch an assault on the Turkish forces who arrived from Chania to assist their escape, as they were afraid of catching the plague, which by that time had struck Chania. As a result, half of the Turks from Selino managed to reach Chania, thus increasing the number of families taking shelter in the town and the number of armed men ready to fight the rebels.

Tombazis then made the tactical mistake of not attempting to capture Chania now that he had a large army at his disposal and cannons to bombard the walls from land and sea. Instead, he convened a conference to decide on new government structures and assign leadership roles, some say at the behest of the Sfakians, who wanted to ensure that their men were appointed to all the top regional positions. The conference lasted a number of weeks, and there were many debates and arguments about the Sfakians' future role in the uprising, since rebels from other areas preferred their own leaders.

In mid June, a fleet of 50 Egyptian vessels carrying 5,000 Egyptian and 2,000 Albanian troops, ammunition and supplies, arrived in Heraklion to

[280] Mourellos (1931-4), p. 564

reinforce Hussein's men, who were preparing to advance on the rebels who controlled the west of the island. Tombazis relocated to Amari in order to coordinate efforts to stop Hussein. A fighting force of more than 3,000 rebels was assembled, and the Sfakian *Kapetanios* Vourdoumbas was appointed as its leader. When they discovered that Hussein's 12,000-strong army was camped at Agia Varvara (26 km south of Heraklion), they drew up a meticulous plan of attack. But again, lack of discipline amongst the rebels led to disaster. A group of rebels decided to steal some animals and horses from the Turko-Egyptian forces before the agreed start of the attack; they were pursued, and the situation developed into a full-scale battle near the village of Amourgieles, some 15 km to the east. By the end of the day, the rebels had lost 300 men and were forced to flee in the face of a much larger and better equipped army. This defeat alerted Tombazis to the fact that his plan had been to no avail due to infighting amongst their leaders and poor discipline; they were also very low on ammunition, especially after this last disastrous battle. Tombazis realized the danger to the uprising and, accompanied by some rebel leaders, made his way south to Kali Limenes, boarded one of his naval vessels and sailed off to Kasteli Kissamos, leaving Hussein free to continue subduing the island.

Hussein now turned his attention to the Messara plains; all civilians and rebels there fled before him. His troops then headed north, one battalion towards Amari and the other towards Rethymnon. At Melidoni, 20 km east of Rethymnon, they came across 340 women and children who had taken refuge in a cave, defended by 30 armed men. After bombarding them for weeks, his troops suffocated them by throwing burning rags and branches through a hole in the roof of the cave.

Meanwhile, Tombazis coordinated attacks against the few remaining Turkish strongholds in the west and renewed the siege of Gramvousa. On the night of the 11th of December, 500 rebels set off for Gramvousa, 150 of them in rowing boats while the rest followed in Tombazis' ship. The first group scaled the walls of the fort using ladders without being noticed and captured the guard, who they found asleep with his wife. They killed the guard, but before they could attack the other sleeping Turks they were discovered, in part due to the woman's screams. Fierce hand-to-hand fighting ensued, during which only 60 of the 150 rebels managed to escape. The rest of the rebels who were waiting to enter the fort were stranded, since those who had scaled the walls had failed to open the gate.

One of the rebels who perished was a brave young Sfakian *Kapetanios* from Askifou who had fought valiantly over the previous two years in the east. He was Markos Bouzakis, known also as Bouzomarkos. His death is celebrated in a Sfakian *rizitiko*:[281]

[281] Kelaidis (1983), pp. 121-122.

Bouzomarkos first scales the walls
he single-handed kills seven with his dagger alone,
"Come up boys to attack the Turks,
because I will not leave as I will die here."
The first to be killed was Bouzomarkos,
the brave, the good, the famous dragon.

The fourth year of the uprising: Hussein invades Sfakia

By March 1824, Tombazis was desperate for help and wrote to the provisional government on the mainland seeking urgent aid and pleading with them to "take measures, for the beautiful island of Crete is being lost".[282] But the mainland Greeks were again preoccupied with political infighting and attempts to rein in the power of their supreme military commander, Kolokotronis.

Hussein was ready to attack the rebels in the west and quash the uprising throughout Crete once and for all. He sent messages to the inhabitants of the Apokoronas district, demanding that they submit to his troops or be destroyed; people reacted by fleeing to the mountains in the knowledge that Hussein would not show them any mercy. Most headed for Sfakia, where their numbers swelled far beyond the district's ability to provide them with even the most basic shelter; some historians state that there were 30,000 refugees in an area that normally sustained only about 3,000 people.

Hussein's huge army – claimed to numbered 26,000 – crossed Apokoronas without meeting a soul; nevertheless, they burned and destroyed anything in their path that had survived the onslaught from Hassan's troops some eighteen months before. They then headed for the pass at Katre, the site of the massacre of Turkish troops in 1821, without encountering any resistance, and by the 19th of March they had reached Askifou. Again there were no rebels in sight; all had taken shelter with their families in the mountains. Hussein's army proceeded to Imbros, Mouri and Anopoli in an attempt to catch those fleeing to Loutro and onward to the Samaria Gorge. As in 1821, most of the Sfakians and refugees had already left. Dozens of boats, some Sfakian and others chartered from the mainland, transported refugees from Loutro to Gavdos and the Peloponnese; 10,000 people managed to escape this way. Before Hussein's army could reach Loutro, the rebels blew up all the ammunition stored there, which represented a huge loss for them since Loutro held their main arsenals.

A detachment of enemy troops in Anopoli were sent to Aradena, where some of the Cretans were trying to escape across the gorge. A band of 300 rebels managed to keep them at bay long enough for those fleeing to

[282] Mourellos (1931-4) p. 821

Approaching the narrows of the Samaria gorge

reach Agios Ioannis and from there continue on to Samaria. But the Turko-Egyptian troops caught up with them at Agios Ioannis, where a heroic stand by 35 rebels, all but two of them Sfakians, allowed the women and children to reach the safety of the Samaria Gorge. Only one of the rebels survived; the dead included the celebrated Sfakian *Kapetanios* Chatzi Giorgis Kelaidis,[283] also known as Mouriotis.

Hussein's men, fearing another ambush and uncertain about the difficult mountain terrain leading to Samaria, returned to Loutro. Hussein dispatched a large contingent to Agia Roumeli tasked with entering the Samaria Gorge, where the Cretan women and children had taken refuge, but for some reason they did not advance deep into the gorge. All his troops then assembled at Frangokastello, from where Hussein sent messages to the Sfakians demanding that they submit to his rule, but to no avail. He remained there until the 28th of March, then returned to Rethymnon.

Tombazis, while sailing along the south coast out of Sfakia and witnessing this latest destruction of the province, realized there was little more he could do to unify the Cretans and provide them with the leadership needed to stop Hussein' forces. He announced his resignation, urging the rebels to set aside their differences, stop their infighting, and continue with their struggle. He promised that he would encourage the authorities on the mainland to offer them more support than they had received up to that point. With Tombazis' departure, the 1821 uprising had almost run its course.

However, there was one more area that Hussein had not yet brought under control: the Kissamos and Selino districts in the far west of the island. He issued an offer of a general amnesty to all Christians, provided that they submit to his rule, but he was not prepared to wait for a reply. His troops had already advanced into Kissamos and Selino, meeting no resistance on the way and chasing all the inhabitants south. Their pursuit of the fleeing populace ended in tragedy on the 16th of April when more than 600 women and children were massacred on the small island of Elafonissos, off the southwest tip of Crete, after they had waded across the shallows to evade the troops.

This was not the only large-scale massacre to take place in this area. Many of those who were trying to escape by boat to Kythera, other islands and the Peloponnese were attacked by Turko-Egyptian ships patrolling the south-western seas. Many of their boats were captured or sunk; others

[283] Chatzi Giorgis Kelaidis was from the Mouri branch of the Kelaidis family, which is why he was known as Mouriotis. He initially fought with Alexander Ypsilantis at Dragashani in Wallachia in June 1821, then travelled to the island of Samos, where he fought against the Turks who were attempting to capture the island. Afterwards, he recruited a number of volunteers and sailed to Crete to participate in the uprising. He fought in the east of the island, but returned to Sfakia following Hussein's successful campaign there. Kelaidis (2007), p. 162.

that sought shelter near the coast were attacked and killed by the Muslim Cretans of Selino, who had scores to settle and were merciless. The Cretan historian Psilakis estimates that more than 1,500 people perished in this way along the coast between Tripiti and Kissamos,[284] many of them Sfakians or refugee families. Others were seized by the Turks and either sold, ransomed, or exchanged for captured Turkish families.

By May 1824, the uprising in Crete had essentially been suppressed, and Hussein was free to redeploy some of his Egyptian forces on the mainland. By now some 60,000 Cretans[285] had died as a result of the conflict, while another 60,000 had left Crete[286] for the Peloponnese and nearby islands, some in boats chartered with Sfakian money, to escape from the killing, slavery and starvation. Many of those with families who had remained behind took up Hussein's offer of an amnesty and returned to their villages to rebuild their houses and cultivate the land again in order to feed their starving dependents. Soon afterwards Hussein was replaced by Mustafa Naili Pasha, an Albanian who had been raised in Egypt and who was to play a significant role in Crete's history over the next forty years.

But those with no families to look after continued to fight the oppressors – Egyptians, Albanians, Turks and Muslim Cretans. The spectre of the *Hainides* re-emerged, and countless Muslim Cretan families lived in fear of the nightly visits of avenging Cretans. These *Hainides* included a band led by Manousakis (Manousos Mavropateros) from Askifou and other Sfakians, such as Stratis Deligiannakis from Asfendou, and Giorgis and Androulis Tsoutsounides from Anopoli. Small groups of rebels continued to operate around the island, ambushing passing army convoys or attacking small, isolated settlements, primarily to acquire arms, ammunition and food supplies.

The Cretans resumed acts of piracy against their enemies with great zeal. Many either bought or, more often, seized Turkish boats for this purpose. They were based on the islands of Kasos and Karpathos to the northeast of Crete, and Kythera to the northwest, from where they ruthlessly attacked Turkish and Egyptian ships, as well as those whose governments supported the Turks, such as Algeria and Austria. Hussein feared that these islands would also be used by Cretan pirates and the very active Greek fleet to attack his lines of supply, so he destroyed Kasos in June 1824, and left behind an army to secure the island and deprive the Cretan rebels of a secure base.

Many of the Cretans who had escaped now joined the Greek forces fighting the Turks on the mainland; others organized the delivery of supplies to those who continued fighting on Crete. It was from these displaced

[284] V. Psilakis (1970 [1906]), Vol. 3, p. 419.
[285] Papadopetrakis (1971 [1888]), pp. 445-446.
[286] Kriaris (1902), p. 71.

Cretans that a new initiative arose which revived the rebellion and gave some hope to those who had capitulated to the Turks on the island.

The fifth year of the uprising: the Gramvousa years

The Cretans on the Greek mainland wanted to bring the struggle against the Turks back to Crete, but they were short of resources, organizational skills and leaders. Eventually they reached consensus amongst themselves, and the mainland Greek government agreed to provide support and financial assistance to take the fortified island of Gramvousa, which was very useful for monitoring and controlling the movements of enemy vessels. The Cretans' plan was to capture Gramvousa and establish it as a base for raids against the Turks, and eventually as a springboard for a full attack with the goal of retaking the entire island.

As we saw earlier, the Turks kept a strong garrison at the Gramvousa fort and had been able to defend it successfully. In late July 1825, Sfakian refugees on Antikythera, 22 nautical miles northwest of Gramvousa off the southeastern tip of the Peloponnese, received information that the fort was only lightly manned, and they urged the Cretans in the Peloponnese to take advantage of this opportunity. A force of 700 Cretan fighters and 13 boats soon gathered at Nafplion, on the northeastern coast of the Peloponnese, with the intention of sailing to Gramvousa. The organizers of this expedition did not inform the Sfakians of their plan, suspecting that they would want to assume the leadership, as they had done in the past. The fleet picked up a further 150 Cretans further south along the coast at Monemvasia, then sailed to Antikythira, where they finally invited the Sfakians to participate in the attack. Incensed at not having been informed earlier, the Sfakians replied that they were not ready but would join in soon. However, they had no intention of following somebody else's battle plan; they were going to show the others what Sfakians could achieve on their own!

Fifteen hardened Sfakian fighters[287] manned a large rowing boat and headed for Gramvousa after the Cretan fleet had departed. An overnight storm forced the Cretan fleet off course, but the Sfakians were able to reach Gramvousa before daybreak. Pretending to be Turks, they managed to deceive the Turkish commander into believing that they were the relief guards he was expecting, and soon they captured the lightly protected fort,

[287] They were: Anagnostis Panagiotou, one of the *Kapetanioi* in the 1821 uprising; Anagnostis Psaroudakis, a founding member of the *Kangelaria*; Pavlos and Ioannis Kriaras, Andreas Pachinakis, Manousos Kouletos, and Ioannis Seimenis, all from Anopoli; Ioannis Roukounas from Askifou; brothers Manousos and Andreas Foundoulakis from Komitades; Emmanouil Vratsolis, the owner of the boat; and A. Toumbas, I. Tsilimpinis, G. Pertsoulinakis and N. Verikakis.

only having to kill one Turk in the process.[288] At daybreak, when the Cretan fleet appeared, the Sfakians fired the fort's guns in salute. The other Cretans were confused and were reluctant to approach the island until the Sfakians sent out their own boat to inform them that they had already seized the fort. Although they were upset that the Sfakians had outmanoeuvred them, everyone was euphoric about their achievement in gaining a fortified base to use in their struggle against the Turks.

Some of the Cretan boats that had been blown off course landed further south at Schinias Bay, just north of Falasarna. Three hundred rebels, under the leadership of Dimitrios Kourmoulis, decided to disembark and proceed east to prevent any Turkish troops from coming to the assistance of those on Gramvousa. On their way they learned that the fort at Kastelli was lightly guarded, so they changed their plan and were able to capture it with ease. However, they abandoned the fort a few days later when they learned that a 2,000-strong Turkish contingent from Chania was heading their way.

News of the capture of Gramvousa spread quickly throughout the island, giving hope to all those who were still suffering under Hussein's rule. Many of them decided to join the rebels on Gramvousa, including some Sfakians whose boats had been roaming the seas attacking enemy ships. However, the brave and cunning achievement of the 15 Sfakians, instead of providing encouragement for future action, caused a further escalation of tensions between Sfakians and other Cretans. One evening soon after Gramvousa was captured, 300 rebels who had been drinking heavily surrounded a house inside the fort where 23 Sfakians were staying. One of the Sfakians who had helped take the fort, N. Verikakis, ventured out to see why there was such a large gathering, and during subsequent verbal exchanges he was shot. The other Sfakians locked themselves inside the house. They were eventually forced to come out, surrender their arms, and leave the island aboard a Sfakian boat.[289]

Once these 22 men arrived in Sfakia with the news of this incident, hatred against those involved, as well as bitterness at their ingratitude, pushed the Sfakians to seek revenge for this grave insult. Civil war was the last thing that Crete needed at this critical juncture. Amongst the leaders on Gramvousa was the cleric and respected political figure Neophytos Oikonomou; he had participated in the earlier provisional government, and now took the initiative to defuse the explosive situation. He convinced the *Kapetanioi* and other leading figures on Gramvousa of the danger created by the thoughtless actions of the drunken rebels, and persuaded them to send a deputation to Sfakia to seek their forgiveness. Two *Kapetanioi* and two clerics, including Oikonomou, travelled to Sfakia, where they gave back the Sfakians' weapons and invited them to return to Gramvousa, but the

[288] Mourellos (1931-4), pp. 861-874; Psilakis (1907 [1906]), Vol. 3, pp. 431-435.
[289] Mourellos (1931-4), pp. 880, 881.

Sfakians were unyielding. They were offered two leadership positions in the provisional government on Gramvousa but turned this down. Andreas Kriaras from Anopoli responded: "I refuse to cooperate with criminals." For the rest of the uprising, the Sfakians stayed away from Gramvousa.

The Turks, fully aware of these events, tried to persuade the Sfakians to come over to their side, but their approaches were rejected. The Sfakians continued their guerrilla warfare against the Turks and Egyptians, but their enthusiasm and commitment to the uprising had significantly diminished.

On Gramvousa, the new permanent residents made long-term preparations, sending delegations to the provisional government on the Greek mainland, establishing a church, and opening a school for the children sheltering there. More rebel bands popped up across Crete, engaging in guerrilla tactics against the Muslim Cretans and the Turkish and Egyptian forces. Mustafa Pasha, the overall commander of the combined Turkish-Egyptian forces on the island, remained in the west of the island in an attempt to control rebel activities emanating from Apokoronas and Gramvousa. His forces attacked a sizeable group of Gramvousan rebels who were camped across from the fort at Tigani and killed a number of them, but he did not have enough resources to lay siege to the fort. Life on Gramvousa became difficult due to the large number of people living there, food shortages, and the lack of assistance from mainland Greece. Raids on nearby areas of the island for supplies were not confined to Muslim Cretan targets, thus creating antagonism between Gramvousans and other Cretans.

The island of Gramvousa with its Venetian era fort at the top

The sixth year of the uprising: Sfakians withdraw from the battlefront

Mustafa was quite different from his predecessor: he was prepared to take a more conciliatory approach, and he also issued firm orders, especially to the Muslim Cretans, not to harass the Christians. However, the Sfakians were a perpetual threat, and he was determined to take a firm line with them. So Mustafa gathered an army of about 7,000 men in Apokoronas and made known his intention to invade Sfakia if he was unable to negotiate a treaty to end the Sfakians' attacks against his troops and gain their acceptance of Ottoman rule. After lengthy discussions and assurances of their safety received through a Sfakian intermediary, a number of Sfakian leaders – Giorgios Morakis, the Protopapas[290] of Sfakia, Roussos Vourdoumbas, and a few others – met Mustafa at Nipos in Apokoronas on the 21st of February, 1826. Although some historians[291] state that Mustafa arrested them immediately and transported them to Chania as prisoners, the French Consul in Chania reported[292] that at this meeting the Sfakians agreed to Mustafa's terms and were allowed to leave.

On the 17th of April, Mustafa sought a further meeting with the Sfakians, during which he arrested all of them and threw them in jail in Chania; the French Consul attributed this action to the Sfakians not fulfilling their part of the agreement. Vourdoumbas and nine others were kept in prison and tortured. A year later their attempt to escape went wrong, with only Protopapas Morakis managing to get away; the rest were injured in a fall and were thrown back into jail, where they were to stay until the end of the uprising in 1830. Sfakia was spared an invasion by Mustafa's troops; but with its leadership significantly diminished, and feeling isolated from other Cretans, given their poor relationship with the Gramvousans, it seemed that Sfakia was not to play any further significant role in the struggle.

Meanwhile, on Gramvousa the rebels had formed a governing committee to formalize and coordinate attacks throughout Crete and to re-establish links with the provisional government on the mainland. Fighters arrived on Gramvousa from their refuges around mainland Greece, as did small numbers of mainland Greeks. With this boost in numbers, they were able to attack the enemy further afield on the island, with mixed results.

By the end of the year, the governing committee realized that the Sfakians' withdrawal from the uprising was harming the general effort, so they asked them to reconsider their stance. The wording of their letter was bound to be seen as a further insult by the proud Sfakians:[293]

---

[290] Chief priest of the district.

[291] Papadopetrakis (1970 [1888]), p. 364; Psilakis (1907 [1906]), Vol. 3, p. 439

[292] Mourellos (1931-4), pp. 906-908

[293] Ibid., p. 912.

> Do not allow the people and the nation to criticize you as being the reason for their misfortunes [by not continuing to fight the enemy], and consider all your great achievements and the privileges that you have gained and which you risk losing now.

It finished with a threat:

> If within 30 days you do not take action in support of the nation in coordination with us ...you will lose all rights that the nation has bestowed upon you, and you will be considered enemies of the nation.

The letter was torn to pieces by the Sfakian leaders. A further approach was made by the government of mainland Greece in an attempt to appeal to the Sfakians' better instincts, encourage them to put all differences behind them, and fight the common enemy together, but this did not achieve the desired result.

The seventh year of the uprising: Sfakia is threatened again

In the meantime, it looked like the uprising on the mainland was about to be quashed by the newly arrived Egyptian forces under the command of Ibrahim Pasha, son of Mehmed Pasha of Egypt, who in early 1825 had transported some 10,000 infantrymen and 1,000 cavalry across to the mainland from Crete. The experienced Egyptian forces soon had the undisciplined Greek rebel bands on the run in the Peloponnese, and by June 1827, after prolonged sieges, the Egyptians took Messolonghi and Athens. The three Great Powers, Britain, France and Russia, had been negotiating unsuccessfully with the Sultan for an end to the fighting in Greece and the establishment of a new state. When they saw that the revolution was going to collapse, they decided to intervene on the side of the Greeks (in an agreement known as the Treaty of London, signed on the 6th of July, 1827). The combined fleets of England, France and Russia imposed a blockade around Greece to prevent the movement of the Turko-Egyptian forces, and they surrounded the Turko-Egyptian fleet that was based at Navarino (today's Pilos) in the southwest corner of the Peloponnese, which was being used as naval and supply centre. Their objective was to negotiate the withdrawal of Ottoman forces from Greece, but the Egyptians fired at the boat carrying the negotiating party on the 20th of October, which started a battle that by the end of the day saw the entire Turko-Egyptian fleet lying at the bottom of the bay. This resulted in the Great Powers' troops landing in Greece and eventually bringing the fighting to an end.

Now a lengthy negotiating process started to establish the borders of the new state. For Crete the implications were twofold. First, Greek troops became available to assist them in their struggle against the Turks. At the same time, there was a new urgency imposed upon the Cretans to prove to the Great Powers that their uprising was a part of the overall Greek revolution, and that the new state had to incorporate Crete.

On Gramvousa, the governing committee had only one vessel at its disposal to secure supplies through raids along the coast of Crete. They managed to buy another boat with money raised from the sale of gold and silver church treasures that had been brought there for safekeeping. Soon Greek pirate boats turned up, and some of the rebels on Gramvousa joined them, returning laden with their share of loot, which encouraged others to do likewise and enrich themselves. The committee was worried about the reaction of the foreign powers whose merchant vessels were being attacked, and felt that these activities worked against the interests of the uprising. Their requests to the mainland Greek government to send a naval vessel to thwart the pirates went unanswered. After the battle at Navarino, the admirals of the three Great Powers demanded that the Greek government put an end to the piracy based at Gramvousa. It, in turn, sent a mere directive to Gramvousa to curtail these activities, but the committee was powerless to act since most of its men were engaged in fighting elsewhere in Crete.

Mustafa could see that control of Gramvousa was the key to suppressing the uprising in Crete. But before tackling this, he had to ensure that Sfakia would not create problems, as the Sfakians were still active in Apokoronas despite their previous assurances of loyalty. On the 25th of May 1827, 10,000 of Mustafa's men set off for the pass at Katre, while another 5,000 armed men proceeded to Argyroupolis, all heading for Askifou. Once there, he demanded that the Sfakians meet him to surrender their weapons and declare their submission to his rule. The Sfakians were few in number, with no allies, and had very little ammunition. They had sent their families into the high mountains for safety and could do nothing other than engage in protracted negotiations with Mustafa; some say these lasted a whole month. Mustafa's army eventually left Askifou without doing any harm to the Sfakians. Some historians speculate that Mustafa was waiting for his Egyptian fleet to reach the shores of Sfakia and thus prevent the Sfakians from escaping via the sea, but the fleet never turned up, as it was engaged in battle with Greek ships on the north of the island.[294]

More Cretan fighters returned from the mainland, and the campaign against the Turks spread to the east, but their success was limited, primarily due to poorly coordinated actions and the lack of leadership. Some fighters, after the bitter experience of these battles, returned to mainland Greece or retreated to the safety of Gramvousa. The absence of the experienced

[294] Papadopetrakis (1970 [1888]), pp. 374-375; V. Psilakis (1970 [1906]), Vol. 4, p. 9.

Sfakians was being felt on most fronts.

It was only in December 1827 that the Sfakians showed they had not totally abandoned their fellow Cretans. A 3,000-strong Turko-Egyptian contingent from Heraklion engaged the rebels at Mochos, just south of Malia, and soundly defeated them. The rebels fled in all directions, leaving behind more than 200 dead. A group of rebels from Gramvousa and the west, including a few Sfakians who had joined them for the plunder, were chased south by the troops. They found themselves trapped on the southwestern slopes of Mount Ida in freezing weather, surrounded by large numbers of armed Muslim Cretans, with little food or ammunition. In desperation, they sought help from Sfakia, pointing out that there were Sfakians amongst them. Andreas Manouselis from Kallikratis and Gero-Christodoulos from Askifou led about 200 Sfakians in snowy conditions along 50 km of treacherous mountain tracks to where the rebels were pinned down. Surprisingly, as they approached, the Muslim Cretans withdrew – it seems they were not prepared to fight on two fronts, and the fearsome Sfakians were now on their rear flank. This intervention not only saved many rebels from certain death, but also indicated that the Sfakians were willing to re-establish their relationship with the other rebel factions.[295] Sfakia soon received a shipment of ammunition from Gramvousa, which reinforced this bond.

The eighth year of the uprising: Gramvousa under siege by the allies; the Frangokastello battle

As fate would have it, on the 5th of January 1828, there were two unexpected arrivals on Gramvousa. One was Hatzi-Michalis Dalianis, a *Kapetanios* from Epirus in northern Greece, which at the time was still under Turkish control. He was an experienced combatant and leader, having fought in a number of campaigns against the Turks. He arrived with 600 men and 100 cavalry to fight against the Turks in Crete, and to the surprise and displeasure of all on Gramvousa, he wanted to launch his campaign from Sfakia.

On the same day, a squadron of six British naval vessels and two French corvettes under the command of Commodore Sir Thomas Staines arrived off Gramvousa to tackle piracy. Aboard HMS Cambrian was a Greek government representative, Alexandros Mavrokordatos. In the harbour were eight pirate boats as well as two merchant vessels captured by the pirates. Mavrokordatos informed the governing committee that they had to relinquish all the pirate ships, as well as the two captured vessels, all looted goods, and 14 criminals who he believed were on the island. The committee were quite happy to get rid of the pirates, but they were not willing to hand

[295] Mourellos (1931-4), pp. 966-971.

over the 14 men, as they considered them crucial in the fight against the Turks.

Before Mavrokordatos had the opportunity to report back to Commodore Staines, there was a huge explosion in the harbour: one of the pirate ships had been blown up by accident while Dalianis' men were secretly unloading the ammunition stored on board. The British fleet, thinking that the rebels were shooting at them, responded with cannon fire, upped anchor, and sailed to the other side of the island. Eventually Mavrokordatos returned to HMS Cambrian and explained that the Gramvousans were willing to surrender the pirate ships, but that the criminals were not on the island. Staines was unhappy with this response and sent a message ordering the rebels to vacate the fort and for Dalianis and his men to leave the island. He then shelled the fort and the pirate ships for the rest of the day; not a single pirate ship was hit,[296] but in the process HMS Isis, Staines' flagship, managed to crash into HMS Cambrian and sink it!

The next day, Staines sent a detachment to take control of the fort. Although piracy had been eliminated on Gramvousa, a number of issues concerning control of the fort, the number of rebels allowed to remain there, and the role and size of the French contingent that was to be stationed there remained unresolved for quite some time. However, the island would continue to be used as a refuge and staging post for Greek and Cretan fighters throughout the uprising.

Dalianis and his troops were stranded for more than a month on Gramvousa, as there was a shortage of small vessels that could land in Sfakia. Eventually some of his men were taken to Agia Roumeli, while his cavalry landed at Loutro. The rest waited on Gramvousa for the supplies and ammunition promised by the mainland government, but by the beginning of March Dalianis had grown impatient and decided to depart with their meagre supplies for Frangokastello, where he was joined by the others.

Mustafa was well aware of all these movements and assembled his own troops at Zouridi and Agouseliana, southwest of Rethymnon, and Vrises. From there he wrote to the Sfakians asking whether they were going to ally themselves with the newcomers from the mainland or stay loyal to him. Their answer was that the elders of Sfakia were considering the matter and would reply soon; Mustafa understood from this that they were playing for time.

Dalianis met with the Sfakian leaders and *Kapetanioi* to determine how

[296] There is some confusion about the exact number of vessels involved and whether any of them were hit. The above description of events comes from Mourellos (1931-4, pp. 982-985). Detorakis (1994, p. 315) writes that the pirate ships were sunk, Psilakis is silent on the matter, while Trikoupis (1994, Vol. 4, p. 230) writes that there were 14 boats, 7 of which were captured and taken to Malta. The one certain detail, though, is that HMS Cambrian was sunk by HMS Isis.

they could assist him with supplies and ammunition; he also wrote to the mainland government urgently seeking money and supplies. The Sfakians helped him the best they could, given their own dismal situation, but in doing so they made enemies with the Cretans whose animals they stole to feed Dalianis' army.

By the end of April, with no help forthcoming from the mainland, Dalianis decided to leave Crete, and it was only on the insistence of the Sfakians and leaders from Messara and Amari that he stayed. Dalianis received a letter from Mustafa giving him 10 days to quit Crete or have his army destroyed. Mustafa knew about Dalianis' supply problems and offered free transport for him and his troops to the mainland if they came to Chania. Dalianis' reply was quite brief: "I came to Crete to fight Turks with my brave men, and wherever God wills, let him give us victory."

Dalianis headed for Rethymnon with most of his troops, accompanied by Sfakians led by Stratis Deligiannakis from Asfendou, Petros Manouselis from Kallikratis, and Anagnostis Manousogiannakis from Imbros, as well as Giorgos Tsouderos and his men from the Agios Vasilios district further to the east. They encountered the Turks at Prines, just west of Rethymnon, and soon put them to flight. The rebels returned to Frangokastello euphoric at their easy victory, bringing with them a large flock of animals they had rounded up on their way to supplement their meagre food supplies.

Mustafa, having heard about his troops' disastrous defeat, set off for Sfakia with 8,000 men via Askifou, Asfendou and Kallikratis; they camped at the bottom of the Kallikratis gorge for two days. The Sfakians discussed with Dalianis what tactics to adopt against the Turkish advance. Dalianis wanted to engage with them on the Frangokastello plain, using the Venetian fort as his base. The Sfakians strongly opposed this strategy and recommended that he take his troops to higher ground from where he could fight more effectively, rather than leave them open to easy attack by the more numerous and better equipped enemy, but Dalianis insisted on his own tactics. Most of the Sfakians, insulted by his insinuations that they were afraid to fight the Turks, took to the higher ground to watch the ensuing battle. Only a small band of 60 Sfakians under Stratis Deligiannakis decided to remain with him. Deligiannakis said to him, frankly: "This is crazy, you are endangering so many lives, but I came to join you to show you that I am not afraid, although I know that we will all die."[297]

On the 18th of May the Turks attacked the ill-defended fort, and by the end of the day Dalianis and 385 of his men lay dead, while the Turks lost over 800 men. Deligiannakis' Sfakians and a few other Greek fighters continued shooting from inside the fort over the next few days, despite continued shelling, lack of food and water, and the stench of rotting corpses left lying in the open. Mustafa, concerned about the prolonged engagement

[297] Mourellos (1931-4) p.1014

and the menace of Sfakian snipers on the surrounding peaks, agreed to a truce, and his troops departed on the 28th. A local nun named Magdalene, moved by the sight of all the dead fighters – Greek, Turkish and Egyptian – together with some locals deposited all the corpses in deep crevasses along the rocky shore, as there was no priest available and no possibility of proper burials.[298]

The fort at Frangokastello, the location of the tragic battle of Hatzi-Michalis Dalianis

Mustafa's plan was to make for Agios Vasilios and Rethymnon via the narrow pass where the Kotsifou river runs down towards Plakias. But shadowing them along higher ground were 600 Sfakians, who were keen to avenge the death of Dalianis and his troops and to show Mustafa that they were still a force to be reckoned with. Their first confrontation took place just beyond Skaloti at a location known as Akastare. The Sfakians had to pull back in the face of the enemy's superior numbers, but the situation quickly changed when they set a fire which, assisted by a strong wind, raced towards the Turks. The rebels attacked the rear-guard of the fleeing

[298] Locals and many visitors talk of seeing the ghosts of these dead soldiers marching over the rising mist early in the morning on the anniversary of their death. The legend is that their souls, not having received a proper burial, revisit the location of their tragic demise. Scientists have tried to explain this phenomenon, but the mystery and the legend still remain. One needs to be at the location well before dawn to see the *Drosoulites*, as they are known, and not on the 18th of May (which is the date from the old Julian calendar) but on the 31st of May. The name *Drosoulites* or *Drositses* comes from the word for dew drops seen on the grass in the early morning in May.

troops near Korakas beach at Kato Rodakino, and then pursued them to the Kotsifou Gorge.

Armed men from Agios Vasilios were waiting in ambush further north, but they were fearful because of Mustafa's past threats and his large army, and decided at the last minute to leave before his troops arrived. At a place known as Halara of Agios Antonios, the Sfakians attacked the enemy again. By the end of the day, the bodies of more than 1,900 Turks and Egyptians were strewn from Rodakino to Kanevos, the narrowest part of the gorge. The slaughter would have continued, but the Sfakians were keen to grab as many supplies as possible and return to their undefended families in Sfakia. The remnants of Mustafa's troops eventually regrouped at Kali Sykia before straggling back to Rethymnon and Chania. This was one of the biggest defeats suffered by any occupying force in Crete's history, and Mustafa's entire army could have been massacred if the fighters from Agios Vasilios had joined them in battle.

While the uprising in Crete was intensifying again, the mainland government was working with the Great Powers to reach an agreement with the Sultan about establishing a Greek state. The President of the new National Assembly of Greece, Capodistrias, who became Greece's first Prime Minister in 1830, sent the German Baron Rheineck as his representative to Crete in June 1828, recommending that the Cretans stop fighting the Turks and Egyptians, as this was causing problems in the negotiations. The Sfakians and other Cretan leaders rejected this request outright and intensified their efforts. Soon they had pinned down the Ottoman troops within the walls of the three big towns, and the rest of the island was again under the control of rebel bands, many of them led by well-known Sfakian *Kapetanioi*. A large rebel detachment took control of the Sitia district in the east, and the Turks and Muslim Cretans sought refuge in local forts, in Ierapetra, and on the island of Spinalonga. At the same time there were terrible retributions exacted against Cretans, with hundreds being massacred in the streets of Heraklion and Chania.

This resulted in the Europeans taking a renewed interest in the Cretan struggle, and a fleet of British and French vessels arrived at Souda Bay in October 1828. Their Commander, Sir Frederick Lewis Maitland, put pressure on the Egyptian authorities to bring those who were carrying out the massacres under control. He spent most of the winter off the coast of Crete on HMS Wellesley endeavouring to arrange an armistice, with no obvious results.[299]

[299] He certainly was not a philhellene, going by his writings after the armistice negotiations in Crete, in which he refers to the Turks as "manly, straightforward, and sincere", whereas he considers the Greeks to be "perfidious, ferocious, and cruel".

The last two years of the uprising, and its sudden end in 1830

Throughout the year battles flared throughout the island, and practically all rural areas came under the control of the rebels, while the Turks, Muslim Cretans and Egyptians barricaded themselves inside the walls of Chania, Rethymnon and Heraklion. Once again the struggle had reached a stalemate. Rheineck was replaced as Capodistria's representative in early 1829 by an Englishman, who in turn was replaced at the end of the year by the Cretan Nicolaos Renieris.

Negotiations about creating the new Greek state were not progressing well. After the Treaty of London, the British position changed with the death of the British Prime Minister George Canning in 1827; he was succeeded by the Duke of Wellington, who took the completely opposite line in his dealings with the Sultan. Britain now wanted a strong Ottoman Empire as a bulwark against the threat emerging from a more aggressive Russia. Sultan Mahmud, encouraged by Wellington's support, intensified hostilities in Greece and abrogated an earlier treaty with the Russians. The Russians declared war on the Ottoman Empire and soon crossed the Danube; not long after they reached Adrianople, Russian cannons could be heard in Constantinople. The Sultan quickly signed a treaty with the Russians in September 1829, but the Russians then became anxious about the possibility of the Ottoman Empire disintegrating and large parts of it being shared out between Britain and France. So the new Russian position was to maintain the status quo in the Ottoman Empire.

These developments were not promising for the Greek President or the Cretans. The political manoeuvring and protracted negotiations between Britain, France and Russia concluded in the London Protocol of February 3rd, 1830, which declared Greece to be an independent state and monarchy, with the three Great Powers as guarantors. Greece's northern border was to run from Thermopiles in the east to the Acheloos river in the west, resulting in a state that consisted of only the lower portion of the mainland, the Peloponnese, Evia, and the Cyclades islands. Crete had been left out of the protocol! Greeks and Cretans alike rejected this. The issue of the Greek border was eventually renegotiated in 1832 when the Sultan agreed to a frontier running along a line from Volos to Arta. Again, Crete was not included.

Cretans' protestations to the Great Powers and to President Capodistrias were in vain. They lobbied influential philhellenes in Britain and the British parliament in order to keep alive the debate about the future of Crete, but these efforts were not sufficient to make Wellington change his position. The man chosen as future King of Greece, German Prince Leopold, wrote to Wellington expressing his strong disagreement about the exclusion of

Crete from the new Greek state, and he eventually refused to accept the role of King in protest. A French naval ship carrying the French ambassador arrived in Chania, and its commander instruct the Cretan fighters to cease hostilities and obey the Sultan's representatives. Their reception was not very cordial. On the 5th of June 1830, three more naval vessels from the Great Powers arrived at Heraklion to inform the Cretans and Turks about the terms of the ceasefire, and the Cretan Assembly had no option but to agree to them.

Thus ended a tragic but heroic chapter in the history of Crete. A new chapter was to open soon, just as tragic and heroic as the ones before it, in which the involvement and interference of the Great Powers continued to influence the future of Crete.

A Sfakian perspective on the collapse of the uprising

Cretans in general felt that mainland Greeks had not assisted them enough against the much larger Turkish military forces. They were especially bitter towards wealthy Greek sea captains, many of whom saw the rebellion as an impediment to their commercial activities and demanded significant payment for their help.

But although such issues contributed to the failure of the Cretan uprising, they were minor in comparison to the impact that disagreements and mistrust amongst Cretans themselves had on the outcome. Initially, there was a consensus that only the Sfakians were well enough prepared and capable of leading the struggle; this was reflected in the decision to appoint Sfakians to a majority of the top military positions. It became quite clear to everyone that it was mainly due to the Sfakians' leadership and experience, and the nucleus of Sfakian fighters, that they were able to win in battle. The first leader of the provisional government, Afendoulis, saw this as a threat to his own authority and personal ambitions, so he appointed less-experienced Cretans to leadership positions, which resulted in discord over tactics, a number of defeats in the field, heated arguments about individual contributions, and accusations between the various factions about their true objectives. Many Sfakians felt betrayed by this development, and suspicion between the Sfakians and other Cretans increased. A variety of incidents during the uprising reinforced their feeling of betrayal, especially the events in March 1824 when the Sfakians were left to face the massive Turko-Egyptian army alone as it invaded Sfakia, even while they were providing shelter to almost 30,000 refugees from other parts of the island.

Before the uprising, the Sfakians were much better off than other Cretans; they had gained significant wealth from their maritime activities and enjoyed specific freedoms that others had not been granted. In addition, no Turks or Muslim Cretans were present in their area. However, Sfakians were prepared to risk all those advantages in order to end the oppression of Cretans throughout the island and win freedom for Crete.

Sfakians made up only about 5% of the Christian population of Crete, but their contribution to the uprising was enormous and quite disproportionate to their numbers. They contributed funding for weapons and food, provided boats to transport refugees and supplies, gave sanctuary to fleeing families, and offered up their bravest men to fight and die for the liberation of all areas of the island – 9 of the 12 Sfakian *Kapetanioi* lost their lives fighting in districts outside Sfakia. After all these sacrifices, it is understandable that they felt betrayed and insulted when their efforts were undermined and their motives questioned.

XIII. Egyptian and Ottoman rule – 1830 to 1866

Crete under Egyptian rule; the Mournies movement

The London Protocol of February 1830 declared Greece to be an independent state under the guarantee of the three Great Powers, but the new state did not include Crete. Instead, the protocol granted the island to the Governor of Egypt, Mehmed Ali Pasha, for services he had provided to the Ottoman Sultan during the rebellions in the Peloponnese and Crete (and as compensation for the loss of his entire fleet at Navarino). Thus Crete now came under the control of Egypt, which was still under the suzerainty of Sultan Mahmud II.

Mehmed Ali's power and success on the battlefield had led him to aspire to overthrow the Sultan and rule over the entire Ottoman Empire himself. The Great Powers wished to avoid war between the two and came to play various roles in this drama. The French were co-operating with Mehmed Ali over their common interests in the north of Africa. The British under Wellington wanted a strong Ottoman Empire to contain the ambitions of the Russians, and they saw an alliance between the French and Mehmed Ali as fatal to the Empire. Finally, the Russians, who had entered into a treaty with the Sultan at the end of the 1828-1829 war, wanted to ensure that the Empire was not going to be divided up between the other powers.

The Sultan was not able to dislodge Mehmed Ali from Crete – and the Great Powers were more interested in avoiding war between him and the Sultan, which is why they had agreed to grant him control of Crete. This did not satisfy Mehmed Ali, who built a new fleet, and in November 1831 invaded Syria, which was then under the control of the Sultan, creating a new international crisis. The Sultan soon had to turn to the Russians for help; they sent their fleet and troops, but the British, fearing an alliance between the Sultan and the Tsar, protested strongly. They negotiated terms for Mehmed Ali to withdraw from the areas of the Ottoman Empire he had conquered, and in exchange conceded Syria, including Damascus, Tripoli and other major towns in the area to him.

Mehmed Ali appointed Mustafa Pasha, who had been in charge of the combined Turkish-Egyptian troops in Crete since 1825, as Governor of Crete, with instructions to introduce laws and controls that would pacify the locals and avoid persecution of the Christian population so as not to provide the Great Powers with a reason for giving Crete back to the Sultan. Mustafa's troops were predominantly Egyptian and Albanian, which antagonized the Turks and Muslim Cretans on the island, many of whom sided with the Orthodox Cretans in their complaints against the general treatment of the island's population. Many Muslim Cretans departed for Asia Minor to be under the Sultan's protection, while Mustafa himself sent others into exile on suspicion that they were undermining his authority and siding with the Sultan. Orthodox Cretans also left the island with their families and settled in towns on the eastern coast of the Peloponnese and on nearby Greek islands. Gramvousa was returned to Mustafa by the European Powers in January 1832, after it changed hands twice between the allies who had initially occupied it in 1830.[300]

Mustafa set up a revised regional administration which included both Christian and Muslim representatives, but this was not proportional and thus usually resulted in Christians being unable to protect and promote their interests. There were some improvements in infrastructure, education and public health under the Egyptian regime, but substantial increases in taxes were levied to pay for these. Sfakia appears to have attracted special attention when a new tax was imposed on alcohol production, which Sfakians had previously been exempt from; a contemporary report indicates that the authorities were having problems gathering the relevant information from Sfakia needed to levy the tax.[301]

Although these changes gave the appearance of significant improvements in comparison with the previous Turkish regime, in reality Mehmed Ali took advantage of his power to exploit opportunities for his own personal benefit. Cretans who had escaped to the mainland and now returned as Greek citizens found that they could not reclaim ownership of their properties or sell them without first renouncing their Greek citizenship. Turks who had moved to Asia Minor also lost their property rights. All proceeds from these confiscated properties ended up in Mehmed Ali's personal coffers. But the island's population was exhausted and was not prepared to undertake another uprising; the Sfakians continued to keep to themselves and were unwilling to initiate any action against the new ruler.

The Sfakian historian Papadopetrakis writes that the British Commander-in-Chief of the Mediterranean Fleet,[302] acting on behalf of the three Great Powers, proposed that Sfakia should become an autonomous district

[300] V. Psilakis (1970 [1906]), Vol. 4, pp. 90-91.
[301] Mourellos (1950), pp. 858, 861.
[302] Admiral Sir Pulteney Malcolm, Commander-in-Chief of the Mediterranean Fleet.

within Crete, with full recognition by the Governor of Egypt and under the guarantee of the three Powers; the intention was to ensure that the Sfakians would not incite any further rebellions in Crete. The Sfakians, according to the same account, rejected this proposal outright, so the Admiral boarded his ship in Loutro and sailed off.[303]

In September 1833, a meeting was organised at Mournies, just outside Chania, involving representatives mostly from the western and central parts of the island, to draw up a document to present to the guarantor powers and the Sultan, airing their grievances against the Egyptian administration. About 7,000 Cretans, including some Muslim Cretans, attended the meeting; all of them were unarmed, in accordance with the conditions of the peace treaty. (A number of Sfakians under the leadership of Stratis Deligiannakis arrived armed, refused to leave their weapons outside, and were turned away.) By September 20th a report was finalized and signed by thousands of citizens, setting out the basis of their grievances and seeking the Great Powers' intervention. The British Admiral, who at the time was stationed at Souda Bay, attended the meeting together with the British Consul to assess the situation, but they proved unwilling to help them. The Cretan historian Mourellos reports that, when the British officials returned to Chania, they told Mustafa that he could take whatever action he wanted to resolve the situation.[304]

Mustafa dispatched troops to Mournies, and they quickly dispersed the gathering, arrested the leaders, and immediately hanged 50 of them. Some of the Muslims attending the meeting were also arrested and sent into exile. The troops pursued the Cretans throughout Apokoronas, arresting and hanging many of them. The governor suspected that the Sfakians were behind the meeting and sent 2,000 troops to the area, under the command of the Albanian Ali Ciazintzi, to arrest and hang the Sfakian leaders. Giazintzi camped at Askifou and invited all the Sfakian leaders to assemble there, saying that he wanted to inform them about the Pasha's latest edicts. The Sfakians, having been warned of his true intentions by the local Ottoman supervisor, who had a good relationship with Sfakians from Kallikratis, arrived in Askifou only two or three at a time, so that Giazintzi did not have the opportunity to arrest all of them at once. After tolerating this ploy for a number of days, Giazintzi arrested 8 of the leaders, and fearing an attack, strangled 7 of them in secret; the last and most popular leader, Androulis Morakis, who was over 100 years old and had fought with Daskalogiannis, was hanged from the plane tree in the centre of Askifou as Gianzintzi was leaving for Apokoronas. The Sfakians followed the departing Egyptian troops with the intention of attacking them at Katre, but by the time they

[303] This story is repeated by V. Psilakis (1970 [1906]), Vol. 4, p. 98, but we have not been able to confirm this from other sources.
[304] Mourellos (1950), Vol. 2, p. 870.

managed to gather their dispersed fighters, most of the Egyptians had made it through the pass. Mustafa's troops continued to arrest and hang suspected leaders in the Apokoronas and Rethymnon districts until the local representatives of the three Great Powers intervened to put an end to this action and thus avert another uprising.

Towards the later part of the decade, Mustafa tried another approach to reduce the threat that the Sfakians posed. He exempted them from the prohibition against transferring property to anyone other than neighbouring landowners, thus hoping to encourage them to move away from rugged and inhospitable Sfakia and settle on better land. The plan was initially quite successful; some of the more influential families left Sfakia, and the hatred that other Cretans felt towards Sfakians increased as a result of this preferential treatment. With the Sfakians becoming substantial property owners as a result of this strategy, it removed some of their enthusiasm for rebellion against Egyptian rule. However, while Mustafa hoped to divide the Sfakians and diminish their threat through this approach,[305] what eventually happened was that the Sfakians, having acquired extensive property holdings elsewhere on the island, especially from Muslim Cretans, urged Orthodox Cretans in these areas to form bases for future revolts, thus creating new "Sfakias" throughout the island! These bases were to play a significant role later on.

In any case, Egyptian rule over Crete was to end soon, as relations between the Sultan and the Governor of Egypt, Mehmed Ali, continued to deteriorate over control of Syria. In 1839 the Sultan invaded Syria, but the result was a disastrous defeat of his army and the embarrassing desertion of his entire fleet to Mehmed in Alexandria. Fearing Russia's intervention, the British pushed for a joint approach with Russia to resolve the precarious situation. The French were unwilling to participate, so an agreement was reached between Britain, Russia and the newly emerging power, Austria, to offer Mehmed Ali terms for his withdrawal from Syria, which he rejected. The allies attacked him by land and sea, and with the assistance of local Arabs succeeded in defeating the Egyptian army. The British fleet then set sail for Alexandria, threatening to shell the Egyptian fleet. Mehmed Ali eventually signed a peace treaty on the 15th of July 1840, in which he agreed to cut the Egyptian armed forces, return the Turkish fleet to the Sultan, abandon his claims over Syria, and withdraw from Crete.

The 1841 uprising; Crete under Ottoman rule again

Although the Turks had regained control of Crete through the 1840 agreement, the handover did not take place until the middle of the next year.

[305] Ibid., pp. 813-814.

The Cretans were very disappointed because the Great Powers once again had ignored their appeals and not seen fit to make them part of the Greek state, something that they had been fighting for since 1821. This provoked Cretans living in mainland Greece to plot another rebellion. By the end of the year, groups of them were in place at various locations around Crete. Their overall leader was Aristides Chairetis, from Anogia, who arrived in Loutro with 65 Cretan fighters; although they were made welcome, they were unpleasantly surprised to find the Sfakians very reluctant to join in the uprising. The Sfakians remembered very clearly how they had been let down on a number of occasions during the unsuccessful 1821 uprising, as well as the bitter infighting for leadership positions and the incident on Gramvousa. Furthermore, they could see that the island was not ready for another insurrection; they were short of weapons and military supplies, funding was non-existent, they lacked political support from external powers, and they knew that British geopolitical interests favoured an Ottoman-controlled Crete.

The Cretans from the mainland were not willing to start an uprising without the support of the Sfakians, since they knew the key role these fighters had always played. During numerous meetings it became clear how strongly the Sfakians resented their fellow Cretans because of their behaviour in the past, and how suspicious they were about other Cretans' willingness to fight the enemy. Mustafa was also aware of these developments and sent a Sfakian intermediary to try to persuade the Sfakians not to join the rebellion. He reported back that the Sfakians, like the rest of the Cretans, were planning to win autonomy for Crete, under the protection of Britain.

Negotiations continued between the rebels and the Sfakians. In February 1841, they signed a remarkable document which recognized the Sfakians' past contributions to the uprisings and set out future standards of conduct towards them. The document noted the sacrifices that the Sfakians had made for the common good, stated that without them nothing would have been achieved, and acknowledged that in the past the rebels had behaved towards them in an ungrateful manner. For their part, the Sfakians declared that they were willing to forget all these injustices provided that the others promised to follow them "till death" and "not abandon them and leave them to fight the Turks alone".[306] This text was signed by some 100 *Kapetanioi* from most parts of Crete. What is remarkable is that the Sfakians demanded a document to be drawn up with such demeaning content, and that the other rebels were willing to sign it in order to secure their participation in the uprising. In April, a similar document was signed by all the island's regional representatives and *Kapetanioi* at a meeting in Vafes in Apokoronas, again recognizing the Sfakians' past contributions and promising, on oath,

[306] Ibid., pp. 900-901.

to fight together until Crete was free, and to ensure the fair distribution of the benefits of nationhood.[307] Following these assurances, the Sfakians agreed to join in the rebellion.

The Cretan leadership held the mistaken view that the British Foreign Secretary was in favour of Crete becoming part of the new Greek state. They sent a deputation to Admiral Stewart, who was in charge of the British naval fleet in Souda Bay, to present their grievances and demand to be freed from Ottoman rule. After protracted discussions about the alternatives – union with Greece, which is what the Cretans aspired to; local autonomy, but under the suzerainty of the Sultan; or becoming a British protectorate, the solution the British were promoting – Stewart asked for a public meeting to hear for himself what the Cretans preferred. The meeting in Vafes was attended by thousands from all over the island. Believing that the British were in favour of Crete joining Greece, and encouraged by Cretans from the mainland, they demanded *Enosis* – union with Greece – stating "that's why we spilled rivers of blood," and they refused to listen to discussions about the other alternatives. The British were very upset by the crowd's behaviour and informed them that union was not possible. Stewart returned to Chania and told Mustafa that he was free to do whatever he believed was appropriate to bring peace and order to the island.

Mustafa ordered the Cretans to disperse and offered an amnesty to all those who had attended the meeting, but they stayed put and awaited the arrival of armed reinforcements from Greece. However, the Turkish fleet and Stewart's navy had blockaded western Crete, so few managed to land. On the 14th of May 1841, a force of 14,000 Egyptian and Albanian troops attacked the rebels. Over the next few months fighting erupted in many parts of the island; the rebels were outnumbered, short of ammunition and supplies, and continuously in retreat. Mustafa's troops cleared the rebels from Apokoronas and pursued them to Theriso. The rebels were furious that the Sfakians had not come to assist them, and accused them of deserting the rebellion. The Sfakians responded that any efforts on their part would have been in vain since Greece had abandoned them under British pressure, and that the campaign was already lost.[308]

Pleas for the Great Powers and Greece to intervene met with no response. By early July, the rebels leaders had retreated to Kallikratis, and fearing that Mustafa's troops would invade Sfakia, they finally decided to call an end to the rebellion. They sent the local priest, Papa-Giannis, to Mustafa to declare their submission to his rule on behalf of all Christians on the island.[309] This was accepted on condition that all the rebels would give assurances about their future obedience; they would then be issued with registration papers that would enable them to circulate freely on the island. Thus ended the

[307] Ibid., pp. 912-914.
[308] Ibid., pp. 943-944.
[309] Ibid., p. 949; Papadopetrakis (1971 [1888]), p. 462.

uprising, with humiliating terms imposed on the rebels.

The return of Crete to Ottoman rule in June 1841 brought few administrative changes. The new young Sultan, Abdul Mejid I, kept Mustafa Pasha as Governor of Crete. The Albanian had no problem changing allegiance from the Egyptians to the Turks, nor did his Albanian and Egyptian troops or the civil servants who stayed on in Crete after the change in governance. Mustafa's control over the island strengthened, and he appointed his sons as governors of the Rethymnon and Heraklion districts. Mustafa ruled Crete for another ten years, becoming known as Mustafa Pasha the Giritli ('the Cretan'), since he had lived on and governed the island for close to thirty years. During his reign, he repressed the Christians on the island and withstood all pressure for changes from the Great Powers and Constantinople, including reforms[310] decreed by the Sultan which were meant to mirror those happening in Western Europe.

In 1851, the Sultan promoted Mustafa to the position of Grand Vizier (Prime Minister) in Constantinople and replaced him with Salih Vamik Pasha, who was friendlier to the Greeks and the representatives of the Great Powers. Salih Vamik moved the capital of Crete to Chania, where all foreign envoys were based; he also introduced reforms, including to taxation, and awarded Christians in rural areas the freedom to establish their own schools.

Britain again pushed for Crete to become a British protectorate. First they approached the Sfakians about this during a Royal Navy visit to Loutro. The Sfakian historian Papadopetrakis tells us that Petros Manouselis from Kallikratis addressed the elders gathered there as follows: "I would ask you one question: the struggles and the sacrifices and the blood that we spilled, did we do all that for the English, or for our own people?" The assembly replied: "For our people and their freedom!"[311] The British tried similar approaches in other parts of the island, but with the same result: the Cretans wanted their freedom, and union with Greece.

New reforms promised; the 1858 uprising[312]

In the early 1850s, war broke out between the Ottoman Empire and Russia. Britain and France were drawn into the conflict and fought against Russia in the Crimean Peninsula during the final stages in 1855. The subsequent peace treaty acknowledged the Sultan's reform initiatives: the *Hatt-i Humayun* edict of 1856 promised religious equality before the law, and

[310] Known as the *Hatti Sherif of Gulhane*, which heralded the Ottoman period of reform commonly referred to as the *Tanzimat*.

[311] Papadopetrakis (1971 [1888]), pp. 462-463.

[312] Known in Crete as the Mavrogenis uprising, after the leader of a group of Cretans who attacked Turkish tax collectors in Lakki, starting the revolt.

reformed the police, prisons and taxes. For the non-Muslim minorities in the Ottoman Empire, this meant equal rights in taxation, justice, military service, education and gaining public office. These changes brought them closer to Western practices; it also defused Russian attempts to annex Ottoman lands with predominantly Christian Orthodox populations on the pretext of freeing them from discriminatory Muslim rule. Thus, while the *Hatt-i Humayun's* provisions brought benefits to the Christian population of Crete, it resulted in them losing Russia as a possible ally in their struggle to liberate themselves from Ottoman rule.

Implementing the edict was going to be a formidable task, as the ingrained apathy and corruption of the ruling classes first had to be overcome. Exploitation of the masses was rife, not only by Muslims but also by the Christian church authorities and many of the more wealthy Christian tax collectors, who did not hesitate to maltreat their co-religionists. The authorities in Crete chose to ignore the edict, but its existence gave the Cretans additional grounds for complaining to the Great Powers; indeed, the Orthodox population's demands for the full implementation of the provisions of the *Hatt-i Humayun* was the main basis of their claims and grievances over the next forty years.

Salih Vamik was replaced as governor by Mehmed Emin Pasha; during his rule, conditions deteriorated again, and he in turn was succeeded in 1856 by Veli-uddin Pasha, son of Mustafa Pasha the Giritli. Veli had been born in Crete, spoke Greek fluently, and had received a traditional Muslim education. He had also studied French and spent a considerable time in Paris. But instead of implementing changes influenced by the *Hatt-i Humayun* and his long exposure to Western customs and thinking, he presided over a harsher regime, which extorted higher levels of taxes to support the more extravagant life-style he had become used to in Paris. His father's position as Grand Vizier made him immune to criticism from any quarter, including from the Great Powers' consuls in Crete.

These harsh taxes soon provoked the Cretans to plan another uprising. A number of them met at Lakki and decided to refuse to pay the levies Veli had imposed, then travelled to Sfakia to ascertain intentions there. Armed rebels in Lakki sent tax collectors away with a message for the authorities that they were not prepared to accept these financial burdens any longer. Preparations for the rebellion accelerated, and many more men were recruited from nearby districts. The Greek consul in Chania was also sounded out about support from the mainland government; the rebels' main concern again was the lack of weapons and finances. More than 6,000 armed rebels gathered southwest of Chania at Boutsounaria-Perivolia on the 14th of May 1858 to demonstrate peacefully against Veli's unjust tax regime. The leaders sent messages to all the consuls in Chania indicating the purpose of the gathering and seeking their support.

Veli initially wanted to send his troops to disperse the demonstrators, but his military commander refused to carry out the order since the protest was against Veli and not the Sultan, whose policy towards his subjects was very different. Veli then tried to placate the Sfakians; he sent emissaries to convince them that it was not in their interests to join the revolt, offering them special privileges and money if they distanced themselves from the rebels. Twice the Sfakians rejected his proposals. His next tactic was to get Constantinople to agree to his plan of breaking up the protest by force, but this was rejected, because the consuls sent messages to Constantinople indicated that the rebels' demands were justified. Finally, the Turkish General Aali Pasha was dispatched to Chania from Constantinople to defuse the situation. He immediately began negotiations with the rebel committee, headed by the much respected Sfakian *Kapetanios* Anagnostis Manousogiannakis from Imbros. The protracted deliberations ended peacefully, most of the rebels' grievances were accepted as legitimate, and Veli was sent back to Constantinople.

On the 7th of July 1858, the new Governor of Crete, Sami Abdurrahman Pasha, issued an edict declaring an amnesty for all those who had participated in the meeting at Boutsounaria, cancelling a number of taxes, and reiterating that the provisions of the *Hatt-i Humayun* were to be respected by the island's authorities. Amongst the provisions highlighted in this edict was the right to own weapons, although both Christians and Muslims were prohibited from bearing arms in public places. In addition, Christians were allowed to form their own elected district councils of elders. The power to adjudicate over disputes amongst Christians about family matters and inheritance law was given to these councils and removed from the jurisdiction of Muslim courts. Muslims could form their own separate councils. Higher-level district councils were established with one Christian elder and one Muslim elder to represent the smaller areas in the district; but Sfakia was represented by one Christian elder only, since no Muslims ever lived in Sfakia.

Over the next few years, Crete had a succession of new governors, each one harassing the Christians more than the previous one and ignoring the provisions of the 1858 edict and the *Hatt-i Humayun* when it suited them. The Cretans now firmly believed that the Sultan was taking his revenge on them. Greece was also undergoing changes that would influence the Sultan's approach to governing Crete. King Otto of Greece had been deposed through a revolution, and the Great Powers chose Prince William George of the Danish Glucksberg dynasty to replace him on the throne as King George I, King of Hellenes. Greece was granted the Ionian Islands by the British upon his appointment, with the clear understanding that he was not to encourage any future uprisings against the Ottoman Empire. So the Sultan was now free to exercise tougher control over his subjects in Crete without fear of support from the Greek mainland for another uprising.

During the first few years of the 1860s, the Sfakians attracted special attention from the Turkish governors of Crete. The Turks' main strategy was to create disunity amongst the more rebellious factions within the island, especially in the western districts. To achieve this, they spread exaggerated stories in the Selino and Chania districts about the Sfakians – that they were receiving special privileges from the Turks, that they were perpetrating heinous crimes, and that without the Sfakians relations between the authorities and the Christian population on the island would be more harmonious. To promote this agenda, Governor Hosni Hussein Pasha called a meeting of elders from across the island to agree on taking appropriate measures against law-breakers, especially the "criminal Sfakians". The delegates did not give him the authorisation that he was seeking, as they suspected that his real objective was to abolish the right for all Cretans to own weapons. Furious at their refusal, Hosni Hussein kept all of them under armed guard until the consuls of the Great Powers intervened.

The anti-Sfakian propaganda continued, and at a meeting of Cretan elders in 1863, a new governor, Ismail Pasha, accused a number of Sfakian elders and *Kapetanioi* of committing crimes against fellow Cretans in nearby areas. The Sfakian representative refuted the accusations but made the great mistake of allowing the Turkish governor to come to Sfakia, arrest the accused, and put them through proper court proceedings, where they would be able to prove their innocence. To their dismay, 6,000 troops invaded Sfakia to arrest men charged with stealing flocks of sheep, and one charged with bride stealing. These were frequent events in Crete's high mountains, not serious crimes! They eventually arrested 19 Sfakians and, fearing an escalation of the already tense situation, quickly left Sfakia for Apokoronas.[313] The Sfakians were tempted to attack the Turkish forces at Katre, but since they were not prepared for a full-blown war, and 19 of their own men were with the troops, they let the opportunity pass.

Cretans from nearby areas now realized what the true objectives of the Turks were, and agreed that a combined effort was required to force the authorities to change their policies and abide by the provisions of the *Hatt-i Humayun*. They wrote to the Sultan outlining their complaints and delivered the document to Ismail for submission to the Sultan. Ismail was certainly displeased, and a month later told them that the Sultan refused to accept their submission and threatened them with exile if they sent another such document. The deteriorating situation caused by the harsh taxation measures and the unwillingness of the Turkish authorities to discuss grievances had set the stage for the "big uprising of 1866", as it is referred to by Cretans.

[313] Mourellos (1950), Vol. 2, pp. 1008-1009; Papadopetrakis (1971 [1888]), pp. 492-494.

XIV. The last major uprising against Ottoman rule – 1866 to 1869

Events leading to the uprising

Early in 1865, another event stirred up anger among many prominent Cretans against the authoritarian approach of Ismail Pasha. There was a dispute between the Christian population and the clergy in eastern Crete about control of the income generated by monastic properties. The local elders demanded that this revenue be allocated for new schools, but the clergy refused. To resolve the issue, the elders intended to appeal directly to the Patriarch in Constantinople. Ismail Pasha intervened on the side of the clergy, dissolved the committee that was to travel to Constantinople, and exiled four of the more vocal proponents of the proposal.

Early in the spring of 1866, discussions were taking place in many villages about how to deal with the increasingly harsh levels of taxation and the authoritarian regime. On the 30th of March at the church of Agios Antonios in Lakki, a group of local elders, incensed at the deteriorating situation, signed a document under oath declaring their intention to protect their legal rights and free their island of Ottoman tyranny. The next day they sent letters to the nearby districts of Chania, Selino and Sfakia urging them to join their cause.[314] Elders and *Kapetanioi* from the western districts arrived in Omalos by mid April, amongst them a fiery Sfakian cleric, Parthenios Kelaidis, who urged them to take up the struggle. They decided to convene a pan-Cretan assembly at Boutzounaria, just south of Chania, to air their grievances. All participants were to arrive unarmed, since at that stage they were taking a non-violent approach to the issue. If Turkish troops demanded to know the purpose of the gathering, they would reply that as representatives of their people, they were exercising their right of peaceful assembly to draft a submission to the Sultan in Constantinople.

By the 23rd of April some 4,000 Cretans from all over the island had

[314] Mourellos (1950), pp. 1018-1019.

gathered to begin the slow process of forming regional committees and then choosing an overall coordinating group. Sfakia's committee consisted of some celebrated rebels, amongst them Anagnostis Manouselis and Anagnostis Vougioukalakis from Kallikratis, Sifis Vourdoubakis and Roussos Koundouros from Chora Sfakion, Anagnostis Birakis from Komitades, and Anagnostis Manousogiannakis from Imbros; all of them were to play leading roles during the uprising. Their deliberations were held up for some time by the delayed arrival of representatives from the eastern districts, but while waiting they published a notice addressed to all Christian and Muslim Cretans proclaiming the assembly's peaceful intentions and asking them to join in seeking justice for everyone from the Sultan.

Ismail Pasha reacted immediately by issuing an announcement to all Christians in which he accused the assembly of acting out of self-interest and stated that the proper way to air their complaints was approach him directly. Anticipating another uprising, Ismail requested reinforcements, which arrived on the 6th of May. He also attempted to orchestrate a clash between Muslims and Christians by calling on the entire Muslim population to withdraw into the walled cities, supposedly due to an imminent threat of a Christian insurrection. This caused panic; the cities were overflowing with Muslim refugees, who attacked the few Christians remaining in the towns. Many Christians also fled by sea to nearby Greek islands and the mainland.

The pan-Cretan assembly presented its petition to the Sultan on the 14th of May. It called for relief from the exorbitant levies which had been imposed since 1858, as well as from the complex, onerous and unequal system of taxes on farming activities. It also requested improvements to the road system, the opening of ports other than the three on the north coast for trade, abolition of monopolies on specified goods, amendments to the way that tribunals operated in order to provide fairer outcomes, provision of schools, freedom to practice their religion without impediment, and aired many other grievances which are too numerous to list here.[315] The petition was sent to the Governor to be forwarded to the Sultan, and copies were distributed to all the foreign consuls in Chania. The next day, the representatives who had stayed behind wrote letters to the Queen of Great Britain, the King of France and the Tsar of Russia, seeking their understanding (and therefore support) about the Cretans' efforts to achieve union with Greece. In their letter to the British Queen they added:

> Should that, however, be impossible at present, we beg your Majesty to endeavour to obtain for us a political organization, under which there

[315] A translation of the full document can be found in Stillman (1874), pp. 179-183. William J. Stillman was US Consul in Crete at the time.

may be laws and regular tribunals, less grievous and better imposed taxes, ... and generally that our just grievances may be redressed by a Christian and paternal administration.[316]

Soon after the petition was delivered, Ismail Pasha ordered all those who had participated at the assembly and were still at Boutzounaria to go home and wait for a reply; they initially refused, but soon many of them did return to their villages. Only a small committee stayed behind to await the Sultan's reply. Ismail had acknowledged that the assembly was legal since members had gathered unarmed, but he now wanted to declare the committee illegal on the basis that they disobeyed his order to disperse. He called the foreign consuls together to inform them that he proposed taking military action against the committee, and sought their support for this. The French and English consuls backed him, but the Italian, US, Russian, Swedish and Greek consuls were in favour of peaceful negotiations. Eventually the committee withdrew to the mountains, thus avoiding open conflict. During this time, more Turkish ships arrived in Souda Bay, bringing some 5,000 Egyptian troops[317] under the command of Schahin Pasha as further reinforcements against an insurrection.

The committee moved around from place to place to avoid capture. While at Embrosneros, they were confronted by some Sfakians who were worried about the situation developing into a fully-fledged rebellion. They had been informed through their own private channels that Athens was unwilling to support another insurrection against Ottoman rule, either morally or materially. Furthermore, Athens believed that the Great Powers would not back any movement that threatened the political balance with the Ottoman Empire. This assessment was shared by quite a few Sfakians, who could see that the island was not prepared for total conflict against the superior Ottoman forces.[318] They argued with the committee against instigating a new insurrection, pointing out all the negative factors.[319] This difference of opinion about Crete's readiness for another uprising developed into political conflict amongst Sfakians as well as with other Cretans, many of whom accused the Sfakians of betraying the cause and being pro-Turkish; this was to get much worse, as we will see further on.

The Sultan's response arrived on the 18th of July: he rejected all their requests and demanded that they return immediately to their villages, threatening severe punishment if they disobeyed and continued with these "acts of rebellion that cannot be tolerated".[320] The committee quickly

[316] The full text of this letter can be found in Stillman (1874), pp. 184-186.

[317] US Consul Stillman reported that there were 8,000 Egyptian troops.

[318] Papadopetrakis (1971 [1888]), pp. 507-508.

[319] Mourellos (1950), pp. 1044-1046.

[320] Stillman (1874), pp. 187-190.

responded by sending letters to the foreign consuls in Chania strongly objecting the Sultan's response and indicating that the only avenue left to them was armed insurrection. They also dispatched letters to regional leaders in Crete urging them to prepare for an uprising, and to their supporters in Athens urgently requesting arms and volunteers. The committee, still being pursued by Turkish and Egyptian forces, eventually moved to the more inaccessible Sfakia area, from where it sent proclamations about the imminent rebellion to all parts of Crete. They persevered in their attempts to get the foreign consuls to intervene against the campaign of terror the Turks had begun in earnest against them.

On the 21st of August 1866, from their base near Askifou, the committee officially announced the start of a new uprising, issuing a proclamation that rejected Ottoman rule and declared the union of Crete with Greece.

The first battles of the uprising

The first major clash with Ismail Pasha's forces took place soon after this, when rebels surrounded the 4,000 Egyptian troops stationed near Vrises. Fighters from the districts of Sfakia, Apokoronas and Kydonia blocked all the roads the Egyptians could have used to retreat towards Chania and cut off their only supply of running water. The Egyptian commander, Schahin Pasha, who up till then was following a policy of appeasement towards the Cretan elders on instructions from the Viceroy of Egypt, had no option but to fight back and try to extricate his troops from this difficult situation. Turkish reinforcements on their way from Chania were defeated by the rebels, who anticipated such a move, thus preventing the Egyptian troops' retreat. The heat and lack of water pushed Schahin Pasha to seek a truce after five days. The timing of his request was most welcome to the rebels, as they had just learned that 6,000 Turkish soldiers were on their way to assist the Egyptians, and the rebels were running out of ammunition. The truce permitted the Egyptian troops to leave carrying all that they could. It was also agreed that they could send men the next day to collect the supplies they had left behind. Other clashes between rebels and Turks were taking place in the Selino district, as well as near Heraklion, where some of the most brutal massacres of unarmed civilians occurred when villages and monasteries were razed to the ground.

To bring the rebellion under control, the Sultan sent Mustafa Giritli Pasha, the former Grand Vizier and ex-Governor of Crete (1825-1849), to replace Ismail. Mustafa Giritli arrived in Crete on the 31st of August bearing the impressive title of Imperial Commissioner, reflecting his more senior status. He immediately made contact with most of the elders on the island, who he knew from his earlier period as Governor; he offered them inducements to forego the rebellion and tried to spread dissent amongst the various rebel groups. Mustafa promised to address their grievances and gave them five days to lay down their arms; if they did not, he would take all necessary measures to restore order to the island. This tactic, which he had used before, did not succeed. The general revolutionary committee issued two proclamations (on the 7th and 9th of September) addressed to all Cretans, stating that they rejected Mustafa's demands and urging them to continue the struggle; their declared ultimate objective was "Union or Death".[321]

Battles continued in many parts of the island, but the rebels did not have the numbers or the resources to defeat the better-armed enemy. Clashes around Malaxa resulted in the destruction of the village, with numerous deaths on both sides, events that were witnessed by many foreign observers from within the walls of Chania and Souda. Mustafa's troops, numbering more than 12,000, freed the Turks and Muslim Cretans besieged at Kasteli and Kandanos and other fortified locations, with the rebels unable to stop them. Some of these Turks were escorted to Paleochora, where they were taken by boat to the safety of Chania, while many more, together with their animals and possessions, were accompanied overland to Chania. The rebels chose not to attack the fleeing Turks, believing this would make it easier to control the region, but others disagreed and tried to inflict as much damage as they could on them. The decision to allow the besieged Turks to be escorted back to Chania unhindered was criticised later, as this gave them more scope to pursue the rebels. This situation once again reflected the consequences of the rebels having no effective central military leadership.

Mustafa was also unhappy at the outcome of his campaign in the Selino district, which highlighted his inability to bring this area, which was previously heavily populated by Muslims, under control. His forces regrouped and reinforced, and they now headed to Lakki, where some of the rebels were located; others had gone home to their families, as they usually did after the end of a battle. Mustafa was well aware of the rebels' lack of central military command, discipline and preparedness for a protracted offensive campaign. The Turkish troops, meeting little effective resistance on the way, destroyed Lakki and moved on to Meskla and Theriso, which they also burned down. In the meantime, rebels from the nearby areas were regrouping south of Theriso at Aliakes, a difficult location for the Turks to reach and which Mustafa's troops attacked a number of times with no effect. During their retreat the Turks were ambushed by rebels, forcing them to withdraw further to Meskla and then nearer to Chania, under constant harassment.

[321] Mourellos (1950), p. 1090.

In the east, more Egyptian forces arrived, led by Ismail Ferik Pasha,[322] who took over command of the Egyptian forces after Schahin Pasha's defeat at Vrises. Ismail Ferik's mission was to reinforce the Turkish troops in Heraklion, who were unable to contain the rebellion in the eastern provinces, which was growing on a daily basis under the charismatic leadership of "Korakas",[323] a *Kapetanios* from Messara. Battles raged unabated in the area around the Almyros river near Heraklion starting in early September, and then spread south and east of Heraklion, as well as south of Rethymnon, continuing throughout October.

Assistance arrives from Greece

Greece was in a difficult situation from an economic, military and diplomatic point of view. It was feeling threatened by large concentrations of Ottoman forces on its northern borders who were there to put an end to the sporadic uprisings and widespread banditry in Thessaly and Macedonia. Greece only had a small army with obsolete weaponry. Economically, it was still suffering from the effects of previous wars, as well as from maladministration, and its government was divided on whether the time was right to engage in more hostilities with its larger and better-prepared neighbour.[324] On the diplomatic front, Greece was only supported by Russia, who still harboured the desire to lead the Christian Orthodox countries.

Mainland Greece immediately responded to calls for help from Crete by collecting money and supplies, and many men volunteered to join the fighting there. Some of these were army officers who took leave of absence from the Greek army; three of them were to play leading roles in the Cretan uprising over the next years.

At the end of September, Lieutenant Colonel Panos Koroneos landed in Bali, near Rethymnon, bringing food and military supplies with him, and accompanied by a group of officers and other volunteers. He immediately

[322] An interesting historical novel by the Cretan writer Rea Galanaki, *The Life of Ismail Ferik Pasha* (available in English), covers the story of this young Christian Cretan boy from Lasithi, who was taken as a slave to Egypt, converted to the Muslim religion, and reached the high post of Minister of the Army in Egypt prior to his appointment in Crete.

[323] His name was Michalis Karouzos, but he was given the nickname Korakas ('raven' in Greek) by the Turks for the fierceness of his attacks against them. He participated in all the uprisings against the Turks from 1821 onwards.

[324] Greece had got into this dramatic situation as a result of bitter infighting between various political factions. It had five different governments in the space of a year, then another 12 governments in three years. The government in power at the time was headed by Dimitrios Voulgaris, who could only offer some vague promises of help to the Cretans.

assumed command of the forces around Rethymnon, and his plan was to attack the city using the few rebel troops available, in spite of the local *Kapetanioi* advising that this was unwise. Soon afterwards, Koroneos and the rebels advanced on Rethymnon; they were repelled by a strong Turkish contingent, and only the offer of a fast horse by one of the *Kapetanioi* saved Koroneos' life.

The second officer to arrive on Crete was Major Ioannis Zymvakakis, the brother of the Greek Minister of the Army, who had been invited by the central committee to assume leadership of the rebel forces in western Crete. He arrived in Loutro on the 1st of October aboard a small blockade-running ship, the *Panhellenion,* along with 275 volunteer officers and soldiers, ammunition, weapons, three mountain cannons, and flour. A Turkish frigate which had pursued the *Panhellenion* shelled the ship, and the disembarking forces responded, with the assistance of Sfakians, by setting up their artillery and returning fire. Meanwhile, the *Panhellenion* manage to escape. Zymvakakis and his troops advanced through Anopoli, Mouri and Askifou to reach Vafes, to the southeast of Chania, by the 4th of October, where he called a meeting of all the *Kapetanioi* of the western districts. He and his men were totally unprepared for the rebels' tough living conditions, with only a few olives and onions for food, exposed to the bitterly cold weather of an early winter, and with a large concentration of Turkish forces not far away.

The third officer to arrive from the mainland was the retired Colonel Christos Vyzantios, who disembarked from the *Panhellenion* west of Paleochora on the 5th of November. With him were a number of volunteer officers and men, as well as a group of 70 troops from Garibaldi's International Brigades under the command of a French officer. The ship also carried ammunition, weapons, four mountain cannons, and supplies of food. Other reinforcements followed on three of the blockade-running ships that were plying between Greece and Crete, bringing in ammunition, supplies and volunteers and returning with women, children and older people who were fleeing from the Turks, harsh winter conditions, and starvation.

The battle of Vafes and the capitulation of Sfakia

As we saw earlier, Zymvakakis had called for a meeting with the *Kapetanioi* of the western district to decide on their next move against the 12,000 Turks camped at Vamos. Zymvakakis' forces, consisting of mainland volunteers and rebels, and numbering only 800, were confronted by Turkish advance parties on the 10th and 11th of October, without any losses on either side. By then Zymvakakis had realised the disparity between the two armies' numbers, weapons and supplies, so he sought advice from the *Kapetanioi* on how to deal with the enemy. The rebels advised him to keep his troops on the high ground above Vafes and fight the Turks from this vantage point. But Zymvakakis and his officers, in their enthusiasm to take on the Turkish army, decided to engage the Turks on the lower ground outside Vafes. Out of respect for the officers' military rank, enthusiasm and conviction, the rebels acceded to this proposal.

The next day, Mustafa's troops attacked the rebel position on two fronts. In the initial clashes, Zymvakakis lost 17 fighters, forcing the rest to retreat, and soon they were running for their lives to higher ground where they could safely attend to the wounded. Stormy weather kept the Turks from pursuing them. This defeat is reminiscent of similar events at Frangokastello some 40 years earlier, when Hatzi-Michalis Dalianis ignored the Sfakians' advice with disastrous results.

When Zymvakakis' men reached Askifou, they found a huge concentration of unarmed, hungry and cold Cretans seeking refuge in Sfakia in the face of the advancing Turkish troops. Zymvakakis was criticised at the time by the locals for this catastrophic situation, and also later on by many historians, including the Sfakian Papadopetrakis. But this sudden and unexpected defeat held more serious consequences. Mustafa wanted to take advantage of the psychological impact on the Cretans, so he offered an amnesty, plus safe passage to Greece, to all volunteers from the mainland who laid down their arms. He also agreed to pardon locals who submitted to his rule, and promised not to destroy their villages. Numerous localities acquiesced, including many villages in Mirabello, Pediada, Vianos, Lasithi and Sfakia. Crucially, however, not all Sfakians agreed to this capitulation; the consequences, and the rights and wrongs, of this are still debated today.

Mustafa demanded that the Sfakians submit to his rule in writing, surrender their weapons, and expel any volunteers and rebels from their region. He also sent personal letters to the Sfakian elders he knew from his period as governor laying out the conditions of his offer.[325] The Sfakian leaders were in an extremely difficult position. There were 12,000 Turkish troops in Vrises at the northern approach to Sfakia, ready to invade the area. The Sfakians, on the other hand, had no more than 1,000 fighters at their disposal, since many of them were fighting against the Turks in other parts of the island, and assistance from outside Crete was highly unlikely. Moreover, more than 25,000 women, children and elderly people from all over the island had taken refuge in Sfakia. Food was non-existent, and the few supplies that were delivered infrequently had to be shared with the combatants. Severe winter weather had arrived early, adding to their misery. Given this crisis, many Sfakians could see no alternative but to give in to Mustafa's demands. Others from Kallikratis and Askifou were more

[325] Mourellos (1950), p. 1127.

optimistic about the Great Powers intervening and strongly disagreed with the decision to capitulate. And, fatefully, this led to accusations of treason against those who reluctantly wanted to accept Mustafa's terms.

Later on, we shall see interesting echoes of this fight-and-be-destroyed versus submit-and-survive dilemma in events which took place towards the end of the German occupation in World War II, when attacks by resistance fighters against the Germans led to increasing levels of reprisal against villages on Crete, to the extent that the Allied Forces actually removed Cretan guerrillas from the island.

The decision to accept Mustafa's terms was taken by Sfakian elders who did not believe the Great Powers would come to their assistance – correctly, as it turned out.[326] Their strategy was to gain time and prevent the invasion of Sfakia, which would have led to the certain death of thousands of refugees. It seemed to them that they had no other option, although this did not imply that they intended to submit to Ottoman rule in the long run. Instead of appearing together in front of Mustafa as instructed, they sent only seven representatives. Mustafa was most displeased, but they explained that many of their leaders were simply too ashamed to present themselves and would come sometime in the future. Mustafa was also annoyed that the elders had not brought the Sfakians' weapons along, but he was prepared to let that pass. This successful manoeuvring for time and the avoidance of the certain destruction of Sfakia and the massacre of thousands of refugees was to have very serious repercussions for the Sfakian elders who signed the submission papers, as the leaders from Askifou and Kallikratis, who did not put their names to the document, declared them to be traitors.

An incident involving the *Panhellinion,* which was delivering supplies to the rebels, further inflamed the situation. The ship arrived in Sfakia in the early hours of the 21st of October, two days after their capitulation, in order to unload a small amount of flour, but the crew were told that the supplies should be delivered further to the east where the rebels were still fighting, since Sfakia had capitulated two days earlier and there were no rebels there requiring the goods in Sfakia. But a mainland volunteer who wanted to escape from Crete – so the story goes – told them, untruthfully, that as a result of Sfakia's submission, all of Crete had capitulated. The captain immediately abandoned his mission and returned to the island of Syros, announcing there that the uprising had failed. There was an enormous outcry on Syros, and then in mainland Greece, at the "treachery" of the Sfakians.

[326] Ibid., p. 1132. Twenty-nine elders signed a letter addressed to Zymvakakis, who was still in Askifou, advising him of why they had submitted to Mustafa's demands, and asking him to take his volunteers and continue his fight away from Sfakia. Some elders hand-delivered the letter to him in order to explain their reasons in person and to assure him that many Sfakians would join him in the struggle elsewhere, as their intention at that point was to keep the struggle outside Sfakia because of the refugee problem.

The controversy about this continues to this day. Papadopetrakis (who came from Kallikratis) does not defend Sfakia's capitulation in his *History of Sfakia*,[327] but he recognises that thousands of women and children's lives were saved because of their "fake" surrender.[328] The Cretan historian Psilakis is more critical than this, as is Kriaris. Some modern historians have been more understanding about the Sfakian strategy. Mourellos, for instance, is rather sympathetic,[329] acknowledging the desperate situation in which Sfakia and the refugees found themselves, and he supports the Sfakian elders' assessment of the situation which led them to submit to the Turks. Furthermore, he attributes some of the nineteenth-century hostility to these "traitors" to the central committee's need to find a scapegoat for the disastrous turn of events that ended in defeat at Vafes and the apparent collapse of the uprising.[330] The contemporary and well-respected local Sfakian historian Paris Kelaidis has also supported Papadopetrakis' view that there was no treachery involved, that the elders who signed the document provided no assistance to the Turks, and that none of them gained personally from their decision.[331] The controversy undoubtedly will continue.

The Arkadi Monastery tragedy

Mustafa and his troops remained near Vafes for almost three weeks negotiating terms with the Sfakians. He was uncertain whether he had secured an agreement that was going to last or whether he should invade Sfakia and put an end their constant threat. Eventually, events further to the east convinced him that his army would be better deployed quelling the continuing unrest south of Rethymnon.

After Koroneos' rebel troops failed to wrest control of Rethymnon from the Turks, they withdrew to Arkadi Monastery, some 20 kilometres south of Rethymnon, which was the base for the regional revolutionary committee under the chairmanship of Abbot Gabriel Marinakis. As well as housing monks, the monastery provided a temporary refuge for a large number of rebels together with more than 700 women and children. Koroneos' assessment of the situation was that the monastery was not defendable and was unsuitable for sheltering such a large number of civilians, but the Abbot and monks disagreed, arguing that no enemy had ever captured the monastery. Leaving some volunteers behind and one of his officers in charge, Koroneos left to help the rebel forces nearby prepare to defend the monastery.

[327] Papadopetrakis (1971 [1888]), pp. 511-512.
[328] Ibid., pp. 517-518.
[329] Mourellos (1950), pp. 1124-1128.
[330] Ibid., pp. 1143.
[331] Kelaidis (2007), p. 329.

For some months the Pasha of Rethymnon had demanded that the Abbot expel the committee from Arkadi Monastery and stop the rebels from using it as a base, but he had refused to take any action and ignored an ultimatum that was given to the Abbot towards the end of September. On the 20th of October, Turkish forces heading for the monastery engaged the rebels in battle; fighting continued over the next few days, with the rebels managing to keep the Turks away from their target. Mustafa gathered 7,000 troops in Episkopi and sent reinforcements to Rethymnon by sea to join those who were marching on Arkadi. Despite the rebels' best efforts, 15,000 Ottoman soldiers[332] deploying 30 cannons surrounded the monastery on the morning of the 8th of November. Within the buildings were more than 700 women and children and 259 armed men, including 45 monks. All of them could have escaped to Mylopotamos, but they believed they were safer behind the monastery walls and did not want to abandon the holy place to the Turks.

The Turks shelled the monastery, as well as the road leading to it to prevent rebels from assisting those inside. They attacked in waves throughout the day, but the few rebels inside the monastery repelled them, assisted by snipers situated in a nearby windmill outside the walls; but by the end of the day these brave men were dead. A messenger who slipped out of the monastery at night to seek help returned with the bad news that none was on its way. Despite the shelling and the multiple attacks, the walls held, so the Turks requested larger cannons from Rethymnon. Under the heavier shelling, the walls and gate soon began to collapse, and by evening masses of Turkish troops had breached the walls. The rebels, whose ammunition had run out, engaged them in hand-to-hand combat, while the others had barricaded themselves into various parts of the monastery. The women and children had hidden in the monastery's gunpowder magazine, where they were saying their final prayers, since it had been decided that they would blow themselves up rather than surrender to the Turks. When the doors to their room were battered down and Turkish troops flooded in, one of the rebels set light to the barrels of gunpowder and the entire building exploded, killing everyone. At the end of that day, 846 Cretans lay dead, mostly as a result of the explosion, and more than 1,500 Turks had been killed during the two-day siege. The 114 Cretans who survived were taken to Rethymnon by the Turkish forces; after suffering public humiliation, they were thrown into jail.

The dramatic events at Arkadi turned world opinion in favour of the long-suffering Cretans, and many countries quickly established charities and committees to send aid to the refugees who were flooding out of Crete, and to promote diplomatic action to stop this unnecessary carnage.

[332] The American Consul in Crete, William Stillman, reported that the Ottoman force that surrounded Arkadi totalled about 23,000 men, including regular and irregular troops, based on information from Mustafa Pasha's secretary (Stillman 1874, p. 85).

Prominent supporters of the Cretan cause, such as the French writer Victor Hugo and the Italian general Giuseppe Garibaldi, wrote letters of support, and many of Garibaldi's followers travelled to Crete to fight alongside the rebels. This widespread backing encouraged the Cretans to continue with their struggle after such a devastating setback.

But the Arkadi tragedy held another unforseen consequence for Greece. Just a month after this tragic event, elections in Greece brought a new government to power headed by Alexandros Koumoundouros. He was a strong believer in Crete's aspirations for independence and was prepared to take a firm line against the Turks. He immediately started to build up a strong army equipped with modern weapons, and he ordered three destroyers and two battleships built, all funded by government bonds sold primarily to Greeks. Koumoundouros became very active on the diplomatic front in pressing for the liberation of Crete and the northern Greek districts of Thessaly and Epirus. From the day he took power, more money, supplies and volunteers were funnelled to Crete, paid for in great part by the Greek treasury.

The church at the Arkadi monastery

Mustafa returns to western Crete

Fighting continued in the east of the island, and the Turks took refuge in the forts at Mirabello and Ierapetra. The rebels, encouraged by their successes, advanced on the well-defended Turkish villages in the Sitia district. Supplies were arriving from Greece on the *Panhellinion* and *Hydra,* soon to be joined by the legendary *Arkadi.* Besides bringing arms, ammunition, other supplies, and volunteers, they sailed back to Greece loaded with refugees. On one of these runs in late December, a group of about 700 well-armed Maniot volunteers, led by Colonel Dimitrios Petropoulakis, landed between Heraklion and Rethymnon, but the Turks soon attacked and forced them to retreat inland. Turkish forces from Heraklion attempted to advance on the Mylopotamos district, but they withdrew after being defeated at the narrow Tylissos pass.

While all this was going on, Mustafa's attention was again drawn to the western districts of Crete south of Chania, as well as to Kissamos, where Kasteli was under siege by the rebels, and to Selino. But his main focus was on Sfakia. Reports of Sfakians attacking his troops and harassing Muslim Cretans led him to realise that the threat from the Sfakians had not yet been eliminated, despite their purported capitulation. The Turks had been unable to take control of the west despite their incursions a few months earlier, so to demonstrate to the Sultan that he had finally quashed the rebellion, Mustafa led 15,000 troops into western Crete. The rebels were still plagued by leadership disputes, uncoordinated operations against besieged Turkish forces, and shortages of weapons and ammunition, despite the more frequent arrival of supplies and volunteer fighters.

At the end of November, Mustafa's forces headed to Lakki and Theriso, which his troops had destroyed just two months earlier, to attack the rebels based there. Despite putting up a spirited fight, the rebels were driven south to Zourva, which they also had to abandon, and finally sought refuge in the higher reaches of the Lefka Ori. The Turkish troops suffered hundreds of deaths and injuries in the battle, while the rebels' toll was 20 dead and 15 injured. But what was worse for the rebel leadership was the loss of all control over their fighting forces, who were now engaged in an undisciplined retreat. This situation has been attributed to infighting between Zymvakakis, Koroneos and Vyzantios; the latter was now demanding to be made overall leader because of his higher rank.

The winter weather was most punishing for the women and children, who had taken refuge in the mountains and caves with very little food or clothing. The Europeans came to their rescue. The British consul in Chania requested that the gunboat HMS *Assurance,* under Commander William Pym, provide humanitarian assistance, and in contravention of instructions to maintain neutrality, the ship sailed to Selino and evacuated 320 refugees from Paleochora.[333] This was the only time the British participated in the rescue effort. France, Russia, Austria, Italy and Prussia also sent warships along the southwest coast of Crete to evacuate refugees from Paleochora, Sougia, Tripiti and Agia Roumeli.

An earlier incident on the 10th of October, involving the Russian frigate the *General Admiral* under Admiral Bukatov's command,[334] demonstrates the tense relations with the Ottoman authorities concerning these humanitarian efforts. When three Turkish naval vessels attempted to stop Bukatov from rescuing 1,200 refugees at Tripiti, he opened the ship's cannon doors to indicate that he was ready to take them on. The Turks retreated, and so the families and injured fighters sailed off to Piraeus and safety. These rescue missions, which were a clear breach of the Ottoman maritime embargo, increased tensions between the Ottoman and British governments on the one hand, and the governments of other countries who were influenced by public opinion over the ongoing carnage and tragedy in Crete.

Mustafa in Sfakia

Mustafa's troops soon took control of most of the Selino district, first forcing the rebels out of Agia Irini and then Koustogerako, from where they retreated up to the Omalos plateau and the Lefka Ori. As Mustafa's forces gradually occupied the lower reaches of the Lefka Ori, he offered an amnesty to those who agreed to yield to his rule and lay down their arms. From Selino, he wrote to the Sfakians informing them that he would come to Chora Sfakion to obtain a reaffirmation of their submission to his rule. A small detachment of soldiers that he sent to Agia Roumeli on the 13th of December were forced to turn back by rebels defending the entrance to the Samaria Gorge, where 1,000 refugees had taken shelter.

On the 19th of December, Mustafa dispatched a naval vessel to Chora Sfakion with letters addressed to the elders and *Kapetanioi* of the 10 Sfakian villages demanding that three or four representatives from each village return with the ship that evening for urgent discussions. The Sfakians replied that most of the leaders were away, so it would take some time before they could assemble and consider his demand. This stalling tactic continued for some days, with the Sfakians offering a series of excuses for why they couldn't come to Mustafa. Eventually, on the 28th of December, Mustafa himself arrived in Chora Sfakion and met the few elders who were present, but he demanded a meeting with those from the other villages to

[333] Although Pym was praised by the public, by the press and by politicians who supported the Cretan uprising, the British government was not happy about this, and Pym's naval career languished after this incident.

[334] Aleksei Ivanovich Butakov 1816-69, a Russian admiral and hydrographer.

obtain confirmation of their submission. Excuses and threats continued for a number of days. The Sfakians claimed that most of the other elders had not yet returned, and that in any case they had no weapons to be surrendered; they also gave assurances that there were no rebels staying amongst them. The Sfakians were playing their old game of avoiding confrontation unless they could choose favourable ground, and at a time that suited them.

Mustafa heard that the rebels' central committee was in Agia Roumeli, along with fighters and many refugees, so on the 30th of December he dispatched three naval ships to attack them. Over the course of the day, about 50 rebels managed to prevent the Turkish troops from landing, which provided an opportunity for the refugees to move further up the Samaria Gorge, and for the central committee to escape to Aradena and from there to Mouri. But the next day 300 Turks landed further to the east and attacked the rebels on their flank, forcing them deeper into the gorge. Eventually some 1,500 Turkish troops arrived, but they were unable to advance up the gorge in the face of fierce gunfire from the rebels.

Word of the attack on Agia Roumeli reached nearby areas, and fighters, including many from Anopoli and Agios Ioannis, made their way to the area, taking up positions on either side of Agia Roumeli and the Samaria Gorge. On the 8th of January, while the Turks were going about their morning preparations in a leisurely fashion, several hundred rebels decided that the opportunity was ripe to make their presence felt and attacked. Panic and confusion ensued amongst the Turkish troops as partially dressed soldiers ran for cover or tried to grab their weapons. Cannon fire from the Turkish ships gave them a chance to get organised and take cover. Mustafa heard the cannons from Chora Sfakion and ordered one of his ships to go to their assistance, but as the bombardment continued, he decided to send two more troop carriers from Frangokastello; they arrived in the afternoon with 2,000 fresh troops. The battle in Agia Roumeli went on for 10 days, with fewer than 10 rebels being killed or wounded. This was a massive defeat for the Turks, who suffered around 600 casualties and eventually had to abandon their attempt to penetrate into the Samaria Gorge.

The stalemate between Mustafa and the Sfakians was proving difficult for both sides. The bitter winter weather and food shortages put pressure on Sfakians living on the coast to reach a settlement. Mustafa needed to return to Chania, but he wanted to be able to tell the Sultan that he had succeeded in his campaign in western Crete and had secured the Sfakians' capitulation. He ordered Mehmed Pasha,[335] whose troops were camped at Embrosneros just north of Krapi, to send a detachment to Askifou in order to ensure his own safe passage back from Sfakia; but Mehmed's 2,500 men were unprepared for an attack by about 200 Sfakian rebels who were

[335] According to Mourellos (1950, p. 1279), Mehmed Pasha was a French-Prussian named Alfred Detroit who had joined the Turkish Army after converting.

guarding the entrance to Askifou. On the 14th of January, after only a few hours, the Turks were forced to retreat, and when rebels from Apokoronas joined the battle, the Turks fled to the safety of their fortified positions in Embrosneros.

The previous day, a Turkish naval ship had arrived in Sfakia bringing a envoy of the Sultan, Server Effendi, to assist Mustafa with his negotiations. He told the Sfakian elders that the Sultan was willing to meet all the Cretans' reasonable demands and negotiate a new constitution. To this end, he was inviting two representatives each from the two religious communities in every district of Crete to gather in Chania, and from there travel to Constantinople. Because there were no Muslims in Sfakia, they were allowed to send four Christian representatives; but it was impossible for the Sfakians to overcome their mistrust of the Turks, so they refused. Server Effendi departed, and Mustafa continued negotiations in a more conciliatory manner. He abandoned his demand that the Sfakians surrender their weapons – they would be allowed to carry their arms without being harassed by Turkish troops or Muslim Cretans – and he offered to send food supplies for their starving families; but in return they would have to expel any rebels still in their district and sign letters of submission once more. The Sfakian elders eventually agreed to Mustafa's demands, promising that once all Sfakians had been consulted they would send four representatives to Chania.

Mustafa had no option but to accept their assurances and return to Chania. He left Frangokastello with his 8,000 troops on the 17th of January and camped in Askifou, but due to difficult weather conditions they remained there for another day, departing in the early morning darkness for the Katre pass. Fearing that the Sfakians might attack as his troops negotiated the pass, which had happened a number of times before with devastating results, Mustafa had sent soldiers ahead to establish defensive positions. His fears were realised: about 250 rebels from all the nearby villages, plus Apokoronas and Agios Vasilios, were in place for an ambush, but their plan was made more difficult by the Turkish advance party's positions. The rebels attacked at daybreak. Mehmed heard the sounds of battle from Embrosneros, and his forces rushed to the Krapi plateau, hauling cannons to bombard the rebels perched on the ridges above the Katre pass. The noise of the battle also attracted rebels from nearby, who joined in with great zeal, swelling the rebel numbers to 400. Fighting continued well into the night, until the last Turks had reached the safety of Embrosneros. This was another crushing defeat for the Turks against a far smaller rebel force; they lost more than 1,000 men, whereas the rebels sustained only 20 casualties.[336]

[336] Reliable figures for casualties are hard to obtain. Papadopetrakis claims that 1,013 Turks were killed and 1,500 were injured, based on information from a doctor working with the Turkish forces (Papadoperakis 1970 [1888], p. 528). Detorakis gives a more conservative figure of 500 Turks killed (Detorakis 1994, p. 339).

Mustafa's mission in Crete had proved to be a complete failure by that stage. Fighting continued to flare up in both the west and east of the island. Although the Sfakians had signed a declaration of submission, they were still very active in the rebellion. There was dissent amongst the senior Turkish officials about Mustafa's more cautious handling of the rebels, while the foreign powers' envoys were becoming more alarmed and vocal about the suffering of the local population, spurred on by public outcries back home. Operations against the rebels continued throughout Crete over the next few months, with no clear victory in sight for the Turks. It is estimated that more than 10,000 of Mustafa's troops lay dead,[337] the equivalent of between a quarter and a third of his total armed forces. The Sultan was becoming more perturbed by the day; he kept receiving requests from Crete for more troops, while at the same time being assured that the insurrection had nearly been quashed. Server Effendi's efforts to convince the Cretans about sending a deputation to negotiate a new constitution for the island were again being frustrated by the Orthodox Cretans, who failed to agree amongst themselves about participating in this initiative; many of them felt that this was another trap laid by the Sultan.[338]

Omer Pasha replaces Mustafa

By March the Sultan had recalled Mustafa and replaced him with one of his more able generals, Omer Pasha, a Croat who had converted to Islam. Omer had a proven track record of putting down rebellions, having quelled several across the Ottoman Empire; and as a commander during the Crimean War, he had helped defeat the Russians at Sevastopol. His mission was to crush the Cretan uprising, which had gone on for far too long and was causing the Sultan serious problems in his dealings with the Great Powers. This change in approach was supported only by the British,[339] while the other Great Powers were against any increase in hostilities and put pressure on the Sultan to grant some form of autonomy to the people of Crete. Omer's plan was to attack and destroy the two districts that had

337 Stillman (1874), p. 104.

338 This effort to bring a deputation to Constantinople degenerated into farce. Eventually, 31 Christian Cretans were forced onto a ship with a number of Muslim Cretans and sent to Constantinople for the conference. Seven of them escaped from Constantinople on a Greek boat before the proceedings were completed, after having first complained to a number of consuls in Constantinople about their forced inclusion in a process which did not represent the wishes of the people of Crete (Mourellos 1950, pp. 1246-1249).

339 The appointment in the previous year of Lord Stanley (Edward Henry Stanley, 15th Earl of Derby) as Secretary of State for Foreign Affairs was followed by adherence to a strict policy of non-intervention in the affairs of the Ottoman Empire, as he feared its imminent collapse with unforeseen consequences for Great Britain's interests.

been the most troublesome to the Turks – Sfakia in the west and Lasithi in the east – believing that this would cause the uprising to collapse.

Omer arrived in Souda Bay on the 27th of March 1867 and immediately started recruiting all able-bodied Muslim Cretans into his army. By the 16th of April, his 12,000 men were joined by Mehmed's contingent of about 5,000 soldiers from Apokoronas; they made for Vrises, from where they could advance on Sfakia. The rebels were aware of the Turks' movements and, anticipating an invasion of Sfakia, once again took up positions along the Katre pass, under the command of Zymvakakis. Hundreds of rebels streamed in from Sfakia and nearby districts, determined not to allow the Turks a victory. Another group of rebels led by Koroneos, which included men from Asfendou and Kallikratis, gathered to the east of Kallikratis, anticipating that the enemy would also approach from the east as they had done previously. Further to the east was yet another group of local rebels and volunteers from the mainland, commanded by Vyzantios. Altogether, there were 5,000 rebel forces guarding the approaches to Sfakia, the largest concentration since the uprising had started.

Omer knew that Sfakia was vulnerable from the southeastern approaches to Kallikratis and decided to launch a two-pronged attack. A contingent led by Mehmed was to attack Sfakia via the Katre pass, the most hazardous approach. Although they expected to meet resistance, they were well prepared for it. A second force of 10,000 under Omer's command was to be joined by Hassan Pasha's 4,000 soldiers from Rethymnon and then head to Kallikratis through Episkopi, Argyroupoli and Asi Gonia. Their first skirmish with rebels took place at Argyroupoli, but the few rebels involved quickly retreated. On the 23rd of April, the Turkish attack began in earnest on both fronts. Mehmed's men encountered resistence much sooner than they expected: the rebels attacked them on their way to the Krapi plateau, near Embrosneros and Alikampos, without waiting for them to enter the Katre pass. At the end of the day-long battle, the Turks were sent fleeing, abandoning their dead as well as many weapons and supplies. Estimates at the time put the Turkish casualties at more than 200, while the rebels only lost 20 fighters. Omer did not fare much better. After a three-hour battle at Myriokefala, southeast of Asi Gonia, his troops were forced to retreat, leaving behind 100 dead. Bad weather over the next four days may have saved the Turks, since it halted the rebels' pursuit, but it also caused great hardship and many deaths amongst Sfakian families and refugees who were hiding in the mountains and caves facing heavy, continuous rain and snow.

Omer's troops retreated to the north coast to resupply, all the time shadowed and harassed by the rebels. It is unclear why Omer did not then resume his campaign against Sfakia. Instead, he headed for Rethymnon, arriving on the 28th of April with an army of about 9,000. His target and final destination was Lasithi, the base for many of eastern Crete's most active rebels, but on the way there his troops also destroyed everything in their path. Mustafa's soldiers had set fire to villages, but Omer's razed them to the ground, burning even the olive and fruit trees, and killing women and children, who Mustafa would have spared. These stories of extreme cruelty reached the foreign consuls in Chania and Rethymnon on a daily basis, but they had no way of expressing their abhorrence about what was happening other than by writing to their respective governments.

Resit Pasha's 9,000 Turkish soldiers and Muslim Cretans from Heraklion, who were in the vanguard of the forces heading for Lasithi, engaged with rebels east of Rethymnon. Rebel groups were now under the command of the various mainland leaders – Zymvakakis, Petropoulakis, and Koroneos – as well as numerous other local *Kapetanioi*, including the legendary Korakas, and Skoulas from Anogia; this lack of central control would again plague their campaign. Omer's troops reached Heraklion on the 10th of May, after razing a large number of villages between Apokoronas and Mylopotamos, and despite the heroic efforts of the rebels to slow down their progress, and moved on to the Lasithi plateau, engaging in some clashes with rebels on the way. Omer's 30,000-stong army, which included Ismail Ferik's Egyptian contingent, approached Lasithi from a number of different directions, making it more difficult for the rebels to defend the plateau. The battle for Lasithi lasted ten full days, during which the Turks suffered significant losses,[340] including the death of Ismail Ferik,[341] while the rebels lost 150 of their men. But more devastating were the brutal massacres of civilians, and the destruction of their villages, crops, fruit trees and flocks. This was the second time in 40 years that Lasithi had been razed to the ground by the Turks.

In the west, Mehmed's troops had retreated to the areas around Vrises after his defeat at Krapi, waiting to see what the rebels would do next. Unfortunately, the lack of a strong, unified rebel command structure again stifled the uprising's momentum from their two heroic victories, and rebels started drifting back to their villages. Mehmed was informed about their reduced numbers and decided to attack, calling for reinforcements from Chania. Zymvakakis found out about Mehmed's preparations and urgently called for the rebels who had left a few weeks earlier to return. The two forces – about 5,000 Turks against well under 1,000 rebels – clashed initially

[340] Mourellos writes that more than 500 Turks were killed and up to 1,000 injured (Mourellos 1950, p. 1327).

[341] While other historians report that Ismail was wounded during a battle at Lasithi and eventually died at Kastelli, Mourellos reports that Ismail was poisoned by Omer, possibly because of his insistence on the more humane treatment of the civilian population (Mourellos 1950, pp. 1330-1332). As mentioned earlier, Ismail was originally a Cretan from the Lasithi district; he was taken to Egypt as a child and forced to convert to the Muslim faith.

on the 20th of May around Vafes, and the Turkish army was driven off. The rebels repulsed three more attacks by the Turks, including one made along three fronts.

Over these two weeks of battles, the rebels had held off the enemy remarkably well, given their own small numbers; however, disagreements erupted amongst them, especially with Zymvakakis about strategy, and with the Sfakians about the distribution of weapons and supplies from Greece. As a result, some of the *Kapetanioi* departed, leaving Zymvakakis and the Sfakians to deal with the dangerous situation on their own. Their bitter infighting had blinded the rebels to the fact that this situation could result in the eventual collapse of the uprising. By the 9th of June, fewer than 500 rebels remained to protect the approaches to Sfakia; they were attacked once again at Embrosneros and were forced to retreat to Alikambos. Another Turkish assault on the 24th of June pushed them further back to the Krapi plateau, and from there they had no other option than to take up positions along the Katre pass in preparation for the next Turkish attack. Mehmed's troops had now managed to pin down the rebels at one of the access points to Sfakia, while further to the west Turkish forces from Chania engaged with the rebels in Kissamos to prevent them from coming to the assistance of Zymvakakis' depleted forces.

Omer Pasha's attack on Sfakia

Having dispersed the rebel forces in Lasithi, Omer left behind two battalions to deal with the rebels who had withdrawn to Vianos and Kastelli, and then departed for Heraklion to prepare for his next campaign against the Sfakians. His plan was to launch a three-pronged attack: Mehmed's troops would approach from the north; Resit's would advance from the southeast via Kallikratis; and his own 8,000 troops would proceed to the south coast at Timbaki, on Messara Bay, where they would board 12 Turkish naval vessels for Frangokastello and approach Sfakia from there. Mehmed recruited additional Muslim Cretan forces from Apokoronas and Kissamos, then pushed towards Sfakia via Krapi with more than 10,000 troops. Zymvakakis was informed of this increase in activity and asked the area's *Kapetanioi* for reinforcements as a matter of urgency. Resit proceeded down the Amari valley with more than 20,000 men; despite harassment from rebels along the way, he was unstoppable. The rebels in Kallikratis and Asfendou sent their families away to safety and prepared for battle.

Omer's men disembarked just east of Frangokastello on the morning of the 24th of June and took up positions around Kapsodasos, Patsianos and Kolokasia. As previously agreed, Mehmed began his campaign along the Katre pass on the 25th of June, tying down any rebels in the area to prevent them reaching their comrades fighting on the south coast. By the 27th of June, Resit's army made their first contact with rebels near Kallikratis, establishing the third front. The 1,500-strong rebel force, headed by Koroneos and including men from Sfakia, Rethymnon and Agios Vasilios, managed to pin down the much larger Turkish army for a number of days. By the 28th of June, Mehmed's troops had reached the northern Askifou plateau and dug in at Kares, while the rebels still controlled the southern end of the plateau around Amoudari, Stavrorachi and Petres. The rebels managed to trap the Turks there for a number of days by cutting off the Katre pass, thus also preventing any reinforcements from reaching them and severing Mehmed's lines of communication with Omer. Koroneos' rebels near Kallikratis were holding off Resit's forces so they could not come to Mehmed's rescue. Thus the majority of the Turkish forces were stopped from joining Omer's men on the south coast. It was not until the 5th of July that Omer's forces managed to break through the rebel lines and free Mehmed's forces in Askifou, as well as Resit's men, who had joined them there. After setting fire to all the villages on the Askifou plateau, the combined Ottoman armies marched to Imbros, where the rebels hoped they could stop them, but the far larger Turkish force easily dispersed the rebels.

Omer, unnerved by the strong resistance his troops had met at the northern and eastern approaches to Sfakia, sent an envoy by boat to Chora Sfakion on the 28th of June to demand the Sfakians' immediate capitulation, but the envoy was arrested and taken to the central revolutionary committee in Mouri and the boat was confiscated. Outraged at this insult, Omer burned down the village of Komitades and dispatched more emissaries to Mouri and Asfendou, again demanding immediate surrender. At the same time, to cover up his failure, he sent messages to the foreign consuls in Chania announcing that the Sfakians had capitulated and surrendered their weapons. This misinformation was refuted by the rebels' central committee via circulars denouncing these lies and seeking the foreign governments' support. Omer also put pressure on the Sfakians by hunting down the families who had taken refuge in the many caves in the area (e.g. Agiasmatsi and Schisti), attacking them, threatening them with starvation, smoking them out by placing burning bushes in the cave entrances, and demanding their surrender. The consuls became very alarmed by these events, but Omer claimed that his intention was simply to relocate these families to safer places. Intervention by the French consul, who travelled to Sfakia to see the situation for himself, resulted in Omer giving a personal undertaking about the families' safe passage, which was eventually accomplished.

On the 9th of July, Omer issued an ultimatum addressed to all Cretans, especially the Sfakians, giving them 24 hours to lay down their arms or else he would destroy Sfakia. Before the 24 hours was over, Omer's forces attacked Anopoli; a rebel contingent of 600 men were forced to retreat to the western ridge of the Aradena Gorge. The Turks destroyed all the settlements on the Anopoli plateau but were prevented from moving higher up towards Mouri. A huge Turkish force was deployed along the eastern ridge of the Aradena Gorge, from Dialiskari on Marmara Bay all the way up to the northern end, creating a front 7 kilometres in length. The troops at Dialiskari had arrived on foot via Loutro and Livaniana, and by boat from Kissamos. The rebel forces were stretched very thin, since Zymvakakis' men had to protect the Imbros pass in case Resit's forces attempted to come across through Kali Lakki, while Koromeos' rebels were holding the Kallikratis-Asfendou area to stop the Turks there from advancing to Anopoli.

Spread out along the western ridge of the Aradena Gorge were rebels from Sfakia and Apokoronas and volunteers from the mainland at the centre and southern end, with men from Selino and Kydonia at the northern end. The two sides fired at each other for two days without the Turks managing to cross the gorge, but on the third day, the 13th of July, a large contingent of Turks attacked at the northern end to create a diversion from their main objective of getting troops across the gorge lower down. Some 4,000 Turks crossed from Livaniana, while the 2,000 men at Marmara Bay, supported by cannon fire from the four naval vessels which had brought the troops from Kissamos, advanced north along the western ridge of the gorge. The rebels were soon obliged to withdraw to Aradena, as it was impossible to stop the huge tide of Turks that was surging northward. With additional pressure from the Turks at the northern end of the gorge, the rebels were forced to retreat to higher ground at Krousia, north of Agios Ioannis. The disastrous outcome of this battle was also the beginning of the end of the uprising; and the battle resembled one fought at the same location during the Daskalogiannis uprising some 100 years previously, which had also heralded the end of that tragic rebellion.

The rebels dispersed, many returning to their villages to protect their families, who they feared were to be the next targets of the Turks. While the battle at Aradena was drawing to an end, five Turkish naval vessels took troops to Agia Roumeli, where the rebels kept some of their stores and where large numbers of refugees had taken shelter. The rebels had constructed fortifications there in anticipation of another attempt by the Turks to enter the Samaria Gorge, and they managed to prevent the Turks from disembarking, despite heavy cannon fire from the ships for more than five hours. Another attempted landing two days later was also repelled, but the ships then sailed further west to Fournoti beach, where 4,000 Turks disembarked and headed for Agia Roumeli. The rebels tried to stop their progress but were pushed back. Simultaneously, another Turkish contingent descended to the coast from Agios Ioannis and advanced to Agia Roumeli along the beach, posing a threat from another direction. The rebels, seeing that they were in danger, set fire to their stores and ammunition in Agia Roumeli and retreated into the gorge. The Turks were unable to pursue them and had to abandon their attempt to dislodge the rebels from the Samaria Gorge.

Resit's troops returned to Heraklion, harassed all along the way by rebels, and Mehmed's forces went back to Apokoronas to await new developments. Omer took his men by ship to Sougia, where they were joined by those who had been unsuccessful at taking the Samaria Gorge. Omer then sailed to Chania to deal with the foreign consuls, who were becoming increasingly outspoken about the plight of the civilian population. His troops in Sougia were joined by local Muslim Cretan irregulars and other locally posted Turkish troops, bringing this force to more than 10,000; they began operations against the few rebels who had returned to the area, and on the 24th of July they took control of Kandanos.

On Omer's orders, Mehmed left Apokoronas with some 5,000 troops on the 29th of July to join the Turks in the west, whose goal was now to seize control of the Omalos plateau, which many of the rebels had escaped to after the battles in Sfakia. The rebels took up positions around Agia Irini, Livada and Koustogerako, but the Turks cut through their defences, taking the villages of Kambanos, Livada and Epanochori; however, they were not able to break through to the plateau. A concentrated attack on the 31st of July eventually enabled them to reach Omalos, but by that time the rebels' families had escaped to higher ground. This was the first time that the Turks had ever penetrated this far. But they were soon attacked by rebels from all directions and had to retreat without reaching Xyloskalo, the northern entrance to the Samaria Gorge. More rebels arrived from the north, and the Turks fled the next day to Agia Irini and on to Livada, abandoning their pursuit of the rebels in the higher reaches of the Lefka Ori.[342]

[342] The unsuccessful campaign of Omer Pasha in Sfakia was discussed by the American consul in Crete, William Stillman, in his report to the Secretary of State on the 17th of August, 1867, where he stated, amongst other things: "Omer Pasha…claims…complete control of Sfakia; but from complete and reliable information I am able to inform you that his pretensions are contrary to the actual fact. … All attempts [to enter the Samaria Gorge] failed and this wild fortress made good its ancient reputation of the impregnable Cretan stronghold and the troops were withdrawn, having lost, by the more reliable accounts I can obtain, about seven hundred killed and wounded. … They [the Turks] have never succeeded in defeating the Christians decisively or in holding a position which made reconquest easier, but, on the contrary, the tactics of the Christians have succeeded in wearing the army out and causing losses by sickness and fatigue, which amount to thousands, including some of the best officers and utterly discouraging the rest, who find an enemy always retiring yet always harassing, but over whom no victory is possible. … All the highland districts are again in the hands of the insurgents and to be occupied must be won by the same tedious and costly operations by which they have been once, though very partially and briefly, occupied, which the army now in the island would not suffer for." Stillman (1976), pp. 78, 79.

Omer's campaign continues without a clear outcome

Although the Turkish army could overcome the rebels because of their superior numbers, modern arms and better supply lines, they could not maintain continuous control over the areas they had taken. As soon as the troops returned to their bases or moved on to their next target, the rebels would reappear, regroup and attack. Skirmishes continued throughout the island over the course of the next two months. Resit's troops destroyed villages in the Agios Vasilios district, but the rebels took revenge by seizing opportunities to attack the Turks whenever they could. In the east, fighting erupted in the Mirabello district, and Korakas recaptured the Lasithi plateau, while in the west more battles were fought in Kissamos. The Turks entered Sfakia once again on the 16th of August in pursuit of Zymvakakis, who was in Askifou at the time. They arrived in Chora Sfakion by ship, walked up to Mouri, and from there crossed to Askifou. The Sfakians followed them, waiting for the right opportunity to attack. Eventually the chance arose when the Turkish troops were returning to their ship; the Sfakians ambushed them in Komitades, inflicting some losses on the Turks before they escaped.[343]

Omer's campaign, although not successful from a military view point, was distinguished from other efforts at suppression by his brutal policy of totally destroying villages and persecuting the civilian population in the most barbarous way. This resulted in the foreign consuls[344] sending urgent reports to their respective governments requesting them to intervene politically and provide more ships to transport the refugees to safer locations. French and Russian naval vessels again disregarded the Turkish blockade and approached the southwest coast to rescue civilians who were being hunted down by Muslim Cretans and other irregulars, doing so even when Turkish troops and ships were present. The day that the Turks abandoned their attempt to enter the Samaria Gorge, a French naval destroyer, the *Prométhée,* along with two other French frigates, took refugees on board at Agia Roumeli while a Turkish battleship stood by uncertain whether to intervene; they then sailed on to Tripiti and Sougia, picking up more refugees. Russian, Italian and Prussian vessels joined this

---

[343] Mourellos (1950), pp. 1384-1386.

[344] The American Consul Stillman reported "attacks from irregulars both Cretan Mussulmen and others, who, without any regard to the protection accorded by the Government, commit the most barbarous outrages on these districts – murdering, raping, robbing, desolating whole districts guilty of no acts of hostility, so that those who have submitted to the Government are in worse state than those who are still in rebellion. We have today news of whole villages being surrounded at night and their inhabitants all massacred in districts which Omar Pasha has announced as completely pacified and which surrendered their arms on assurance of protection." Stillman (1976), p. 77.

evacuation mission, scouring the coast for civilians.[345] Similar reports were filed by consuls in Heraklion about thousands of refugees fleeing from Muslim Cretans to the north coast of Mylopotamos district and along the southern coast at Messara, where they waited under the protection of rebel forces for foreign vessels to take them to safety. As happened in the west of the island, Italian, French and other foreign naval vessels disregarded the Turkish blockade and picked up the desperate refugees. This in turn left the rebels, who had been protecting their families, free to rejoin the rebellion.

While the Turks were trying to reach Omalos, the Greek blockade runner *Arkadi* was lost off the southwest coast of Crete. The *Arkadi* had arrived at night in Agia Roumeli, bringing supplies and taking on civilian refugees. Three Turkish naval vessels gave chase, firing their cannons. A cannon ball hit and disabled one of the *Arkadi's* engines, slowing it down enough for the Turks to catch up, but the captain ran the ship aground near Palaeochora, enabling all those on board to escape. Although the loss of the *Arkadi* was a serious blow to the uprising, two other Greek vessels, the *Enosis* and the *Kriti,* joined the mission.

The Sultan's campaign was not producing the desired results; he could see that the continuous fighting had not diminished the rebels' determination. Furthermore, the inhumane treatment of civilians was having a negative impact on the Ottoman Empire's image among Western nations. Pressure was being put on the Ottoman government by Great Britain, France, and Russia, and to a lesser degree by Italy and Prussia, although each country supported a different solution to the governance of Crete.

Aali Pasha replaces Omer Pasha; the Organic Act

Early in September 1867, the Sultan announced that Omer was to be recalled. A five-week ceasefire was arranged, and an amnesty was granted to all rebels in the run-up to the arrival of the new governor, Grand Vizier Aali Pasha. He arrived in Chania on the 22nd of September with a fresh assignment: to introduce new laws for the governance of Crete, preferably with the agreement of the locals. Aali immediately invited representatives from every district, two Christians and two Muslims each, to meet with him and agree to a new form of government for the island. The central revolutionary committee rejected this proposal at once; they were suspicious of Aali and were still in favour of union with Greece, although some of them were prepared to compromise on a form of independence guaranteed by the Great Powers. Aali insisted on forming a committee to provide at least the appearance of general popular consent and recruited 30 Christians through pressure, blackmail and bribes, as well as 20 Muslims.

[345] Mourellos (1950), p. 1378.

On the 11th of October, Aali presented the committee with the Sultan's proposed new laws for governing Crete, known as the Organic Act. Two days later the Act was printed in both languages and distributed throughout Crete, and the committee was given eight days to study and comment on it. The proposals included the formation of a general assembly, lower taxes, use of the Greek language alongside Turkish in official documents, and recognition of assemblies of Christian elders. Crete was to continue to be a province (*vilayet*) of the Ottoman Empire governed by a representative of the Sultan, the Governor General (*Vali*), and was to be divided into five districts and 20 provinces. Sfakia was one of the five districts, containing the provinces of Sfakia, Apokoronas and Agios Vasilios. District and council employees were to include a pre-determined proportion of Christians and Muslims. Law courts were also to have both Christian and Muslim representation. The committee was given to understand that it had no option but to endorse the new law under which Crete was to be governed for the next ten years.

The central revolutionary committee rejected the Organic Act and carried on fighting in most parts of the island. Aali tighten the blockade of the island by employing eight new destroyers; he knew very well the pressure that starving refugees would put on the rebels' will to continue. Early in November, a large Turkish contingent once again invaded the Lakki area and pursued the rebels near Alikianos and Zourva, with battles continuing until mid-December, when the cold and lack of food forced the rebels to disperse. However, they returned in mid-January to continue the struggle. In Rethymnon, the Turks rarely attempted to leave the safety of the fortifications to engage with the rebels. Battles in the areas between Mirabello, Vianos and Ierapetra continued throughout the winter.

Sfakia was not spared from occasional incursions by the Turks. In late December, two Turkish naval vessels arrived at Dialiskari, on Marmara Bay, and put to flight a number of refugees who were waiting there for a passing foreign vessel to take them to safety. The Turks advanced on Anopoli, and the few rebels still there fought valiantly, but their small numbers could not inflict any serious harm on the enemy.[346] Turkish troops arrived in Chora Sfakion by ship in late January 1868 and attacked some villages, but they found very few people there, since most had been warned that the Turks were on their way and had taken refuge in the mountains. There was no real resistance, as most rebels had either already moved up to difficult terrain or were fighting in other parts of Crete.[347]

The Organic Act was issued as an Imperial Decree on the 8th of January 1868 and put into circulation throughout the island on the 3rd of February; it incorporated some minor changes to satisfy some of the Cretans'

[346] Mourellos (1950), p. 1405.
[347] Ibid., p. 1422.

demands. Aali tried to convene a pan-Cretan conference to convince the Great Powers and the Sultan that there was general acceptance of the new law, but he was unsuccessful. Clashes continued throughout Crete, but the rebels' enthusiasm had waned, and civilians were still trying to leave the island. Disagreements between rebels and civilians over the meagre and diminishing food supplies discouraged the population even further from continuing with the rebellion. To further break their unity of purpose, in mid-February Aali started delivering food to all the villages that were prepared to declare their submission to his rule. But this did not continue for long, since the villagers would sign the submission document, receive the supplies, return to the mountains where their families had taken refuge, and continue with their opportunistic attacks. The Turks soon realised that this plan was not going to work and stopped distributing food.

A new strategy for conducting the war against the rebels was attempted on the recommendation of a British former naval officer, Hobart-Hampden,[348] who was now in the employ of the Ottomans. The Turks began building a chain of forts within sight of each other; this would enable them to keep an eye on rebel activities in known insurgent areas and monitor where outside help was coming in. There were 150 such forts built throughout Crete during this period; Sfakia, a rebel stronghold, had twenty.[349] Some were fairly large and contained permanent garrisons, while others were simply small observation posts. They are known in Crete by the Turkish

[348] Augustus Charles Hobart-Hampden, a former British Navy officer who entered the service of the Ottomans in 1867. He was immediately given command over the Ottoman fleet to help suppress the insurrection in Crete and was rewarded by the Sultan with the title of Pasha in 1869.

[349] Starting with the northern approaches to Sfakia, the Turks built a fort on Rogdio peak looking north to Embrosneros, where there were two more forts, and looking south to the two forts at the northern end of the Askifou plateau There is some speculation that the northern one was initially Venetian because of its different design, but there is nothing in the Venetian era reports to indicate that there was a fort there. From Askifou one can see the ruins of a small fort at Imbros, located at the northern approach to the village on a small hill above the road. In the south, there were already Venetian fortresses at Frangokastello and Chora Sfakion. The Turks built a fort higher above Chora Sfakion on the northeastern edge of the village, just above Agioi Apostoloi church. To the west, one was erected on the eastern ridge of the Illingas gorge and another further west at Kambia in Anopoli, with a separate observation post which overlooked the Sfakia district to the east all the way to Frangokastello. Further to the west on the Anopoli plateau there are forts at Agia Ekaterini and Agios Dimitrios, in sight of the one below at Loutro. Above Agios Ioannis are two forts with clear views eastwards to those on the Anopoli plateau and westwards to those above Agia Roumeli. There are four forts at Agia Roumeli, two on each side of the Samaria Gorge; another was constructed above Samaria village which can be seen from Xyloskalo, where a fort provided a line of communication with those on the Omalos plateau and Lakki. To the west of Agia Roumeli, there is a Turkish fort at Tripiti which looks west to Sougia, and from there a line of forts ran northwards to Chania. See www.dalidakis.com

name for a fortified structure, *kale* (in Greek *koules*, plural *kouledes*). Most of these forts remained intact while the Ottomans controlled Crete, and some of them survive today as tourist attractions and a reminder of the bitter wars that were fought. In Sfakia, the better-preserved Turkish forts are in Askifou (the southern of the two forts there), Loutro, Agia Roumeli (the lower fort), and Tripiti. The others are in various stages of collapse; some are now no more than a pile of rocks. There is nothing left of the Turkish fort above Chora Sfakion, as the location has been converted to a water pumping facility for the village.

Aali departed for Constantinople at the end of February 1868, leaving Hussein Avni Pasha as the new governor tasked with overseeing the implementation of the Organic Act and bringing the uprising to an end. Aali reported to the Sultan that his mission had not been entirely successful since the rebellion had not been crushed.

Diplomatic events outside Crete, 1867-1869[350]

While battles raged all over Crete in 1867, the Great Powers, who had agreed to maintain the integrity of the Ottoman Empire at the Paris Treaty of 1856, were trying to reach a compromise solution to the Cretan problem. The Greek Koumoundouros government's preparations for war added to the complexity of the problem. As mentioned earlier, the British were in favour of non-intervention in the Cretan uprising, and they maintained this position throughout the discussions. The French had no intention of intervening directly, although they had initially promoted the formation of a commission of inquiry to examine the Cretans' grievances. As negotiations dragged on, the French proposed granting some sort of local autonomy to the Cretans, a line that at times was also favoured by Russia; the two countries tended to side with each other, although they argued about who would take the lead in exerting pressure on the Ottoman government. Britain appeared to agree with the autonomy option but was not prepared to actively promote it. Greece's call for Crete to declare independence from Ottoman rule was rejected outright by Britain, which feared that this would lead to the unravelling of the Ottoman Empire, as other occupied areas would make similar demands. But Britain also did not want Greece to gain control of such an important base in the eastern Mediterranean, which would provide a link to the sea route to India via the Suez canal when it opened in 1869. The French proposal for a form of autonomy for Crete was finally tabled on the 14th of June, 1867, and it was eventually supported by all the Great Powers, but the plan was rejected by the Ottoman government. The Sultan's visit to London and Paris in the summer of 1867 gave these

[350] Besides drawing on Greek historical sources, this section is also based on material from Bourne (1956), pp. 74-94.

The ruins of two of the forts built by the Turks in 1868 at Askifou

countries the opportunity to put more pressure on him, as he had to face the increasing criticism in their press about the barbarous treatment of the starving refugees.

As we saw earlier, the Sultan appointed Aali Pasha as governor of Crete and gave him the task of introducing a set of reforms (the Organic Act) as a way of breaking the deadlock with the Great Powers and offering a solution that partially met their demands. The Great Powers, with the exception of Britain, complained that the changes fell well short of what was required, but they received no response to their legitimate concerns.

Throughout 1867, the Greek government continued to support the Cretan uprising by shipping supplies, volunteers and arms to Crete, to the great annoyance of the Ottomans. At the end of 1868, an event took place that brought things to a head. An expedition of around 1,000 volunteers headed by the son of the Maniot Colonel Petropoulakis was preparing to leave for Crete on the 24th of November 1868. This well-publicised mission was further than the Ottoman government was prepared to allow the Greek government to go, and they had the full backing of all the Great Powers in this decision. On the 29th of November, the Ottoman government's ambassador in Greece issued the Greek government with an ultimatum, stating the following conditions: 1) All volunteer organizations supporting the Cretan insurrection had to be disbanded immediately; 2) Armaments must be removed from the "pirate" naval vessels the *Enosis, Panhellenion* and *Kriti,* and they were forbidden access to Greek ports; 3) All Cretan refugees must be allowed to return to Crete, with full assistance provided; 4) All those guilty of attacking Ottoman soldiers and citizens were to be punished and compensation paid to their families; 5) The Greek government's policies must in future be in line with common law and current international law. If the Greek government did not agree to these demands within 8 days, diplomatic relations would be suspended. This meant war!

At the same time another crisis was unfolding, involving the blockade runner *Enosis* and three Turkish naval vessels commanded by Hobart-Hampden. He had received new instructions from the Ottoman government to capture or sink the blockade runners, which he was allowed to do in Greek territorial waters but not in Greek ports; however, if the ship had fired on a Turkish vessel, he could enter the port and arrest the crew on the basis that it was a "pirate" vessel. The Turkish fleet soon caught up with the *Enosis* on its way to the Greek island of Syros on the morning of the 2nd of December, after it had delivered the Petropoulakis volunteers and other supplies to Crete. A gun battle ensued during which the *Enosis* landed several direct hits on one of the Turkish ships, killing and injuring some of the sailors on board. The *Enosis* managed to escape to the port on Syros, pursued by the other two Turkish vessels. Hobart-Hampden immediately wrote to the district governor of the Cyclades[351] outlining the events that had just taken place, accusing the *Enosis* of an act of piracy, demanding that the matter be brought before the consuls of the Great Powers and that Greek laws on piracy should be used against the *Enosis'* crew. The governor convened a meeting with the consuls, including the Turkish consul, and expressed his outrage at this insult to Greece. The Greek government, despite advice from the Great Powers, ordered the Greek frigate *Hellas* to sail immediately to Syros with instructions to attack the Turkish vessels. Fortunately, the French consul in Athens rushed to Pireaus, where the French corvette *Forbin* was moored, and despatched the ship to Syros to intervene. The *Forbin* reached Syros before the *Hellas,* which had to restock on its way, and a confrontation was averted. Because the Greek authorities did not respond to Hobart-Hampden's demands, he left Syros port but blockaded the island using three other Turkish naval vessels.[352] Following pressure by the Great Powers, the Greek government had to back down, and the governor of the Cyclades, on instructions from Athens, passed a letter to the English consul informing him that Hobart-Hampden's accusations had been submitted to the Greek courts, who would examine the case, and that the *Enosis* was prohibited from leaving the port. Although this diffused the situation, Hobart-Hampden and his fleet remained stationed outside Syros for a few more days to ensure that *Enosis* did not leave.

[351] The group of islands to which Syros belongs.

[352] Mourellos (1950), pp. 1501-1504.

While this was going on, the eight-day timeframe of the Turkish ultimatum had expired, and the Turkish ambassador and his staff had left for Constantinople. The Great Powers, alarmed at the escalation of events, convened a conference in Paris early in January and declared that the Greek government should prohibit men being recruited to attack Ottoman territories (i.e. Crete) and ships being fitted out in Greek ports to transport aid to the rebels in Crete, and that it should allow Cretan refugees to return to the island. An additional note advised that if the Greek government failed to accept the terms of this declaration within a week, the Great Powers would abandon Greece to the consequences. Greece had no option left but to accept the Paris declaration. From a Cretan perspective, this sealed the fate of the 1866 uprising.

Battles continue throughout 1868: focus on Sfakia

Throughout 1868, the fighting continued in most parts of Crete but with less intensity, as a number of areas gradually submitted to Ottoman rule in the expectation that the Organic Act would make life more bearable for their families. Sfakians continued with their aggressive struggle throughout the island, many of them taking on leadership positions.

Sometime after Omer Pasha's destruction of Sfakia in July 1867, the Turks established permanent army camps in Chora Sfakion and Frangokastello. The number of troops reported to be stationed at these two locations varies from writer to writer, but there must have been more than 1,000 in Chora Sfakion and several thousand in Frangokastello.[353] Turkish forces arrived in Chora Sfakion by boat and camped in the old Venetian fort above the harbour and the newly built structure at the northeastern end of the village. The village had been nearly abandoned by the locals, who must have been pushed up to higher ground with difficult living conditions by such a large number of enemies practically living amongst them. As well as keeping the Sfakians under control, the Turkish garrisons supported the effort mentioned earlier to construct forts for a permanent army in this area, one of the major initiatives taken by the Turks to prevent new rebellions erupting across the island, as well as supporting the troops in Frangokastello.

The presence of enemy forces so close by was too much of a temptation for the rebels. When troops moved between these two locations, the Sfakians ambushed them and then withdrew to the mountains. On one such occasion, on the 25th of April a large group of about 900 rebels gathered in Kallikratis and attacked the Turks in Chora Sfakion, who were defended by cannon

[353] V. Psilakis (1970 [1906]), Vol. 4. pp. 322 and 342, claims there were 1,600 Turks stationed in Chora Sfakion and 6,000 in Frangokastello. Papadopetrakis (1971 [1888]), p. 560, puts the number at 6,000, which must include those in Frangokastello.

fire from four ships anchored in the bay.[354] Although after a day-long battle the Sfakians were not able to dislodge the Turks from the village, they demonstrated that the rebellion had not yet been suppressed. In another skirmish on the 20th of June, the rebels made an assault on Turkish forces camped in Anopoli,[355] during which they lost one of the most celebrated Sfakian *Kapetanioi* of this period, Tselepis Daskalogiannis.[356] The next day they learned that some of the Turks from the Chora Sfakion garrison were going to Frangokastello and prepared to attack them. Sfakians from nearby areas joined them at Komitades and inflicted heavy losses on the Turks, forcing them to return to Chora Sfakion. The rebels engaged the Turkish troops again in July as they attempted to move beyond Frangokastello, and drove them back into the fortress there. Later that month, enemy troops managed to advance further east with the support of cannon fire from two Turkish naval vessels which shadowed their progress along the coast to prevent the rebels from getting near them.[357] The rebels attacked Turkish troops twice again in August while they moved from one location to the other, both times near Komitades.[358]

During this time, the Turks had also taken control of the Omalos plateau and were similarly busy erecting a line of forts linking Omalos with the main army base in Chania. One of their ultimate targets was to take the Samaria Gorge. On the 14th of June, Turkish troops approached Xyloskalo, the northern entrance to the gorge, but they were soon driven back, with serious losses, by rebels who had taken up positions on higher ground around the northern approaches. The Turks made a second attempt to enter the gorge on the 20th of June from another entrance at Poria,[359] but the rebels forced them to retreat, again with heavy losses.[360] However, the gorge was to remain free of Turks for only a few more months.

Askifou was another area that the Turks wanted to seize control of, since many of the Sfakian rebels used it as their base; furthermore, they needed to build forts in this area in order to link the coastal forts of Sfakia with the heavier troop concentrations in the north of the island. Early that September, some 5,000 Turks headed for Askifou from Frangokastello, while another contingent approached it via the Krapi plateau and the Katre pass. Rebels, some of them Sfakians, and volunteers were already in

[354] Mourellos (1950), p. 1448.

[355] Ibid., p. 1457. The historian does not tell us why the Turks were in Anopoli at the time, but we can safely assume that this again involved support for building forts, since three were erected there.

[356] Ibid., p. 1457. He was the great-grandson of the tragic hero of the 1770 uprising and nephew of Tselepis Daskalogiannis, who was killed in 1821.

[357] Ibid. pp. 1469-1470; V. Psilakis (1970 [1906]), Vol. 4, pp. 343 and 345.

[358] Mourellos (1950), p. 1477; V. Psilakis (1970 [1906]), Vol. 4, p. 353.

[359] Northeast of Xyloskalo, a short distance beyond today's Kallergi refuge hut.

[360] Mourellos (1950), p. 1462.

Askifou when they learned that the Turkish army was heading their way up the Katre pass. They immediately took up positions on either side of the pass and ambushed the Turks as they entered it, causing many casualties. But when the Turkish forces arrived from the south, the rebels were forced back towards Amoudari, and from there up to the Tavri plateau, and finally to Mouri.[361] And so another stronghold of the Sfakians had been seized by the Turks, who immediately started constructing forts in this area to link Embrosneros with the south coast.

During this period, the blockade runner *Enosis* was a frequent presence on the Sfakian coast, bringing in supplies and ammunition for the rebels and their families. There are reports of deliveries on the 2nd of July in Tripiti, where the ship also deposited a few volunteers, on the 16th of July again in Tripiti, and early in September in Phoenix, when the *Enosis* was pursued by a Turkish naval vessel but managed to escape to Gavdos. On the 6th of November, the *Enosis* arrived in Loutro with supplies, ammunition and 60 Cretan rebels returning from mainland Greece. The Turks found out about this, rushed down to Loutro from Anopoli, and confiscated most of the supplies.[362] This was the beginning of the end to the rebels' access to outside help in this part of the island. The Turks soon built a large fort at Loutro, and other Turkish troops shifted westwards towards Agia Roumeli and Tripiti. The Turkish governor of Sfakia, Savas Pasha,[363] had established himself in Chora Sfakion by that time and called a conference of all Sfakian elders on the 22nd of November to announce the terms that the Sultan was prepared to offer in order to end the fighting; those who did not attend would continue to be persecuted. The majority of the Sfakian elders,[364] including most from the mountain villages, capitulated.[365]

By that time the only free area in Sfakia was around the mountain villages of Asfendou and Kallikratis, where the central revolutionary committee had gathered to assess the impact that these calls for submission and offers of amnesty were having. Petropoulakis' rebel force and other volunteers had just arrived in Kallikratis from further east on the 9th of December, pursued by Turks; soon the enemy caught up with them and attacked, forcing the rebels to disperse above Askifou, while the committee headed for Asi Gonia in the hope of finding safety amongst rebels there.

[361] Ibid., p. 1480, V. Psilakis (1970 [1906]), Vol. 4, p. 360.
[362] V. Psilakis (1970 [1906]), Vol. 4, p. 378.
[363] Ioannis Savas was a Greek Christian from Ioannina, in northern Greece. He became a doctor in Constantinople and worked for the Ottoman government in administrative positions. His appointment as governor of the province of Sfakia, with his base in Vamos, was his first post outside Constantinople. In 1887 he became Governor of Crete.
[364] Mourellos (1950), p. 1508.
[365] Ibid., p. 1494. Papadopetrakis (1971 [1888]), p. 570 says that "all the elders of Sfakia came by the end of December to Ombrosgialos (Chora Sfakion) to give their submission officially to Savas Pasha".

The Turks destroyed Kallikratis, Asfendou and Imbros and massacred most of the civilians they encountered. On the night of the 11th, the committee found themselves surrounded by Turks before they could reach Asi Gonia, and although some managed to escape, others were killed while fleeing or were executed as soon as they were arrested. This was a tragic end for those who had provided leadership and inspiration for the uprising.

Petropoulakis received a letter from the French consul in Chania telling him that Greece had been issued with an ultimatum, that the Great Powers would not support Greece or the rebellion in Crete in any way, and strongly advising him to surrender.[366] Surrounded by Turks and with no hope of outside support, the rebel leaders agreed to surrender under terms that allowed them to leave Crete with their weapons, while the Cretans amongst their group were given an amnesty but had to surrender their weapons.[367]

About 250 rebels from nearby areas were trapped in the Samaria Gorge, since all access routes to the outside had been cut off by Turkish troops. They received a message from the Sfakian elders on the 19th of December urging them to try to escape, and if this was impossible, to give themselves up, since Savas Pasha had promised them amnesty. They were given a week to decide what to do. Exposed to the bitter cold and snow, with little food to sustain them, and surrounded by the enemy on all sides, they were left with no option but to surrender. All of Sfakia was now under Turkish control.

The end of the uprising

By the end of January 1869, Greece had given in to the Ottoman ultimatum and pressure from the Great Powers to stop providing any further support to the uprising in Crete. The rebellion continued in the eastern districts into early January, but soon word of the rebels' capitulation in the west reached those still fighting, as did news of the Ottoman government's ultimatum to Greece and the Great Powers' demands at the Paris conference. A renewed attack on the 10th of January by a large Turkish force from Heraklion left the rebels with very few options.

The *Kapetanioi* leading the fight in the east hastily gathered to try to reach an agreement on the future direction of their struggle. Some refused to give in to Turkish pressure to surrender and took to the mountains, others decided to leave for mainland Greece, while yet others reluctantly agreed to surrender and accept the amnesty terms offered by the Turks, which were in line with the agreement negotiated by the Great Powers at the Paris conference. By the end of the month, Sfakianakis, the leader of

366 Mourellos (1950), pp. 1509-1511.
367 Ibid., pp. 1514-1515.

the rebel forces in the east, and Korakas, the celebrated *Kapetanios* from the east, along with some others gave themselves up, signalling the end of the rebellion. Rebels who refused to surrender were hunted down by the Turks over the next few months, and many were killed in skirmishes with Turkish troops or by Muslim Cretans, who wanted to collect the bounty money that had been placed on their heads.

This unsuccessful three-year rebellion once again demonstrated that without clear support from the Great Powers, Crete would not be able to achieve its desired goal of independence and union with Greece. The cost to both the Cretan population and the Ottoman state in terms of lives lost and human suffering was enormous; there are no reliable estimates, but both sides lost tens of thousands of lives. The Cretan countryside and its productive resources took more than a decade to recover, and rural life continued to be gruelling for those who had survived. The only positive outcome for the Cretans was the introduction of the Organic Act, which provided some improvements to their legal rights and living conditions; but, as we will see later, a huge gap still remained between what the Act provided for and the benefits the Cretans were actually able to obtain.

Sfakia was one of the most heavily devastated districts in Crete, having been attacked by Turkish troops on a number of occasions. After Omer Pasha invaded and destroyed the area in June 1867, large parts of the district were occupied by the Turkish army while they built their network of forts. The Turks maintained a permanent garrison there for a number of years, depriving the Sfakians of their cherished freedom for the first time in their long history. In terms of lives lost amongst Sfakians during this uprising, the only information that we have is from the Sfakian historian Papadopetrakis, who writes that "during the battles of this uprising 325 Sfakians were killed, which is one third of the Sfakian fighting force". His estimate does not include Sfakians who died from hunger, illness and other causes related to the struggle. He also does not count Sfakians who relocated outside the district and fought and died there.[368] Although it is hard to say how accurate his estimate is, given that the district's population in the 1881 Turkish census, 12 years after the uprising ended, was 5,183, his suggestion that there was one fighter for every four non-combats, and a third of these fighters were killed, seems reasonable.

[368] Papadopetrakis (1971 [1888]), p. 569.

XV. The period leading to union with Greece – 1869 to 1913

Towards autonomy for Crete

After the devastation of the three-year uprising, Crete was in need of economic development and rapprochement between the two warring populations. Unfortunately, the failure to fully implement the Organic Act and the string of governors appointed to rule the island did little to achieve either of these goals. Unequal representation and violations of the Act continued to anger the Christian population, while the governors were all military figures who were hostile to any change and were generally fanatically anti-Christian.

Bosnia Herzegovina rose up against the Ottoman Empire in the summer of 1875, soon joined by the Bulgarians. This initially led to war between Serbia and Turkey in 1876, and the next year to war between Turkey and Russia, later joined by Romania. These uprisings and the Russo–Turkish war inspired the Cretans to revolt against Turkish rule once again, this time with support from the Greek government. On the 4th of February 1878, the leaders of this latest rebellion met at Fre[369] and issued a statement which declared an end to the Sultan's rule over Crete and the union of Crete with Greece.[370] The rebels were in a great hurry, as they could see the end of the Russo–Turkish war coming and wanted to have a seat at the negotiating table where the future of all Ottoman vassal territories would be determined. The rebellion soon spread throughout the island, forcing the Turks to withdraw once again behind the walls of major towns and forts.

As expected, the impending collapse of the Ottoman Empire led to

[369] In the Apokoronas district of western Crete.
[370] Mourellos (1950), p. 1536.

intervention by the Great Powers and to a treaty[371] in March 1878, which was further amended at a conference in Berlin that July. Crete featured very little in the negotiations with Turkey, other than extracting an obligation from the Turks to fully implement the Organic Act, including any changes required under the new circumstances. Further negotiations between the Turks and the Cretans were conducted under the auspices of the British Consul in Chania, resulting in October 1878 in the Haleppa[372] Agreement, which provided better representation for the Christian population and included a number of other improvements in conditions for the local population,[373] and gave Crete semi-autonomous status within the Ottoman Empire.

The next ten years in Crete were marred by political infighting between leaders entrenched in two newly-established political parties. One party was dominated by the better-educated and more powerful members of society, some of whom held high positions in the island's administration; they espoused more conservative values and were referred to derogatorily by their opponents as *Karavanades*.[374] The other party, referred to by their opponents as *Xipolitoi*,[375] represented the more progressive and liberal sections of society. Political fanaticism led to widespread violence, including murder, and everyone seemed to have forgotten their higher aspirations for freedom and union with Greece.

Following a bitterly fought election early in 1889, which was won by *Xipolitoi*, the opposition unexpectedly tabled a motion at the General Assembly in May supporting union with Greece. The proposal received universal support from Christian members of both parties, but it inflamed the feelings of all the Muslim members and was declared illegal by the Governor General. He dissolved the Assembly and issued arrest warrants for members of *Karavanades*, who by then had gone into the mountains and declared an uprising. The wider population enthusiastically backed the rebellion, but Greece was not ready for such an unexpected turn of events, and the Greek government disassociated itself from this move. The Ottoman government soon replaced the Christian Governor General with one of their own military men, Sakir Pasha, who established martial law. The Turkish army took control of the entire island, supported by Muslim

[371] The treaty of San Stefano, in which the Ottoman Empire conceded independence to Romania, Serbia, and Montenegro and autonomy to Bulgaria.

[372] Haleppa was an outer suburb of Chania where the meetings took place.

[373] The main clauses were: the Governor General was to be a Christian, but not necessarily a Cretan, appointed for a five-year term and supported by a Muslim councillor; the General Assembly was to have 49 Christian and 31 Muslim deputies; a Cretan gendarmerie was to be established; Greek was to be recognised as the official language; certain tax exemptions were granted, as well as a general amnesty.

[374] 'Those aspiring to higher positions by becoming army officers.'

[375] 'One who has nothing of value and walks around without shoes.'

Cretans, who immediately attacked unprotected Christians. The hapless population was unprepared for this and had no means of resisting a return to brutal Turkish suppression. The Haleppa Agreement and the previously granted civil and religious privileges were revoked in December 1889, heavy taxation was imposed, and the old style of Turkish government was reintroduced.

The next five years were some of the worst that the Cretans experienced during all of the years of Ottoman rule. Small bands of rebels, including volunteers from Greece, recommenced opportunistic attacks against Turks and Muslim Cretans, while brutal assaults by Muslim Cretans against remote Christian villages became widespread. By 1891, Cretan leaders had held a number of meetings and discussions, mainly in the western districts, to consider how to deal with this deteriorating situation. The most significant meeting took place in Sfakia in June 1892, where the Sfakian Abbot Parthenios Kelaidis, one of the leaders of the 1866-69 uprising, promoted the option of autonomy as a step towards eventually achieving union with Greece when conditions were more favourable.[376] They were discouraged from pursuing this idea further by the cool response from the Greek government, which was embroiled in political infighting and faced significant financial problems, as well as by the unwillingness of other areas of Crete to support this.

Nevertheless, early in 1894 a secret brotherhood was formed in Sfakia with the aim of starting a new uprising. They formed the *Metapoliteftiki*[377] rebellion committee; its chairman was the charismatic Sfakian leader Manousos Koundouros.[378] Members of this new movement believed that autonomy was an acceptable first move towards union with Greece, a view which was also supported by the Great Power consuls in Chania, with the exception of the Greek consul, although a number of Cretan politicians were also against it. On the 10th of September 1895, about 1,500 armed Cretans gathered on the Krapi plateau where, following a religious service at the chapel of Agios Ioannis, they signed a declaration of support for the revolutionary committee, which sought "autonomy under the leadership of a Christian Orthodox leader" and laid out other demands, including the reinstatement of the Haleppa Agreement with improved terms. The proposal was forwarded to the Governor General and the foreign consuls in Chania. The Governor declared these demands illegal and ordered the committee's arrest. The Ottoman government also rejected every demand, but offered an amnesty to all those involved in order to avoid escalating the situation; however, the committee rejected their offer.

---

[376] Detorakis (1994), p. 359; Mourellos (1950), p. 1549.

[377] 'Regime changing'.

[378] Kelaidis had fled from Crete to Italy, as he was about to be arrested by the Turks for his revolutionary activities.

By mid-1896, conditions had deteriorated throughout the island, with Turkish-inspired violence spreading to many parts and volunteers once again arriving from Greece to support the Cretans. This prompted the Great Powers to intervene once more by putting pressure on the Ottoman government in Constantinople to agree to a negotiated settlement. The foreign consuls in Chania entered into protracted negotiations with the revolutionary committee, and by August 1896 an agreement was finally reached. This provided for a Christian governor of the island, appointed by the Ottoman government for a five-year period but requiring the approval of the Great Powers; enhanced representation for the Christian population in public positions; a reorganised Cretan gendarmerie under the command of European officers; and full economic and judicial independence under the guarantee of the Great Powers. Furthermore, they extracted a promise that Turkish troops would remain within their barracks in the larger towns. It was thought at the time that this agreement had brought an end to the rebellion, but soon the situation worsened with the appointment in September 1896 of George Verovich Pasha as the new Governor General, as he was not able to stop the violence against the Orthodox citizens around the island. Pressure by the Great Powers to implement the provisions of the agreement proved ineffective, as the Turks undermined their efforts.

By January 1897, there were clashes between rebels and the Turkish army and Muslim Cretans in many parts of Crete. Public pressure forced the Greek government to intervene; they dispatched naval vessels to prevent the Turks from bringing reinforcements into Crete and sent an army of 1,500 men with orders to take control of the island. The Greek army landed at Kolymbari, in western Crete, on the 1st of February 1897, declared that they were taking control of Crete in the name of the King, and announced the union of Crete with Greece. The Great Powers, concerned about these developments, decided to seize control of the island themselves, using the few armed men at their disposal who were stationed around Crete on the naval ships. They prevented the Greek army from reaching Chania and declared an exclusion zone around the town, but the Turks broke their agreement of non-interference by shelling the Greek troops. The Great Powers blockaded the coasts to prevent both the Turks and Greece from bringing additional men and supplies onto the island, but battles continued unabated throughout Crete, with the most bitter fighting taking place around Heraklion.

The Great Powers' solution to the situation was autonomy for Crete, with Greece's Prince George becoming Governor General, but their proposal was rejected by both the Cretans and Greeks, who still insisted on union. On the 5th of April 1897, the Ottoman government, supported by Germany and the Austro-Hungarian Empire, declared war on Greece on the basis that Ottoman Crete had been invaded by Greek irregular forces, and invaded the Greek mainland. Greece was totally unprepared for war and soon had to retreat on a number of fronts while remaining engaged in frantic diplomatic efforts to get the Great Powers to intervene and stop the war. It was the intercession of the Russian Tsar Nicholas II that convinced the Sultan to stop hostilities, and a truce was signed on the 22nd of May. Negotiations between the two nations about how to resolve the dispute dragged on, until on the 27th of November they reached an agreement whereby most of the mainland territory captured by the Turks was returned to Greece, which for its part was obliged to pay significant damages. Further discussions with the Great Powers, who were to provide loans for these reparations, lasted another four months.

But the Cretan problem was still unresolved. Greek forces had left the island when the war with Turkey began. Widespread fighting continued in Crete throughout the remainder of 1897 and the first half of 1898. Negotiations with the Greek government about autonomy for Crete were not progressing at all; the Turks were prepared to accept this solution on condition that Turkish troops remained on the island, but not union, which the Greeks and Cretans still insisted on. Eventually, the leaders of the uprising agreed to accept autonomy as a first step towards union with Greece in the not too distant future. Negotiations about who would become the governor resulted in the Great Powers restating their proposal to appoint Prince George of Greece as High Commissioner of Crete. On the 18th of July 1898, the General Assembly announced it had agreed to the Great Powers' proposals and would form an Executive Council to formulate the rules and regulations for governing the island.

The local Muslim Cretans were very unhappy with these developments and continued their violence in many parts of the island. During a massacre of hundreds of Christians in Heraklion on the 25th of August 1898, a detachment of British troops also fell victim to the Muslim Cretans, and 17 of their soldiers and the British Consul were murdered. The British reaction was swift – they immediately arrested and hanged the 17 Muslim Cretans who were considered to be the ringleaders. The British fleet sailed into Heraklion harbour and ordered the Turkish army and navy to leave the island. On the 2nd of November, the last Turkish soldier departed, and on the 9th of November 1898, to great jubilation by all Cretans, Prince George arrived at Souda Bay to become the leader of an autonomous Crete. This was the end of the Turkish occupation of the island, which had lasted 250 years.

From autonomy to union with Greece

The Prince arrived at Souda Bay aboard the Russian battleship *Nicholas I*, escorted by the other Great Powers' fleets, and was welcomed by the Admirals of the Great Powers and enthusiastic Cretan crowds. He was escorted into Chania to attend a service of thanks, and then continued on to the government building where the Admirals officially handed over control of the island to him. The new Cretan flag[379] was raised, and was saluted with cannon fire from the naval vessels anchored outside the harbour.

The Prince quickly appointed a committee of 12 Christian and 4 Muslim leaders to draft a new constitution. Elections were called for the 24th of January 1899 to choose new Assembly members, to consist of 138 Christian and 50 Muslim Cretans. These new representatives approved the new constitution, which was then ratified by the High Commissioner and the Great Powers, and it finally came into effect on the 16th of April 1899. The High Commissioner appointed his first government on the 27th of April, which included five ministers; one was Eleftherios Venizelos, a young lawyer and emerging charismatic political leader, who became Minister of Justice, and another was Manousos Koundouros, the Sfakian political activist mentioned earlier, who was appointed as Minister of Foreign Affairs.[380] On the 18th of May, Venizelos submitted a proposal for a new legal framework for the island, and introduced other initiatives, including the creation of a central bank, a new form of currency, public health and education programmes, and a reformed gendarmerie.

The Prince travelled to Moscow, London, Paris and Rome on his own initiative in an attempt to convince the Great Powers to push for the union of Crete with Greece, but all four countries were unwilling to change the status quo. Venizelos held a different view of how union could be achieved, favouring a gradual and steady move towards that goal. The differences between the two men's plans soon became public knowledge, and this escalated into an open conflict between them, to the point that the Prince dismissed Venizelos on the 18th of March 1901 (after refusing to accept his resignation, which was submitted twice). Venizelos formed an opposition party, which remained very critical of the way the High Commissioner was interfering in the process of government. The Prince, upset by continuing criticism from the Venizelos camp in the Cretan and Greek press, became

---

[379] The Cretan flag was based on the Greek flag of the time. It consisted of a white cross dividing the flag into four quadrants, three of which were blue, as on the Greek flag, but the top left quadrant was red and contained a white star, symbolising the Sultan's claim to the island.

[380] The other three were: Nikolaos Giamalakis as Minister of Public education and Religion; Constantinos Foumis as Minister of Economic Affairs; and Hussein Yenitsarakis as Minister of Public Order.

more authoritarian, censoring the press and harassing and arresting leading members of the opposition. The island had reached another crisis point.

On the 26th of February 1905, the opposition issued a statement demanding changes to the Cretan constitution in order to free the island of authoritarianism and pursue the objective of union with Greece, with the interim step of full independence; they also declared that they were prepared to resort to armed insurrection to achieve these objectives. A few days later, on the 10th of March, opposition members under the leadership of Eleftherios Venizelos gathered at Theriso, in the northern foothills of the Lefka Ori, together with an armed force of about 1,000 men, where they announced the start of an armed uprising in pursuit of union with Greece and raised the Greek flag. The rebellion spread very quickly throughout the island, but the gendarmerie remained loyal to the Prince. The Great Powers showed restraint and were not prepared to interfere at that stage, with the exception of the Russians, who came to the aid of the Prince by shelling some of the rebel positions.

The Prince issued a thirty-six hour deadline for the rebels to lay down their arms, and after the time passed he declared martial law, with the agreement of the Great Powers. He also asked the foreign consuls to urgently take all necessary measures to help put down the uprising. They in turn sent a message to the rebels requesting that they lay down their weapons, and threatening to use their armed forces to put an end to the uprising if the rebels did not. In response to this, more members of the Cretan Assembly travelled to Theriso to join the rebel government.

The representatives of the Great Powers, seeing the lack of public support for the Prince, decided to pursue a diplomatic solution and travelled to Mournies, just south of Chania, to meet the leaders of the rebel government. Negotiations continued on and off for months; an agreement to end the uprising was finally reached on the 15th of November 1906. This was the first step in a protracted series of negotiations between Venizelos' opposition party and the Great Powers. The agreement included the restructuring of the gendarmerie and the formation of a new militia, both under the control of officers seconded from the Greek army; the departure of all foreign troops after law and order had been restored; securing additional foreign loans; and a review of the Cretan constitution. Finally, the Great Powers conceded the right to appoint the High Commissioner to the King of Hellenes, George I, subject to their own approval. This decision was made public on the 14th of September 1906, and a few days later the King announced the resignation of Prince George as High Commissioner. In his place he appointed Alexander Zaimis, an experienced and well-respected Greek political figure who had served previously as Prime Minister of Greece. Soon a new government was formed, a new constitution was passed by the Cretan Assembly, a new civil guard was established, and by July 1907 a large proportion of the foreign troops had departed from the island. The remainder of the foreign forces gradually left Crete over the following twelve months after securing guarantees for the safety of the Muslim population.

In the middle of 1908, events started unfolding elsewhere that would have a significant impact on the situation in Crete. First, the opposition movement in Turkey, known as the "Young Turks", won power in July. On the 5th of October, the Bulgarians took advantage of the confused situation in Turkey and proclaimed full independence, annexing the eastern part of Macedonia in the process. The following day the Austro-Hungarian Empire unilaterally annexed Bosnia and Herzegovina. The impact of these events in Athens and Crete was unprecedented, with public demonstrations condemning Bulgaria's seizure of eastern Macedonia and demanding the immediate union of Crete with Greece.

On the 6th of October, the Cretan Assembly passed a resolution forming an interim government to administer the island in the name of the King of the Hellenes under the laws of the Greek state, until such time as the King was ready to assume control of the island himself. The Cretan flag was lowered, and in its place the blue and white flag of Greece was raised over Firka fort in Chania. The Greek government, although entirely supportive of these developments, refrained from officially recognising the actions of the Cretan Assembly, as it first wanted to secure the full backing of the Great Powers. They appeared to accept the developments in Crete, but were not prepared to inflame the delicate diplomatic situation with the new Turkish government, which demanded that the Greek government disavow the Cretans' actions. Following insistent complaints from the Turks, the Great Powers demanded that the Cretan government take down the Greek flag. Finally, when they saw that the Cretans had no intention of obeying this instruction, they sent a military detachment to Chania to chop down the flagpole.

The situation remained unresolved for a while. The Greek government was overthrown in a coup d'état by a group of young military officers who had formed a "Military League" and forced the Greek Prime Minister to resign. Recognising that they lacked political expertise, they invited the Cretan opposition leader Venizelos to become their political advisor, and he joined them in January 1910. At the next elections in September, Venizelos was elected to the Greek Assembly, and by October he was the new Prime Minister of Greece. In the meantime, Crete experienced a number of interim governments, resulting in political instability, and Greece remained unwilling to annex Crete, since it was trying to avoid open conflict with the Great Powers and Turkey. Venizelos' refusal to allow Cretan representatives to participate in the Greek Assembly led to another uprising in Crete in January 1912.

The start of the first Balkan War against Turkey in October 1912 was the catalyst to a resolution of this difficult state of affairs. The Greek Assembly immediately invited members of the Cretan Assembly to join them as a first step towards full annexation. Turkey's defeat led to the Treaty of London on the 30th of May 1913 in which Turkey relinquished its title to Crete, amongst other provisions. In a separate treaty between Turkey and Greece signed on the 1st of November, the Sultan renounced all claims over Crete, thus ratifying the annexation of Crete by Greece. One month later, on the 1st of December, the Greek flag was raised on a newly erected flagpole over Firka fort in Chania in front of King Constantine, Eleftherios Venizelos – the Cretan who was Prime Minister of a united Greek nation – and a throng of ecstatic and tearful Cretans. Crete had been waiting for this moment for 267 years, 7 months and 7 days.

The ceremony of the Union of Crete with Greece in Chania

Sfakia during this period

Historians tell us little about Sfakia after the dramatic events of the 1866-69 uprising, as their focus turned away from the armed rebellion in which the Sfakians had taken a leading role to political developments and international negotiations where only a few of the protagonists were Sfakians. The scant references to Sfakia during this period provide an incomplete picture of the region's recovery from this dramatic and painful three-year struggle.

The first report we have is from 1879, a year after the brief uprising that led to the Haleppa Agreement. It was written by a Greek doctor from the island of Syros, Iosif Hatzidakis (his mother was from the village of Asfendou), who travelled around Crete in the summer of 1879.[381] During this trip he visited Sfakia, journeying to Kallikratis, Asfendou, Imbros, Chora Sfakion, Loutro, Phoenix, Anopoli, Mouri and finally Askifou; and he described seeing the ruins of forts[382] erected ten years earlier which had been destroyed by the Sfakians during the 1878 uprising. He wrote about being welcomed with the Sfakian tradition of firing guns in the air, gave details of the damage inflicted by the Turks ten years earlier,[383] and mentioned the total absence of Turks in the area.

There was a similar report 15 years later by an Italian visitor, Vittorio Simonelli.[384] He stayed overnight in Chora Sfakion on the 26th of August 1893, accommodated by the Turkish garrison's commander in the barracks in the upper village; he was suffering from a high fever and the garrison's doctor looked after him. Simonelli described the army unit as

> not war-like … badly dressed, some wearing slippers while others are without any shoes at all … they go to fetch water and for every soldier carrying back the water there are two armed guards with him … when a soldier goes to the sea to wash, another one sits guard with his finger on the trigger. … They have to take these measures because the rebels are circling there like wolves! (p.157)

He also mentioned that the second fort down by the harbour was still a functioning structure. This gives us some evidence that the Turkish army had returned to Chora Sfakion and rebuilt the two forts which had been destroyed in 1878. But the description of the situation indicates that the Sfakians had somewhat recovered and were posing a threat to the Turkish forces lodged there.

As mentioned earlier, following the Haleppa Agreement in 1878 a Cretan gendarmerie was established, with many Christians as well as Turks

---

381 Hatzidakis (1881), pp. 74-91.

382 He specifically mentioned the ruined fort in Imbros, the Frangokastello fortress, which had been abandoned by the Turks, and the ruins of the two forts in Chora Sfakion and Askifou, but there was no mention of those in Loutro or Anopoli, although he visited both areas.

383 He mentioned that the Turks had destroyed 4-5,000 olive trees in Chora Sfakion in 1868, that there were only two families living in Loutro, that only 100 families lived in Anopoli where before there had been more than 300, and that in Mouri there were only 45 families instead of the more than 200 before. He also commented on the ruined houses from the earlier uprisings in most of these villages.

384 Simonelli (1996 [1897]), pp.148-158.

and Muslim Cretans serving in its ranks.[385] The more senior posts were held by Turks. This body functioned until the uprising in 1889 and served to demonstrate that the two religions could cooperate with each other. What is of great interest here is that many Sfakians joined the gendarmerie, and some were appointed to the higher ranks (five Sfakians were Majors). Of the nearly 2,000 police, 340 covered the extended region of Sfakia, although this was reduced to 260 by 1889. After the 1889 uprising, all the Christians left the gendarmerie, but during those first ten years, there were police stations in Chora Sfakion, Agia Roumeli, Agios Ioannis, Anopoli, Askifou, Patsianos and Gavdos.[386]

Visitors to the district of Sfakia today cannot fail to notice the many monuments that have been erected in its villages, some of which mention achievements in battles during the years 1903–1914 in the north of Greece.[387] These relate to another chapter of Sfakian heroism, when they fought in areas that today form the Greek districts of Epirus, Macedonia and Thrace, which had populations of Turks, Greeks, Albanians and Slavs. Many Sfakians volunteered to defend the Greeks living in Turkish-controlled areas from the Bulgarians, who were trying to expand the boundaries of their newly established state following the 1875-1878 Balkan wars and the Treaty of San Stefano, mentioned earlier. By the time of these battles, five years had elapsed since the last Turkish soldier had left Crete. The Muslim Cretans were resigned to living under the control of the Orthodox Cretans with the supervision of the Great Powers, so the battle-hardened Cretans no longer had to deal with threats at home. The challenges that their fellow Greeks faced in Macedonia and Thrace were to become their next cause.

The first wave of battles in these areas took place between 1903 and 1908, during which bands of Greek volunteers, including from Sfakia and other areas of Crete, fought against Bulgarian irregular forces. Neither Greece nor Crete was at war with Turkey, and Turkey was reluctant to get involved in these clashes for control of territory as long as the warring factions did not challenge Turkey's right to these areas. The second period of war in the north in which Sfakian volunteers were involved was in 1912-13, when Greece, Montenegro, Serbia and Bulgaria formed an alliance and

[385] There was a gendarmerie before this, but it was mostly manned by Muslims, as very few Christians were willing to join, and then only in the lowest ranks.

[386] Information in this section comes from a thesis by Dimitrios Papalas written in 2003 at the University of Crete, *The 2nd Regiment of the Cretan Gendarmerie, District of Sfakia, 1884-1889.*

[387] These monuments can be seen at: www.dalidakis.com, "The monuments of the district of Sfakia". The monuments covered there are for Giorgos Tsondos-Vardas, Stavrianos Polentas-Sisanes, Nikolaos Psarros, Anastasios Chobitis, Giorgos Perros, Ioannis Karavitis. There is also a monument in Frangokastello to the people from the village of Patsianos who fought in Macedonia and Epirus during the years 1903–1914 (35 names).

achieved independence for virtually all the Ottoman Empire's territories in the Balkans. This was followed by a brief war against Bulgaria, which was not satisfied with how Macedonian lands had been divided amongst its other allies; during this conflict Bulgaria lost most of the territories that it had gained. The Cretans could not serve as regular soldiers in this war against Turkey, since they were still Ottoman subjects at the time, according to the Autonomy agreement. The third period of Sfakian engagement in the north occurred in 1914, when bands of Sfakians, together with other Cretans and mainland Greeks, fought unsuccessfully to defend the short-lived Autonomous Republic of Northern Epirus and protect Greek civilians living in that area, which had been declared part of the new state of Albania after the treaty settling the 1912-13 Balkan war.[388]

The achievements of Sfakians who fought and died in these wars are discussed in three books written by the Sfakian historian Paris Kelaidis, who pays tribute to their dedication in attempting to gain freedom for their fellow Greeks in other occupied regions.

[388] Albania's independence was recognized by the Conference of London on the 29th of July 1913 (where the six Great Powers negotiated about how to divide up the acquired territories), but the borders of Albania were drawn disregarding the demographic realities of the time, and many Greek villages were forced to become part of the new, mainly Muslim Albanian state. At the beginning of the Second World War, the Greek army took control of this area, but subsequent political upheavals in Greece led to the Italians invading and seizing most of Epirus and Albania. At the end of the war, the allies returned northern Epirus to Albania at the Paris Conference of 1919.

XVI. Sfakia in Greece – 1913 to 1950

Sfakia after the Union

The union of Crete with Greece was due in no little measure to efforts by the people of Sfakia and their centuries of rebellion against foreign domination. However, Sfakia was still paying the price for its leading role in the struggle for independence: the failure of the 1770 revolt, the economic consequences of the 1821-8 rebellion, the devastation suffered during the uprising of 1866-9, and the long-term failure of Crete to become part of Greece continued to affect the area for decades. The Ottoman destruction of Sfakia, and the loss of manpower through death and exile, were colossal. Between 1821 and 1834, the population of the Sfakia area dropped to about 4,000; in 1834 Chora Sfakion had only about 60 families, and there were many areas of the province which were abandoned.

After World War I came a disastrous war between Greece and Turkey, with Sfakian men involved as regular members of the Greek army. The conditions of the truce involved ethnic cleansing on a massive scale in 1922, with Muslims in Greece being transferred to Turkey, and Christians in Turkey being sent to Greece, including to Crete. But there were no Muslims in Sfakia to send away, and Christian refugees from Asia Minor who came to Crete tended to settle in the urban areas on the north coast. The population of Sfakia recovered somewhat; in 1928 Chora Sfakion had 407 inhabitants, with Anopoli and Askifou both being about twice that size.

Sfakia became involved in another political event in the mid-1930s. Very many Cretans at that time were liberals, Venizelists, and republicans, and were very much opposed to the fascist-royalist Metaxas dictatorship which had been installed in Athens in 1936. It was therefore not surprising that an armed uprising against Metaxas began in Chania on the 29th of July that year as part of a planned nationwide coup organised by democrats in Athens. The radio station in Chania was seized, and appeals were made to the King and the army to restore democracy. According to Paris Kelaidis, one of the leaders of the revolt was a Sfakian politician, Manousos Voloudakis who, together with Thrasyvoulos Klados from Askifou, led armed men from Sfakia to Chania to take part in this uprising. One group of Sfakians took over the army barracks, where some officers agreed to join them, while another group occupied government offices. The dictatorship reacted quickly, however, and it soon became clear that no further support for the uprising would be forthcoming. Realising that their cause was hopeless, the leaders escaped to Askifou, and then up into the mountains around the Niatos plateau. They stayed there for several weeks until arrangements were made for a boat to pick them up from Chora Sfakion and take them to Cyprus, where they remained until 1945.

Throughout the 1930s, maritime trade flourished in Sfakia, based in Ombrosgialos, the shoreside area of Chora Sfakion.[389] Ombrosgialos looked prosperous for an isolated village. It had thirty or so different shops and businesses, with three grocery stores, a dairy, a blacksmith, a butcher, a tailor, a cobbler, and tavernas and cafes – one exclusively for professional people such as doctors and teachers. Their main trade was with Chania, but because of the absence of roads, it was much easier to move goods to and from the north coast by ship than overland. The Sfakians also traded along the south coast of Crete with places such as Agia Galini. And they also established direct commercial ties with Piraeus, the main port of Athens.

The road from Chania went only as far as Askifou, and older Sfakians today remember vividly the absence of roads and, as a consequence, of any wheeled vehicles. In Chora Sfakion there was a mule track leading up from the beach at Ombrosgialos to Mesochori, which provided the main link by land to the outside world; another *kalderimi* ran up to Anopoli. There was not even a real harbour as such in the village, so the bay would be full of trading vessels, mostly sailing boats riding at anchor, with smaller boats hauled up onto the shallow stony beach that gave onto the backs of warehouses. Scores of mules and donkeys stood by ready to transport goods to the villages along the coast to the east, to Anopoli or to Askifou.

So Sfakia was just beginning to thrive again when it was struck by another disaster, not even slightly of its own making.

Sfakia and the Battle of Crete

It is often said (especially in Britain) that after the fall of France at the beginning of World War II, Britain stood alone against the Axis alliance of Germany, Italy and Japan. However, on the other side of Europe, Greece was also courageously engaged in a successful armed conflict with the Axis

[389] Some of the information in what follows is based on the personal recollections of Sfakians born in the 1920s and 1930s.

enemies. Although it was a predominantly rural country with a population of only seven million, Greece had been fighting back against an Italian invasion since October 1940. Decisions taken in London and elsewhere about supporting the Greeks in this heroic struggle were quite soon to have serious consequences for Crete, and not least for Sfakia.

Many events combined to put Sfakia, briefly but dramatically, at the centre of world news in 1941. Italian forces invaded Albania in April 1939 and annexed the country. The Italians already held sovereignty over the Greek Dodecanese islands, which had been ceded to them when control was taken away from the Turks in 1913. These islands include Kasos, which is only 25 miles from Crete.

Mussolini then decided to invade Greece, much against the wishes of Hitler, using neighbouring Albania as a springboard. Mussolini's Greek counterpart, the fascist dictator General Metaxas, refused Mussolini's ultimatum to allow Italian forces into Greece to occupy strategic positions. It is widely believed that Metaxas simply replied to the ultimatum with the single word *ochi* 'no' - although it is much more likely that he actually spoke to the German ambassador who had delivered the ultimatum in French; and a few hours later, in the early hours of the 28th of October 1940, the Italians invaded the northern part of Greek Epirus and western Greek Macedonia. October 28th is still commemorated in Greece as *Ochi* Day. Mussolini's army performed very badly against the Greeks, and soon the Greek army had turned them back and were themselves advancing into Albania.

Hitler was greatly worried by these Axis losses and was determined to seize control of the Balkans. In anticipation of a German invasion, British troops, a majority of them Australians and New Zealanders, began landing in Greece from Egypt on the 7th of March 1941, after lengthy discussions involving Winston Churchill, Anthony Eden, and the governments of Greece, New Zealand and Australia. Their primary aim was to defend Thessaloniki from an invasion coming from the north. On the 6th of April, German, Hungarian and Bulgarian forces invaded Yugoslavia and Greece. The Greek and British soldiers were overwhelmed by the Axis troops, and Thessaloniki fell to the Germans on April 9th, with the Allied troops retreating south towards Athens. On April 16th, the general in command of the Greek forces asked the British to withdraw from their defensive positions at Thermopylae, and the Greek army in Epirus surrendered on April 20th. Between April 25th and 28th, the Allied forces were for the most part successfully evacuated from mainland Greece to either Crete or Egypt.

After this retreat, Churchill appointed a retired New Zealand general, the World War I hero Bernard "Tiny" Freyberg, as Commander-in-Chief of the Allied forces in Crete. The withdrawal to Crete had been rather disorderly, with the British troops being forced to use any boats they could lay their hands on. In fact, the confusion was so bad that even today we do not really know how many men General Freyberg had at his disposal to counter the expected German invasion of the island. There were perhaps 30,000 British and Allied forces, which included 7,000 New Zealanders and about the same number of Australians, as well as some thousands of Cypriots and Palestinians – both Arab Palestinians and Jews had volunteered in large numbers. However, many of the men had been forced to leave their weapons and equipment behind on the Greek mainland in the rush to evacuate; and there were undoubtedly deserters who had deliberately abandoned their guns. The total also included a large number of non-combatant clerks and orderlies.

On Crete, there were also about 10,500 lightly armed Greeks under the leadership of General Skoulas. This included some Cretans but consisted mainly of 7,000 raw recruits who had an assortment of weapons and little ammunition, plus 2,500 gendarmes with little fighting experience and 1,000 reservists, together with Greek soldiers who had managed to escape from the mainland. But most of the Greek army, including unfortunately a majority of the regular Cretan units, were still in Epirus and Macedonia, where they had gone to oppose the Italians. (The general who had surrendered in Epirus and then returned to Crete without his troops was very soon assassinated by outraged Cretans in Kasteli Kissamos.)

On the 20th of May 1941, the German invasion of Crete began. The Germans attacked British positions along the north coast by dropping gliders and paratroopers at strategic positions. The fighting was extremely fierce and was notable for the fact that a good number of incredibly brave Cretan civilians, including women and children, many of them unarmed, joined in. This was one of the very few places in Europe where a German invasion was countered by the civilian population as well as the military. Their courage was especially remarkable because they knew that the Germans would execute captured civilians, women as well as men, who were involved in the fighting, arguing that they were guerrillas who were not protected by the Geneva Convention. But Cretans had enjoyed full independence for less than thirty years after suffering many centuries of foreign control, and they were not prepared to lose it again without putting up a fight. Indeed, many of the older men who were involved in these battles had fought against the Turks in the 1870s and 1880s, as well as in the Macedonian Wars of 1912-13.

King George of Greece, other members of the royal family, and the Greek government, who had crossed over to Crete from mainland Greece before the Germans arrived in Athens, now brought about Sfakia's involvement in the situation. They escaped from Crete on the night of May 22nd by walking down the Samaria Gorge, where they were reportedly fed roasted lamb by members of the local Viglis family. A Royal Navy submarine picked them up at Agia Roumeli and evacuated them to Egypt. They were escorted down the gorge by New Zealand soldiers, who subsequently had to walk all the way back up the gorge to join the fray.

The military historians Ian Stewart and Alan Clark are agreed that in actual fact the Allied forces could have won the Battle of Crete, and were quite close to doing so. It seems that the British forces were in a winning position, but their commanders did not know this because of bad communications facilities, which meant that Freyberg was not able to gain an accurate overall picture of the situation. By May 27th, the British High Command had decided, probably incorrectly, that victory was impossible, and the Allied forces were ordered to retreat to the south coast. The first the Sfakians knew of the impending retreat was when two battalions of Colonel Robert Laycock's British Layforce Commandos, consisting of 200 men, landed there from Egypt between the 24th and 27th of May to protect the intended disembarkation point at Chora Sfakion. A larger force of commandos were also put ashore at Souda Bay.

Now tens of thousands of British and Commonwealth soldiers, very many on foot, made their way to Vrises, which was already under bombardment from the Luftwaffe, and from there began the long trek south to Chora Sfakion to await evacuation. It was a 25-mile walk from Vrises, starting from near sea level, going up to 2,000 feet and back down again. After the men left Vrises, it was increasingly hard to find water. It took most of them three days to complete the journey because of the difficult terrain and congestion along the narrow track, with abandoned vehicles making conditions worse; in addition, they could only travel at night because of Luftwaffe attacks. Some soldiers marched together as organised units, but there were also some disorganised rabbles without their weapons, as well as many men who were badly injured. This massive retreat along the road was only made possible because it was being defended, unbeknown to the troops, by the 8th Greek Regiment. Together with a collection of local Greek irregulars, they were heroically protecting the retreating column from attacks by German mountain troops who were cutting across the hills from the northwest, a danger the British High Command seems not to have thought of.

After leaving Vrises, the New Zealand 5th Brigade and two Australian battalions, the 2/7th and the 2/8th, plus three tanks, were given the task of bringing up the rear. These units took it in turns to hold a position while the others drew back through their lines. Their initial defensive position was at the narrow pass into Sfakia at Katre, the scene of many earlier battles between the Sfakians and the Turks. This initial rear-guard position was attacked by the Germans at about 4 pm on May 29th, with the New Zealanders withdrawing first and moving on to Amoudari (Askifou). By evening the main Allied defensive position was at Askifou, in the area of Petres. The rest of the retreating forces found that the road from the north coast turned into a small track after Imbros where, according to Theodore Stephanides[390] in his book *Climax in Crete,* Freyberg had established his headquarters. All the retreating Allies' vehicles that had made it that far (many had run out of petrol) had to be abandoned and pushed over cliffs to prevent the Germans from using them.

An easier route to the coast for those on foot lay down the Imbros Gorge, which the soldiers nicknamed Rhododendron Valley (though the plants they saw were actually oleander) and on to Komitades. The crowding, chaos and confusion in the gorge, with thousands of exhausted men passing through the narrow, rocky confines, must have been incredible – at one time there were at least 8,000 men in the gorge. The local historian Kanakis Geronimakis relates how he escaped from Imbros into the hills to the east of the village, together with half a dozen other families who were trying to avoid the German advance. He describes very vividly that, from the ridge above the Kapnis Gorge (which runs down to Nomikiana), they heard the sound of thousands of army boots ringing up from inside the Imbros Gorge as the Allied army passed through.

From Komitades, the troops continued by *kalderimi* to Chora Sfakion. Royal Navy evacuation ships coming from Egypt and Libya were able to approach the shore only under the cover of darkness, again because of Luftwaffe attacks – the German planes swooped in from the north, but because of the high mountains immediately behind the village, roared out to sea first and turned back inland to attack. When night fell, the naval ships would move closer, moor offshore at about 11 pm, and send in landing craft to pick up the troops. Many Sfakians, including even young boys, rowed out to the warships with their small boats crammed full of Allied soldiers. The naval vessels could remain offshore only briefly, since they had to withdraw a sufficient distance towards Africa before daybreak to get beyond the range of the bombers.

The first night of the evacuation, May 28th, three destroyers[391] arrived from Africa and were able to evacuate more than 700 Allied soldiers. By May 29th, a German unit had outflanked the defensive battalions at Askifou and broken through to Vouvas, only a few miles from Chora Sfakion. That night, eight Royal Navy vessels[392] managed to evacuate more than 6,000 men to Egypt. In an event which was to prove significant later on, that same night also saw seven political prisoners of the Metaxas regime take advantage of the situation by seizing a rowing boat and escaping from Gavdos, which was being used as a prison island for the dictatorship's

390 Stephanides was actually there.

391 *The Khandahar, Kelvin* and *Nizam.*

392 The destroyers *Calcutta, Coventry, Hasty, Janus, Jervis,* and *Perth*, the cruiser *Phoebe,* and the troop carrier *Glengyle*; the *Glengyle* was particularly useful because of its landing craft. During the voyage back to Africa, the *Perth* received a direct hit which killed four crew and nine soldiers.

left-wing opponents. These men were able to reach Crete, landing east of Chora Sfakion, and later went on to form a significant part of the Resistance movement against the Germans.

By May 30th, the Germans were stopped at the Imbros pass by the 5th New Zealand Brigade, while the Germans who had fanned out into the hills above the pass were being held up by the Royal Marines between Komitades and Asfendou, and by the Layforce commandos between Chora Sfakion and Mouri. Four Allied destroyers[393] were making their way again to Crete, and although two of them had to turn back to Alexandria, the other two vessels were able to take over 1,500 men off the island that night.[394]

The Allied High Command decided that the evacuations would not be able to continue safely after the night of May 31st. A flying boat picked up General Freyberg and 53 others that night, while other ships managed to evacuate more than 3,700 troops from the beach.[395] On that last evening of the evacuation, the exhausted New Zealand 5th Brigade, who had been carrying out the rear-guard action to defend Sfakia, were given priority in embarking, with platoons of Australians remaining in defensive positions up the hills to prevent the Germans slipping through the Sfakian Gorge and the Imbros Gorge. The Kiwis marched into Chora Sfakion through the ranks of the other, by now half-starving and thirsty, waiting men; many of these were not front-line soldiers and included clerks, mechanics, labourers from Palestine and Cyprus who had been abandoned by their officers, stragglers from units destroyed in the battle, demoralised soldiers who had been evacuated from the mainland and never been given new weapons or attached to new units, and Greeks.[396] To this day, Sfakians have a special friendship and respect for New Zealanders. Sadly, like so many of the other soldiers who were evacuated to North Africa and survived the Luftwaffe's bombing raids on the ships, many of them died later in campaigns fighting the enemy in the Western Desert.

---

[393] The *Nizam, Khandahar, Kelvin,* and *Napier.*

[394] The *Khandahar* had engine trouble and the *Kelvin* was hit by the Luftwaffe; the *Napier* took a hit on the way back.

[395] The *Phoebe,* and the destroyers *Hotspur, Jackal and Kimberley,* plus the minelayer *Abdiel.*

[396] As a precaution, the New Zealanders protected themselves by a cordon of troops with fixed bayonets and sub-machine guns, on the assumption that not all the other retreating men could be relied upon to observe the best military discipline under the circumstances.

The military historian Ian Stewart, who was Medical Officer to the 1st Welsh Regiment, wrote:

> As it grew dark, the Brigade closed up and began to come down from the hills. All had shaved. Every man carried a weapon. They moved in silence save for the creaking of their equipment and the rattle of pebbles as they stumbled down the rocky path. Other men got to their feet to watch them pass. There were murmurs in the darkness, "It's the New Zealanders, the New Zealanders". But most of the watchers stood without sound or movement among the shadows cast by the rising moon. Their envy was touched by admiration.

The rear-guard of Australians were supposed to be given the next priority in the evacuation; but by the time they arrived at Ombrosgialos, their progress had been slowed so much by the masses of waiting troops, some of them resentful at this privilege and deliberately blocking their way, that the ships had gone – they got there just in time to hear the sound of lifting anchor chains echoing round the bay. The last ships left the bay at 3 am on the 1st of June.

Colonel Laycock and some of his staff, including his intelligence officer, the famous English novelist Evelyn Waugh, escaped on the last ships, but a majority of the Layforce commandos had to remain behind on the island and were captured. Waugh reported that in spite of the priorities laid down by the army, many of the troops who were taken on board were from the "rabble", and many of the genuine fighting men were left behind: one report stated that the majority of the commandos failed to be evacuated because they were not able to "penetrate the rabble".[397] The following morning, the soldiers remaining on the beach were attacked by dive-bombing Stukas, in spite of the fact that they were waving white flags.

The first Germans to advance as far as the edge of Chora Sfakion were part of a westward flanking movement which had taken them down the Sfakian Gorge from Kali Lakki, but they were repulsed at the end of the gorge by the British, who killed twelve of them. When the main German force finally made it to the village, their soldiers who had retreated up the Sfakian Gorge returned via Mouri. The Luftwaffe's bombing of the village had forced many of the locals to flee into caves above the village, and then further into the hills towards Mouri, where they encountered these German troops on their way back down. One young blond man from the Sfakian Tzardis family had to show his Greek identity papers to the soldiers, who suspected that he might be British. Other German troops broke through to the evacuation area from Komitades.

The official Allied surrender was ordered to take place at 9 am on the 1st of June. The Australian Commander of the 2/7th Battalion, Lieutenant Colonel Theo Walker, walked to Komitades and delivered the surrender documents to the Austrian Commander of the German 5th Mountain Division. Walker had actually made it onto one of the rescue ships, but when he realised that

[397] After the New Zealanders had been evacuated, their cordons were withdrawn, and control was handed over to an ill-prepared British Artillery unit. While they were setting up, according to Stewart,

> rabble rushed down on them. The Maoris raced back with fixed bayonets and amid "scenes best forgotten" fiercely restored the line. But after that, access to the beach ... was severely impeded. Resentful "rabble," who had often arrived at Sphakia much earlier than the "fighting troops", sat down in the narrow, sunken track to stop them passing. Badly briefed "Movement Control Officers" mistakenly forbade some "fighting" units to move forward. And because every Creforce officer had decamped by seaplane before midnight, no one on the island had the knowledge or authority to settle disputes and keep troops moving.

his men were not going to be evacuated, he asked to be put ashore again.

Something like 14,000 Commonwealth and Greek troops had been successfully ferried to North Africa from the beaches of Sfakia, as well as from Plakias and the Timbaki area to the east, while about 13,000 had been killed or captured. After less than two weeks of fighting, the Germans had taken control of the island, but in terms of the enormous casualties they suffered, the Battle of Crete was a "disastrous victory" for them, according to the German General, Kurt Student. Hitler decided never to use paratroopers in any significant assault again. And because of the huge number of German casualties, and the length of time the defenders were able to hold out against them, the Allied army is credited with having significantly delayed the Nazi invasion of the Soviet Union, and so in the long run contributed greatly to Hitler's defeat on the eastern front. Hitler was also compelled to postpone indefinitely a planned invasion of Cyprus.

The captured Allied soldiers were eventually forced to walk back north, exhausted, hungry and thirsty, the same way they had come, a three-day trek over the mountains. One prisoner who collapsed and could not get back up was shot dead by a German, who was in turn shot dead by a German officer for what he had just done. Some reported that their captors had relieved them of their rings and watches. The soldiers were incarcerated in abysmal prison camps near Chania and, eventually, loaded onto ships – except for some officers who were airlifted – and sent to the Greek mainland, and from there by train to Germany.

Today, there is a plaque in Greek and English commemorating this historic evacuation on the east side of the bay where these awful and dramatic scenes took place. The English reads:

> From this bay between 28th May and 1st June 1941 the last Australian, British and New Zealand forces which fought alongside the Greek forces in the fierce struggles of the Battle of Crete against the Germans were evacuated by British and Australian warships.

When the people of Chora Sfakion eventually dared to return to the village, they found much destruction from the bombing, and the stench of dead animals. There was barely any food left for the villagers, because the soldiers had eaten everything – even most of the flour was gone, because the local women had cooked wheat cakes from flour and water for thousands of the hungry men. The retreating British army had left behind them a harbour filled with rifles and a bay full of sunken landing craft – two of them were still there 40 years later. When Xan Fielding revisited the village in 1952, even then he found the beach littered with "rusty steel helmets, rotting respirator tubes, old boots and empty bully-beef tins".

But these were by no means the worst problems experienced by the inhabitants of Chora Sfakion. Many of the Allied soldiers who had not made it onto the evacuation ships avoided capture. Some of them attempted to reach the island Gavdos about 20 miles away by commandeering small boats belonging to the Sfakians – or even by floating out to sea on doors. Some of them actually made it to Africa. Others dispersed along the coast, to Agia Roumeli, for instance, where no Germans arrived until June 6th. But large numbers of them fled into the hills to hide, and many of these were protected and fed by local families in their houses or shepherds' huts. Soldiers who escaped from the prisoner-of-war camps – which was often easy enough to do since the Germans at first sometimes allowed POWs to come and go as they pleased – also benefitted from local care and hospitality. The best estimate is that there were a maximum of about 1,000 Commonwealth troops in western Crete trying to evade the Germans.

In the summer of 1942, in an attempt to terrorise civilians into denying this kind of aid to the Allies on the run, and to discourage opposition on the part of the local population generally, Gestapo and SS units arrived in the area. The German commandant of Chora Sfakion alerted those villagers who he thought were most in danger from these arriving Nazis, and they were able to flee. But the Gestapo arrested many civilians from Sfakia who they suspected of harbouring escapees or of carrying out other activities against the occupation.

One Gestapo trick was to assemble the male population of a village in the church and ask if anyone had seen British soldiers, and if so where. Those who answered that they had seen Allied personnel were stood to one side and then taken to Chora Sfakion, were they were imprisoned in a house on the western edge of Ombrosgialos, above the bay at Vrissi. They were kept in appalling conditions in the terrible August heat in a room with no windows, no sanitation, and no food or water. The local people were eventually able to get water to them, but after some days the prisoners were taken out in groups of three and marched by a squad of eight soldiers to the hill below the Venetian fort, where they were shot, and their bodies thrown into a crevasse in the rocks.

Georgis Dourountakis, a shepherd from Chora Sfakian who had earlier given shelter to two British soldiers up in the mountains, was unwittingly if foolishly betrayed by them when, after they had been captured and brought down to the village, they greeted him like an old friend. He was imprisoned with the others and taken to the hill to be shot. An immensely strong man, he managed to break the ropes which bound him and run away, but he was cut down by machine gun fire. To prevent any of the other men from attempting to escape execution, a young local boy, Giannis Tzardis, was forced to row two armed German soldiers out into the bay below the hill to cut off any escape route. He had to witness the victims first being shot by

The monument to the departing allied forces in the village of Sfakia

the firing squad then being shot once more in the back of the head. The last group of three men who were taken to be executed were made to carry cans of petrol on their backs to the site. After all the executions were over, this petrol was poured on the bodies, which the Germans then set alight. Then the entire population of the village, young and old, were forced out of their houses and compelled to cover the charred remains as best they could in the rocky terrain with their spades and other tools.

After the war, a monument to this dreadful event was erected in the pine trees on the hill. At the bottom of the monument, in a glass-fronted case, is a pile of skulls, several with visible bullet holes. The wording in Greek on the stone above them reads: "Compatriots executed by barbarous Germans". There then follows a list of the people who were executed,[398] who came not only from Chora Sfakion but also from Komitades, Agia Roumeli, Livaniana, Anopoli, and elsewhere.

[398] Those executed were: Sifis Dourountakis, Giannis Foundoulakis, Dimitris Gioukakis, Giorgis Dourountakis, Andreas Athitakis, Andreas Zacharias, Giorgos Kontorinis, Grigoris Athitakis, Nikolas Glimenos, Manolis Saviolis, Stilianos Mavrogiannis, Stilianos Saviolis, Nikolas Papaderos, Giannis Kriaras, Giorgis Kriaras, Nikolas Athitakis, Spiros Papaderos, Angelos Roukounakis, Stilianos Koumakakis, Giorgis Tzatzimos, Manolis Tzatzimos, Andreas Kritikos, Giorgos Kantounatos, Giannis Koufakis, and Giorgos Katsias.

Sfakia under the Germans

The German occupation of Sfakia lasted for three years and four months. During that time, as on the rest of the island, the Cretans' resistance to the occupation was continuous. All over the island, fighters took to the hills and harassed the Germans at every opportunity. In Sfakia, a resistance unit had been formed during the invasion, led by Giannis Katsias.

The groundwork for the Cretan Resistance had been prepared before the German invasion by the remarkable English archaeologist John Pendlebury (see Chapter I), who had been recruited by British Military Intelligence and had returned to Crete in June 1940. He had used his intimate knowledge of the terrain of Crete, but more particularly his equally deep knowledge of the local dialects, and contacts all over the island who respected and trusted him, to set up networks of fighters headed by village men. The task of these villagers was to lead the opposition to the invasion, and to continue with resistance activities afterwards. Pendlebury's pre-war organisational activities became known to German intelligence, and he was killed in cold blood near Heraklion by German soldiers, who captured him very soon after the invasion.

Pendlebury also organised reconnaissance missions along the south coast to locate beaches and coves where boats could be secreted so that the Resistance could be supplied after an invasion. His navy colleague Mike Cumberledge, who sailed the naval schooner they had at their disposal, was helped in this search by one of the local men appointed by Pendlebury who met them, as Imogen Grundon says, in "the tiny quiet harbour of Sphakia". Cumberledge reported that the Sfakian man was "a good sailor, and, neither inquisitive nor talkative, he was the right type and knew the dangerous south coast well".

The harassment by the Cretan Resistance was such that the Axis powers had to keep on Crete a force of 40,000 Germans and Italians, who they would have preferred to employ elsewhere, in order to maintain order. As Antony Beevor says, "few other populations in occupied Europe demonstrated such unity in the face of oppression". The Cretan landscape favoured guerrilla operations, and by 1943 the Axis forces and their collaborators remained in control of only the main towns and connecting roads, ceding the mountainous countryside to the Resistance.

But resistance activities did not just involve harassment. Many of their actions were coordinated by a small group of men from the British Special Operations Executive (SOE), including Greek officers as well as notable British figures such as Xan Fielding, Patrick Leigh Fermor, Monty Woodhouse, and the Australian Tom Dunbabin. They were often based in the Lefka Ori, and were in touch by radio with the British High Command in Cairo whenever possible. Some of these men had been in the mountains

The monument to those executed by the Germans in the village of Sfakia

since the Allied surrender, but a number of Cretan partisans and British operatives were also parachuted in or were put ashore from submarines starting very soon after the 1941 evacuation. One of the favourite landing sites was Koraka beach below Kato Rodakino, just to the east of Sfakia; and Xan Fielding was put ashore once near Tripiti at the western edge of Sfakia. As late as Easter 1943, a submarine on such a mission evacuated 180 of the hundreds of Allied soldiers who had evaded capture, many of whom had very good reason to be extraordinarily grateful to Cretan families who had helped and sheltered them. On the 7th of May 1943, the last group of 59 British, Australian and New Zealand soldiers were rescued by a Royal Navy launch from the beach at the end of Tripiti gorge. Those men had been hidden, sheltered and protected for two whole years by brave Cretan villagers, who had risked their lives in doing so.

The achievements of this organised Resistance were many. Their networks were able to provide information via radio of German troop and naval movements, which was particularly important at the time of the North African conflict. The departure of convoys from Souda Bay bringing fuel and supplies to Rommel's troops in North Africa were signalled ahead so that the ships could be intercepted and attacked by the RAF or the Royal Navy. Crucially, the Cretan Resistance was able to supply information about Rommel's lack of supplies as he moved from Libya into Egypt. This intelligence led to a vital change of plan by the Allies: they were able to halt their withdrawal from Egypt, including from the harbour at Alexandria, which had been planned on the mistaken assumption that they would not be able to hold out against Rommel's forces. And so the key British victory at El Alamein, the turning point in the desert war, owed much to the Cretan Resistance.

The Cretans and their allies – British, New Zealand, Free French, Danish and many more – also performed vital acts of sabotage at German airfields and fuel stores. In 1943 they successfully deployed their men in such a way that the Germans were persuaded there was to going be an invasion of the island. As a result, Axis troops and aircraft were kept on Crete, and plans for combatting invasions of other Axis-held locations were less than thoroughly carried through – and when the actual Allied invasion from North Africa took place, it occurred on Sicily. The Resistance also played an important role in liaising with Italian troops when many of them wanted to surrender after Italy capitulated later in 1943.

During the occupation, there was a large German garrison in Askifou, and another in Chora Sfakion. The Germans also used Anopoli as a base from which to mount patrols against the guerrillas. The Askifou garrison constructed a radio transmitter station on the top of the hill at Akones, between Asfendou and Imbros, using local people as forced labour. This station was protected by barbed wire and mines (after the German withdrawal, several Sfakians were killed or maimed by these mines). Sfakian fighters under Manousos Kelaidis attacked the station at Akones in July 1943.

The use of forced labour at Akones was not an isolated case. In 1943, men from Asfendou were forcibly taken to Agia Galini, where they were made to work for two weeks building defences as part of the *Festung Kreta* or Fortress Crete plan against an Allied invasion from the south. They were used instead of horses and forced to pull heavy carts at gun-point, and were fed only small amounts of bread and beans.

But in spite of this heavy German presence, the terrain of the White Mountains, and the local knowledge which gave the Sfakians an advantage over the occupiers, meant that the area was one of the focal points of the Resistance. Sfakian men, many of them shepherds, were very prominent in the Resistance, and the bravery of these fighters was remarkable, not least because anyone found carrying arms by the Germans was generally killed on the spot or publicly executed. Places in Sfakia which were used as bases by the Resistance fighters at various times included Manikas, a grazing area in the mountains above Skaloti; the small Niatos plateau, above and to the west of Askifou; Kali Lakki; and Tripiti. A cave between Asfendou and Kallikratis was used for radio transmissions throughout April and May 1942. In June 1942, Germans hunting for the Cretan leader Andreas Papadakis and the radio transmitter he controlled raided the area of Xerokambos, southwest of Askifou and east of Kali Lakki. But he had been warned, and Papadakis, Xan Fielding and others were able to escape into the hills further east beyond Sfakia. They left just in time, as the Germans combed the hills as far as Kallikratis and into the Krioneritis mountains above Rodakino.

By August 1942, radio transmissions were again coming from Sfakia to the British High Command in Egypt. Patrick Leigh Fermor had a radio on the Niatos plateau. This is a flat area at about 1200m where the Resistance fighter Vangelis Vandoulas had established a refuge located at the sheepfolds used by the Karkanakis brothers. It was here that news was brought by Vangelis' cousin Giannis about the success of the crucial RAF attack on the massive German ammunition dump at Vamvakopoulo, southwest of Chania, so that this vital information could be relayed to Cairo.

The radio transmitter could not remain at Niatos for long, however, as word came that the Germans had learnt of an RAF parachute drop of provisions at Niatos to supply the radio station and local guerrillas; two of the parachutes missed their target by quite a way and were found by Sfakian villagers at Kali Lakki. In anticipation of a German raid, Leigh Fermor therefore had his colleague, the famous "Cretan Runner" Georgos Psychountakis[399] – who once ran over the mountains from Kasteli Kissamos to Paleochora overnight – move the radio out of Sfakia and east into Rethymnon province.

Many of the bands of Resistance fighters were politically organised, and the Middle East Command encouraged them to cooperate against the common enemy. An agreement was signed on the 7th of November 1943 in the White Mountains between the Cretan units of ELAS (the leftist National Popular Liberation Army) and the rightist guerrillas of the monarchist-nationalist EOK (the National Organisation of Cretans), in hope of avoiding the infighting occurring on the mainland which saw guerrillas fighting each other as well as the Germans. Further cooperation agreements were signed over the next few months in an attempt to overcome issues which arose from time to time.

After attacks on the Germans by Resistance fighters, vicious reprisals were often carried out. Perhaps the most infamous of these occurred in June 1942 when, after Free French fighters successfully carried out a sabotage raid on Kastelli Pediados airfield, 62 leading citizens of Heraklion, including businessmen, scientists, lawyers, bankers, engineers and senior police officers, were rounded up and executed. Ordinary people were also often taken hostage, and some were even sent to Germany. Over the course of the occupation, 25,000 Cretan houses were totally or partly destroyed in reprisals.

Some of the guerrilla actions were rash and poorly conceived, and led to dreadful consequences. The level of German reprisals eventually became

[399] After the war, Georgos Psychountakis was imprisoned for 16 months as a deserter because there was no record of his service during this period!

so shocking that the British High Command decided that something had to be done. They argued that major clashes between Germans and increasingly large, concentrated bands of guerrillas – which they had never wanted in the first place – were having appalling consequences for the civilian population. They urged that the guerrillas should break up into smaller more dispersed groups, and that the most important leader, Manolis Bandouvas, who the Germans were determined to capture, should be taken off the island together with some of his more high-profile men. Bandouvas, a wealthy peasant who owned so many sheep that he was given the code-name Bo-Peep by the British, had initially been recruited by John Pendlebury. He was an impetuous man, and some of his group's actions were considered, by the local Cretans as well as by the British, to have been tragically ill thought out in view of the consequences for the local populations who, as he well knew, would suffer for them.

What happened next is described in Xan Fielding's book *Hide and Seek,* and by Georgos Harokopos, a well-known Cretan member of the Resistance, in his book *The Fortress Crete.* In October 1943, Bandouvas and a group of 80 or so men made the long trek from central Crete towards Rodakino, another village which the Germans had destroyed, to meet up with an evacuation boat on one of the beaches, countering attacks from Germans on the way. They were not successful in making contact with the boat, however, and withdrew to Sfakia, spending the night in the gorge between Skaloti and the highland Sfakian summer settlement of Manikas. Some of the men, including Harokopos, then headed east, while Fielding and Bandouvas travelled west, dodging German patrols on the way, and spent the night camped above the Kallikratis plateau.

The morning of October 8th, they discovered that the Germans, as a reprisal, had surrounded Kallikratis and at daybreak had broken into the houses scattered over the plateau, driving out the inhabitants - just some elderly men, plus women and children, since the younger men were in the habit of sleeping outdoors as a precautionary measure. The women and children were forced into the church, and the old men were taken away and executed nearby. The women and children were then marched off to Chora Sfakion under armed guard, and the village was set on fire. Reports say those who were too feeble to walk were burnt alive. The monument to the atrocity in Kallikratis today lists the victims who were shot or burnt to death.[400]

[400] Georgios Manouselis, Emmanouil Manouselis, Manousos N. Manouselis, Manousos G. Manouselis, Stratis Manouselis, Roussos Gantadakis, Spiros Hairetis, Nikos Hairetis, Stratis Hairetis, Nikos G. Vougioukalos, Ioannis Sifostratoudakis, Emannouil Konstantoudakis, Alexandros Vougioukalos, Emmanouil G. Vougioukalos, Georgios Kandiros, Manousos Vougioukalos, Pavlos Polakis, Markos Markoutsakis, Stavros Likakis, Eleni Polaki, Xanthippi Kandirou, Angeliki Gantadaki, Athina Tsivoledaki, Maria Haireti, Aikaterini Giannakaki, Evangelia Tsivoledaki, Zambia Papadosiphaki. Paris Kelaidis cites the additional names of Nikos Harogiannakis and Fania Vlahaki.

On their way back from Kallikratis, the Germans sacked and plundered Asfendou as well. A message was sent out that other villages would receive the same treatment unless Bandouvas was handed over. The unit that was mainly responsible for carrying out this atrocity was a paramilitary group of Greek criminals and Nazi sympathisers, commanded by a Greek-speaking German sergeant called Fritz Schubert. He had been born in Smyrna (Izmir), Turkey, and emigrated to Germany at a young age. He was so infamous that the Cretans referred to his unit as the Souberites – they were also involved in many other sadistic atrocities such as the sacking of Rodakino. N.A. Kokonas, in his book *The Cretan Resistance* writes:

> Sonderfuhrer Schubert, who already had a record of criminal brutality in Heraklion province, was charged with the formation of a Greek unit in German uniform. This unit, the Jagd-Kommando Schubert, mustered a hundred criminals and thugs, about half of them from the village of Kroussonas.[401]

Bandouvas and some of his men set off in an easterly direction, and he was eventually evacuated to Egypt about a month later. Fielding in the meantime undertook a four-day trek across the White Mountains via Kali Lakki to the western edges of Sfakia and into Selino province, where there was a refuge with a radio transmitter at Koustogerako. The most dangerous part of this journey was crossing the road from the north coast that runs through Askifou but as he approached his base more tragic news reached him.

The three villages of Koustogerako, Livada and Moni in Selino, which had been providing him and the ISLD (Inter-Services Liaison Department, a branch of British Secret Intelligence Service) team with support since their arrival in November the previous year, had been attacked by a large German force, including Stuka dive-bombers and long-range cannon fire from Palaeochora, over a five-day period from the 29th of September, and had been totally destroyed. Seventeen locals, including ten women, were killed, while some three hundred people, including women and children, were arrested and taken to Ayia prison outside Chania for interrogation. The local andartes – the Cretan guerrillas – fought back, killing 37 of the enemy and wounding more than 100, but their villages were gone; they were not able to return until the Germans had withdrawn to their northern enclave twelve months later. The two Allied teams had to abandon the Selino district, as it was now unsafe and lacked the local support structure that they required to continue with their operation.

A few weeks later, however, a recent addition to the SOE team, the New Zealander Dudley Perkins, a soldier who had escaped from Crete

[401] Kokonas (1993), p. 72. Kroussonas is a village to the southwest of Heraklion.

and then returned, came back to regroup the dispersed andartes teams and re-established a new, larger force of more than one hundred andartes. By February 1944, the radio transmitter had started operating again from a new location at Achlada, between Koustogerako and Omalos, under Perkins' control. The Germans located the position of the radio and organised a sortie to capture it, but they were ambushed and routed. Quite soon afterwards, Perkins himself – who was called Vasilis by the Cretans and became known as the "Lion of Crete" – was ambushed and killed by the Germans on the northern side of the Omalos plateau at Lakki, where today there is a plaque commemorating his bravery.

Life was not easy for anyone in Sfakia during those years – even in Chora Sfakion, especially in the early months of occupation, people suffered from random acts of cruelty by the Germans. And everyone was afflicted by hunger. The worst time in Sfakia was the very cold winter of 1942, when some people actually starved to death. Meat had always been in short supply, but from the time of the British evacuation there were very few animals left, and people who did own some had to keep a close eye on them to prevent their theft. There was no milk available. The Germans did issue permits for in-shore fishing from boats – but most of the boats had been taken by Allied soldiers or destroyed during the Battle of Crete.

So the Sfakians often had to rely on snails and wild greens for food, and because of the absence of sheep and goats, these greens were plentiful in season. They also cooked carob beans – they called it "chocolate" – which they then ground by hand. Schoolchildren used to steal carobs from the fodder store that the Germans kept for their mules, and this was mostly perpetrated by girls, who hid the pods in their aprons. The villagers resorted to making bread from a mixture of a small amount of barley flour together with ground acorns or carob beans.

Sfakians also undertook long journeys by horse or mule to trade for food. Geronimakis, just a boy at the time, took olive oil from Asfendou to the western area of Sfakia, where there were not so many olive trees, and exchanged it for salt. He describes how he would then carry some of the salt east into the province of Rethymnon to exchange it for broad beans and potatoes. Adults travelled much further than this, for example to the Messara plain and back, a journey which took a week by donkey, to trade for barley. And on one occasion the German commander of Chora Sfakion permitted a rowing boat to travel from the village down the coast to Matala – a two-day trip – to pick up food.

In Chora Sfakion, a *modus vivendi* gradually developed between the occupying troops under this German commander, an Austrian, who was not unsympathetic to the plight of the locals. Germans had seized a number of local houses in the centre of Chora Sfakion and lived cheek-by-jowl with the Sfakians. This did not prevent a certain amount of bullying and harassment of the local teenagers by the German troops, however. Older villagers today remember frightening pranks, such as having their oars shot in half by German sharpshooters as they rowed in the harbour.

The German soldier/writer Erhart Kästner describes how during the war he and two companions were hunting in the area of the Samaria Gorge when they encountered some members of the Viglis clan who lived there – they were all partisans, including some of the women. When the Germans tried to leave, they were not allowed to do so: the rules of Cretan hospitality required that the hunters be fed and given a bed for the night. The next day they were escorted by a group of locals to the top of the gorge, where their Sfakian companions suddenly melted away. The hunters rounded a bend and came upon an armed German patrol, who gave them the astonishing information that, the previous day, they had been conducting a mission against partisans in the gorge.

The End of the Occupation

The German occupation of Sfakia ended in 1944. In August that year, the Germans had taken the decision to withdraw all units from the Aegean islands to the Greek mainland. On September 8th the order came to leave eastern Crete, with the plan being to transfer most of the German troops to the mainland, leaving a skeleton force behind to hold the island. On September 21st, however, they decided to halt their withdrawal to the mainland: they were suffering too many losses because of superior British forces, and progress was too slow.

The Germans on the mainland, fearful of being cut off in Greece by the advancing Russians, began a retreat from Attica, which made any withdrawal of further troops from Crete to the mainland pointless. On October 3rd the order was given to halt the troop transfer from Crete. All the Axis troops in Crete, by now numbering about 15,000 Germans and 5,000 Italians,[402] were to withdraw to the *Kernfestung* – a central stronghold. This was an area running along the western part of the north coast, focussed on Chania. The defensive line surrounding this stronghold passed just to the east of Giorgioupoli and to the south of Vrises. It then ran west along the foothills of the White Mountains and down to the coast again, just east of Nopigia. It did not include any areas of Sfakia.

The British forces and the resistance group favoured by the British government, the rightist EOK, did not try to hinder this German retreat into their stronghold. They wanted to avoid bloodshed, and it would of course be advantageous for them to have the rest of the island free of Germans. The leftist members of ELAS, the larger of the two resistance groups, similarly

[402] Kavvos (1991), p. 677.

held off because of the strength of the German forces. Major Bruce Mitford arrived on the island in August 1944 as the British liaison officer working with ELAS, who were by now hostile to Fielding. This was no doubt because, although Fielding sympathised with them, as he told Mitford, he had been given direct orders not to collaborate with them.

Some sources say that, during their withdrawal, the Germans, officially but secretly, gave weapons and munitions to rightist bands for them to use against ELAS. The Germans had planned to destroy Heraklion harbour, but this did not happen – one theory is that some of the German plotters may have been bribed by the Cretans and/or British. The German retreat from Lasithi was completed by September 21st. ELAS took control of Heraklion on October 12th, and of Rethymnon on October 13th. All areas evacuated by the Germans were taken over by EOK and/or ELAS, with agreement between two groups, meaning that the process for the most part happened peacefully.

That November, with the whole island outside the German stronghold having been liberated, a pitched battle took place between the Germans and the andartes at Panagia, outside Chania. This was the largest battle fought by the Resistance in Crete. The brunt of the fighting was borne by a unit of Sfakians, the 8th Independent Sfakian Company, which by that time had been wound down to only 18 men. Between the 12th and 14th of November, 600 ELAS guerrillas, with support from EOK units, both supplied as before with boots and clothing by the British Special Operations Executive under Bruce Mitford, inflicted significant casualties on the 2,000 or so Germans involved.

The ELAS forces and their allies took up positions above Katochori and Gerolakkos, inland from Mournies in the foothills of the White Mountains. The first attacks at dawn on the 12th occurred at the villages of Kontopoula and Katochori, southeast of Mournies. German forces approached from Stilos, west of Armeni, moving towards Samonas and Kambi in order to strike at the andartes from the south. Other German units closed in from the north on Loulos and Agios Georgos, to the northwest of the ELAS positions. The largest number of German troops, however, mobilised due south of Mournies and Perivolia with the aim of reaching Panagia. By 9 am, battle was engaged on all fronts, with German artillery directed at the ELAS lines. The fighting was extremely fierce, with bloody encounters between the Sfakians from the 8th ELAS company and the Germans at the Kleftoperama Gorge, where they were reinforced later on in the day by a larger company of ELAS fighters from Rethymnon. Together they managed to hold back the Germans, with the loss of only three dead and 11 injured. Two of those killed were Sfakians: the heroic leader Manousos Manouselis from Kallikratis; and Sifis Manousakis from Imbros. By November 14th, the Sfakian unit was just 11 strong, but it still repelled another German attack.

But under heavy artillery bombardment, they were forced to withdraw further south from their position, enabling the Germans to take the village of Panagia; however, by the evening the Germans had to retreat again.

One of the Sfakian fighters who was wounded in the battle was the famous Theodoros Viglis (also known as Viglothodoris), from the village of Samaria in that gorge; he was well known as a brilliant sharpshooter and had taken part in many smaller actions against the Germans during the occupation. He was an ELAS andartis who had once been offered a post as a bodyguard to Eleftherios Venizelos, and was described by Bruce Mitford as fearless, impulsive, and generous, as well as being a complex and interesting character who was "redoubtable" and "of splendid physique".

Altogether, nine ELAS men were killed and 20 were injured. German losses are not known, but estimates vary between 20 and 200. About 100 Axis soldiers deserted to the Cretan side, most of them Italians but also including some Russians and other nationalities. Territorially, the battle was not conclusive: Nazi troops were still holding out in Chania even after the German government in Berlin had surrendered in May 1945.

This was not the last battle fought between the andartes and the Germans, however. On the 8th of December 1944, there was another battle, at Vafes, in which soldiers from the German garrison in Vrises, supported by seven tanks, took on the andartes in an attempt to discourage guerrilla attacks on the base. Both EOK and ELAS andartes fought there. The Sfakians who took part were from the 1st Sfakian Company, "the national organization of Sfakians" that had been formed for the purpose of joining the EOK forces at Apokoronas.

A most remarkable, legendary figure was involved in this battle, a Sfakian from Askifou, Stavrianos Polentas (1856-1959), known as Sissanes after the type of large rifle that he used to carry. He was nearly 90 and had started his military career fighting against the Turks in the 1877 uprising. When the German attack started, his nephew Panagiotis Polentas sent fleet-footed young men up to Askifou, where church bells were rung to summon fighters – most of the men in the village – to defend Vafes, an action which turned out to be decisive. Sissanes grabbed a machine gun and rushed down the hill towards Vafes on foot. Paris Kelaidis relates in his biography of Sissanes that the only concession made to his age was that he allowed another nephew, Lasthenis Polentas, to carry this heavy weapon for him.[403] Men from nearby villages also came to the aid of the guerrillas. Ten Cretans died in the intense fighting at Vafes, while 60 Germans were killed or injured. The Germans pulled back to Vrises when their commander was wounded.

In January 1945, with the Germans confined to their stronghold, fighting

[403] Sissanes did not actually take part in the fighting – by the time he arrived, the battle was over.

between EOK and ELAS erupted in Rethymnon. ELAS was the stronger of the two Resistance armies and had achieved considerable popular support through, for example, tracking down and destroying the Schuberitis who had committed the massacre at Kallikratis. After the Greek government was reinstated in Athens in October 1944 and ordered guerrilla forces to disband, andartes in the Chania area of Crete were officially allowed to continue to be armed because of the presence of the several thousand German troops in the fortified enclave after the liberation of the rest of the island. ELAS was officially disbanded in May 1945, but in a number of Cretan villages, former ELAS men formed "self-protection" groups, fearing reprisals from right-wingers.

In Sfakia itself, the food situation had improved after the German withdrawal in September 1944, and life gradually returned to something a bit more like normal. Fishing could start again in earnest. Young boys walked, often barefoot, from Chora Sfakion to Anopoli and Askifou to exchange fish for flour and vegetables. Then in December 1944, the Royal Navy began a relief service from Egypt to deliver supplies, although there were reports from elsewhere in western Crete that these were totally inadequate. The British Special Operations Executive under Sergeants Watson and Luscombe had been active in having a prisoner of war pen constructed in Chora Sfakion, and the Navy removed some German prisoners that the Cretan guerrillas had captured.

The strange situation in western Crete with the German forces controlling their defensive enclave continued well past the collapse of Germany, the death of Hitler, and the official surrender of the German army on the 8th of May 1945. General Benthag, the commander of the German forces on the island, received orders from Germany to capitulate and was flown to Heraklion, where he surrendered unconditionally on the 9th of May. But this did not mean total surrender for the Germans in western Crete. They had a tacit agreement with the British and Greek authorities on the island which has perplexed many commentators. Over the next two months, the Germans were allowed to keep their weapons, supposedly for their own protection, and retain control of their enclave. During this time, the Allies supervised the destruction of German armaments and their dispersal at sea, and provided protection to the Germans while they completed this task: there was concern that the weapons might fall into the hands of EAM (National Liberation Front) forces who still surrounded the Germans. It was not until the end of June, almost two months after the war ended, that Crete was finally free of all armed German troops. During this period, the British remained worried about acts of revenge against the Germans and allowed them to take probable war criminals as well as the spoils of their looting with them.

In the aftermath of the war, General Bruno Brauer, the German Governor of Crete, was tried by a Greek military court in Athens, charged with responsibility for the deaths of some 3,000 people during the occupation of the island. The indictment cited murders, massacres, pillage, destruction, torture and ill-treatment of civilians. He was sentenced to death on the 9th of December 1946 and was shot on the 20th of May 1947. General Friedrich Müller, the Military Governor of Crete, was also tried in Athens for massacres of hostages as reprisals, such as those carried out in Chora Sfakion and Kallikratis, and was sentenced to death and shot on these same dates. Fritz Schubert, who had led the massacre in Kallikratis, was executed as a war criminal in northern Greece in 1947.

Sfakia after World War II

After the war, the relative prosperity that the Sfakia region had known in the 1930s was not at all quick to return. Many people left, including a number of young men who joined the merchant marine and travelled the world. And the aftermath of the war was by no means entirely peaceful.

Crete did not experience the full horror of the Greek Civil War as it unfolded on the mainland from 1946 to 1949. On the one side was the government of monarchists and rightists, supported by the British and other western governments; their adversaries were the guerrilla forces composed of communists, Venizelist anti-monarchists, and other leftists who had played a very prominent role in the resistance against the Nazis, with support from Yugoslavia and other Eastern European communist governments.

It is possible that Crete was spared some of the worst excesses of the Civil War because there was a long tradition of liberal republicanism in Crete, reflecting their support for the political ideology of Eleftherios Venizelos, so there was a tendency for some of the population to be both anti-communist and anti-monarchist. Also, there were no sizeable groups of ethnic or linguistic minorities in Crete, unlike in northern Greece, where before World War I there had been perhaps as many as half a million Slavs.[404] The two main Resistance groups had agreed to cooperate against the German enemy during the years 1943 and 1944, encouraged by the Special Operations Executive operatives on the island and the Middle East Command in Egypt, although these agreements were often broken by both parties. This all meant that there was less inter-Greek fighting than had

[404] These Greek Slavs, who played a prominent role in the Resistance after the German invasion, had been subject to heavy repression and persecution under the fascist-nationalist Metaxas dictatorship in the 1930s, so it was no surprise that many of them supported anti-government guerrilla forces during the Civil War. See also references in the previous chapter to the multi-ethnic composition of this region.

occurred on the mainland before the German withdrawal. And, as we just saw, the two groups fought together a year later at the Battle of Panagia.

But the fighting in Rethymnon in January 1945 mentioned above turned out to be a harbinger of much worse things to come. The EOK guerrillas officially disbanded, and some of their members were absorbed into the Greek Army, but ELAS members who applied were generally rejected. A local government-sponsored anti-communist gendarmerie was formed, with many of their recruits being petty criminals or suspected German collaborators. Some ELAS fighters did declare allegiance to the reconstituted right-wing Greek government in Athens, but most did not and held onto their weapons. Giannis Manousakas, a communist originally from Agios Konstantinos in Rethymnon province, travelled around Crete gathering former ELAS units into "The Democratic Army of Greece"; this was in line with the December 1946 policy of the mainland communist leadership to unite all anti-government partisans into a new unified army unit. In western Crete, Manousakas cooperated with figures such as Nikos Tsamantis, a wartime ELAS leader who had taken part in the Battle of Panagia against the Germans.

Civil war broke out in eastern Crete in earnest in April 1947 with the escape of 60 left-wing sympathisers from mainland Greece who had been forcibly conscripted as labourers (*skapaneis*) and held in an army camp at Agios Nikolaos; they were assisted by local andartes.[405] Initially they were successful in taking control of Ierapetra but were soon forced westwards towards the Psiloritis mountains, where they were joined by other local andartes. A three-day battle at the end of June saw most of them killed or captured, with only eight escaping; these men headed to Kallikratis, where they joined the far stronger ELAS units in the White Mountains.[406] The government forces fighting against them included the private army of Manolis Bandouvas, the *Kapetanios* from Heraklion whose deeds in western Crete in 1943 were recounted earlier, and who by now had become a strong government supporter and fervent anti-communist. The head and the right arm of the slain ELAS andartes leader, Podias, were triumphantly paraded through the streets of Heraklion by right-wing supporters. Bandouvas later criticised his brother for the unauthorised mutilation of Podias body.[407]

In the west of the island, civil war also erupted in April when ten leftists were arrested and expelled from Crete. Over the next two days, ELAS took over police stations at Fre, Theriso and elsewhere in Kissamos, and there were bloody battles around Tavronitis and Voukolia.[408] In July, the ELAS andartes seized Maleme airport, securing arms; and some Air Force

[405] Kokolakis (1988), pp. 243-249.
[406] Christoforakis (1984), pp. 159-168.
[407] Sanoudakis (1979), p. 439
[408] Iliakis (2002), pp. 36-47

personnel took the opportunity to join them. Over the next few months, clashes with the gendarmerie continued in the northwest of Crete.

In January 1947, Pavlos Gyparis, a well-known republican but anti-communist military figure who had already played a role in the fighting in Rethymnon, was appointed military governor of Chania and assumed the task of suppressing left-wing opposition to the government. Many measures were taken against communist and non-combatant left-wing groups, and people who had been imprisoned by the Germans for their resistance activities were now imprisoned again by the Greeks. Demonstrations were banned. Many who were unsympathetic to Gyparis and his gendarmerie's methods of operation were found dead in mysterious circumstances, or were arrested and pronounced guilty by military tribunals and quickly executed or sent into exile.

In Sfakia, Geronimakis relates how he once saw local communist guerrillas come down from the mountains to Vouvas and join fellow villagers, including some known rightists, for a glass of wine; they talked amicably for a while, and then the guerrillas returned to the mountains. But tensions were running high. In May 1947, an EOK leader from Imbros was killed by ELAS; and the gendarmes in Patsianos were disarmed by a 17-year-old boy from Kallikratis. The situation was becoming very unstable, with the guerrilla forces gathering in the mountains and military activity increasing. The number of ELAS guerrillas in the hills increased for a while, as some young men who had been conscripted into the Greek army to fight on the government side on the mainland chose to join up with the Cretan andartes instead. Punishments instigated by Gyparis against guerrillas' families – such as imprisonment, exile, forced labour, and burning their houses down – led to further recruitment, as brothers and even sisters of fighters joined guerrilla units rather than stay at home and face such reprisals. As the months went by, there were many atrocities carried out by both sides, including innocent people being killed in bus ambushes; the bodies and severed heads of male and female ELAS fighters were even displayed on the bridge over the Kladissos River by Chania.

Gavdos, too, was once again being used as a prison island. The British newspaper *Reynolds News* published an article in 1946 written by an American entitled "Gavdos, Island of Hell". It stated that there were 42 men and 8 women exiled on the island, some communists and some democrats. Some of the women were being held because they refused to answer questions about where their sons were. A further 450 prisoners were said to be on their way to the island.

Gyparis and his forces attempted to combat the leftists in the hills and foothills by punishing villagers for giving food to the guerrillas, whether they had done so willingly or not. There were many forced signings of written declarations of loyalty – at one stage all the adult male inhabitants of

Agia Roumeli were compelled to sign one. Many curfews came into effect, as did prohibitions such as restrictions on the movement of shepherds' flocks in the White Mountains. Rural Security Units (MAY) were compulsorily formed to deter attacks and food raids by guerrillas: there was a MAY unit of 85 men in Anopoli and one of 30 men in Agia Roumeli.

Following a spectacular ELAS attack on the motorcade of the Greek government minister Sophocles Venizelos, son of the former Prime Minister, and a large group of other politicians and diplomats travelling on the road between Georgioupoli and Neo Chorio in March 1948, Gyparis was replaced, as was the Military Commander of Crete and the Commander of the Gendarmerie. The new head of the Gendarmerie was Lieutenant-Colonel Georgos Vardoulakis, who was from Anopoli. The government sent Vardoulakis reinforcements of gendarmes from the mainland, and at one point in the campaign he actually led a large patrol to Anopoli itself, where he announced an amnesty for army deserters and those who had failed to report for compulsory military service.

The ELAS fighters frequently used the Omalos plateau as a base, and mid-May 1948 saw a large force of Cretan ELAS guerrillas camped inside and around the Samaria Gorge. A group of them set out to blow up two buildings on the edge of Anopoli where the government gendarmerie were garrisoned. Their approach was betrayed and, learning from local people that most of the gendarmes had left, and that the few that had stayed behind had taken up defensive positions, they aborted the attack and crossed back over the Aradena Gorge. They then walked up to Krousia, above Agios Ioannis, where cheese-making was in progress; exhausted and hungry, they requisitioned cheese from the local shepherds who, it is reported, were unwilling to give it to them voluntarily.[409] After returning to Samaria, they planned to regroup, leaving two or three small groups in place there to surprise any search parties, and move the majority of the andartes out of the gorge and on to other targets. However, there was now a general government order for a large-scale operation against the guerrillas in western Crete and, enclosed in the gorge as they were, the next day the andartes found themselves trapped.

The government forces, consisting of army units, gendarmes, and MAY units, numbered perhaps well over 1,000 men. Troops from Paleochora disembarked at the bottom of the gorge, others arrived from Selino and took up positions on the north-western ridge of the gorge, while yet others approached from Omalos, Poria and Psari in the north and from Agios Ioannis in the east. Fleeing from this encirclement was not possible, so the andartes spread out and barred the approaches to the various entry points to prevent the government forces from entering the gorge. The Air Force supported the government troops by strafing and bombarding the area,

[409] Ibid., p. 85.

while the Army units fired mortar bombs at the andartes' positions around the gorge. This attack on the 4th of June was frightening in its intensity, but the andartes held fast.

After four days of heavy fighting, however, the government forces succeeded in penetrating into the gorge and killed eight andartes who were defending the position near Agios Nikolaos church between Xiloskala and Samaria village. But most of the andartes were saved from capture by an extraordinary escape which was made possible only through the local knowledge of two Sfakians from Samaria village, Giannis and Vangelis Viglis.[410]

The memoirs[411] of two survivors of this battle, Agryro Kokovli and Giorgis Tzompanakis, give us a very vivid picture of how the Viglis cousins led an evacuation of 90 guerrillas, including women, by getting them to climb up the apparently impassable western wall of the gorge along an extraordinarily dangerous route known only to very few locals. After escaping from the gorge, the majority of the andartes assembled at Prinias, high up on the southwest side of the gorge, from where they embarked towards safety on paths that only the Viglis men knew. The majority of the guerrillas were suffering badly from exhaustion, hunger and thirst, and some of them were injured, five seriously. Vangelis Viglis courageously walked back down to Agia Roumeli and returned with two large loaves of bread for the 90 starving andartes.

The majority of them then laboured across the Kladou and Tripiti gorges – some with no shoes – finding stagnant water only once, and shooting three stray goats, which provided their only nourishment during the three days that it eventually took them to reach the mountains above Koustogerako where support, sustenance and help were available to them at last. A smaller group, consisting of the injured who could not follow the rest, descended to Agia Roumeli after resting for two days, helped by a local Sfakian who provided them with food. The Sfakian Georgos Manouselis, a former Athens policeman from Kallikratis, led them from Agia Roumeli eastwards along the beach and up the Eligia Gorge; they hid in a cave with running water in the Kormokopou Gorge, a branch of the Eligia which leads to Agios Ioannis, where they eventually made their way. At Agios Ioannis they met a Sfakian from Aradena who helped them reach Apokoronas. Another group of some 20 andartes who had been cut off from the others dispersed from Lagoudolivada on the southwest side of the gorge and headed in small bands north towards Meskla, Zourva and Therisso. Two of them were arrested and shot, while a third was shot when found injured and unable to move.

Back in Samaria, Theodoros Viglis, the leader of the Samaria Viglis clan

---

[410] A brother and a cousin of Theodoros Viglis.

[411] Kokovlis and Kokovlis (2002); Blazakis and Tzompanakis (1977).

and brother of Giannis, who had led the guerrillas out of the gorge, was killed in November 1947. He had fought with ELAS against the Germans, as we have seen, but was not an active participant in the Civil War. Nevertheless, in the hills above Omalos between the villages of Lakki and Zourva, he was ambushed on November 13th and shot dead by members of the local MAY unit from Lakki, which had been a predominantly EOK village. In his book *The Stronghold*, Xan Fielding describes how, when challenged to give himself up, Theodoros shouted "a Viglis never surrenders!" and opened fire single-handed against the troops, among whom was Matthaios Skoulas, who had fought along with EOK against the Germans. The following lament was composed and sung in Samaria:

> All the mothers are full of joy and happiness.
> Only the mother of Viglothodoris weeps inconsolably and tells her sons
> "Giorgi my youngest, Gianni my eldest,
> May you kill the Lakkiotes ..." [*and there followed some names*][412]

Shortly after Theodoros died, Skoulas was killed in a revenge attack, and thereafter, Fielding says, no Sfakians from Samaria ventured onto the Omalos plateau from the south, and no men from Lakki dared enter from the north – Omalos became a kind of no-man's land.

Colin Janes, who has carried out extensive research on this period and written a book about the Civil War in Crete,[413] supplies further invaluable information about the aftermath of the Battle of Samaria. He says that at the beginning of 1949 there were 32 male and 8 female guerrillas still left at large in western Crete. In the Sfakia area, the local tradition of hospitality and sheltering fugitives – which had led Sfakians to risk their lives aiding Allied troops during the war – meant that assistance was sometimes available to the guerrillas in places such as Aradena and Livaniana.

In February 1949, Georgos Manouselis and his group who had escaped from Samaria were hiding above Agios Ioannis in the forest by Kato (Lower) Krousia, where local people supplied them with food. In early March, feeling less secure, they relocated eastwards to Kali Lakki, which would not be occupied by Sfakian shepherds until later in the spring; they then walked over the mountains to the northern slopes of the Lefka Ori. In April, Manouselis moved back to Kato Krousia with seven others, and then to a cave above Kallikratis where, as a local man, he was able to ensure help

[412] Ούλες οι μάνες χαίρουνται κι ούλες καλή καρδιά 'χουν, μόνο του Βιγγλοθοδωρή η γι-εδική ντου μάνα κλαίει απαρηγόρητα και λέει των υγιώ τζη:- Γιώργη μου πλιο μικρότερε, Γιάννη μου πλιο μεγάλε, Λακκιώτες να σκοτώνετε...

[413] Janes (2012) has made a detailed study of the Greek and English-language literature on the Civil War in Crete. His archival research into the records of Cretan newspapers from the period, and his interviews with surviving fighters and their families, provides us with unique and invaluable information about this turbulent period.

and supplies of food from relatives. However, their hideout was eventually discovered and attacked by gendarmes, and six ELAS members, including Manouselis, were killed. Two escaped: one hid near Vouvas, but was soon found and shot dead when he refused to surrender; the other evaded capture by heading west, but two days later was caught and brought to Chora Sfakion, where he was shot dead when he refused to answer questions or, according to another report, when he tried to escape.[414]

Many of the other guerrillas who had escaped and scattered stayed up in mountainous areas such as Agios Ioannis and Asfendou for months. Some eventually surrendered, often as a result of pressure from their families. A number of them died of disease as a result of the hardships of living through winters in the mountains. Others were tracked down and killed, in one instance near Livaniana. Some were captured, tried in military courts and executed. Yet others were imprisoned and eventually freed during the 1950s, sometimes after courts had been petitioned for their release by fellow villagers, and once after the intervention of Xan Fielding.

On the northern slopes of the White Mountains, guerrillas were able to stay in hiding for much longer. In October 1952, there were still 13 guerrillas, including two women, who had evaded capture. Eight of them were still at large in 1960. Six of these managed to leave Crete and make their way via Athens to Italy, whence with the help of the Italian Communist Party they travelled to the Soviet Union (to Tashkent, now in Uzbekistan), where there were 20,000 leftist Greek refugees.[415] And extraordinarily, the other two guerrillas stayed in the mountains until 1975, when an amnesty granted after pressure from prominent figures such as Mikis Theodorakis following the collapse of the military junta persuaded them after more than 25 years to come down from the mountains.[416] One of these men, Giorgis Tzompanakis, later went on to make a career leading walking parties through the Samaria Gorge, where he had fought against the government forces in 1948; he could often be found in the summer months in Agia Roumeli.

---

[414] Kokovlis and Kokovlis (2002), pp. 265-266.

[415] Kokovlis and Kokovlis provide details of this difficult period of the lives of these andartes.

[416] Blazakis and Tzompanakis (1997). This book gives the life story of these two andartes up to when they received their amnesty and rejoined the free society.

XVII. Epilogue

Many of the famous names of the heroic figures from the past that we have mentioned in this book live on in modern Sfakia. It is still easy to meet people in Sfakia called Deligiannakis, Fasoulis, Kelaidis, Manouselis, Manousogiannakis, Saviolakis – to name just a few. And very many Sfakians today can trace their ancestry back to the Skordilis *archondopoula* clan. Modern Sfakians live *in* their history. They live surrounded by it. Their past is still very much alive in their monuments, *kalderimia,* forts, and churches, but also in their mountains, gorges, and caves. If you listen to an elderly Sfakian talking today about the Daskalogiannis rebellion, you can tell that for them it is something which happened only yesterday.

The Sfakians are still shepherds, fishermen, farmers. But since the last quarter of the 20th century, they have started to regain something of their past wealth, through a very modern phenomenon. Apart from a few young adventurers, after 1944 no Germans returned to Chora Sfakion until the early 1970s, when an official peace-and-friendship visit was organised: a group of 30 Germans, with a large escort of Greek police for protection, visited Sfakia for the first time in 30 years. But today Sfakia is, like the rest of Crete, full of German and Austrian tourists in the summer months – as well as visitors from very many other parts of the world. Agia Roumeli, Loutro, Chora Sfakion and Frangokastello in particular now benefit from the tourist trade. But throughout the region, the hospitality for which Sfakia is famous helps to attract people from other lands and keep them coming back. Some of these foreigners arrive with knowledge of how the history of their own country – Italy, Australia, New Zealand, Britain, Germany, Turkey – is intertwined with that of the Sfakians. Many others come with no idea of the historical significance of the area.

The Samaria Gorge, especially, attracts thousands of tourists every year who walk down from the Omalos plateau to Agia Roumeli in their shorts and sunhats, admiring the splendour and wild beauty of Europe's longest and deepest gorge, and are then taken by boat to Chora Sfakion. Most of them are probably not aware that thousands of terrified women and children once huddled in the gorge for protection; or that defensive battles were fought near the Iron Gates to prevent the murderous incursions of Venetian troops; or that there were many failed attempts by Turkish troops to penetrate into this Sfakian defensive stronghold. And most of them will also certainly find it impossible, if they glance upwards, to imagine the Viglis cousins, not so very long ago, leading a band of guerrillas on their escape route up the apparently impassable cliffs on the west side of the gorge. just as it will be difficult for them, as they enter the peaceful harbour of Chora Sfakion on the ferry back from Agia Roumeli, to visualise the Luftwaffe aircraft roaring in over the mountains to attack the tens of thousands of Allied soldiers crammed into the village in 1941.

In *The Stronghold,* Fielding relates that when he himself returned to the White Mountains in 1952 and descended into the Samaria Gorge from the north, he and his party were met by armed men – he assumed from the Viglis family – still standing guard in the gorge just north of Samaria village, five years after the Battle of Samaria. Ten years after that, in 1962, the Greek government achieved something which the Arabs, Venetians, Turks and Germans had never managed. The Samaria Gorge was designated a National Park, and its Sfakian inhabitants, against the promise of financial compensation, moved out of Samaria village. For the first time in 4,000 years, there was no human habitation in the Samaria Gorge.

And west of Chora Sfakion, there is still absolutely no wheeled traffic along the Sfakian coast.

Bibliography

Andrianakis, Michalis (1982), *Ο Νομός Χανίων κατά την παλαιοχριστιανική περίοδο (κατάλογος μνημείων)* [*The district of Chania during the Paleo-Christian period – Documentation of Monuments*]. Χανιά: Ετήσια έκδοση Δήμου Χανίων.
Agelis, Nikos (1962), *Δασκαλογιάννης* [*Daskalogiannis*]. Athens: Mavrakis
Antill, Peter (2005), *Crete 1941.* Oxford: Osprey.
Beevor, Antony (1991), *Crete: the battle and the resistance.* London: Penguin.
Bendiner, Elmer (1983), *The rise and fall of paradise.* New York: Putnam
Blazakis, Spiros and Giorgis Tzompanakis (1977), *35 Χρόνια Αντίσταση. Οι δυο αντάρτες της Κρήτης αφηγούνται την ζωή τους* [*35 years of resistance. The two Cretan insurgents describe their lives*].
Bounialis, Marinos Tzane (1979), *Ο Κρητικός Πόλεμος (1645-1669)* [*The Cretan War (1645-1669)*]. Athens: A. Nenedakis.
Bourne, Kenneth (1956), *Great Britain and the Cretan Revolt, 1866-1869.* In: *The Slavonic and East European Review*, Vol. 35, No. 84, pp. 74-94.
Chadwick, John (1958), *The decipherment of Linear B.* Cambridge: Cambridge University Press.
Clark, Alan (1962), *The fall of Crete.* London: Blond.
Christides, Vassilios (1984), *The conquest of Crete by the Arabs (CA 824). A turning point in the struggle between Byzantium and Islam.* Academy of Athens.
Christoforakis, Michalis (1984), *Εθνική Αντίσταση και Δημοκρατικοί αγώνες στην Κρήτη* [*National resistance and democratic struggle in Crete*]. Athens: Σύγχρονη Εποχή.
Damer, Sean and Ian Frazer (2007), *On the run: Anzac escape and evasion in enemy-occupied Crete.* Melbourne: Penguin.
Detorakis, Theoharis (1988) *Κρήτη, Ιστορία και Πολιτισμός, Τόμος Β* [*Crete, History and Civilization, Vol. II*]. Heraklion: Σύνδεσμος τοπικών ενώσεων Δήμων και Κοινοτήτων Κρήτης.
— (1994), *History of Crete.* Heraklion.
Dueck, Daniela, Hugh Lindsey and Sarah Pothecary (eds.) (2005), *Strabo's cultural geography.* Cambridge: Cambridge University Press.
Elliot, Murray (1987), *Vasili: the Lion of Crete.* London: Hutchinson.
Fielding, Xan (1954), *Hide and seek.* London: Secker and Warburg.
— (1955), *The stronghold.* London: Secker and Warburg.
Gallagher, Donat (2007), *Inventing invention.* In: *Evelyn Waugh Newsletter & Studies* 37, 3.
Geronimakis, Kanakis (1996), *Κοινότης Ασφένδου Σφακίων, [Community of Asfendou, Sfakia].* Chania.
Giannopoulos, I.G. (1978), *Η Κρήτη κατά τον τέταρτο Βενετοτουρκικό πόλεμο (1570-1571)* [*Crete during the fourth Veneto-Turkish war (1570–1571)*]. Athens.
Harokopos, George (1993), *The fortress Crete 1941-1944.* Athens: B. Giannikos & Co.
Hatzidakis Iosif (1881), *Περιήγησις εις Κρήτην* [*Touring in Crete*]. Athens: Αναστατικές Εκδόσεις.
Holton, David (ed).(1991), *Literature and society in Renaissance Crete.* Cambridge:

Cambridge University Press.
Hood, Sinclair (1971), *The Minoans: Crete in the Bronze Age.* London: Thames and Hudson.
— **(1974)**, *Primitive rock engravings from Crete.* In: *The J. Paul Getty Museum Journal* 1, pp. 101-111.
Hopkins, Adam (1977), *Crete: its past, present and people.* London: Faber and Faber.
Hutchinson, R.W. (1962), *Prehistoric Crete.* London: Penguin.
Iliakis, Lefteris I. (2002), *Ο Εμφύλιος πόλεμος στην Κρήτη* [*The Civil War in Crete*]. Chania: self-published.
Janes, Colin (2012), *The eagles of Crete: an untold story of civil war.* Amazon.
Karathanasis, Athanasios E. (1973), *Ανέκδοτη αλληλογραφία του Φρ. Μοροζίνη και άλλων Βενετών με Κρητικούς στα χρόνια του πολέμου 1659-1660* [*Unpublished correspondence of F. Morosini and other Venetians with Cretans during the years of the war 1659-1660*]. *Kretika Chronika*, Vol. 2, pp. 21-124. Heraklion
Kavvos, Giorgios, (1991), *Γερμανό-Ιταλική Κατοχή και Αντίσταση Κρήτης, 1941-1945*, [*German-Italian Occupation and Resistance in Crete, 1941-1945*]. Heraklion
Kelaidis, Paris (1982), *Αρχαίες πόλεις στα Σφακιά* [*Ancient cities of Sfakia*]. Athens: Καράβι και Τόξο.
— **(1983)**, *Ριζίτικα για τα Σφακιά* [*Rizitika songs for Sfakia*]. Volume 1. Athens: Καράβι και Τόξο.
— **(1984)**, *Ριζίτικα για τα Σφακιά* [*Rizitika songs for Sfakia*]. Volume 2. Athens: Καράβι και Τόξο.
— **(1988)**, *Ο καπετάν Πολέντας – Σισανές από τα Σφακιά* [*Captain Polentas – Sisanes from Sfakia*]. Athens: Καράβι και Τόξο.
— **(1992)**, *Οι Σφακιανοί στον «Κρητικό πόλεμο» (1645-1669)* [*Sfakians during the "Cretan war"*]. Athens: Καράβι και Τόξο.
— **(2004)**, *Τα 12 Αρχοντοπουλα του Βυζαντίου στην Κρήτη του 1182, Β': Φωκάς–Καλλέργης* [*The twelve Archondopoula of Byzantium in Crete of 1182, B': Fokas-Kallergis*]. Athens: Καράβι και τόξο.
— **(2007)**, *Εγκυκλοπαίδεια των Σφακίων* [*Encyclopedia of Sfakia*]. Athens: Καράβι και Τόξο.
Kokolakis, Michalis (1988), *Ανατολική Κρήτη, Κατοχή, Αντίσταση, Εμφύλιος* [*East Crete, Occupation, Resistance, Civil War*]. Athens: Γνώσεις.
Kokonas, N.A. (1993), *The Cretan Resistance 1941-1945.* London.
Kokovlis, Nikos and Argyro Kokovlis (2002) *Άλλος δρόμος δεν υπήρχε. Αντίσταση – Εμφύλιος – Προσφυγιά* [*There was no other road – Resistance – Civil War – Refugees*]. Athens: Polytypo.
Kopaka, Katerina and Christos Matzanas (2009), *Palaeolithic industries from the island of Gavdos, near neighbour to Crete in Greece.* In: *Antiquity* 83. http://antiquity.ac.uk/projgall/kopaka321.
Krantonelli, Alexandra (1998), *Ελληνική πειρατεία και κούρσος τον ΙΗ' αιωνα και μέχρι την Ελληνική επανάσταση* [*Greek piracy and corsairs during the 18th century and until the Greek revolution*]. Athens: Estia.
Kriaris, Panagiotis K. (1902), *Ιστορία της Κρήτης, Από των αρχαιοτάτων χρόνων μέχρι της επαναστάσεως του 1866* [*History of Crete, From the most ancient period to the uprising of 1866*]. Chania: Η. Πρόοδος.

Laourdas, Vasilios (1947), *Η επανάσταση των Σφακιών και ο Δασκαλογιάννης, κατά τα έγγραφα του Τουρκικού Αρχείου Ηρακλείου [The uprising of Sfakia and Daskalogiannis according to documents from the Turkish Archives of Heraklion]*. *Kretika Chronika*, Vol. 1. Heraklion.

Llewellyn Smith, Michael (1973), *The Great Island. A study of Crete*. Thetford, Norfolk: Lowe & Brydone.

Madden, Thomas (2003), *Enrico Dandolo and the rise of Venice*. Baltimore: Johns Hopkins University Press.

Maltezou, Chrysa (1988) *Η Κρήτη στη διάρκεια της περιόδου της Βενετοκρατίας (1211-1669) [Crete during the period of the Venetian occupation (1211-1669)]*. In: *Κρήτη, Ιστορία και Πολιτισμός [Crete, History and Civilization]*, Vol. II. Heraklion.

Manousakas, Giannis (1980), *Ο Φυγόδικος [The fugitive]*. Athens: Odysseas.

Markopoulos G. (1981), *Το πέρασμα του Ναπολέοντα από την Ιεράπετρα. Θρύλος ή πραγματικότητα [The passage of Napoleon from Ierapetra. Legend or Reality]*. Cretologial conference papers. pp. 115-120. Heraklion

Matton, Raymond (1957), *Le Crète au cours des siècles*. Athens: Institut Français.

Meillet, Antoine (1975), *Aperçu d'une histoire de la langue greque*, 8th edn. Paris: Klincksieck.

Moniou Dimitra I. (2007), *Μνήμες Αλώσεως, Κωνσταντινούπολη 1453 [Memories of the fall of Constantinople 1453]*. Athens: Kiriakides Publications.

Mortensen, Peder (2008), *Lower to Middle Palaeolithic artefacts from Loutró on the south coast of Crete*. In: *Antiquity* 82. http://www.antiquity.ac.uk/ProjGall/mortensen/index.html.

Mourellos, I.D. (1931-1934), *Ιστορία της Κρήτης [History of Crete]*, 4 volumes. Heraklion: Elefthera Skepsis.

— (1950), *Ιστορία της Κρήτης [History of Crete]*, 2nd edn., 3 volumes. Heraklion: Elefthera Skepsis.

Nixon, Lucia (2006), *Making a landscape sacred*. Oxford: Oxbow.

Norwich, John Julius (1990) *Byzantium. The early centuries*. London: Penguin Books.

— (1993), *Byzantium. The apogee*. London: Penguin Books.

— (1996), *Byzantium. The decline and fall*. London: Penguin Books.

— (2003), *A history of Venice*. London: Penguin Books.

— (2006), *The middle sea. A history of the Mediterranean*. London: Vintage Books.

Nowicki, Krzysztof (2011), *Settlement in crisis: the end of the LM /LH IIIB and early IIIC in Crete and other south Aegean islands*. In: A. Mazarakis Ainian (ed.), *The "Dark Ages" revisited: acts of an international symposium in memory of William Coulson, I.*

Palmer, Leonard R. (1965), *Myceneans and Minoans*. London: Faber and Faber.

Pandelakis, Helen S. (2006), *A Byzantine twelfth century family in Crete: the Skordyles*. In: *T. Detorakis and A. Kalokairinos (eds), Proceedings of the 9th International Congress of Cretan Studies*, Elounda, Crete 2001. Heraklion: The Society of Cretan Historical Studies.

Papadia-Lala, Anastasia (1983), *Αγροτικές ταραχές και εξεγέρσεις στη Βενετοκρατούμενη Κρήτη (1509-1528), Η «Επανάσταση» του Γεωργίου Γαδανολέου – Λυσσογιώργη [Rural unrest and rebellions in Venetian occupied Crete (1509-1528), The "Revolution" of Georgios Gadanoleos-Lissogiorgi]*. Athens: Doctoral thesis.

Papadopetrakis, Grigorios (1971 [1888]), *Ιστορία των Σφακίων, ήτοι μέρος της*

Κρητικής ιστορίας [*History of Sfakia, being part of the history of Crete*]. Athens: Vardinogiannis Brothers.

Papadopoulos, Gerassimos A. (2011), *A seismic history of Crete, The Hellenic Arc and Trench*. Athens: Ocelotos Publications.

Papalas, Dimitrios (2003), *Το Β' Τάγμα της Κρητικής Χωροφυλακής: Νομός Σφακίων, 1884-1889* [*The 2nd Regiment of the Cretan Gendamerie, District of Sfakia. 1884-1889*]. Herakion: Postgraduate thesis, University of Crete.

Papayianni, Aphrodite (2010), *He Polis healo: The Fall of Constantinople in 1453 in Post-Byzantine Popular Literature*. In: *Al-Masaq*, Vol. 22, No. 1, p. 27-44.

Pashley, Robert (1989 [1837]), *Travels in Crete*. London: John Murray, Dion. Athens: N. Karavias Reprints.

Pendlebury, J.D.S. (1939), *The archaeology of Crete: an introduction*. 2nd edn. London: Methuen.

Pissanos, Antonios (1971), *Ο Ιωάννης Κόντος ως συγγραφεύς, ως εθνικός αγωνιστής και ως άνθρωπος* [*Ioannis Kontos as writer, national fighter and as a man*]. Athens: self-published.

Ploumidis, G.S. (1972), *Η έκθεση του Ρέκτορα Χανίων Λεονάρδου Λορεντάν (1554) [The report of rector of Chania Leonardo Loredan (1554)]*. Heraklion: *Kretika Chronika*, Volume 14 II, pp. 435-447.

Plymakis, Antonis G. (2010), *Μνήμες Σαμαριάς* [*Memories of Samaria*]. Chania: self-published.

Psilakis, Nikos (2009), *Τα ντοκουμέντα που συνθέτουν το πορτρέτο ενός ήρωα [Documents that contribute to the portrait of a hero*]. *Istoria tou Ethnous*, July, Athens: Ethnos.

Psilakis, Vasilios (1970 [1906]), *Ιστορία της Κρήτης, (Μεταγλωττισμένη)* [*History of Crete*], 4 volumes. Athens: Αρκάδι.

Psychountakis, Giorgos (1998 [1955]), *The Cretan runner*. London: Penguin.

Rackham, Oliver and Jennifer Moody (1996), *The making of the Cretan landscape*. Manchester: Manchester University Press.

Runciman, Steven (2005), *The fall of Constantinople, 1453*. Cambridge: Cambridge University Press.

Sanders, I.F. (1982), *Roman Crete*. Warminster: Aris and Phillips.

Sanoudakis, Antonis (1979), *Καπετάν Μπαντουβά Απομνημονεύματα* [*Kapetan Bandouvas Memoirs*]. Athens: Κνωσός.

Simonelli, Vittorio (1996 [1897]), *Κρήτη – 1893. Οι περιηγητικές αναμνήσεις του Vittorio Simonelli* [*Crete – 1893. Touring memoirs of Vittorio Simonelli*]. Translation into Greek of the book *Candia. Ricordi di escursione di Vittorio Simonelli*. Parma: L. Battei. Rethymnon.

Spanakis, Stergios. *Μνημεία της Κρητικής Ιστορίας* [*Monuments of Cretan History*], 6 volumes of reports to Venice, translated into Greek. Heraklion: Sfakianos.

— **(1940)**, Vol. I, *Relazione Zuanne Mocenigo, Provveditore Generale del Regno di Candia, 17 April 1589.*

— **(1950)**, Vol. II, *Relatione di Cania del General Francesco Moresini, 1629.*

— **(1953)**, Vol. III, *Relatione di Filippo Pasqualigo, Capitano di Candia et Provveditore della Canea, 1594.*

— **(1958)**, Vol. IV, *Relatione dell Benetto Moro, Provveditor General del Regno di Candia, 25*

June 1602.

— **(1969)**, Vol. V, *Francesco Basilicata, Relazione, 6 December 1630.*

— **(1976)**, Vol.VI, *Relatione del Antonio Priuli, Provveditor Generale delle Armi in Candia, 30 March 1667 and Relatione del Antonio Barbaro, Provveditor General dell' Armi in Candia 24 February.*

— **(1981)**, *Κρήτη. Τουρισμός–Ιστορία–Αρχαιολογία* [*Crete. Tourism–History–Archaeology*], Vol. 1: Central and Eastern Crete; Volume 2: Western Crete. 3rd edn. Heraklion: Sfakianakis.

— **(1991)**, *Πόλεις και Χωριά της Κρήτης, στο πέρασμα των αιώνων, Τομος Α και Β.* [*Cities and Villages of Crete through the centuries, Volumes A and B*]. Heraklion, G. Detorakis A.E.B.E.

Sphrantzes, Giorgios and Nicolo Barbaro (1993), *Η Πόλις Εάλω, Το χρονικό της πολιορκίας και της άλωσης της Κωνσταντινούπολης* [*The City has fallen, A chronicle of the siege and the fall of Constantinople*]. Translation by G. Kousounelis and Vanessa A. Lappa. Athens: Livanis Press.

Spratt, Captain T.A.B. (1865), *Travels and researches in Crete.* London: John Van Voorst. Facsimile Reproduction (2004), Elibron Classics.

Stavrinidis Nikolaos S. (1955), *Συμβολή εις την Ιστορία των Σφακιών, Περίοδος του 1645-1770* [*Contribution to the history of Sfakia, 1645-1770*]. *Kretika Chronika,* Vol. 9. Pp. 213-333.Heraklion.

— **(1981)**, *Πώς έχει η υπόθεσις Ναπολέοντος Βοναπάρτη εν Σφακίοις και Ιεράπετρα* [*Current position regarding Napoleon Bonaparte at Sfakia and Ierapetra*]. Cretological conference papers. pp. 187-191. Heraklion

Stephanides, Theodore (1966), *Climax in Crete.* London: Faber and Faber.

Stewart, Ian M.G. (1991), *The struggle for Crete.* Oxford: Oxford University Press.

Stillman, William J. (1874), *The Cretan Insurrection of 1866-7-8.* New York: Henry Holt and Company.

— **(1966)**, *American Consul in a Cretan War. The Cretan insurrection of 1866-7-8.* Revised edition with introduction notes by George Georgiades Arnakis. University of Texas, Austin: Centre for Neo-Hellenic Studies.

— **(1976)**, *Articles and despatches from Crete.* Edited with introduction and notes by George Georgiades Arnakis. University of Texas, Austin. Centre for Neo-Hellenic Studies.

Theotokis, S. (1933) Η *Κρήτη του 1570* [*Crete of 1570*]. To Imerologion tis Megalis Ellados. pp. 315-337.

Trikoupis, Spiridon (1994), *Ιστορία της Ελληνικής Επανάστασης* [*History of the Greek revolution*]. Athens: Λιβάνη.

Trudgill, Peter (2008), *In Sfakia: passing time in the wilds of Crete.* Athens: Lycabettus.

Tsivis, Giannis D. (1993), *Χανιά 1252-1940* [*Chania 1252-1940*]. Athens: Γνώση.

Tsougarakis, Dimitris (1987), *Η Βυζαντινή Κρήτη* [*Byzantine Crete*]. *In: Κρήτη, Ιστορία και Πολιτισμός* [*Crete, History and Civilization*], Vol. I. Heraklion.

— **(1988)**, *Byzantine Crete, from the 5th century to the Venetian conquest.* Athens: St. D. Basilopoulos.

Vincent, A.L. (2001), *The Calergi case, Crime and politics in Western Crete under Venetian rule.* In: *Thesavrismata* Vol. 31. Venice: Greek Institute of Byzantine and Post-Byzantine studies in Venice.

Webster, T.B.L. (1958), *From Mycenae to Homer.* London: Methuen.
Willetts, R.F. (1965), *Ancient Crete: a social history from early times until Roman occupation.* London: Routledge and Kegan Paul.
— **(1977)**, *The civilization of ancient Crete.* London: Batsford.
Xanthoudides, S. (1939a), *Η Ενετοκρατία εν Κρήτη και οι κατά των Ενετών αγώνες των Κρητών* [*The Venetian occupation of Crete and the struggle of the Cretans against the Venetians*]. Athens: Byzantinisch–Neugriechischen Jahrbucher.
— **(1939b)** *Το δίπλωμα (Προβελέγιον) των Σκορδίλων Κρήτης* [*The Diploma of the Skordilises of Crete*] Published in a Collection of papers by Επετηρίς Εταιρίας Κρητικών Σπουδών [Annual of the Society of Cretan Studies], pp. 299-312.
Xylander, Marlen von (1989), *Die deutsche Besatzungsherrschaft auf Kreta 1941-1945.* Freiburg: Rombach.
Younger, John, and Paul Rehak (2008), *Minoan culture: religion, burial customs, and administration.* In: Cynthia Shelmerdine (ed.), *The Aegean Bronze Age.* Cambridge: Cambridge University Press, 165-185.
Zampelios, Spiridon (2003), *Οι Κρητικοί Γάμοι* [*The Cretan Weddings*]. Athens: Dorikos.
— and **K. Kritovoulidis (2004 [1893])**, *Ιστορία των επαναστάσεων της Κρήτης, συμπληρωθείσα υπό Ιωάννου Δ. Κονδυλάκη [History of the Cretan revolutions, completed by Ioannis D. Kondylakis]. Athens: Eleftheri Skepsis.*

Index